The Impact of Feminism in English Renaissance Studies

The Impact of Feminism in English Renaissance Studies

Edited by

Dympna Callaghan

First published 2007 by
PALGRAVE MACMILLAN
Houndmills, Basingstoke, Hampshire RG21 6XS and
175 Fifth Avenue, New York, N.Y. 10010
Companies and representatives throughout the world

PALGRAVE MACMILLAN is the global academic imprint of the Palgrave
Macmillan division of St. Martin's Press, LLC and of Palgrave Macmillan Ltd.
Macmillan® is a registered trademark in the United States, United Kingdom
and other countries. Palgrave is a registered trademark in the European
Union and other countries.

ISBN-13: 978–1–4039–9212–3
ISBN-10: 1–4039–9212–6

This book is printed on paper suitable for recycling and made from fully
managed and sustained forest sources.

A catalogue record for this book is available from the British Library.

A catalog record for this book is available from the Library of Congress.

10   9   8   7   6   5   4   3   2   1
16   15   14   13   12   11   10   09   08   07

Printed and bound in Great Britain by
Antony Rowe Ltd, Chippenham and Eastbourne

In memory of
Sasha Roberts

While this book was in the final stages of preparation for the press, one of our contributors, Sasha Roberts, was tragically killed in a road accident. Sasha was a magnificently gifted scholar and a valued friend whose loss is felt in academic communities across the globe. This book is dedicated to her memory.

THE CONTRIBUTORS

Contents

Part III Histories

11 Hermione's Ghost: Catholicism, the Feminine, and the Undead   213
    Frances E. Dolan

12 No Man's Elizabeth: Frances A. Yates and the History of History   238
    Deanne Williams

13 Women's Informal Commerce and the "All-Male" Stage   259
    Natasha Korda

14 Why did Widows Remarry? Remarriage, Male Authority, and
    Feminist Criticism   281
    Jennifer Panek

15 "I desire to be helde in your memory": Reading Penelope Rich
    through Her Letters   299
    Grace Ioppolo

16 Hormonal Conclusions   326
    Gail Kern Paster

Index   334

List of Figures

Notes on the Contributors

Dympna Callaghan is Dean's Professor in the Humanities at Syracuse University. Her books include *Woman and Gender in Renaissance Tragedy* (Harvester, 1989), *Shakespeare Without Women* (Routledge, 2000), *Romeo and Juliet* (Bedford St. Martins, 2003), and (with Jyotsna Singh and Lorraine Helms), *The Weyward Sisters: Shakespeare and Feminist Politics* (Blackwell, 1994). She is the editor of *The Feminist Companion to Shakespeare* (Blackwell, 2000), winner of the Choice Award for Outstanding Academic Title. She is currently working on *The Oxford Anthology of Early Modern English Verse* (Oxford University Press).

Pamela Allen Brown is Associate Professor of English at the University of Connecticut, Stamford. She is author of *Better a Shrew than a Sheep: Women, Drama and the Culture of Jest in Early Modern England* (Comparative Drama, 2004), and co-editor (with Peter Parolin) of *Women Players in England 1500– 1660: Beyond the All-Male Stage* (Ashgate, 2005). With Jean E. Howard, she is preparing a volume for Bedford/St Martins on As You Like It: Texts & Contexts. She is also working on a project about 'bad fun' among the British – laughter at the expense of Jews, blacks, Catholics, Muslims and the deformed – from the early modern period to the present day.

Kate Chedgzoy is Professor of Renaissance Literature at the University of Newcastle, and has published widely on Shakespeare, women's writing, gender, and sexuality. Her current research interests are women's writing in the early modern British Atlantic world, and the construction of childhood in early modern culture.

Kimberly Anne Coles is an Assistant Professor in English at the University of Maryland. Her recently completed manuscript, *Making Sects: Women as Reformers, Writers and Subjects in Reformation England*, examines the influence of women writers on religious identity and its cultural expression in the sixteenth century.

Frances E. Dolan is Professor of English at the University of California, Davis. She is the author of *Whores of Babylon: Gender, Catholicism, and Seventeenth-Century Print Culture* (Cornell, 1999), and *Dangerous Familiars: Representations of Domestic Crime in England, 1550–1700* (Cornell, 1994). She is also the editor of *The Taming of the Shrew: Texts and Contexts* (Bedford, 1996), and of five plays for the new Pelican Shakespeare. She was the President of the

Shakespeare Association of America, 2004–5. Her current project is a study of representations of marital conflict in seventeenth- and twentieth-century England and America.

Jonathan Gil Harris is Professor of English at George Washington University. He is the author of *Foreign Bodies and the Body Politic: Discourses of Social Pathology in Early Modern England* (Cambridge, 1998), and *Sick Economies: Drama, Mercantilism and Disease in Shakespeare's England* (University of Pennsylvania Press, 2004); he is also the co-editor, with Natasha Korda, of *Staged Properties in Early Modern English Drama* (Cambridge, 2002). He is currently working on a book project entitled *Untimely Matter: Reworking Materiality in the Time of Shakespeare*.

Heather Hirschfeld is Associate Professor of English at the University of Tennessee, Knoxville. She is the author of *Joint Enterprises: Collaborative Drama and the Institutionalization of the English Renaissance Theater* (University of Massachusetts, 2004) as well as several articles appearing in journals such as *ELH, Shakespeare Quarterly, Shakespeare Studies, Renaissance Drama* and *PMLA*.

Jean E. Howard is William B. Ransford Professor of English at Columbia University where she teaches early modern literature and gender studies. One of the four editors of *The Norton Shakespeare*, she is author of several books, including *The Stage and Social Struggle in Early Early Modern England,Shakespeare's Art of Orchestration: Stagecraft and Audience Response* (Routledge, 1994), (with Phyllis Rackin) *Engendering a Nation: A Feminist Account of Shakespeare's English Histories* (Routledge, 1997), and *Theater of a City: The Places of London Comedy 1598–1642* (University of Pennsylvania Press, 2006). She is a past President of the Shakespeare Association of America and the recipient of a number of awards and honors including a Guggenheim Fellowship and Folger, Newberry, and Huntington Library Fellowships. She is currently working on a study of the plays of Caryl Churchill.

Grace Ioppolo is Reader in English and American Literature at the University of Reading. She is the author of *Dramatists and their Manuscripts in the Age of Shakespeare, Jonson, Middleton and Heywood: Authorship, Authority and the Playhouse* (Routledge, 2006) and *Revising Shakespeare* (Harvard University Press, 1991), the editor of *Shakespeare Performed: Essays in Honor of R. A. Foakes* (University of Delaware Press, 2000), and the co-editor of *Elizabeth I and the Culture of Writing* (British Library Press, 2006) and *English Manuscripts Studies*, Volume 11 (British Library Press, 2002). She has edited plays by Shakespeare and by Middleton and has published widely on the transmission of the early modern text from manuscript to print.

Natasha Korda, Associate Professor of English at Wesleyan University, is author of *Shakespeare's Domestic Economies: Gender and Property in Early Modern England* (University of Pennsylvania Press, 2002), and co-editor of *Staged Properties in Early Modern English Drama* (Cambridge University Press, 2002).

Jennifer Panek is Associate Professor of English at the University of Ottawa. She is the author of *Widows and Suitors in Early Modern English Comedy* (Cambridge University Press, 2004) and several articles on gender issues in early modern drama.

Patricia Parker is the Margery Bailey Professor of English and Comparative Literature at Stanford. Author of *Inescapable Romance* (Princeton, 1979), *Literary Fat Ladies: Rhetoric, Gender, Property* (Routledge, 1987), and *Shakespeare from the Margins* (Chicago, 1996) and co-editor of numerous collections of criticism including *Shakespeare and the Question of Theory* (with Geoffrey Hartman, Routledge, 1985) and *Women, 'Race,' and Writing in the Early Modern Period* (with Margo Hendricks, Routledge, 1993), she is currently preparing a new Arden edition of *A Midsummer Night's Dream* and new Norton Critical Editions of *Much Ado About Nothing* and *Twelfth Night* and writing a book on *Turks, Moors, and the Barbary Coast* in Shakespeare and other early modern contexts.

Gail Kern Paster is Director of the Folger Shakespeare Library in Washington, DC. Among her publications are *The Body Embarrassed: Drama and the Disciplines of Shame in Early Modern England* (Cornell University Press, 1993) and *Humoring the Body: Emotions on the Shakespearean Stage* (University of Chicago Press, 2004). She is also a co-editor of *Reading the Early Modern Passions: Essays in the Cultural History of Emotion* (University of Pennsylvania Press, 2004).

Sasha Roberts is Senior Lecturer at the University of Kent, and has published extensively on Shakespeare, the history of the book, and women in literary culture. Her books include *Reading Shakespeare's Poems in Early Modern England* (Palgrave, 2003), the first comprehensive study of early modern texts and readings of Shakespeare's poems, and (co-edited with Ann Thompson) *Women Reading Shakespeare 1660-1900: A Critical Anthology* (Manchester University Press, 1997). She is currently editing *The Witch of Edmonton* for Arden, and working on a provocative study of early modern print and manuscript culture, *Between Truth and Beauty: Reclaiming Renaissance Poetry*.

R. S. White, after teaching at the University of Newcastle Upon Tyne, became Professor of English, Communication and Cultural Studies at the University of Western Australia. He has published many books and articles on

Shakespeare, Keats, and Hazlitt, and his publications include *Constructing Gender* (with Hilary Fraser, University of Western Australia Press,1994), *Natural Law in English Renaissance Literature* (Cambridge University Press, 1996), *Natural Rights and the Birth of Romanticism in the 1790s* (Palgrave, 2005). He is a fellow of the Australian Academy and was awarded the Australian Centenary medal for contributions to the Humanities through the teaching of English.

Deanne Williams is Associate Professor of English at York University, Toronto. She is the author of *The French Fetish from Chaucer to Shakespeare* (Cambridge University Press, 2004) which won the 2004 Roland H. Bainton Prize for Best Book in Literature from the Sixteenth Century Society and Conference.

1

Introduction

Dympna Callaghan

Imagine there was a form of cultural performance—understood in the expanded sense of that term to mean active participation involving "actors" or "agents" in the rituals, habits, or practices of a society—that demonstrated beyond a shadow of a doubt women's presence and participation in an enactment central to one of the most important institutions in early modern England. Imagine too that women's presence in this enactment was not simply occasional or optional, but vitally necessary to its function and effectiveness, as was their freely given vocal assent to the proceedings. Moreover, in this particular cultural performance, the principal actors were both male and female, and women had significant speaking parts. Further, women of all classes, from aristocratic court ladies to women from the very lowest ranks of the social order, might participate and were even encouraged to do so. Suppose further that records and documents attesting to these circumstances existed in considerable number, together with the names of the female participants, and that extant copies of a script for the performance itself survived in abundance. What might we infer from this information? Would feminist criticism beat a hasty retreat from the political commitments that led to the feminist lexicon of "oppression" and "exclusion" forged in the heat and dust of the 1980s when scholars sought to put women indelibly on the cognitive map of early modern England?

Before I attempt to address these questions, let me first say a little about current understandings of the nature of cultural performance itself. A widely held feminist argument describes the following trajectory: if we are to understand women's role in the social order and particularly women's participation in cultural life, we must expand our horizons from the narrow confines of theatrical representation and women's writing to encompass the vast range of cultural activities women were engaged in that, among other things, enabled and sustained more specifically aesthetic modes of cultural engagement. When we consider aesthetic performance practices such as theater and literature in isolation, we invariably exclude and occlude the way women were highly vigorous participants in early modern culture. From this

1

perspective, those feminists who have sought to address women's marginal place in literary history, or alternatively, women's exclusion from it altogether, are themselves guilty, however unwittingly, of perpetuating women's oppression. Phyllis Rackin cautions that the "exclusion" argument may be itself a patriarchal trap: "For feminists, there are obvious dangers in contemplating our past from the point of view of late twentieth century academic men, who may—consciously or not—be anxious or ambivalent about the progress women have made in the wake of the contemporary women's movement."[1] Cultural performances (again understood in the more comprehensive sense), so this line of argument goes, merit deeper consideration because they are more inclusive of women and, rather than being completely different from specifically aesthetic practices (that is, non-cultural or merely social), such performances exist on a continuum with them.

There is in fact a cultural performance such as the one postulated at the start of this introduction. It was ubiquitously enacted in early modern England, and its script survives as "the Solemnization of Matrimony" in The Book of Common Prayer (1559). The nuptial rite is a form of cultural performance indispensable to patriarchy, and, following on the social and legal transactions of courtship and dowry, ritually inaugurates the conjugal bond. There is also arguably a distinct cultural trajectory from the wedding script in The Book of Common Prayer to Jonson's court masque *Hymenaie*, which aristocratic women performers were able to appropriate for their own purposes, and the arrival of Hymen at the end of *As You Like It*. It remains the case, however, that despite the achievement of conjugal felicity by individual women, historically, marriage is an institution not much associated with women's emancipation. Tongue in cheek, then, for the purposes of elucidating a bone of current critical contention, and one which has contoured the impact of feminism on Renaissance and early modern literary studies,[2] I propose to take the solemnization of matrimony from The Book of Common Prayer as the script for a cultural performance that offers sober and illuminating insights into the problem of interpreting women's participation in early modern culture faced by feminist criticism.

I Revisionism and performance

From one feminist point of view, the marriage ceremony is potentially an under-examined performance in which women have a key speaking part. Thus, in the marriage service we see a cultural enactment in which women play an active and vital role. There can be no marriage without the woman's consent, and in this little drama with three speaking parts (and potentially a fourth, if someone from the audience/congregation decides to object to the legality or legitimacy of the proceedings), the woman is enjoined to speak. She is not a transvestite actor, but a woman enacting and enabling a ritual on which the social order is founded. We know that large numbers of early modern women performed this role, and while the role is not identical with that of her male counterpart in the ceremony, to address only women's lesser part in this ritual is to deny women's agency in their destinies and their autonomous choices about marriage, which were probably exercised in the period more often than they were curtailed. This remains the case despite the fact that "victim feminism" has given almost all of its attention to enforced marriage.

Women who gave their vocal and bodily consent to marriage in the words "I do" and in the act of giving of hands (both the right hand, and the left hand for the receiving of the ring), should not be represented as being like manikins under the control of men. We might note, for example, that at the end of the ceremony, both the man *and* the woman have their hands, the somatic representations of their agency, taken by the priest: "*Then shall the Priest join their right hands together, and say. Those whom God hath joined together, let no man put asunder.*" Thus, *both* man and woman are enjoined to the rights and duties to which they have sworn. More importantly, the marriage is only effectively solemnized with the consent of the congregation. Thus the "audience" of this particular cultural performance, invariably of both genders, also plays a key role:

> Forasmuch as *N.* and *N.* have consented together in holy wedlock, and have witnessed the same before God and this company, and thereto have given and pledged their troth, either to other, and have declared the same by giving and receiving of a Ring, and by joining of hands: I pronounce that they be man and wife together.[3]

While it was axiomatic until recently in feminist thinking that marriage was an oppressive institution, from the perspective of a feminism less invested in oppression and victimization, we cannot aver that in the complex cultural performance of the wedding ceremony women did not exercise agency, nor can we deny the fact that marriage afforded women protection and privileges they would not have enjoyed as unmarried women. We know, for instance, that on marriage, women exercised control over their household and often over their husband's business affairs. Indeed, historical research has shown that despite the patriarchal propaganda issued from pulpit and printing house to the contrary, most early modern women were *not* in fact married and were thus unfettered by whatever limitations conjugality was alleged to impose.[4] The wedding ceremony can be seen in some sense then as a public act of initiation into what was potentially a more empowered standing in the social realm than could be enjoyed by single women.

While many of the oft-quoted marriage manuals and advice books urged women to submission and obedience within the married state, there are those, such as Thomas Hilder's remarkable and truly benevolent *Conjugal Counsel* (1653), which sought to lay the way for marital happiness for his children of both sexes. Hilder charts a path to conjugal felicity by championing the virtues of mutuality. He also includes an encomium to his deceased wife, "a most choice and blessed mother," in an account which is far from unique in the period and suggests that marital relations in this era might be very satisfying indeed:

> Truly, I might here dip a golden pen in odiferous oil . . . She was indeed a *Margaret* [a pearl] by name and much more by sweetness of nature . . . She was full of the overflowings of love to her most unworthy (yet much endeared) comfort. She was of a very peaceable and amiable life toward all persons. She did live much in a little time.[5]

These remarks serve as a reminder that women's actual experience of marriage was probably as varied then as it is now, and very much dependent on the personalities of the marriage partners.

To conclude what is currently the most prominent feminist line of argument in early modern studies, patriarchy itself has had an unduly bad press, as Debora Kuller Shuger reminds us: "[t]he image of the father need not belong to the realm of power and oppression but to an explicitly opposed arena of love and forgiveness."[6] In other words, not all patriarchal discourse concerns whitewashing coercive power relations. Thus, whatever the limitations of specific marriages, the wedding ceremony itself is hardly a document of women's abject oppression. Rather, the nuptial rite stresses the rights and responsibilities of both parties so that even the Pauline injunction to female submission is balanced by the duties of husbands to "love your wives, even as Christ loved the church, and hath given himself for it," placing the onus on husbands to be Christ-like to the point of self-abnegation.

II Female subjugation

From another feminist point of view, one whose contours, since they are more familiar, require only a brief summary, marriage was the single most important instrument of women's social inferiority. Early modern women's subjugation was inscribed in the marriage ceremony itself where woman's arguably ventriloquized assent to even the most pernicious excesses of patriarchal power, committed her to a life of perpetual submission, to which it singularly failed to commit her husband.[7] Upon marriage, a woman became a non-person, a *feme covert*, whose legal identity was subsumed under that of her husband, as T. E., *The Law's Resolutions of Women's Rights* (1632) puts it: "[F]or they are but one person. And by this a married woman perhaps may either doubt whether she be either none or no more than half a person"[8] Further, a woman's agency was circumscribed even before she was bound by the yoke of conjugality. The bride was given away by her father, or "friends," an all-encompassing early modern category which might refer to any and all parties who had an interest, emotional or financial (and very often both), in the match. In fact, the wedding ceremony contains a considerable amount of fast footwork. The law of coverture put a woman's property rights in jeopardy once she married, and, in the case of an unhappy match, she might be condemned to a life of abject subjection or to a power struggle with her husband in which "violence is the fundamental arbiter."[9] The law afforded no protection against abuse unless the woman was actually beaten to death; though there was vigilant social and legal enforcement of women who were believed to usurp the power of their husbands, a situation reflected in the "comic" rhymes of John Taylor's *Juniper Lecture*:

> Dub a dub, kill her with a club,
> Be thy wife's master. . . .
> But if she persist, and will have her will,
> Oh, then bang her, bang her, bang her still.[10]

Brutality is the model of conjugality here, and even the rhythms of the verse imply a certain relish at the prospect of what we would now call marital rape.

The nuptial rite is at best the instantiation of wifely inferiority, one that informs virtually every aspect of early modern life. Thus its relationship to more specifically cultural texts and aesthetic performances inheres in its status as their contextual premise. In other words, the wedding ceremony, whose function was to reiterate the gender hierarchy derived from Genesis, had some bearing on all other cultural representations of gender. Whether literary texts re-inscribe, reinforce, or strive to rewrite the foundational rules of the gender hierarchy, so the argument of this line of criticism contends, they must always in some sense refer to them.

III Revisionism and "exclusionism"

I offer the above (only slightly caricatured) interpretations because I believe they recapitulate the central currents of feminist reading at the moment. The first position is that of feminist revisionism, which crucially stresses women's agency and participation in culture and pulls back from the more traditional feminist emphasis on women's oppression and subjugation. Revisionism's key and invaluable contribution to the feminist debate about early modern women is its questioning of the specificity and integrity of the aesthetic realm. Revisionism takes a far more comprehensive view of culture, understanding it as a much broader category which, even taking into account a more inclusive canon, includes a vastly expanded range of persons and cultural practices than the more restricted notion of "the literary." The latter interpretation of marriage described above, on the other hand, emphasizes women's subordinate position within patriarchal structures and within more strictly defined modes of cultural representation.

The perplexing status of women is in part a consequence of the fact that gender hierarchy is changed and modified once it abuts the class hierarchy, which is the other major structuring principle of early modern power relations. Thus, at the very top of the social hierarchy, women might well function as the shapers of culture. Further, since women were subordinated *within* the patriarchal structure of early modern society rather than well-nigh annihilated from it (unlike, for example, the indigenous peoples of the Americas in colonial culture), in a certain and significant sense, it goes without saying that "Women were everywhere in Shakespeare's England" (Rackin, 25). Women were, as a consequence, engaged in a great range of activities, some of which comport with patriarchal precept and some of which, invariably, do not. Like all overarching structures and institutions, no matter how large and looming they may be, patriarchy functions in part precisely because it is so completely normalized and naturalized. There are, then, certain political and methodological perils attendant on the revisionist "inclusion thesis." Methodologically, there is a tendency to return to a pre-feminist treatment of woman-as-theme ("women were everywhere so let's just look at everywhere they were"), and politically the graver danger is that revisionism is simply oblivious to, or in denial about, the structural inequities in early modern and, for that matter, contemporary patriarchy.

Patriarchy is a system organized around the gender hierarchy, and while that system largely benefits men at the expense of women, it is not, as indeed revisionists rightly point out, applied evenly everywhere and without exception. It is also true, as the revisionist critique of women's subjugation as wives suggests, that most women in early modern England were not in fact married. However, unmarried women, far from being "liberated" by this condition, often struggled to survive: the poorest of the poor were "spinsters" in the textile trades, who did not earn even subsistence wages.[11] Women were, on the whole, indeed offered economic protection by marriage, and those who did not or could not marry (perhaps because it was beyond their economic means to provide a dowry) might suffer extraordinary hardship. Revisionist claims that women gained access to power and agency within the system, and even within the household, are also true. This agency might take the form, for example, of controlling aesthetic and ideological agenda of court entertainments. On the other hand, revisionism is reluctant to acknowledge that one of the most everyday forms of women's power and agency was that of being authorized to beat and abuse household subordinates. As Frances E. Dolan's work on women and household chastisement reminds us, agency and authority are not necessarily good in themselves.[12]

The revisionist account of early modern marriage outlined above emphasizes the *experience* of individual women in marriage in the early modern period; while the second reading emphasizes marriage as an *institution*. Institutions, of course, do not exist apart from individual experience of them, but nor do individuals have experiences that are not shaped by social institutions. Even practices that seem wholly somatic can function as part of the social and institutional organization of patriarchy. Gail Kern Paster, for example, has argued the "the institution of wet-nursing" worked to enforce class differences.[13] While the revisionist perspective, then, offers some useful correctives of the feminist critique of patriarchy, it is not a substitute for it. We thus need information from both these approaches if we are to arrive at a properly comprehensive view of women's relation to cultural representation in the period.

Feminist scholarship thus far, then, presents us with two divergent perspectives, which nonetheless have the potential to add up to a valuably complex, nuanced picture of women's simultaneous participation in *and* exclusion from early modern culture. Women's status in early modern England is, paradoxically, that of *excluded participants*. The instance of marriage is a case in point. One of its most notorious legal consequences was, for all practical purposes—which cannot be dispatched by any number of instances of marital bliss—the erasure of female identity, except in the case of criminal transgression:

> Now because Adam hath so pronounced that man and wife shall be but one flesh, and our Law is that. . . . they are but one person. And by this a married woman perhaps may either doubt whether she be either none or no more than half a person. But let her be of good cheer. Though for the near conjunction which is between man and wife, add to them a perfect love, agreement, and adherence, they by intent and wise fiction of Law, one person, yet in nature and in some other cases by the Law of God and Man, they remain divers. For as Adam's punishment was several from Eve's, so in criminal and other special causes our Law argues them several persons. . . .
>
> See here the reason of that which I touched on before, that women have no voice in Parliament; they make no laws; they consent to none; they abrogate none.
>
> T. E., *The Law's Resolutions of Women's Rights* (1632)[14]

While some women might have been coerced into marriage, the law did not officially recognize such marriages, and at least the letter of the law (from which, admittedly, practice might deviate) required the freely given consent of both parties. In one of the most famous of early modern love matches, that between John Donne and Ann More, Donne's letter to the bride's father after the wedding claims her active participation and eagerness to be joined with the poet in his description of their small, secret ceremony: "We both knew the obligations that lay upon us, and we adventured equally; and about three weeks before Christmas we married. And as at the doing there were not used above five persons."[15] Although all the evidence suggests that this was indeed a mutual arrangement, Donne needed to insist that they both "adventured equally"; otherwise he could be charged with abduction.

The predicament of this couple is instructive, insofar as the early modern concern about marriage manifests not so much as concern for the status of women in conjugal arrangements as the fact that *both men and women* might be prevented from exercising free choice in the selection of a marriage partner. Donne's argument to Sir George More is that knowing he would have been disqualified as a potential suitor on grounds of his social and financial status ("my present estate less than fit for her"), he and Ann decided that their best and only option was a clandestine marriage:

> I knew that to have given any intimation of it had been to impossibilitate the whole matter. And then having these honest purposes in our hearts, and those fetters in our consciences, methinks we should be pardoned if our fault be both this, that we did not, by fore-revealing of it consent to our hindrance and torment.[16]

Though evidence suggests that in most cases families sought to accommodate the needs of eloping couples, Donne's planned career was ruined by his marriage.[17] In fact, in early modern England probably the most common problem faced by young people of both sexes in relation to marriage was that of being prevented from marrying the person they had an inclination to marry, or alternatively being compelled to espouse someone they disliked. This had especially disastrous consequences for women, but it did not affect women alone. Enforced marriage was probably the most significant debate about marriage in the period, and within that discussion, the issue of the status of women *per se* was somewhat overshadowed.

Weddings themselves did, however, constitute the complex performance of social rituals that often departed from the scripted solemnities envisaged by The Book of Common Prayer. In Kendal, the minister complained in 1601:

> [W]hereas many young persons and others, void of all reverence and civil behaviour, have been and are accustomed to stand upon the stall and seats to gaze about them in the time of any wedding or marriage . . . it is enjoined that none shall use any unreverent gestures or behaviour but quietly keep their places . . . at the time of any wedding or otherwise.
>
> (quoted in Cressy, 354)

All manner of disorderly, carnivalesque conduct might be engaged in during the wedding festivities. Henry Gray of Southweald, Essex danced during the wedding sermon in 1604, and John Wilkins, the parish clerk of Whitstable, Kent, who was married in 1599, donned his wife's bridal gown (Cressy, 354). At the wedding, the bride might be subject to patent misogyny and/or take the performance into her own hands. Brides were sometimes taunted with horns, a symbol of the fact that the groom was very likely to become a cuckold. Alternatively, Richard Brathwaite's *Batchelars Banquet* represents the nuptial day as one where the bride and her guests formed "a frolic gamesome crew" (Cressy, 353).

There remains, however, the historically indisputable fact that men and women were patently unequal partners in the institution of marriage. This structural inequity can be overlooked only if we examine the nuptial rite in isolation. Solemnization was not in fact a legal requirement to make marriage, defined as "an agreement between two persons," valid. Indeed, the church rite was merely one ritualized, sacramentalized event in a long chain involving a very large number of people, who were also, incidentally, of both genders: kin networks, interested parties, "friends" who sought to parcel out property and power by means of matches designed to further their own interests, which might be quite ancillary to those of the proposed conjugal couple, or even antithetical to those interests. Even those aspects of the wedding ceremony which most reveal the operations of patriarchy, are, on the face of it, at least as registered in the words of the wedding service, relatively benign: "And the Minister receiving the woman at her father or friend's hands, shall cause the man to take the woman by the right hand, and so either to give their troth to the other."[18] It is only in the amplification of these rights by commentators that the real operations being effected are disclosed. Richard Hooker, the Anglican divine, observes in *Of the Lawes of Ecclesiasticall politie* (1597) that the custom of giving the bride away "putteth wemen in mind of a dutie whereunto the verie imbecillitie of their nature and sex doth binde them, namely to be always directed, guided and ordered by others."[19] While there are unquestionably myopic tendencies inherent in the revisionist trend in current feminist scholarship, and from one point of view, these tendencies indeed may represent the erosion of political commitment, from another, they reflect the sheer complexity of scholarship that is invested in examining the cultural experiences of more than half the population of early modern England. Indeed, it is from a perspective that rightly insists on this reality that Phyllis Rackin claims "women were everywhere":

'In historical research,' as a wise old teacher once warned me, 'you're likely to find what you are looking for'; and what most of us have been looking for in recent years in a history of men's anxiety in the face of female power, or women's disempowerment, and of outright misogyny. We need to interrogate that history (and . . . our reasons for preferring it), not because it is necessarily incorrect but because it is incomplete. It constitutes only one of many stories that could be told about women's place in Shakespeare's world . . . [20]

Women's exercise of agency is not to be found in the precepts of patriarchy itself, that is within the orthodox dicta of the system of male property ownership, male political power, and social hierarchy, but rather in the contradictions, gaps, and "wiggle-room" of patriarchal order. As the author of *The Law's Resolutions of Women's Rights* put it: "All of them are understood either married or to be married, and their desires subject to their husband. I know no remedy, *though some women can shift it well enough*" (my emphasis).[21] T. E. notes both the restrictions on women *and* the gap between patriarchal precept and social practice, precisely the space in which women made room for themselves as social actors in all manner of situations from the writing of literature, the assumption of sovereignty (in the absence of a male heir), the execution of wills, the control of businesses, and even (as we shall see) control over parliamentary elections. Increasingly, feminist attention has turned its gaze on precisely this space as a way of seeing not so much how women were constrained from acting—in the social as well as the more narrowly cultural sense—but rather how they maneuvered within it. Famously, for example, by rendering her relationship with her English subjects as a mystical marriage, Elizabeth I managed to oust the idea of a flesh-and-blood husband entirely and reserve center stage for herself. However, even this notion of women's manipulation and maneuvering is in danger of ignoring the fact that while *some* women could "shift it well enough," others (potentially the majority) were so constrained by structures and circumstances that they simply could not.

Crucially, women may get the short end of the stick in the patriarchal order, but they are not outside it—patriarchy is a cultural horizon in which both men and women define their identities, perform their social functions, exercise their religious duties, and fashion their desires—and thus they have an investment in it, and very often an investment in the status quo around gender and sexuality as much as around any other issues. When we consider the magnitude of the task involved in assessing the relation of over half the population as a group to the issue of cultural representation and participation, it becomes clear that any generalization about women and women's cultural production is almost bound to be wrong. There are almost *always* exceptions. Even T. E.'s assertion that "Women have no voice in Parliament; they make no laws; they consent to none; they abrogate none," a seemingly incontrovertible statement, requires some qualification when we look in sufficient detail at the extraordinary diversity of women's experience. For example, during the reign of Elizabeth, the Pakington family of Aylesbury, Buckinghamshire controlled elections. The town was incorporated in 1554, but even this move offered no challenge to them. In 1572, power lay in the hands of the widow of Sir Thomas Pakington, and the election return for that year reads as follows: "... know ye, me, the said Dame Dorothy Pakington to have chosen ... my trusty and well beloved Thomas Lichfield and George Burden, esquires, to be my burgesses of my said town of Aylesbury."[22] Since

Dame Dorothy controlled the selection of Members of Parliament in *her* town, she probably also had a considerable say in their behavior once they arrived at the Palace of Westminster, especially perhaps as Lichfield shortly afterwards became her son-in-law.

Nor is Aylesbury the only place where women managed to "shift it" (as T. E. so eloquently puts it) sufficiently to give themselves a voice in Parliament. Sole electoral patronage in the town of Gatton, Surrey was twice in the hands of women. Elizabeth Copley, widow of Sir Roger Copley, controlled elections from 1549 until the manor passed into the hands of her son, Thomas, in 1559.[23] Eventually, Thomas's widow, Katherine, received, under the terms of her jointure, "the nomination of the two burgesses for the town of Gatton" to Parliament. The Privy Council in this instance stepped in, not on the grounds of Katherine Copley's gender but because of her involvement in the Babington Plot: "she is known to be evil affected."[24] In an election in Westminster in 1621, there is an account of a whole range of people, women among them, who attempted to vote (in the customary manner, by acclamation) for a candidate: "a verie great number of them who cried for Mr. Manne were weemen children and other people who had no voice."[25]

The contiguity between political and cultural representation is an interesting one. Just as there were no written legal prohibitions against women on the stage, nor was there any law which actually debarred women from suffrage. When in Suffolk in 1640 women property-owners, empowered by the internecine struggles of the turbulent mid-century, tried to exercise the power to vote, Sir Simonds D'Ewes prevented them, but admitted that he could find no law to support him:

> [B]y the ignorance of some of the clerks at the other two tables the oaths of some single women that were freeholders were taken without the knowledge of the said High Sheriff who as soon as he had notice thereof instantly sent to forbid the same, conceiving it a matter very unworthy of any gentleman and most dishonourable in such an election to make use of their voices although they might in law have been allowed.[26]

The "ignorance of the clerks" is itself instructive, but should not distract us from the fact that this is an extraordinary event in a period which saw a surge in women's attempts to assert political power by petitioning Parliament, making loyalty oaths to the government, and raising money for favored causes (Mendelson and Crawford, 397). It is important to register that this kind of activity was part of the newly galvanized political consciousness of the civil war that generated a challenge to all hierarchies in the 1640s.[27] Even in the more egalitarian political climate of that era, however, the upshot of the Suffolk election was that the votes were excised from the record and, further, were removed at the behest of the two candidates ("the knights") for whom the women had attempted to vote:

> [A]s soon as Mr High Sheriff had intelligence of it we had word brought to our table where Mr Clerk & my self wrote that Mr Sheriff would have us take no women's oaths & both the knights desired that those that were taken might be put out & that we should take no more, & so we refused the rest of the women after that notice from Mr High Sheriff & when Mr High Sheriff cased up the books he cast out the women of the general sum.[28]

As Mendelson and Crawford cautiously observe, "We cannot be certain that there were no elections in which single women's votes were accepted in some form rather than disqualified" (437). The point is that we can never be certain about potential exceptions for which there is no extant evidence; we can only be certain about the rule.

The prohibition against voting, like the prohibition against women on the public stage, is not legally articulated because, in this culture, *it goes without saying*. The absence of a legal specification does not, however, mean that women were in practice permitted to act or to vote—or that, at least, that they were not prevented from doing so. Rather, the absence of legal restriction means that the nature of the prohibition is so deeply embedded in the culture that no one found need to specify it: a law becomes necessary only if there some likelihood of it being broken.

A further point needs to be made here: while women might, as we have seen, have had control over the electoral process or challenged their lack of access to that process, they did not sit as Members of Parliament in the House of Commons; furthermore, there are absolutely no exceptions to this prohibition. Similarly, no matter how much control aristocratic women had over court masques, estate management, or anything else, they *never* sat in the House of Lords. Women, in other words, were categorically *not* everywhere in early modern England, and it is just as important to acknowledge that indisputable historical fact as it is to acknowledge the myriad unexpected ways women found to participate in political culture.[29]

The argument of feminist revisionism would have it that female "performance"—from women rope dancers to hairy women exhibited in fairgrounds,[30] to a handful of powerful aristocratic ladies, some of whom had speaking parts in court performances over which they had considerable artistic control[31]—belie notions of women's exclusion and oppression. The revisionist tendency is to privilege cultural representation and performance as a form of quasi-political power and to suggest that the embedded structure of power relations is reversible in any given historical moment. (It is exceedingly doubtful that hirsute women on exhibition in fairs had much power at all.) As I have noted elsewhere, women are not found clamoring to get access to the English Renaissance stage because this was a disreputable rather than a privileged site.[32]

From a more nuanced perspective, from a dialogue between the "revisionist" and "exclusionist" feminist positions, the fact that there are records of women rope dancing, while is hardly evidence of women's equal participation in early modern culture, *is* evidence of an activity that is almost intrinsically inimical to the prescribed behaviors for women, namely those of the conduct book chastity, silence, and obedience. Furthermore, the evidence for female rope dancers does indicate activities and behaviors that are beyond the scope of the rigid model of the conduct book. And therein lies its importance.

The exception does not mitigate the patriarchal rule. We must keep looking at exceptions, but it is equally urgent that we keep in mind that they were just that.

IV Post-revisionism

There is no denying that feminism has been in something of an impasse in recent early modern studies. Largely because of the success of feminist studies, tried-and-true feminist arguments against the evils of patriarchy in the field and in the canon have become obsolete. As a result, some of its detractors now declare, feminism is over. In contrast, the essays in this volume argue that feminism is far from over, but it is much altered.

Crucially, this volume looks to a post-revisionist phase in feminist scholarship in the field, to a new paradigm that moves away from the adversarial politics of blame and from feminism as advocacy, but also away from the revisionist dilution of feminist politics. While revisionism sought in the interests of accuracy to nuance and correct the sometimes sweeping claims made by feminist "exclusionism," the revisionist move to "accentuate the positive and eliminate the negative" has had the unfortunate consequence of denying the reasons for feminist cultural history in the first place. Revisionism has spent its intellectual capital not on a critique of patriarchy, but of feminism itself. Its reversal of feminist arguments is such that attention to historical facts that do not place women in positions of power and agency are, as we have noted, claimed to be themselves instances of the erasure of women from the cultural and historical record, and that Moll Frith played her lute on the stage of the Fortune theater on one occasion in 1611 is routinely adduced as evidence of women's performance on the public stage.

Nor is the revisionist emphasis on women's inclusion in culture at all celebratory. Celebrating women in history and celebrating women in literature, either as authors and characters, is a notion tainted with associations of allegedly retrograde 1970s and 1980s feminism. Revisionism eschews such celebration because this "naively" suggests that celebration is in order because obstacles to recognition and representation have been overcome. Instead, revisionism implies that early modern patriarchy was a rather benign and marvelously malleable state of affairs which endowed "many women" with considerable power. ("Many" is the favorite revisionist adjective, allowing for maximum flexibility in the absence of hard evidence.) There is an alarming proximity between the revisionist position and Frances Yates's pre- (and for that matter anti-) feminist pronouncement: "[T]he injustice of discrimination between the sexes is (in my opinion) enormously over-emphasized today."[33] If that were a statement about early modern England, revisionist feminism would heartily concur with it.

While the political destination of revisionism is indeed questionable, it remains important to stress that feminist revisionism is not so much a critical affiliation or identity of the kind that a list of guilty parties can be provided in the footnotes, as an important discursive strand in an ongoing discussion and dialog across early modern feminist studies to which this volume is everywhere indebted. It is nonetheless vital to elucidate the terms of this argument with bold strokes if we are to assess where we have been, where we are, and to determine future directions. The pendulum has swung rather wildly in the revisionist direction of late, and it is time now to reassess, and reset the course.

The Impact of Feminism, then, does not so much take revisionism to task as draw the outlines of the post-revisionist phase of feminist criticism. Essays in this volume take their impetus from the recognition that the energy of feminism now resides in its full integration into and with other knowledge-making projects. Indeed, feminism has become part of the fabric of nearly all important work in the field. So what does it means for feminism (and indeed identity in general) to become digested and integrated without evacuating its specificity? Feminism is moving on, metamorphosing, and with the all the bounce, brio, and unpredictability of an Ovidian union, coupling with (and sometimes uncoupling from) a range of other political and intellectual projects as it takes its rightful place in the intellectual mainstream. As a whole, this volume seeks a subtle and comprehensive answer to the question "Where, in relation to early modern studies, is feminism now?"

Key to the volume is the hope of articulating precisely the intellectual contours of the post-revisionist phase. These are characterized by an exploration of the deep philosophical underpinnings of feminist work, as well as by the recent return to history, to the archive, and to the new materials that are being uncovered there. Thus, alongside more theoretical reflections, the book includes essays on the specifically historical work done on women and the increasingly complicated questions being asked about women's status and their relation to power. Contributors are especially interested in modes of inquiry that operate in relation to, or as consequence of, a wave of political and theoretical thinking which includes feminism and dialogues with it, and which are, in considerable measure, inspired by its intellectual and political impetus. In other words, there emerges from the contributions collected here a critical-theoretical and empirical reflection on the trajectory of work by feminists (who are to be understood to espouse their feminism more as an allegiance than as an identity), which has increasingly evaded direct labeling.

All of the essays acknowledge the specificity of the aesthetic and of the literary as well as the complicated ways in which art is and is not simply part of the rest of culture. Similarly, the essays attest to the fact that feminism's capacity for both exchange (however heated) and change signals how far beyond the structures in which it was originally conceived feminism has moved, and demonstrate beyond the shadow of a doubt that Feminist Renaissance Studies is more alive than ever.

* * *

The book is divided into three large organizing categories: *Theories*, which emphasizes the theoretical dimensions of the post-revisionist phase of feminist criticism, including psychoanalysis, Marxism and formalism; *Women*, which stresses actual lives or the impact of cultural represent-ations of women's lived experience; and *Histories*, which emphasizes a post-revisionist intervention into received wisdom and feminist histories of the period. The topics addressed under these broad headings include language, representation, ideas about space and cities, as well as ques-tions about epistemological consequences of feminism as a shaping force in new, theoretically informed modes of inquiry and in relation to specifically archival work.

Theories

The book's opening chapter sets the course for completely new feminist territories by staging a dialogue between early modern studies and the epistemological transformations wrought by French feminism. Jonathan Gil Harris's "Cleopatran Affinities: Hélène Cixous, Margaret Cavendish, and the Writing of Dialogic Matter" uses this dialogue to go beyond the limited horizons—and errors—of positive materialism, which, he argues, is currently the conceptual norm of our field. This depoliticized brand of materialism unearths "matter" as literally raw material, conceived as a kind of blank slate devoid of any kind of cultural inscription. Harris also uses this juxtaposition of French feminism with the early modern to challenge what he argues is the antiquarian but popular notion of an irreducible difference between the past and the present.

In particular, Harris emphasizes feminism's far-reaching legacies to early modern studies that increasingly embrace areas of scholarship that might at first glance have little directly to do with cultural histories and/or critiques of patriarchy, gender, or sexuality. One such area is the burgeoning field of "material culture." The latter has been distinguished by two discrete yet mutually supporting foci: objects and bodies. The current scholarly vogue for objects was arguably enabled by the trailblazing, feminist-inflected studies of women's management of properties undertaken by Joan Thirsk in the 1980s; yet its current popularity seems to be fueled largely by a fetishistic longing for the "real" that vitiates questions of theory or praxis. Similarly, scholarship on the Renaissance body is greatly indebted to other feminist work from the 1980s, including adaptations of Mikhail Bakhtin and studies of early modern biology and gender. More recent work, however, has become increasingly preoccupied with less identifiably feminist concerns such as the phenomenology of bodily experience, the physiology of the passions, and even the ethics of digestion.

Despite material culture's loosely feminist genealogy, its increasingly anti-quarian, positivistic, and synchronic conception of the "material" marks a striking renunciation of two of the other critical methodologies with which feminism productively engaged in the 1970s and 1980s: poststructuralism and Marxism. Harris teases out these two strands within a dynamic feminist tradition of writing about the body that has come to be all but ignored in recent early modern studies. This tradition starts with French feminist theories of *écriture feminine* in the 1970s, and culminates in Judith Butler's *Bodies That Matter* (1993).[34] "The body" and "the material" signify very differently in these theorists' writing from how each has been refigured in the recent wave of scholarship on material culture. In ways that critically challenge and refine Bakhtin's theory of the "grotesque" and Marx's theory of "matter," French feminists and Butler alike insist on a diachronic, dynamic conception of bodily materiality. Harris argues that these feminist theories of corporeality and materiality have not impacted the study of early modern material culture sufficiently. Through a rereading of Cixous's lengthy digression on *Antony and Cleopatra* in her essay "Sorties"[35] in relation to the work of Margaret Cavendish, he suggests how French feminism and its related discourses can return "material culture" to earlier feminist questions of political agency.

Heather Hirschfeld's "Confessing Mothers: The Maternal Penitent in Early Modern Revenge Tragedy" takes up two issues which have been sidelined by revisionism—the misogyny of revenge tragedy and psychoanalysis—but does so in the context of a newly urgent issue in Renaissance Studies, that of religion. While psychoanalysis was hugely important to feminist scholarship in the 1970s and 1980s with path-breaking work such as Juliet Mitchell's *Feminism and Psychoanlysis* (1974), Jacqueline Rose's "*Hamlet* the Mona Lisa of Literature" (1986), and their co-authored edition of Jacques Lacan's *Feminine Sexuality* (1982),[36] the 1990s saw an anti-intellectual backlash against the supposed "ahistoricism" as well as gender bias of psychoanalysis among Renaissance scholars, who maintained that Freud's formulations had nothing to offer the analysis of gender and sexuality in a period far removed from *fin-de-siècle* Vienna. This chapter makes explicit the ways in which Freud's paradigms are sensitive to as well as coherent with Renaissance figurations of masculinity and femininity, suggesting that one important element of post-revisionist feminism in Renaissance Studies should be a return, in newly inflected modes, to Freud. Hirschfeld is especially concerned with the "psychotheological" elements of revenge tragedy, that is with the way this genre responds to Reformation desacralization of auricular confession, a practice that is often cited as the precursor of "the talking cure." Revenge tragedy comes to require, Hirschfeld argues, a spectacle of specifically female penitence. Female characters, most famously Gertrude, become ways of negotiating sudden and significant changes in religious prescription as well as their psychological consequences.

Sasha Roberts' "Feminist Criticism and the new Formalism: Early Modern Women and Literary Engagement" asks whether formalist literary analysis which takes form rather than content as its central organizing category can be reconciled with feminist criticism, which takes precisely gender content as its central organizing trope. While we have become more alert to how particular literary forms, such as romance, were gendered in the early modern period, questions of form have generally taken second place to an analysis of content in the feminist and historicist paradigms that have become mainstream in Renaissance literary studies. In the "mutual irrelevance" of feminism and formalism, Roberts discovers a way to resist synthesis and instead to forge a dialogic connection between the two methodologies. The literary terrain she covers is the ostensibly intractable texts of misogynist verse. Margaret Ferguson has noted how women in the past felt themselves "expropriated by a misogynistic discursive tradition," unable to find "a refuge from her culture's definition of her sex."[37] Yet early modern women, Roberts shows, were also readers of some of the most pernicious misogynist literature, prompting the question of how such dynamics of literary expropriation—and appropriation—really operated in the period. Further, in manuscript miscellanies autographed by women, misogynist verse is countered by a range of writing on and by women. It is not simply that genre is crucial to the treatment of gender and sexuality in literature; rather, the multiplicity of genres, modes, and personae encompassed by the miscellany serve to draw attention to the specificities of literary form; to the literary process; to literary artifice. In this respect misogynist verse in the miscellany emerges as less striking, and perhaps significant, for its treatment of women than as an exploration of literary form. This (at one level heretical) observation has implications far beyond manuscript miscellanies or misogynist literature.

Gender and sexuality constitute the central "tropes" of feminist literary criticism. But should they always be? This essay tussles with key questions facing feminist criticism today, particularly in the context of Renaissance studies: given current emphasis on cultural and historical contexts, how should feminist criticism engage with questions of literary form? What possibilities and limitations does the 'new formalism'—a nascent critical movement—present to feminist criticism?

R. S. White's "Ophelia's Sisters" is in part a review of and return to ostensibly pre-theoretical feminist character criticism; it is also a radical re-reading of *Hamlet* from a feminist perspective, which addresses not only the consequences of the play's afterlife for the text(s) of *Hamlet*, but also for examination of the specifically textual detail around the typically female occupations of stitching and mending. This feminist cultural history of Ophelia considers how Shakespeare's most famous tragedy was or has become a "botched" play. "Botching" —meaning to mend, repair, or patch up—is one of several textile references in the play, and is used to describe the creative lyricism of Ophelia's deranged utterances. White addresses these "material" references as points in Shakespeare's text that have been especially generative of appropriation, recuperation, reinterpretations, and indeed wholesale reinvention: White takes up the cultural reinvention and addresses the long tradition of pathologizing her character, and asks what, in Shakespeare's creation, might give Ophelia such open and flexible signification, whether as the demure daughter, the submissive victim of patriarchy, female rebellion, or study in hysteria. Mary Pipher in *Reviving Ophelia: Saving the Selves of Adolescent Girls* and Sara Shandler's *Ophelia Speaks: Adolescent Girls Write About Their Search for Self*—neither of them remotely claiming to be Shakespearean criticism—link the character with adolescent females today; Cheryl Dellasega's *Surviving Ophelia: Mothers Share Their Wisdom in Navigating the Tumultuous Teenage Years* gives her paradigm status for "oppositional defiant disorder."[38] The internet "Ophelia Project" associates her with "relational aggression" and, more specifically, eating disorders in young women. White traces these related appropriations through channels of popular psychology during the 1990s, and argues both that they give Ophelia a new identity for new times and that they constitute the cultural reverberations of the ways in which "Ophelia in reverie provides a distraction into some other quite spellbinding dimension, a different narrative that nobody can either ignore or incorporate, 'botch' or repair to fit the history of the Prince of Denmark."

Women

Jean Howard addresses the way city comedy as an urban literary genre with an urban chorography invites a fresh look at women's place in culture. Arguing that generic hierarchies have determined in part the course of scholarship on women in our field, Howard claims that as long as dramatic genres such as tragedy and history have priority, it takes some powerful reading against the grain to locate women as more than tangential players within these fictions. However, reclaiming the domain of social historians for literary scholars, which means attention to less privileged genres such as housewifery manuals, diaries, domestic tragedy, and city comedies, allows for a re-charting of the position of women within both literary fictions and many of the central institutions of culture. This in turn allows for a re-reading of texts in which the domain of the daily/the everyday/the domestic is underplayed. Howard's goal is to use these texts to talk about women's actual engagement with life in London, both discursive and actual, and to discuss ways of reading cultural texts that draw on the political energies of feminism to query the norms of our discipline.

"Sex and the Early Modern City: Staging the Bawdy Houses of London," then, examines afresh the organizing categories of feminist scholarship on early modern women, looking in particular at the identity categories of "wife," "maid," and "whore" in the "brothel comedies" of the early seventeenth century. Howard argues for the breakdown of discrete identities which have thus far structured feminist thinking about women in the period. That there are simply no whorehouse plays before the end of the sixteenth century suggests that these representations speak to issues that take on specific coloration in the burgeoning metropolis of seventeenth-century London. However, historicizing this relation is complex: the urban whore neither reflects the lives of actual prostitutes nor the prescriptions of conduct literature. Rather, these figures are discursive stress-points, created in response to the material demands of urban commercial theater as well as those of comic genre. In the city, maids and wives could easily turn whore. More importantly, however, Howard argues that not only are these identity categories porous, they are also reversible. The capacity of femininity to metamorphose in response to specific opportunities, constraints, circumstances, and locations is surprising since it is in complete contradiction to the fictions of femininity articulated by the conduct literature. However, the bawdy house plays, which are arguably closer to life on the streets of the new metropolis, show that far from living out polarized conditions of femininity, a woman can be a wife *and* engage in prostitution. Further, prostitutes, at least in these comedies, can attain a legitimate married status, and fallen maids often recover themselves sufficiently in these urban settings to thrive and attain a happy ending. Interestingly, Howard suggests that these reversed feminine identities are analogous to racial and religious transformations articulated in the narratives of conversion in popular contemporary Turk plays. In the latter, "turning Turk," since it necessarily entails circumcision, involves a rather more drastic and irreversible alteration of masculine identity than any of the transformations of women's sexual identity suggested on the early modern stage.

All the contributions to this volume work open up the boundaries of temporality, disciplinarity, genre, and geography as they reconfigure and re-chart extant knowledge about women and representations of women in the sixteenth and seventeenth centuries. Kate Chedgzoy's "Women, Gender, and the Politics of Location" uses the techniques of feminist geography to open up spatial boundaries that can represent not just topological specificity, but also demarcation and containment in relation to Renaissance women's writing. This essay opens up fresh possibilities for theoretical dialogue by bringing together the new theorizations of the politics and meanings of space and place with recent historical analyses of the major geopolitical changes that took place in the early modern period. Chedgzoy exposes the gendered assumptions that excluded women from the period's master-narratives of religious, political, and espistemological change. In her account, intimate domestic detail meets grand narrative; in particular, Chedgzoy addresses the ways in which women's lives were transformed by changes in the meaning of location, at the local, regional, national, and transnational levels that effectively shaped the early modern period; and thus the ways in which women's opportunities for understanding themselves as geopolitical subjects were also transformed. She argues that our understanding of early modern women's relation to the political needs to be articulated through the dimension of place and location. Chedgzoy demonstrates the arguments about women's inclusion and exclusion look very different when considered in the light of women's own accounts about dislocations from the country to the city or from one country or territory to another. This work has important implications for the ways in which early modern women experienced, engaged with, and commented on processes of state-formation and nation-building in the early modern British Isles, and for the ways in which they contributed to the imagining and representation of alternative communities. Chedgzoy also critiques new theorizations of the production and experience of locations charged with social meaning that have not been adequately engaged with by early modernists, with the result that studies of the changing geopolitics of early modern Britain have both neglected the intimate consequences of those large-scale processes for people's lives, and in general have been under-theorized and oblivious to gender. Conversely, while feminist studies of modern and contemporary culture have richly analyzed the over-determinations of women's experience and representation of place and belonging, these perspectives have not, on the whole, been sufficiently alert to historical difference.

Kimberly Anne Coles' "'The 'diffrence...in degree': Social Rank and Gendered Expression" examines the consequences—both practical and theoretical—of the end of essentialism in Renaissance Studies. Among the first of these is that, especially the wake of new scholarly discoveries related to manuscript production, circulation, and the history of the book, it is no longer possible or viable to isolate women writers and women's writing from the myriad texts and writing practices circulating and operating in Renaissance intellectual culture. Especially since *imitatio* was one of the most valued aesthetic practices of the period, women, like men, wrote in imitation, as well as in response and in resistance to the prevailing discursive currents and literary forms. As the works of feminist theorists, including and perhaps most prominently Judith Butler, have pointed out, femininity is a performance and a discursive sign that can therefore be used and manipulated by both sexes. This insight, Coles argues, allows feminist criticism to unearth a more complicated history than we presently have of early modern English culture and its literary representation. She cites the specific case of Amelia Lanyer's poem "Salve Deus Rex Judæorum," which has made Lanyer one of the most recognized poets in the canon of early modern women's writing even though, among those women authors in print circulation in the early modern period, she was one of the least influential. Feminist critics, Cole argues, take Lanyer's apparent "proto-feminist" position as a somewhat straightforward expression of gendered identity. While Lanyer's proto-feminism is undeniable (Lanyer claims, among other things, that women are better able to receive Christ), her position is better and more accurately understood in the context of other early modern poems about the Passion, especially those of Nicholas Breton and Abraham Fraunce. Lanyer's proto-feminism, then, manifests itself as a marketing strategy, a kind of product differentiation as she strives to make her own work stand out from male contemporaries when appealing to the aristocratic women she woos as patrons. Cole shows that questions of identity and the writer's market converge in Lanyer's work even though literary criticism has tended to offer discrete treatments of these issues. This is particularly important since it is her engagement with the patronage system that has produced the most prized literary qualities of Lanyer's work. Cole further seeks to understand the extent to which this political/polemical quality in Lanyer's work has led to her critical appeal. If there is to be no "essentialist freezing" of the ideas of gender, race, and class, then probing the basis for differences (en)gendered in the expression of a middle-class woman's work and those of women of the upper classes becomes particularly productive, and some sense of how these distinctions have been ushered into our own critical understanding similarly becomes crucial.

Pamela Allen Brown's "A New Fable of the Belly: Vulgar Curiosity and the Persian Lady's Loose Bodies" offers a critical reading and cultural history of Marcus Gheeraerts's portrait known as *The Persian Lady*, and does so by putting on a distinctively retro-feminist critical persona that confronts the status quo and rocks the boat of established values. Brown argues the case for "barging in" on other disciplines, and in doing so takes on the issues of feminist inter-disciplinarity in relation to a portrait which would seem to invite and require such a perspective since the painting bears a sonnet in the fretwork on the cartouche in its right-hand corner. The painting has in its history attracted the attention of Britain's most eminent art historians and the great Renaissance cultural historian, Frances Yates. The portrait is an enigma: the lady *appears to be* pregnant, but since one of the most famous paintings of a full-bellied woman, Jan Van Eyck's *The Betrothal of the Arnolfini*, depicts a woman whom art historians have established is not in fact pregnant, it is impossible to make a definitive determination. The subject of the portrait also appears to be in a masquing costume, thus becoming a racialized image as well as one whose sexuality is put on display by her belly—whether or not it contains a fetus. Brown's reading is deliberately, provocatively interrogative, and committed to asking "rude" questions about long-held verities in order to explore issues of identity, anonymity, not in relation to some absolute "truth" behind the painting, but rather in relation to its subject as a type of female performance. Looking at the painting from this perspective, as a scholar who has worked on women's performance during a period when women did not act on the public stage, Brown is able to analyze the enigma of the painting and its poem beyond the confines of the traditional critical pursuit for the sitter's elusive, historical identity.

Patricia Parker's "Construing Gender: Mastering Bianca in *The Taming of the Shrew*" returns with a twist in a radical re-reading of Bianca to the issues of feminist character criticism. Rather than being an early Shakespeare farce, Parker demonstrates that *Shrew* is essentially a play about humanist arts and learning, and further that these issues are not merely an addendum to the play's focus on the battle of the sexes, but rather are integral to the construction and dismantling of all manner of social and linguistic hierarchies that constitute the core themes of the play. Parker takes up the rivalry between Kate and Bianca in terms of the rivalries of "the sister arts" in the humanist educational paradigm and in relation to the role of music as "handmaiden" to the arts of rhetoric and philosophy. The epistemological ordering of music as an ancillary and feminine art is, Parker argues, directly related to the friction the play stages and generates both between the sisters and between men and women, the upper social orders and the lower ones. Building on her earlier path-breaking work in *Shakespeare from the Margins* (1996), Parker argues that the disruption of hierarchy is often effected in Renaissance culture by means of reversal, of the *arsy versy* reconfigurations of the high and low limits of the cultural spectrum rather than by a paradigm that might conform more readily to our own (unrealistic or perhaps fictional) expectations, namely their obliteration. The gender hierarchy, Parker demonstrates, makes these epistemological configurations and rearrangements visible to us by offering an access route to territory that is now linguistically obscure in a way that it was not to early moderns. From this perspective, newly attuned to linguistic and imagistic resonances, and especially to the period's understanding of music, the Bianca subplot, as well as Bianca herself, serve as echoes and resonances of the nuptial rite from The Book of Common Prayer. In this reading, Bianca is never the conduct book model of femininity the other characters, and crucially, other feminist critics, assume. Rather, she is always shown to have a capacity for mastery that Katherine, "the designated shrew," is never permitted.

Histories

Frances E. Dolan's "Hermione's Ghost: Catholicism, the Feminine, and the Undead" takes as its starting point the paucity of female specters on the Renaissance stage. The fact that ghosts who return to demand vengeance are overwhelmingly male suggests not that gender is irrelevant to the spectral dimension of revenge tragedy, but rather that there the gender paradigm needs to be urgently applied. The problem with the Renaissance dead is that they may walk abroad at any moment. Grief, loss, and closure might be deferred indefinitely in the anxious anticipation that the deceased might revive. Closely associated with the idea we see very little of in the drama, namely the female apparition, is the specter of Catholicism, which simply never died and whose afterlife in the cultural imaginary of Protestant England was as the supernatural feminine figure of the Blessed Virgin, and who was, Dolan argues, an object of veneration and of fear. Dolan's detailed reading of the figure of Hermione in *The Winter's Tale* is cast in the light of a culture in which it was widely believed that those who destroyed and defaced statues of the Virgin would suffer similar mutilation. However, Dolan's point is not only to demonstrate the analogy between Hermione's statue and Mariology, but also to show that Elizabethan and Jacobean Catholics have only very recently become visible to cultural critics of the period. In deliberate violation of temporal and geographic boundaries, Dolan suggests an analogy between allegedly vanishing indigenous people, Catholics, and feminism. Now that critics are newly attentive to the Catholic resonances of Shakespeare's plays and to the Catholicism which permeates post-Reformation culture, Catholics are everywhere. Of course, Dolan argues, Roman Catholics never vanished; rather, in their assimilation they became invisible to the gaze of literary critics and historians. The "problem" of Catholicism, its status in English culture, and its visibility or lack thereof, is usefully analogous to the issue of feminist criticism, which is similarly in danger of being assimilated beyond the horizon of visibility.

Deanne Williams offers a fresh examination of the scholarship of the twentieth century's doyenne of Renaissance studies, Frances A. Yates. A female scholar among men, Yates thought feminists were whiners and wanted to be "one of the boys." Williams's biographical account of Yates, "No Man's Elizabeth: Frances A. Yates and the History of History," works to historicize Yates's path-breaking scholarship on Elizabeth I. Yates's work was remarkably innovative and was, at least at its first presentation, an unpopular departure from the prevailing Victorian view of Elizabeth as an aging queen whose fragile mortality was ill-concealed under the paint, power, and wigs which shored up her sovereignty. Yates rigorous inter-disciplinarity, in contrast, drew attention to the importance of Elizabeth's virginity and that the iconography of her sovereignty derived from classical sources and (in a move that struck a discordant note with the strains of "Rule Britannia" to which

England was swaying in 1947) was in several instances indistinguishable from the absolutist ideology of the French court. Although, as we have noted, she was notoriously devoid of feminist sentiments, Yates nonetheless succeeded in providing insights into Elizabeth's reign which have been far more amenable to subsequent feminist scholarship than the Victorian myths of Elizabeth expounded by Virginia Woolf, who had impeccable feminist credentials.

Williams' essay weaves Yates's biography—her reaction to the First World War, the loss of her brother, her bourgeois metropolitan background, the fact that she was possessed of a room of her own which was equipped with a very handsome writing desk—with the founding of the Warburg Institute. Indeed, it was the arrival in London from Germany of the Jewish exile Aby Warburg, with his splendid library, that gave her an intellectual niche at all, and Williams shows how Yates forged a path—and in this regard a decidedly unpopular one—in the pursuit of knowledge of her period. Otherwise, she would have been institutionally homeless, the room and desk not withstanding. Williams combines insights about Elizabeth's self-fashioning through dialogue with learned men and ancient ideals of female power and sovereignty, with the problematic sense of feminine identity presented by Yates and, in a very different manner, by Virginia Woolf. This is a reflexive historicization of women as both scholars and queens which, like Jonathan Gil Harris's essay, seeks to traverse hitherto discrete boundaries between the past, present, and some key moments in between.

In its focus on the daily lives of women in the marketplace, Natasha Korda shares the feminist theoretical concerns expressed by Jean Howard and Kate Chedgzoy about women as cultural players. In "Women's Informal Commerce and the 'All-Male' Stage" she acknowledges that the stage was all-male, but argues that the theatre was not. Turning her attention away from the revisionist emphasis on representation, she investigates the cultural and material foundation of women's labor which made such representation possible at all. That is, instead of dwelling on women who were the exception to the implicit but systematic prohibition against female mimesis, Korda examines the theatre's reliance on female labor for many of its vital operations. Focusing in particular on the women who worked in London's informal economy of unregulated crafts and trades, which flourished in the very suburbs and liberties that gave rise to the commercial theaters, Korda looks to the ordinary women who worked within the networks of commerce surrounding London's public theaters. Korda argues that if we take into account the full range of social and economic interdependencies and collaborations that went into theatrical production, we must redefine the "all-male" stage as a network of commerce between active economic agents of both genders. The public and private theaters were entangled in an immense web of commercial activity in early modern London, many of whose strands were taken up and woven into innovative enterprises by women.

Korda provides a theoretical framework that explores the usefulness of the concept of informality to an understanding of early modern women's work, and considers the ways in which such work contributed to early modern theatrical production and its representation on the stage. As such, her essay builds on recent feminist archival research into early modern women's economic agency and departs from earlier feminist work on the commodification of or "traffic in women" by focusing on the "traffic *of* women." Korda's work entails a return to the archives to recover the many different forms of commerce in which women were engaged. Yet it also entails the elaboration of new theoretical paradigms, such as the concept of "informality," through which such archival material may be reframed. The latter notion captures the blurred contours of this sector of the market which have given rise to a host of descriptive terms—informal, irregular, black, hidden, shadow, parallel, secondary—that reinforce its penumbral or marginal status. The aim of such elaboration is to take better account of the entire gamut of women's economic relation to the singularly aesthetic cultural practices of the theatre.

Jennifer Panek turns her attention to the expression and containment of sexual desire in the conjugal bond. "Why Did Widows Remarry? Remarriage, Male Authority, and Feminist Criticism" responds to this question in relation to the debate about women and early modern marriage in the specific instance of widows and in relation to the period's "prodigal son plays." These dramas frequently end with a feckless youth gladly wedding an older, richer, more responsible widow. Thus her focus is not so much on the performance of marriage as on the reality of its reiteration. That some women in early modern London took a second, third, and even a fourth husband potentially created the conditions, Panek argues, for the remaking of marriage itself. In looking to the potential for metamorphosing the power and gender dynamics of marriage, Panek emphasizes not the social or the economic dimensions of conjugality, but the much neglected realm of the specifically sexual. Instead of resisting as misogynist the most popular early modern answers to the question of why women remarried, namely the widow's desire for sex, Panek appropriates and even embraces the accusation, suggesting that in the middle-class world of urban London at least, notions of dominance and subordination might be more readily overturned in the sexual realm, within the precincts of lawful marriage, than perhaps anywhere else outside it.

Marriage provided, Panek claims, the only socially sanctioned outlet for women's sexuality. And with the tendency of feminist critics to celebrate sexually transgressive women, we have largely ignored the power of respectable sexuality. Pursuing Susan Amussen's hypothesis that women "elevated the importance of sexual behavior" in order to minimize "the contradictions between women's economic roles and their expected subordination,"[39] Panek further suggests that wives may have deliberately deployed married chastity to dispense with the more nebulous and onerous requirements of obedience (Shakespeare's *The Merry Wives of Windsor* is interesting in this context). Potentially then our celebration of "transgression" obscures the extent to which women themselves shaped cultural ideals of female respectability: it was in women's own interests—sexual, economic, domestic, and spiritual—to uphold the value of chastity, and it was easier both to be and to be seen to be chaste as a married woman than as a widow. However, Panek is also interested in the role of men in patriarchy and the limitations of the patriarchal order on their behavior and desires. She asks whether popular culture's obsessive focus on the suitor's sexual mastery of the widow may not always reveal male anxiety about her potential to dominate him, but sometimes constitute a deflective gesture towards the whole concept of domestic power relations. Taking up the feminist commitment to address not just women and femininity but to look at the dynamics of gender more broadly, Panek considers the possibility that the men who heeded the warnings about widows as insubordinate wives and married them anyway were simply ignoring the requirements of their prescribed patriarchal role.[40]

Grace Ioppolo's "'I desire to be helde in your memory': Reading Penelope Rich through Her Letters" is, like Korda's essay, an example of the feminist return to the archives which is symptomatic of a certain frustration with the energy feminist criticism has hitherto spent on abstract philosophical approaches to the conundrum of women's presence/absence in English Renaissance letters. Ioppolo's constructive response draws our attention to the still unexamined yet copious archive of women's writing. Taking Penelope Rich as the exemplary instance of the first-order necessity of feminist archeology, she addresses the letters of the woman "Whose presence absence, absence presence is," as Sir Philip Sidney famously puts in *Astrophil and Stella*. Rich's letters represent a true discovery in the annals of literary criticism, and they are transcribed and analyzed here for the first time.

Rich left letters and other documents in her own handwriting, including a letter to Queen Elizabeth to demand, rather than beg, mercy for her imprisoned brother, and letters to Sir Robert Cecil, Elizabeth's Secretary of State, and one of the most powerful men of the early modern age, to instruct him in her wishes when her husband was absent fighting in the Irish wars. In these letters, Rich speaks for herself: she represents herself, and in many ways can be seen to contradict, if not intentionally damage, early modern standards and boundaries for women. In fact, she more than holds her own against Elizabeth, who was notorious for banishing or punishing women who challenged her power or acted against her wishes in regards to the men in her life and command. Rich has been accused of sexual promiscuity, both before and after her marriage to Lord Rich, whom she divorced in 1605; she has been celebrated, and often condemned, for her beauty and sexuality, but she has, Ioppolo insists, always been represented, through the eyes of men and measured against patriarchal conceptions and idealizations of women. Ioppolo not only attempts to find the historical Penelope Rich using her handwritten letters and other manuscript material, but also uses her as a case study to see how our received feminist images of early modern women and early modern literature change in the light of this new evidence from the archive.

What makes Ioppolo's chapter insistently post-revisionist is its emphasis on the realities of patriarchal power relations that Rich could not evade, and simultaneously its emphasis on the self-representations of a woman who was anything but a victimized "Poor Rich." In its treatment of gender and power, this chapter is avowedly feminist in its motives, but it also provides concrete empirical evidence that no future work on Sidney, Essex, or Elizabeth will be able to ignore.

The volume's finale, Gail Kern Paster's "Hormonal Conclusions," makes the resoundingly revisionist case that the theory-driven retreat from anatomy (branded as crude biologism) toward cultural explanations for women's identities, sexualities, practices, and so forth, in feminist criticism is in need of urgent reconsideration in the case of early modern literary studies. Paster makes the argument for a "fluid interaction" between the biological and the cultural in relation to the specific instance of the connection between hormones and emotions. There *are* hormonally induced tendencies to weepiness, for example, Paster argues, even though feminist critics have sought rigidly rational (and quasi-masculinist) explanations for literary representations of lachrymose women. This is not to revert to the oppressive accounts of female difference, a move back to "biology is destiny." Rather, it is to recognize that biology has itself a culturally acquired negative valuation. When we cease to be so defensive about biology, about the personally and intellectually embarrassing territory of the emotions, poised as they are on the threshold between biology, where they are hormonally produced, and culture, we can, Paster argues, stop being fearful of acknowledging profound connections between early modern women, or their literary representations, and ourselves.

* * *

The contributions to this volume, then, offer a diverse array of post-revisionist feminist treatments of English Renaissance culture. They represent both the absorption of previous phases in feminist criticism and its incorporation into "mainstream" work in the field. The volume also hopes to demonstrate the necessity of feminist scholarship as a constantly growing, changing enterprise, which is not focused on the work of individual critics, but on the accretions, contestations, and accumulations of scholarly labor in a collective enterprise.

Notes

 1. Phyllis Rackin, *Shakespeare and Women* (Oxford: Oxford University Press, 2005), 17.
 2. "Renaissance" is generally used by scholars who emphasize the period's indebtedness to the classical past, whereas "early modern" usually stresses the anticipation of modernity, and especially the advent of capitalism that began in this era. Obviously, such conceptualizations are simultaneously useful and limited, and while they are not synonymous, such terminological distinctions should not be overplayed.
 3. The Book of Common Prayer (1559); see Dympna Callaghan, *Romeo and Juliet: Texts and Contexts* (New York: St. Martin's Press, 2003), 309.
 4. Amy Louise Erickson, *Women and Property in Early Modern England* (New York: Routledge, 1993), 8–9.
 5. Callaghan, *Romeo and Juliet*, 275.
 6. Debora Kuller Shuger, *Habits of Thought in the English Renaissance: Religion, Politics, and the Dominant Culture* (Berkeley, CA: University of California Press, 1990), 233.
 7. Carol Thomas Neely, *Broken Nuptials in Shakespeare's Plays* (New Haven, CT: Yale University Press, 1985), 15.
 8. T. E., *The Law's Resolutions of Women's Rights* (1632) in Frances E. Dolan, *The Taming of the Shrew* (New York: St. Martin's Press, 1996), 198.
 9. Dolan, *The Taming of the Shrew*, 10.
10. Ibid., 13.
11. Alice Clark's *Women and Work in Seventeenth Century England* (London: 1919; repr. 1982).
12. Frances E. Dolan, "Staging Domesticity: Household Work and English Identity in Early Modern Drama," *Shakespeare Quarterly* 54:3 (2003), 318–20.
13. Gail Kern Paster, *The Body Embarrassed: Drama and the Disciplines of Shame in Early Modern England* (Ithaca, NY: Cornell University Press, 1992), 201.
14. Dolan, *The Taming of the Shrew*, 197–8.
15. Callaghan, *Romeo and Juliet*, 296.
16. Ibid., 297.
17. Ibid., 330.
18. Ibid., 307.
19. Quoted in Sara Mendelson and Patricia Crawford, eds., *Women in Early Modern England* (Oxford: Oxford University Press, 1998), 129.
20. Rackin, *Shakespeare and Women*, 9.
21. Dolan, *The Taming of the Shrew*, 198.
22. P. W. Hasler, ed., *The House of Commons, 1558–1603*, Vol. 1 (London: Her Majesty's Stationery Office, 1981), 118.
23. S. T. Bindoff, ed., *The House of Commons 1509–1558*, Vol. 1 (London: History of Parliament Trust, 1982), 194–5.
24. Mendelson and Crawford, *Women in Early Modern England*, 56.
25. Losley MS 1989, "A Certificate of the maner of theleccon [*sic*] of the Burgesses for the Cittie of Westm. For this present Parliament 1620." I am grateful to Chris R. Kyle for this reference.
26. W. Notestein, ed., *The Journal of Sir Simonds D'Ewes* (New Haven, CT, 1923), 463, quoted Mendelson and Crawford, *Women in Early Modern England*, 396.
27. Evidence of women's attempts to exercise power through official channels is largely confined to the mid- and later seventeenth century: "In an election

at Richmond in 1678, women were prevented from voting directly, but were conceded the right to assign their votes to males who would deputize for them" (Mendelson and Crawford, *Women in Early Modern England*, 347).

28. BL, MS Harl. 165, fo. 8; quoted Mendelson and Crawford, *Women in Early Modern England*, 397.

29. In the Introduction to Dympna Callaghan, ed., *The Feminist Companion to Shakespeare* (Oxford: Blackwell, 2000) I also argued against another revisionist precept, namely the anti-essentialist belief that "everyone in the Renaissance was in some respects a woman," by showing gender difference functions as an absolute rather than a relative distinction (xiv).

30. See Ann Thompson, "Women/ 'women' and the stage," in Helen Wilcox, ed., *Women and Literature in Britain 1500–1700* (Cambridge: Cambridge University Press, 1996), 100–16.

31. Excellent recent studies of the questions of women's power in the masque include J. Leeds Barroll, *Anna of Denmark, Queen of England: A Cultural Biography* (Philadelphia: University of Pennsylvania Press, 2001); Clare McManus, *Women on the Renaissance Stage: Anna of Denmark and Female Masquing in the Stuart Court, 1590–1619* (Manchester and New York: Manchester University Press, 2002); *Women and Culture at the Courts of the Stuart Queens*, ed. Clare McManus (New York: Palgrave Macmillan, 2003).

32. Dympna Callaghan, *Shakespeare without Women* (New York: Routledge, 2000), 5.

33. Quoted by Deanne Williams in her essay in this volume from Warburg Library Archive, Frances Yates Papers, "Memorial 1982" TS.

34. Judith Butler, *Bodies that Matter: On the Discursive Limits of Sex* (New York and London: Routledge, 1993).

35. Hélène Cixous, "Sorties: Ways Out/Attacks/ Forays," in Hélène Cixous and Catherine Clément, *The Newly Born Woman*, trans. Betsy Wing (Minneapolis: University of Minnesota Press, 1986), 63–132.

36. Juliet Mitchell, *Psychoanalysis and Feminism: A Radical Reassessment of Freudian Psychoanalysis* (New York: Pantheon Books, 1974); Jacqueline Rose, "*Hamlet*, the Mona Lisa of Literature," in Jacqueline Rose, *Sexuality in the Field of Vision* (London: Verso, 1986); Juliet Mitchell and Jacqueline Rose, eds., *Feminine Sexuality: Jacques Lacan and the école freudienne* (New York: W.W. Norton; Pantheon, 1982).

37. Margaret Ferguson "A Room Not Their Own: Renaissance Women as Readers and Writers," in ed. Clayton Koelb and Susan Noakes, *The Comparative Perspective on Literature: Approaches to Theory and Practice* (Ithaca, NY: Cornell University Press, 1988).

38. Mary Pipher, *Reviving Ophelia: Saving the Selves of Adolescent Girls* (New York: Putnam, 1994); Sara Shandler, *Ophelia Speaks: Adolescent Girls Write about their Search for Self* (New York: HarperCollins 1999); Cheryl Dellasega, *Surviving Ophelia: Mothers Share Their Wisdom in Navigating the Tumultuous Teenage Year* (Boulder, CO: Perseus Publishing, 2001).

39. Susan Amussen, *An Ordered Society: Gender and Class in Early Modern England* (New York: Columbia University Press, 1988), 121–2.

40. See also Dympna Callaghan, "*The Duchess of Malfi* and Early Modern Widows," in Patrick Cheney and Garrett Sullivan, eds., *Early Modern English Drama: A Critical Companion*, (Oxford: Oxford University Press, 2006).

Part I
Theories

2

Cleopatran Affinities: Hélène Cixous, Margaret Cavendish, and the Writing of Dialogic Matter

Jonathan Gil Harris

> Cleopatra [is] infinite intelligence, completely applied to making life, to making love, to make: to invent, to create, from one emotion to draw out ten thousand forms of beauty, from one joy ten thousand games.
>
> Hélène Cixous, "Sorties," 126

> As for *Cleopatra*, I wonder she should be so Infamous for a Whore, since she was constant to those Men she had taken... If they say true Love can dissemble, they may as well say Truth is no Truth, and Love is no Love: but the Lover delivers his whole Soul to the Beloved. Some say she was Proud and Ambitious, because she loved those had most Power: She was a Great Person her self, and born to have Power, therefore it was natural to her to love Power.
>
> Margaret Cavendish, *World's Olio*, 131–2

Two women, from different times, from different worlds, meet in one body—albeit a body that is not one, but multiple, open, becoming. The scene? It, too, is multiple. Paris, 1975: the Algerian-French feminist Hélène Cixous meets the Egyptian Queen Cleopatra in the heterogeneous, intertextual body of Cixous's *écriture feminine*. Antwerp, 1655: the exiled English writer Margaret Cavendish, Duchess of Newcastle, meets Cleopatra in Cavendish's labyrinthine gallery of the mind where, in her words, "so many creatures be, / Like many Commonwealths" (*Sociable Letters*, sig. d). Washington DC, 2005: Cixous meets Cavendish in the "infinite variety" of Cleopatra, or at least does so within the somewhat more finite variety of this essay.

My two epigraphs may seem to set up a circuit of identification that plays out as a transhistorical syllogism. Cixous is Cleopatra (North African queens both, celebrating female fecundity); Cavendish is Cleopatra (powerful women both, loving power); therefore, Cixous is Cavendish. It is precisely these kinds of univocal identification that I want to resist, however, not least because Cixous and Cavendish also resist them. In Cixous's "Sorties," Cleopatra is less a version of Cixous than a fellow traveler, a male-woman whose identity (and sex) is not one: "the feisty queen, to whom everything is becoming—scolding, laughing, crying—at every instant another face, at each breath a passion, flesh struggling with a desire for more love, more life, more pleasure, at every moment, the queen with ten tongues; she spoke them all" (Sorties, 123). Cixous claims to love as Cleopatra but also to love Cleopatra, a mode of association-through-writing that she terms "Other-Love": "It is then that writing makes love other. It is itself this love. Other-Love is writing's first name" (Sorties, 99). Cavendish's Cleopatra also resists univocal identification. Like Cixous, Cavendish is drawn to Cleopatra as a figure of love, but a certain kind of love—one where the Lover delivers his or her "whole Soul" to the Beloved. This is no simple fantasy of union: rather, it bespeaks Cavendish's recurrent interest in the movement of souls from body to body, so that—at least in love—the body becomes multiple, populated by two or more souls. The movement of love she describes here seeks not identity but dialogic contiguity, or what we might call affinity—a sameness-in-difference, and a difference-in-sameness. As we will see, Cleopatra's affinity with Antony (and Caesar, and Pompey) models Cavendish's relation not just to Cleopatra, but also to otherness in all her writing.

   In this chapter, I likewise outline relations not of identity but of affinity between Cixous and Cavendish. The two women cannot be made to speak in one voice: in addition to their different historical, cultural, and linguistic accents, it is impossible to reconcile Cavendish's royalism with Cixous's radical democratism, or Cavendish's pleasures of the rational soul with Cixous's *jouissance* of the flesh. But as their shared investment in Cleopatra suggests, they can be invited to converse. Their dialogue here provides the basis for a plurality of other conversations. Above all, I seek to put early modern studies in dialogue with French feminism. It is less that this dialogue has been silenced than that it has never begun.[1] Many disconcerting tendencies within Cixous's brand of French feminism—her grandiose generalizations about Woman's psychosexual powers, her willful inattention to the cultural and historical specificity of women's experiences, her troubling blindness to race and class, her attenuated understanding of the material conditions of women's oppression—have prevented her from becoming a productive interlocutor in scholarship on early modern literature and culture.[2] Without finessing these problems, I want to insist on French feminism's continuing value for early modern studies by focusing on three of its largely ignored potentialities, each of which is best illuminated by their affinities with Cavendish's writing.

First, Cixous's *écriture féminine* and Cavendish's materialism provide an important potential corrective to the largely untheorized, positivist understandings of the "material" that have become endemic in recent work on early modern material culture.[3] Far from deriving her theory of writing from a universal female body external to language and culture, as has been commonly assumed, Cixous insists on the cultural inscription of corporeal matter. For Cavendish too, matter is less an unmediated given than something that is always already figured, or rather, reconfigured. Within *écriture féminine* and Cavendish's writing, matter (of the body, of the cosmos) becomes an intertextual palimpsest rather than an irreducible physicality. This palimpsest not only rewrites and displaces the phallocentric body-texts of patriarchal writing, but also unsettles the logic of sexual difference that, as Judith Butler has argued, underwrites the Western metaphysical distinction between matter and form (*Bodies*, 55).

Second, Cixous's and Cavendish's different versions of corporeal materialism are inter-articulated with a dialogics of the other. This suggests their affinity also with the work of Mikhail Bakhtin, whose theorization of the other is materialized in the metamorphic openness of the carnivalesque grotesque body.[4] For Bakhtin, the grotesque blurs the boundaries between inside and outside, self and other in a fashion that exemplifies dialogic exchange. Likewise, *écriture féminine* insists that the other embodied in corporeal matter implies not the adversarial alterity of the Hegelian dialectic—a conception of the "other" still dominant in early modern studies, even if now stripped of its teleological thrust[5]—but a companionable difference within the same, and hence a deferral of unitary identity. Cavendish similarly insists that all matter contains within itself other worlds that make a lie of singularity.

Finally, Cixous and Cavendish offer a useful alternative to a historicism that, in its increasingly antiquarian investments, has become wedded to the reflex of "hetero"-history—that is, the assumption of an absolute temporal difference between past and present.[6] Cixous's and Cavendish's dialogics ask that we rethink difference in an historical as much as a synchronic framework: if the "other" is not opposed to but associated with "me," then a dialogic approach to the "other" of the past might seek less to quarantine it from, than palimpsest it within, the present. When read in conjunction, Cixous's and Cavendish's writings—especially their digressions on Cleopatra—open a space for a new historiography grounded not in absolute historical difference, but in what I call anachronic affinity. Cixous and Cavendish both articulate theories of fellow travelers through space and time; these theories, materialized in their rewritings of matter, prompt them to find affinities not only between themselves and other people (whether real or imagined), but also between past and present. In my essay, then, Cixous and Cavendish are themselves fellow travelers, undoing the bar of historical difference in and between their writing.

Cixous and the matter of metonymy

Two women, from different times, from different worlds, meet in one body—albeit a body that is not one, but multiple, open, becoming. In her now canonical essay "The Laugh of the Medusa,"[7] Cixous meets the snake-haired Gorgon of classical myth within the boundlessness of the subversive female body: "we're stormy, and that which is ours breaks loose from us without our fearing any debilitation. Our glances, our smiles, are spent; laughs exude from all our mouths; our blood flows and we extend ourselves without ever reaching an end" (Laugh, 336). Five years later, in her *Vivre l'orange*[8] (1979), Cixous meets the Brazilian writer Clarice Lispector within the multiplicity of "orange," to celebrate Lispector's ability to write about objects in ways that respect their material and semiotic plurality—as suggested by the polysemy of her title's "orange," which is indeterminately fruit and color, noun and adjective.

Cixous's transition between these different affinities, from laughing with the Medusa to savoring the orange with Lispector, uncannily parallels the history of early modern studies' engagement with the "material" in the last quarter of a century. If Cixous's stormy, laughing female body resonates with the 1980s investment in the carnivalesque laughter of Bakhtin's grotesque body and its "material substratum," her turn to objects anticipates the more recent scholarly attention to the things of "material culture."[9] These affinities suggest rich points of departure for dialogue between French feminism and early modern studies on the matter of the "material." Yet they also suggest a productive difference. That difference, for me, concerns Cixous's conception of "matter." Throughout her work, the term possesses a textual dimension that has been largely absent from more positivist analyses of bodies and things in early modern studies.

This may seem a rather surprising claim. After all, Cixous's "The Laugh of the Medusa" and its sister-essay/rewriting, "Sorties," have become infamous for their supposed biological essentialism.[10] "Woman must write her body," Cixous commands (Sorties, 94). Her imperative has been understandably slighted as a naïve deconstructive reversal, a valorization of feminine corporeality over masculine logos.[11] But this critique, I would argue, has misunderstood the very phrase "writing the body." The participle does not presume the ontological priority of the noun; rather, the body is materialized for Cixous in and by writing. *Écriture féminine* is a rewriting and displacement of the western patriarchal text of the body. In its phallocentrism, this text works to articulate not only sexual difference between a male body centered in one organ and a female body marked by that organ's lack, but also metaphysical difference between an active, "convex" Form and a passive, "concave" Matter (Sorties, 63). This second difference is recast, at least in Cixous's reading of Mallarmé, as a distinction between father and son that completely banishes—or "buries"—the woman and her body (Sorties, 65). Hence she is simultaneously inside and outside the phallocentric text. But it is precisely this bi-positionality that lends the female body a power to undermine phallocentrism by enabling "a transformation of each one's relationship to his or her body (and to the other body)" (Sorties, 83). For this banished female body is not just the singular other to the self-same; in standing *both* inside *and* outside the economy of phallocentrism, it discloses the factitiousness of a singular identity that opposes rather than includes the other. "That doesn't mean," Cixous writes, that "she is undifferentiated magma; it means that she doesn't create a monarchy of her body or her desire. Let masculine sexuality gravitate around the penis, engendering this centralized body (political anatomy) under the party dictatorship" (Sorties, 87). Cixous does not so much reclaim a female body prior to language as rewrite the patriarchal text of that body, diverting the agency of inscription from the "centralized" phallocentric body to a non-identitarian (because plural) "she" who "doesn't create a monarchy." In the process, this "she" inscribes a new materiality— "the vast, material, organic, sensuous universe we are" (Sorties, 83)—which undoes the phallocentric oppositions not just of male and female, but also of form and matter.

Luce Irigaray performs a similarly deconstructive rewriting of form and matter in *Speculum of the Other Woman*.[12] In her reading of Plato's *Timaeus*, this key distinction is enabled by even as it excludes the *chora*, the feminized receptacle on which phallic form impresses itself to produce matter. Hence Plato's matter is always already textual, at least in the Derridean sense: it is an effect of pre/inscription (*Speculum*, 243). Judith Butler argues that Irigaray's reading of Plato produces a new text—a palimpsest of Plato—that overwrites the old by finding within it a place for an other that comes to matter even as it is withheld from the domain of matter (Butler, Bodies, 45). The meaning of the *chora* may differ for Irigaray and Butler—for Irigaray, it is the woman's body *tout court*, while for Butler, it is more indeterminate, potentially including various other oppressed bodies such as those of slaves and animals as well as the phallic lesbian.[13] In both cases, however, the *chora* has the deconstructive power to disclose not only the textuality of matter, but also the trace of the other within the folds of matter and text. Hence Irigaray's and Butler's radical textualizations of corporeal matter also provide the basis for a feminist dialogics. And, in the process, both theorists remind us that the "material" is far more than just a synonym for the "physical."

This is equally the case for Cixous. But her dialogics are not articulated in a re-inscription of the matter of Western philosophical tradition; it is in literature that she finds the "other" body—and the "other" in the body.[14] Hence her title, "The Laugh of the Medusa," as well as her extended digressions in "Sorties" through the works of Homer, Kleist, and Shakespeare. Her readings of each male writer further undermine her supposed biological essentialism, even as they disclose how her dialogics are inter-articulated with a textualization of corporeal matter. Notably, the "writing of the body" that undoes the phallocentric text has already been performed by "that being-of-a-thousand beings called Shakespeare"; his plays are scenes of dialogic becoming, where "man turns back into woman, woman into man" (Sorties, 98). For Cixous, *Antony and Cleopatra* exemplifies *écriture féminine* inasmuch as that play writes the body by writing the other into the body. If Antony (dressed in Cleopatra's clothes) and Cleopatra (wearing his sword Phillippan) embody how "man turns back into woman, woman into man," that chiasmus exemplifies Cixous's feminist dialogics, where seeming opposites cross over, find common ground, and enlarge that ground.

This chiasmic strategy characterizes her own textual relation with Shakespeare, who bears the traces of Cixous even as her text bears the traces of Shakespeare. In the English version of "Sorties," Shakespeare is never quoted as such; his words either have been translated back into English from Cixous's French translation, or are paraphrased in her poetic reworking of the play. Similarly, Shakespeare haunts Cixous's own words in the form of numerous intertextual references to *Hamlet* and *Macbeth*.[15] The inscription of the feminine body thus amounts to a dialogic re-inscription—a palimpsesting—of Cixous's and Shakespeare's texts. As Ann Rosalind Jones has noted, we need to recognize Cixous's *écriture féminine* as "a conscious response to socioliterary realities, rather than accept it as an overflow of one woman's unmediated communication with her body . . . [her] work shows that a resistance to culture is always built, at first, of bits and pieces of that culture, however they are disassembled, criticized, and transcended" (367). Cixous proposes a form of textual collaboration, in other words, where she chiasmically locates herself in the other and the other in herself.

The somewhat vexed term that she gives this chiasmic relation is "bisexuality." Cixous has rightly drawn criticism for the heterosexual matrix of her conception of bisexuality, which can seem like a Platonic "wholeness" that leaves no room for anything outside the binary of male and female.[16] But this exclusivity is precisely what Cixous sets out to question. Importantly, she distinguishes between two types of bisexuality. The first is "a fantasy of a complete being, which replaces the fear of castration and veils sexual difference insofar as this is perceived as the mark of a mythical separation . . . Ovid's Hermaphrodite, less bisexual than asexual, not made up of two genders but of two halves. Hence, a fantasy of unity. Two within one, and not even two wholes" (Sorties, 84). By contrast, "the *other bisexuality*" is "the location within oneself of the presence of both sexes, evident and insistent in different ways according to the individual, the non-exclusion of difference or of a sex, and starting with this 'permission' one gives oneself, the multiplication of the effects of desire's inscription on every part of the body and the other body" (Sorties, 85). Cixous's reference to "both sexes" still works to naturalize a totalizing binary division of male and female; but her "other bisexuality" offers a glimpse of a non-binary economy predicated not on the identitarian logic of "either . . . or," but on the dialogics of "both . . . and."

We might characterize this redefinition of bisexuality in more textual terms: it is, in effect, an endorsement of metonymy over metaphor. Cixous's dialogic bisexuality is embodied not in identity or unitary plenitude, but in relations of proximity and affinity. To this extent, Cixous again works in tandem with Irigaray, whose controversial "The Sex That Is Not One"[17] proposes a model of textual pleasure based not on the metaphorical operation of singular identification, but rather on the metonymic register of contiguity. The latter is exemplified by the two lips of the female genitalia, which touch rather than identify; their contiguity models the plurality not only of woman's sexual pleasure, but also of her speech: "what she says is never identical with anything, moreover; rather, it is contiguous. *It touches (upon)*" (Sex, 354). A more textual version of this touching contiguity— materialized in "desire's inscription on every part of the body and the other body" (Sorties, 85)—also informs Cixous's dialogics. *Écriture feminine*, then, is a feminist theory of metonymy that has implications not only for the (re)inscription of matter, but also the formation of new affinities in love, in writing, in political action—and across time. In this, Cixous joins not just with Irigaray, but also with that "being-of-a-thousand beings" called Margaret Cavendish.

Joining Cavendish

Two women, from different times, from different worlds, meet in one body— albeit a body that is not one, but multiple, open, becoming. Throughout her writing, Margaret Cavendish imagines the meetings of two souls in one corporeal location. In her story of "The Propagating Souls" from *Nature's Pictures* (1664), she relates how the souls of two lovers, after death, become permanently bonded in a celestial body: "these Souls being fruitfull, they left many of their issues, called Meteors, which are shining Lights like Stars" (133). Likewise, at the beginning of *CXXI Sociable Letters* (1664),[18] she writes to an unspecified friend that "my mind and thoughts live always with you, although my person is at a distance from you; insomuch, as, if Souls dies not as Bodies do, my Soul will attend you when my Body lies in the grave; and when we are both dead, we may hope to have a Conversation of Souls, where yours and mine will be doubly united, first in Life, and then in Death" (2). If Cavendish fantasizes the souls of Platonic lovers becoming "united" within the body of the cosmos or the body of an individual, it is a union that nonetheless preserves the dialogic capacity of the other so that a "Conversation of Souls" might take place.

Such a conversation is in many ways the governing conceit of *The Blazing World* (1666).[19] Cavendish's remarkable novella portrays the migrations and transmigrations of a nameless young woman, kidnapped by a lustful merchant and transported to another world which joins her own at its north pole. This new world is populated by hybrid creatures—bear-men, fox-men, bird-men, satyrs, etc.—who take her to their emperor. So impressed is he by Cavendish's heroine that he makes her empress and grants her unlimited power. She sets up an academy of knowledge, where she is advised by invisible yet material spirits. Much of her curiosity about the natural world concerns the possibility of conversation between souls: "She asked again, whether souls did choose bodies? They answered, that Platonics believed the souls of lovers lived in the bodies of their beloved" (175). The spirits also speak of a woman from another world, the Duchess of Newcastle (i.e. Margaret Cavendish), who will assist her in the project of writing a "Jewish Cabbala." The duchess's soul transmigrates to the empress's world, and vice versa; the two become firm friends, even Platonic lovers. When they tour England, the duchess and the empress enter the duke's body: "and then the Duke had three souls in one body; and had there been but some such souls more, the Duke would have been like the Grand Signor in his seraglio, only it would have been a platonic seraglio" (194). The final act in this proliferating, quasi-erotic drama of Platonic transmigration comes when the empress realizes that war has been declared against her country of origin in her native world. She seeks counsel from the duchess: "the Duchess told the Empress, that it was requisite that Her Majesty should go her self in body as well as in soul; but, I, said she, can only wait on your Majesty after a spiritual manner, that is, with my soul. Your soul, said the Empress, shall live with my soul, in my body; for I shall only desire your counsel and advice" (206). And, several interruptions notwithstanding, they cohabit happily ever after.

Thus the relationship between Cavendish and the empress resembles Cixous's chiasmic inscriptions of "Other-Love": the empress inhabits Cavendish as a creature of her literary imagination, even as (within the story) Cavendish's soul inhabits the empress's body. In all Cavendish's literary transmigrations, her souls do not merge, but join together in relations based on affinity. Indeed, metonymic "joining" is Cavendish's characteristic mode of relationality. Referring to the simultaneous publication of her *Observations on Experimental Philosophy* and *The Blazing World* in one book[20] (two souls in one body?) Cavendish argues that "I join a work of fancy to my serious philosophical contemplations" (123). This joining is thematized also within *The Blazing World*. When she says in her introduction that "I added this piece of fancy to my philosophical observations, and joined them as two worlds at the ends of their poles" (124), she anticipates the mode of interglobal transmigration that begins the novella: "they were not only driven to the very end or point of the Pole of that world, but even to another Pole of another world, which joined close to it" (126). Joining characterizes not just the relations between Cavendish's worlds, but also the properties of the Blazing World itself. Not only is it populated by fantastical creatures whose hybridity assumes the joining rather than purification of disparate identities; its ships are also metonymically "joined": "in a great tempest they would join their ships in battle array, and when they feared wind and waves would be too strong for them, if they divided their ships, they joined as many together as the compass or advantage of the places of the liquid element would give them leave; for their ships were so ingeniously contrived, that they could fasten them together as close as a honey-comb without waste of place; and being thus united, no wind nor waves were able to separate them" (129).

This joining together of multiple components in contiguous "honeycomb" relations is crucial also to Cavendish's conception of the self, which she views not as unitary and irreducible, but as comprised of myriad "worlds." "By creating a world within yourself," the spirits tell the empress, "you may enjoy all both in whole and in parts, without control or opposition, and may make what world you please, and alter it when you please, and enjoy as much pleasure and delight as a world can afford you" (185). As Geraldine Wagner has noted, the creation of worlds within the self is a leitmotif throughout Cavendish's writing.[21] In her preface to *Natures Pictures*, Cavendish remarks that "in my Brain a large Room I had built, / Most curious furnisht, and as richly gilt, / Fill'd with my Lord, his Children and the rest / Of my near Friends" (sig. A2).[22] And in one of the dedicatory poems to her *Sociable Letters*, we read:

> This Lady only her self she Writes,
> And all her Letters to her self Indites;
> For in her self so many creatures be,
> Like many Commonwealths, yet all Agree.

(sig. d)

Of course, the idea of worlds-within-worlds is a staple *topos* of the time; it features heavily, for example, in the analogical cosmology that pervades early modern European literary as well as medical and political writing, from Rabelais and Paracelsus to Hobbes.[23] But no matter how much the royalist Cavendish may have been influenced by the macrocosmic model of the sovereign body expounded in *Leviathan*, her fantasies of "many Commonwealths" within her do not assume a Hobbesian *corpus politicum* composed of irreducible parts.[24] Despite her avowed desire for a singular identity modeled on imperial sovereignty—she famously asserts in the introduction to *The Blazing World* that "though I cannot be *Henry* the Fifth, or *Charles* the Second, yet I endeavour to be *Margaret* the *First*" (124)—Cavendish's self is infinitely self-dividing. Through her letter-writing and her novellas she repeatedly pluralizes herself, finding an other within herself and herself within the other, as suggested by the many "Conversations of Souls" that she fantasizes.

In some respects, these "Conversations" anticipate Bakhtin's—or Volosinov's—dialogic theory of language: "each and every word expresses the 'one' in relation to the 'other.' I give myself verbal shape from another's point of view."[25] Cavendish's intuition that the other is folded into the word is equally apparent in her attitude to the English language. "English is a compounded Language," she argues, "mithredated of many ingredients . . . so, if I speak the English that is spoken in this age, I must use such words as belongs to other Nations, being mixed therein" (*Natures Picture*, sig. c6). Mixture is equally the basis of Cavendish's theory of literary invention. When the empress's soul tours England with the duchess, she takes great interest in the London theaters, about which the duchess observes, "all or most of their plays were taken out of old stories, but yet they had new actions, which being joined to old stories, together with the addition of new prologues, scenes, music and dancing, made new plays" (192). Cavendish's fascination with linguistic joining and mixtures extends also to her experiments in genre. As we have seen, the fictional *Blazing World* is daringly joined with her scientific treatise *Observations on Experimental Philosophy*; even *The Blazing World* is itself an exercise in mixed genres: "the first part is *romancical*, the second *philosophical*, and the third is merely fancy, or (as I may call it) *fantastical*" (124). Likewise, in the introduction to *Natures Picture*, she claims that "though my work is of Comicall, Tragicall, Poeticall, Philosophicall, Romancicall, Historicall and Morall discourses, yet I could not place them so exactly into severall Books, or parts as I would, but am forced to mix them one amongst another" (sig. c4). Here she redeems Peter Quince's much maligned gallimaufry of "tragical mirth" (*Midsummer Night's Dream*, 5.1.57), making mixture, rather than singularity, the organizing principle of her invention.

As I shall argue, Cavendish's fantasies of Platonic affinity, metonymic joining, infinite self-subdivision, and linguistic mixing are more than feats of the imagination. Even though Virginia Woolf slighted Cavendish's writing, there has been a tendency to regard Cavendish as a proto-Woolf, making a "room of her own" in an entirely privatized imagination.[26] This idealist view is questionable on two counts. As I have argued, there is a persistently dialogic strain throughout Cavendish's writing that qualifies her solipsism; she does not just subdivide internally, but also finds traces of the other in herself, and vice versa. Just as importantly, moreover, Cavendish's fantasies of the other are inter-articulated with a through-going materialist cosmology. Her feats of the imagination are, like Cixous's acts of writing, equally feats of matter. And, also like Cixous, she inscribes matter itself as dialogic.

Cavendish matters

It is difficult to pin down Cavendish's theory of matter. Throughout her writing, she continually reworks her understanding of the natural world. But refashioning is itself integral to her conception of matter. She writes in *The World's Olio* (162) that

> Nature hath not onely made Bodies changeable, but Minds; so to have a Constant Mind, is to be Unnatural; for our Body changeth from the

first beginning to the last end, every minute adds or takes away: so by Nature, we should change every Minute, since Nature hath made nothing to stand at a stay, but to alter as fast as Time runs; wherefore it is Natural to be in one Mind one minute, and in another the next; and yet Men think the Mind Immortal. But the Changes of Nature are like the Sleights of a Juggler, we see many several Shapes, but still but one Matter.[27]

Here we see how Cavendish, even as she seems to respect the body / mind distinction, also destabilizes it; the mind is just as prone to the protean flux of nature as is the body—indeed, she sees in both "but one Matter," a "Matter" so universal that she elsewhere insists on the materiality even of the soul.[28] This theory of universal "Matter" is stated yet more succinctly in her *Philosophical Letters* (1664),[29] where she claims that "the Ground of my Philosophy... is Infinite Matter" (5). But what exactly is this "Infinite Matter" that Cavendish sees as the basic foundational principle of the universe, and what are its properties?

Cavendish's materialism deviates from both the Aristotelian cosmology of the four elements and the mechanistic philosophy that is customarily narrated as replacing it. She rejects the irreducibility of the elements in *Poems and Phancies* (1664): "The several *Elements* are all of one *Matter*" (44).[30] One might think that her "Infinite Matter" would have a greater affinity with the materialism of Epicurus and Lucretius, for whom all compounds are comprised of the basic building blocks of matter—atoms.[31] And indeed, Cavendish early on embraced the idea of atoms: in *Poems and Phancies*, for example, she not only asserts that the universe is comprised of small atoms of various shapes, sizes, and motions, but also compares herself to an "unsettled *Atom*" (sig. b4). Yet in her later writings, she comprehensively rejects atoms:

> I conceive Nature to be an Infinite body, bulk or magnitude, which by its own self-motion is divided into infinite parts, not single or individable parts, but parts of one continued body... it is impossible to have single parts in Nature, that is parts which are individeable in themselves, as Atomes; and may subsist single, or by themselves, precised or separated from all other parts; for although there are perfect and whole figures in Nature, yet are they nothing else but parts of Nature, which consist of a composition of other parts, and their figures make them discernable from other parts or figures of Nature.
>
> (*Observations*, I. 135, 136–7)

As this shows, Cavendish's later theory of matter is corporeal, infinitely divisible, and self-moving. In this, she departs from the then dominant mechanistic philosophy of Hobbes. Instead, she embraces the vitalist theory of matter, a heady brew of Paracelsan cosmology and new science.[32] Paracelsus had proposed that the universe was a self-contained economy within which each part had its own animating soul; for William Harvey and others, this animism provided a necessary corrective to the mechanistic, spiritless physical universe of Descartes, Hobbes and the atomists, for whom the causes of motion could never be immanent within any material body. Like Harvey, Cavendish sought to restore agency to matter, making it rational and capable of choice. Hence for Cavendish, a billiard ball will move when hit by a cue or another ball, not because it is reacting to an outside force, but because it *chooses* to move.[33]

Cavendish's conversion from atomism to vitalism was an unlikely development on two counts. First, the vitalist "moment" had long passed by the time she came to embrace it in 1663, having run its course in the interregnum; and second, Cavendish's royalist politics were at odds with the radical liberalism of other vitalists such as Milton. Yet, as John Rogers has suggested, vitalism appealed to Cavendish inasmuch as it allowed her to articulate a feminist materialism (201). Hobbes's theory of mechanistic matter was masculinist, proposing an external male cause that engenders motion, reducing matter to passive feminine effect. By contrast, Cavendish makes her matter self-moving—that is, she propounds a principle of active femininity. If this very notion is, by the standards of her day, hermaphroditic, she pluralizes it yet further by insisting that matter consists of inseparable rational, sensitive, and inanimate parts. The rational guides the inanimate, and is thus matter's agentic component. Hence Cavendish, in effect, dispenses with a *primum mobile*, as well as the masculinist theory of active form that is pervasive in Western metaphysics from Plato to Hobbes.[34]

Cavendish's feminist understanding of corporeal matter is by no means the same as Cixous's; in contrast to the psychosexual convulsions of Cixous's anarchic female body, Cavendish's body of Nature is orderly in its organization and its movements. If Cixous's flesh is "explosion, diffusion, effervescence, abundance" (Sorties, 91), Cavendish's dutifully heeds the choices of its rational components. Catherine Gallagher has noted that Cavendish's royalist belief in sovereign government paradoxically underwrites her feminism.[35] But in Cavendish's version of vitalism, sovereignty is devolved from an absolute monarch to matter. As a result, all matter is self-ruling—thereby suggesting an unexpected affinity not just between theories of matter and politics, but also between royalism and liberalism. Despite this residue of hierarchical thinking, Cavendish anticipates Cixous in making her corporeal matter the template for a dialogics of the other. Not only is Cavendish's matter divisible into animate and inanimate parts; it is also divisible into infinite worlds. In "Of many *Worlds* in this *World*," she asserts that

> Just like as in a *Nest of Boxes* round,
> *Degrees* of *Sizes* in each *Box* are found;
> So in this *World* may many other be,

> Thinner and less, and less still by degree;
> Although they are not subject to our *Sense*,
> A *World* may be no bigger than *Two-pence*.

(Poems and Phancies, 54)

In this vision, as in her fantasies of the self, worlds lurk within worlds; there is always otherness nested within any seeming whole. The gendered connotation of Cavendish's "nest" is highly suggestive, resonating as it does with Irigaray's discussion of the *chora* in Plato. But whereas Plato seeks to exclude the latter from his distinction between matter and form, the "nest" is for Cavendish the enabling maternal figure for a dialogic matter that necessarily contains, rather than opposes, the other.

As with Cixous, Cavendish's dialogic matter is textual, and in a variety of senses. We might remember that *textum* in Latin is a weaving or a joining together. For Cavendish, matter is textual in just this way; she offers a suggestive counterpart to the Derridean critique of presence, arguing that no matter can be in and of itself, but rather must bear the trace of something else with which it is joined. This underwrites her conviction that, *contra* Aristotle, "there is no such thing as simple bodies in Nature; for if Nature her self consists of a commixture of animate and inanimate Matter, no part can be called simple, as having a composition of the same parts" (*Observations upon Experimental Philosophy*, III. 37–8). This conviction is evident also in the materialist cosmology of *The Blazing World*, where "parts do only assist and join with parts, either in the dissolution or production of other parts and creatures" (153). Nothing is irreducible and individuated, which is why atoms are for her nonsensical; rather, everything is metonymically related to everything else, within the endlessly morphing—yet rational—body of nature.

Despite her insistence on the flux of matter, Cavendish insists that there cannot be anything truly new: all "innovations" are just reconfigurations—or re-compoundings—of extant matter. In the process, she repeatedly resorts to images of writing, or rewriting, to figure matter's transformations. We might recall what she has to say about new plays as rewritings of old stories. Likewise, the "new world" of *The Blazing World* is a self-conscious rewriting of old worlds. The invisible yet material spirits advise the Empress to write a Cabbala with any of the souls of natural philosophers from antiquity ("Aristotle, Pythagoras, Plato, Epicurus or the like") or modern times ("Galileo, Gassendus, Descartes, Helmont, Hobbes, H. More, etc." [181]). The empress instead chooses the duchess as her writing partner, and both write "celestial worlds" of the imagination, one of which is the text of *The Blazing World* (188). But like Cixous, Cavendish does not find in this dialogic union a "female" space completely exterior to male philosophy. Rather, she rewrites Aristotle's matter, Van Helmont's vitalism, and Hobbes's organicism to articulate her own feminist materialism. Likewise in her *Observations*, she devotes an entire book to male philosophers, whose principles she adapts even as she vigorously disputes them. She thus exemplifies what Jones says of Cixous: "a resistance to culture is always built, at first, of bits and pieces of that culture, however they are disassembled, criticized, and transcended" (367). Hence her *writing* of matter thematizes her *theory* of matter; both entail a compounding of self and other, a production of "figures" that seem to possess singular integrity yet are palimpsested—or "nested"—mixtures. John Rogers rightly notes the gendering of matter as "feminine" within the vitalist tradition; but Cavendish's matter is more than any one univocal gender can hope to define.[36] It is "bisexual," in Cixous's words, "compounded," in Cavendish's, or, to use another term favored by Bruno Latour, "hybrid."

In *We Have Never Been Modern*, Latour examines the proliferation of hybrids that both underwrites and undermines the project of modern history. He argues that modern history depends on the progressive purification not only of knowledge systems within space, but also of epochs within time. If pre-modern knowledge systems can strike us as hybrid, mixing the discrete realms of subject and object, modern knowledge has supposedly purified these domains, separating politics (the world of humans) from science (the world of natural things). But according to Latour, this project has always been impossible—which is why, in his words, "we have never been modern." Robert Boyle's air-pump is, for Latour, the material object that both inaugurates modern history and discloses its impossibility. The pump was a hybrid, a non-human agent, and a humanly created thing; as such, it engendered two very different discourses that have come to be seen as incompatible— scientific description of matters of fact in which objects are agents, and social contextualization of phenomena in which humans are prime movers.[37] In 1667, Boyle demonstrated his air-pump at the Royal Society in London; Cavendish was present at the demonstration, the first woman ever admitted by the institution. It is nice to think that at the very moment in Latour's account that history supposedly slides into History—i.e. at the instant where the modernizing project of disciplinary and temporal purification supposedly begins—Cavendish, a committed exemplar of hybridity, should have been in attendance.[38] Just as we might read the *chora* back into Plato's inscription of matter and form, so we might read Cavendish back into the modern purification of politics and science, subjects and objects, humans and things, spirit and matter. Another history emerges here, or rather, in Cixous's words, an "other history" (Sorties, 83)—a history that, in its dialogic embrace of the other, offers an alternative to the modern History critiqued by Latour.

Cavendish was not keen on history as a genre. In "The Anchorite," she criticizes historians as inevitably partial and given to detraction in chronicling the lives of bad men (*Nature's Pictures*, p. 355). But elsewhere she offers a suggestive defence: history, she claims, is "brown and lovely" (*World's Olio*, p. 7). In light of her portrait of Cleopatra, it is tempting to speculate that she was thinking of the Egyptian queen. Cavendish's "brown and lovely" history is perhaps reminiscent of Nietzsche's monumental history, which allows modern men to identify with figures from the past.[39] But Cavendish's is a historiography based not on identification, but on "lovely" affinity, the "Other-Love" advocated by Cixous.[40] The "Other" in Cixous's formulation, we should note, is just as much temporal as it is cultural. Modeled in both Cixous's and Cavendish's affinities with Cleopatra is a movement across time that suggests a mode of historiography resistant to identification or purification. It offers an alternative to historicist paradigms within which past and present are absolutely divorced, whether by the *telos* of the Hegelian Spirit or the rupture of the Foucauldian break. Instead, Cixous's and Cavendish's affinities with Cleopatra—and their Cleopatran affinities with each other—produce a history founded in metonymic "conversations between souls." This is a far cry from the metonymic mode of history that Hayden White attributes to Marx, which is largely a synchronic determinism redolent of Hobbesian mechanism.[41] Rather, Cixous's and Cavendish's metonymic historiographies are anachronic, whereby the past nests in the present, and vice versa. In this, they anticipate Latour, who asserts that every cohort of contemporaneous elements "brings together elements from all times. In such a framework, our actions are recognized at last as polytemporal" (75). Like Latour, Cixous and Cavendish undo the logic of temporal identity and difference by insisting on the dialogic properties of matter, writing, and history.

In this, Cixous and Cavendish are hardly singular. Indeed, one of the greatest gifts that materialist as much as French feminism continues to offer, whether to historical study in general or to early modern studies in particular, is its commitment to an anachronic sensibility: that is, its presumption of affinity—but not identity—between women (and, for that matter, men) in the past and the present. This sensibility is increasingly disguised or disallowed in the name of situating the past within its historical "moment." The dialogue between Cixous and Cavendish, however, suggests that it is time for both feminism and early modern studies to question time—at least the purified time of historicism—and to begin imagining a new historiography grounded in the Cleopatran affinities of past and present.

Notes

1. The absence of French feminism from early modern studies is surprising in light of their shared investment in the body. In particular, early modernists' intense love affair in the 1980s with Mikhail Bakhtin's paradigms of the body might conceivably have led to some kind of dialogue with Cixous. In the grotesque body of early modern carnival, Bakhtin writes, "the stress is laid on those parts of the body that are open to the outside world, that is, the parts through the world enters the body

or emerges from it, or through which the body itself goes out to meet the world" (Mikhail Bakhtin, *Rabelais and his World*, trans Hélène Iswolsky, Cambridge, MA: MIT Press, 1968) 26). With her insistence that the woman's body is multiple, overflowing, and becoming, Cixous complements Bakhtin's theory of the grotesque and underscores its largely suppressed gendered dimensions. Yet while some influential studies of the early modern body have employed Bakhtin's grotesque paradigm to tease out constructions of gender, they have notably made no reference to French feminist theories of the body. See Peter Stallybrass, "Patriarchal Territories: The Body Enclosed," in Margaret W. Ferguson, Maureen Quilligan, and Nancy Vickers, eds., *Rewriting the Renaissance: The Discourses of Sexual Difference in Early Modern Europe* (Chicago: University of Chicago Press, 1986), 123–42; and Gail Kern Paster, *The Body Embarrassed: Drama and the Disciples of Shame in Early Modern England* (Ithaca, NY: Cornell University Press, 1993).

2. See the powerful criticisms of Cixous voiced by Ann Rosalind Jones, "Writing the Body: Toward an Understanding of *l'écriture féminine*," in Robyn R. Warhol and Diane Price Herndl, eds., *Feminisms: An Anthology of Literary Theory and Criticism* (New Brunswick, NJ: Rutgers University Press, 1991), 357–70; Toril Moi, *Textual/Sexual Politics* (New York and London: Methuen, 1985); and Gayatri Chakravorty Spivak, *In Other Worlds: Essays in Cultural Politics* (New York: Routledge, 1986). So when Cixous writes of Woman that "her libido is cosmic, just as her unconscious is worldwide: her writing also can only go on and on, without ever inscribing or distinguishing contours . . . I am spacious singing Flesh," most if not all early modern scholars are likely to share Jones's reservations about "the concept of *fémininité* as a bundle of Everywoman's psychosexual characteristics: it flattens out the lived differences among women"; see Jones, "Writing the Body," p. 365. Somewhat paradoxically, then, the impact of feminism on early modern studies has been to diminish the impact of French feminism on early modern studies.

3. I have written elsewhere on this subject; see Jonathan Gil Harris, "Shakespeare's Hair: Staging the Object of Material Culture," *Shakespeare Quarterly* 52:4 (2001): 445–57; and "The New New Historicism's *Wunderkammer* of Objects," *European Journal of English Studies* 4:3 (2000): 111–23.

4. On Bakhtin's dialogics, see Bakhtin, *Rabelais and his World*; and *The Dialogic Imagination*, trans. Caryl Emerosn and Michael Holquist (Austin, TX: University of Texas Press, 1981); also Valentin Volosinov, *Marxism and the Philosophy of Language*, trans. Ladislav Atejka and I. R. Titunik (New York: Seminar Press, 1973). For affinities between Bakhtin and feminist dialogics, see Dale M. Bauer and S. Jaret McKinstry (eds.), *Feminism, Bakhtin, and the Dialogic* (State University of New York Press: 1991).

5. The "other" has been used in early modern studies to signify the adversarial Other of Hegelian dialectics since Stephen Greenblatt's study of Spenser, *Renaissance Self-Fashioning: From More to Shakespeare* (Chicago: University of Chicago Press, 1980), esp. pp. 177–8. For an attempt to recode early modern "otherness" as a dialogic trace within the body, see Nancy Selleck, "Donne's Body," *Studies in English Language* 41 (2001): 149–74.

6. For the term "hetero-history," I am indebted to Madhavi Menon, who has argued that the reflex underwrites a larger, unwitting project of heteronormativity. See Madhavi Menon, "Queer Time," unpublished MS. presented at the Round Table on "Ten Years after Queering the Renaissance," Modern Languages Association Convention, Philadelphia, December 2004, pp. 1–2.

7. Hélène Cixous, "Laugh of the Medusa," in Robyn Warhol and Diane Price Herndl, eds., *Feminisms: An Anthology of Literary Theory and Criticism* (New Brunswick, NJ: Rutgers University Press, 1991), pp. 334–49.
8. Hélène Cixous, *Vivre l'orange* (Paris: Des Femmes, 1979).
9. Indeed, early modern studies' interest in the body and material culture has been in large part the product of feminist concerns. The now large corpus of scholarship on the Renaissance body is greatly indebted to feminist-inflected work from the 1980s. Similarly, the current scholarly vogue for objects was arguably enabled by the trailblazing, feminist studies of women's management of properties undertaken in the 1980s, even if its current popularity seems to be fuelled largely by a fetishistic longing for the "real" that vitiates questions of theory or praxis.
10. To give just one example, an anthology of literary theory often used in the undergraduate English classroom identifies Cixous's feminism as exemplifying "one strand of essentialist theory"; see Julie Rivkin and Michael Ryan (eds.), *Literary Theory: An Anthology*, 2nd edn. (Malden, MA: Blackwell, 2004), 767.
11. As Gayatri Spivak has objected, Cixous potentially remains trapped within masculinist ideology (Spivak, *In Other Worlds*, p. 149).
12. Luce Irigaray, *Speculum of the Other Woman*, trans. Gillian C. Gill (Ithaca, NY: Cornell University Press, 1985).
13. Referring to Plato's gendering of penetrative form and passive *chora*, Butler asks: "If it were possible to have a relation of penetration between two ostensibly feminine gendered positions, would this be the kind of resemblance that must be prohibited in order for Western metaphysics to get going?" Judith Butler, *Bodies that Matter: On the Discursive Limits of Sex* (New York and London: Routledge, 1993), 51. I would argue that with their theories of feminine writing and self-moving matter, Cixous and Cavendish imagine just this—if not a penetrative femininity, than at least an active femininity that dispenses with a seminal masculinity.
14. Spivak has complained that Cixous has an attenuated understanding of writing; whereas Derrida sees it as *différance*, the principle of differentiation and deferral, Spivak claims that Cixous regards it simply as literary writing. But I think she ignores the extent to which Cixous understands literature as a particularly dialogic province of *différance*.
15. See, for example, her remarks about women's desire: "What does she want? To sleep, perchance to dream" ("Sorties: Ways Out/Attacks/Forays," in Hélène Cixous and Catherine Clément, *The Newly Born Woman*, trans. Betsy Wing (Minneapolis: Univerersity of Minnesota Press, 1986) 67); or about the return of the hitherto repressed active female principle: "They, the feminine ones, are coming back from far away, from forever, from "outside," from the heaths where witches stay alive" ("Sorties," 69).
16. Spivak also notes of Cixous that "in much of her argument for 'bisexuality,' she is sometimes reminiscent of the Freud who silenced female psychoanalysts by calling them as good as men. The question of the political or historical and indeed ideological differential that irreducibly separates the male from the female critic of phallocentrism is not asked" (Spivak, *In Other Worlds*, pp. 146–7).
17. Luce Irigaray, "The Sex that is not One," in Robyn R. Warhol and Diane Price Herndl, *Feminisms: An Anthology of Literary Theory and Criticism* (New Brunswick, NJ: Rutgers University Press, 1991), pp. 351–9.
18. Margaret Cavendish, *Sociable Letters CCXVI* (London, 1664).

19. Margaret Cavendish, *The Blazing World and Other Writings*, ed. Kate Lilley (Harmondsworth: Penguin, 1992).

20. Margaret Cavendish, *Observations upon Experimental Philosophy. To which is added, The Description of a New Blazing World* (London, 1666).

21. Wagner's discussion of Cavendish's multiplicity has many affinities with my own; however, she is more inclined to see synthesis than dialogics in Cavendish's writing—a tendency apparent in her argument that *The Blazing World* is a romance, her conviction that Cavendish's transmigrations of the soul constitute a merger or union, and her assessment that Cavendish's theory of matter entails "oneness." Geraldine Wagner, "Romancing Multiplicity: Female Subjectivity and the Body Divisible in Margaret Cavendish's Blazing World." *Early Modern Literary Studies* 9.1 (May, 2003): 1, 20, 24.

22. Margaret Cavendish, *Natures Pictures Drawn by Fancies Pencil to the Life* (London, 1656).

23. For studies of early modern analogical cosmology, see Leonard Barkan, *Nature's Work of Art: The Human Body as Image of the World* (New Haven, CT: Yale University Press, 1975); and Michel Foucault, *The Order of Things: An Archaeology of the Human Sciences* (New York: Tavistock, 1970), chapter 1.

24. For a useful study of the organicism of Hobbes's *Leviathan*, see Christopher Pye, "The Sovereign, the Theater, and the Kingdome of Darknesse: Hobbes and the Spectacle of Power," in Stephen Greenblatt, ed., *Representing the English Renaissance* (Berkeley, CA: University of California Press, 1988), 279–301.

25. Bakhtin, *Rabelais and his World*; and Volosinov, *Marxism and the Philosophy of Language*, p. 86. Compare Gail M. Schwab, "Irigarayan Dialogism: Play and Power-play," in Dale M. Bauer and S. Jaret McKinstry, eds., *Feminism, Bakhtin, and the Dialogic* (State University of New York Press: 1991), 57–72, 58.

26. Woolf complained Cavendish's "philosophies are futile, and her plays intolerable, and her verses mostly dull"; see Virginia Woolf, *The Common Reader* (New York: Harcourt & Brace, 1946), p. 77. For the view that Cavendish's writing strategy anticipates Woolf's, see Rogers: "she was herself deeply invested (*pace* Virginia Woolf) in building a philosophical 'Cottage' of her own" (Rogers, 200).

27. Margaret Cavendish, *The World's Olio* (London, 1655), 162.

28. See, for example, "Of the Rational Soul of Man": "Of all the opinions concerning the Natural Soul of Man, I like that best which affirms the Soul to be a self-moving substance; but yet I will add a Material self-moving substance" (*Observations*, II. 45).

29. Margaret Cavendish, *Philosophical Letters: Or, Modest Reflections Upon Some Opinions in Natural Philosophy, Maintained by Several Learned and Famous Authors of the Age, Expressed by Way of Letters* (London, 1664).

30. Margaret Cavendish, *Poems, and Phancies, Writtem by the Thrice Noble, Illustrious, and Excellent Princesss the Lady Marchioness of Newcastle: The Second Impression, Much Altered and Corrected* (London, 1664).

31. For a study of the impact of Lucretius on seventeenth-century thought, see Jacques Lezra, *Unspeakable Subjects: The Genealogy of the Event in Early Modern Europe* (Stanford, CA; Stanford University Press, 1997), esp. 15–31.

32. The one extended study of vitalism is Richmond L. Wheeler, *Vitalism: Its History and Validity* (London: Witherby, 1939). See also Walter Pagel, *William Harvey's Biological Ideas: Selected Aspects and Historical Background* (New York: Hafner, 1967), 251–77; and John Yolton, *Thinking Matter: Materialism in Eighteenth-Century Britain* (Oxford: Oxford University Press, 1984), 1–26.

33. See Rogers, 191–2. One might compare Cavendish's critique of mechanistic causality to Fredric Jameson's in *The Political Unconscious: Narrative as Socially Symbolic Act* (New York: Methuen, 1981), 23–25, which also invokes the billiard-ball model of cause and effect. But Cavendish embraces neither the Leibnizian expressive causality nor the Althusserian structural causality that Jameson poses as the alternatives to Cartesian mechanism—unless one sees her theory of the rational parts of matter as a voluntarist model of expressive causality.

34. Although Cavendish repeatedly professes her faith in God, she seems to do so with a measure of anxiety born of the logical consequences of her self-moving, vitalist nature, which has no need of a masculine, transcendent power. It is not surprising, therefore, that Rogers sees Cavendish as the most likely target of the Cambridge Platonist Ralph Cudworth's denunciation, in 1678, of "hylozoic atheism" (Rogers, 194).

35. For qualifications of Gallagher's influential thesis, see Sandra Sherman, "Trembling Texts: Margaret Cavendish and the Dialectic of Authorship," *English Literary Renaissance* 7 (Winter 1994): 184–210, who argues for Cavendish's sense of her historical agency rather than subjection; and Rachel Trubowitz, "The Reenchantment of Utopia and the Female Monarchical Self: Margaret Cavendish's Blazing World," *Tulsa Studies in Women's Literature* 11 (1992): 229–46, who argues for Cavendish's sense of other-connectedness.

36. See also Sarasohn, who argues that "the substance of her philosophy and its exposition justified a revolution in the interpretation of the traditional female role." Lisa T. Sarasohn, "A Science Turned Upside Down: Feminism and the Natural Philosophy of Margaret Cavendish," *Huntington Library Quarterly* 4 (1994): 289–307, 290. Rogers does acknowledge, however, that the masculine is encoded in Cavendish's theory of matter as the inanimate parts that are subservient to the rational female parts (Rogers, 201–2).

37. See Bruno Latour, *We Have Never Been Modern* (Cambridge, MA: Harvard University Press, 1993), pp. 15–32. Latour's analysis of Boyle's air-pump draws largely on the admirable study of Steven Shapin and Simon Schaffer, *Leviathan and the Air-Pump: Hobbes, Boyle, and the Experimental Life* (Princeton, NJ: Princeton University Press, 1985), which focuses on the differences between Hobbes' political and Boyle's scientific interpretations of the pump. Latour points out that Shapin and Schaffer themselves perform the purification characteristic of modern History by insisting ultimately on a political gold standard for interpretation, rather than allowing the proliferation of hybrids that characterize Boyle's and Hobbes's stand-off: "Boyle is not simply creating a scientific discourse while Hobbes is doing the same thing for politics; Boyle is creating a political discourse from which politics is to be excluded, while Hobbes is imagining a scientific politics from which experimental science has to be excluded" (Latour, 27).

38. See Samuel I. Mintz, "The Duchess of Newcastle's Visit to the Royal Society," *Journal of English and Germanic Philology* 51 (1952): 168–76, 168–76, for an account of Cavendish's visit to the Royal Society.

39. Nietzsche writes that monumental history "is the belief in the unity and continuity of the greatness of all times. It is a protest against the changes of the generations and transience." But he also complains: "how forcefully must the individuality of the past be wrenched into a general shape, with all its sharp corners and angles broken off for the sake of the correspondence!" Friedrich Nietzsche, *The Use and Abuse of History*, trans. Adrian Collins (Indianapolis and New York: Bobbs-Merrill Co., 1957), 12.

40. Cavendish's affinities are often qualified, however, by her competitive desire for fame. She observes in *Natures Pictures* that "I have not read much History to inform me of the past Ages, indeed I dare not examin the former times, for fear I should meet with such of my Sex, that have out-done all the glory I can aime at, or hope to attaine" (sig. c1)—a position somewhat at odds with her portrait of Cleopatra.
41. According to White, Marx's dialectical view of history is enabled by a mechanistic materialism whereby the Base determines Superstructure through "a succession of distinctive means of production and the modes of their relationships, a succession that is governed by strict causal laws"; this "cause-effect" relationship he sees as "Metonymical." Hayden White, *Metahistory: The Historical Imagination in Nineteenth-Century Europe* (Baltimore, MD: Johns Hopkins University Press, 1973), p. 286.

3
Confessing Mothers: The Maternal Penitent in Early Modern Revenge Tragedy

Heather Hirschfeld

Harim White's *The Ready Way to True Repentance, or A Godly, and Learned Treatise of the Repentance of Mary Magdalen* (1618), an example of popular post-Reformation literature designed for the self-instruction of the lay penitent, is dedicated to the author's mother: "To the Right, Vertuous, Graue, Wise, and Religious Gentlewoman, Mrs Dorothey Dalby, Widow, his deare and naturall Mother," the parson's guidebook begins, "Harim White, her dutifull and onely Sonne, wisheth in this life prosperity, and in that which is to come, eternall felicity."[1]

Women were, of course, frequent dedicatees of a range of early modern published texts, but White's invocation of his mother at the start of his penitential manual makes explicit a theologically as well as psychically powerful connection between figures of sin, appropriate contrition, and maternal femininity. In what follows I explore the ways in which this connection is dramatized in Renaissance revenge tragedy, a genre whose misogynist tendencies are well noted but have yet to be studied in relation to post-Reformation religious doctrine and practice. This chapter, then, begins to chart a fresh program for understanding the role of women in male-centered revenge tragedies—for seeing them not so much as a model of anti-tyrannical political opposition, as Eileen Allman has suggested, but as a function of the theological and psychological demands of early modern religious change.[2] The religious issue I concentrate on here is the abandonment during the English Reformation of the sacrament of penance, and the subsequent negotiating of penitential practice it brought about. I argue specifically that in *Hamlet* and *The Revenger's Tragedy*, plays central to the genre, mothers are made to assume and enact models of penitence that the revenger, for whom the possibility of atonement has been severely jeopardized if not altogether lost, cannot achieve.

"Revenge tragedy," as Steven Mullaney reminds us, "has long been recognized... for the speed with which it becomes virtually synonymous with stage misogyny."[3] That misogyny finds several outlets in revenge plots, the most frequent being the systematic excoriation of women for traits stereotypically assigned during this period to their gender: duplicity, infidelity, and sexual and economic depravity. Indeed, revenge drama becomes a virtual compendium of the accusations leveled at women during this period, most of which, as critics such as Jean Howard have suggested, testify to widely held anxieties about the instabilities of gender hierarchy and social status.[4] Such bitterness is complemented by both the demand for, and the exaltation of, the ideally chaste woman, whose impossible perfection is the other side of the chauvinist fantasy. John Marston's *Malcontent*, one of the period's few bloodless revenge plots, is exemplary in its portrayal of the vengeful courtier Mendoza's celebration and denigration of women.

> Sweet women, most sweet ladies—nay angels!... You preservers of mankind, life-blood of society, who would love–nay, who can live without you? O paradise, how majestical is your austerer presence! How imperiously chaste is your more modest face![5]

Mendoza's praise quickly fastens on women's potential seductiveness:

> But, O, how full of ravishing attraction is your pretty, petulant, languishing, lasciviously-composed countenance! These amorous smiles, those soul-warming sparkling glances, ardent as those flames that singed the world by heedless Phaeton!
>
> (1.5.40–4)

As the reference to the aspiring and falling Phaeton suggests, Mendoza's depiction traces an inevitable transformation from austerity to passion. Such a description ends in a castigation of female promiscuity:

> O that I could rail against these monsters in nature, models of hell, curse of the earth, women that dare attempt anything, and what they attempt they care not how they accomplish; without all premeditation or prevention, rash in asking, desperate in working, impatient in suffering, extreme in desiring, slaves unto appetite, mistresses in dissembling, only constant in unconstancy, only perfect in counterfeiting.... Their blood is their only god.
>
> (1.6.81–92)

Mendoza's venomous display is typical of the displacement of blame common to the revenge plot (he takes out on his paramour, the duchess Aurelia, a hostility that he harbors not only against her and his attraction to her, but also against the power dynamics of the Genoese court). But the sheer ostentation with which he deploys such vituperative commonplaces suggests their over-determined role in dramas of vengeance. For Mullaney, such misogyny is part of an historically specific emotional economy according to which the male experience of mourning produces an attendant disgust with the female; the revenge tragedy, structured as it is by an original loss and the punitive activities that attempt to accommodate it, dramatizes the way "obsessive misogyny displaces or supplants grief over a male figure."[6] Janet Adelman also charts the convergence of the revenge play and gynophobia: according to her account of *Hamlet,* the protagonist's aggressive stance towards his mother derives from her failure to mourn properly for the lost father. The task of mourning thus falls to the son, and this burden— which takes the form of the quest of revenge—both activates and reinforces Hamlet's revulsion at the "sexualized maternal body" that "subjects the son to [the mother's] annihilating power."[7] For Adelman, the pursuit of revenge becomes the occasion for the son to confront and lament his own as well his father's "vulnerability . . . to the poison" of the mother.[8] Part of the pursuit includes an attempt to "purify" the mother, dramatized in *Hamlet* in the famous closet scene (3.4), where Hamlet and Gertrude exchange blessings. As Adelman points out, this moment results in the "inverting [of] the relation of parent and child."[9]

   What Adelman sees as an inversion, I want to suggest, is part of another dynamic between mother and son: their assumption of the roles of penitent and confessor. This assumption, whereby the son is put (or places himself) in a position to shrive his mother is common to other revenge tragedies, a part of the genre's broader investments—given the theological binary of vengeance and penitence—in post-Reformation formulas for repentance and the quandaries they raise.[10] In this chapter, I explore the ways in which particular revenge tragedies stage versions of penitential ritual that depend on the figure of the confessing mother. It is the treatment of this figure, as the object of her son's penitential as well as vengeful energies, which represents an aspect of revenge misogyny neglected in other critical accounts of the genre.

Forms of penance

The form and structure of Christian repentance underwent a significant shift over the course of the English Reformation. Before this period penance was a sacrament: an experience of sorrow and an achievement of forgiveness enabled by Christ's suffering, worked out on earth as a sign of God's grace by the priest for and with the sinner. Auricular confession was central to the efficacy of the sacrament, the middle step in a three-stage process that moved the penitent from contrition to satisfaction for sin. Eamon Duffy remarks that the proliferation in the late Middle Ages of guidebooks for generating good, complete confessions indicates the importance of the procedure. Such manuals included a range of "exhortations to penitents to encourage them [in] . . . different formulae of absolution and reassurance, prayers for repentance and forgiveness, verses from the psalms, theological notes on contrition, confession, and satisfaction, and procedures to be followed in absolving the dying."[11]

It is against the status and the necessity of the sacrament of penance—and especially the influence of the priest in determining or pronouncing divine forgiveness—that early continental Reformers protest. While some maintained the spiritual value of going to a minister or other "learned figure" for advice and education—indeed, as Ronald Rittgers has explained, German Lutherans "developed a modified version of private confession that they practiced until the end of the eighteenth century"—Reformers contested the scriptural and theological grounds of the priest's sacramental authority.[12] For them it smacked of notions of free will and the possibility of human cooperation in the remittance of sin; it also privileged the role of the priest in a way that they believed denied the centrality and power of Christ's sacrifice. They also challenged the possibility of successful confession. For fallen man complete acknowledgment of sin was by definition impossible, and Luther maintained that requiring it resulted in a debilitating burden that "serve[d] only to frighten hearts into confessing often," rather than to promote the kind of faith that assured forgiveness.[13] Luther's concerns were echoed more bitterly by the Swiss reformers Calvin, Bucer, and Zwingli; Calvin dismissed it as a "butchery of conscience"[14] and Zwingli refuted it in his articles of 1523: "God alone remits sins, through Jesus Christ, His Son, our only Lord. Whoever ascribes the remission of sins to a creature robs God of His honor and gives it to one who is not God. That is pure idolatry. Consequently confession which is made to a priest or to a neighbor is not for the remission of sins, but for counseling."[15]

For the Church of England the institutional rejection of the sacrament and yearly confession took shape under the guiding influence of Thomas Cranmer, Archbishop of Canterbury, who considered confession to be "requisite and expedient" but "not necessary."[16] While the Six Articles of 1539 reaffirmed that "auricular confession is expedient and necessary to be retained and continued, used and frequented in the Church of God," by the end of the 1540s, after Henry's death and the accession of the "hotter" Protestant Protectorate of Edward VI, the sacrament of penance and the rite of private confession were essentially written out of liturgical and devotional practice. Ramie Targoff has chronicled Cranmer's efforts to "reconceive petitions once reserved for the clergy into common acts of prayer." Cranmer's Anglican Order of Communion, which was to become part of the Book of Common Prayer, ensured that private confession was "more or less incorporated into part of the collective liturgy. By the time the second edition of the Prayer Book was published in 1552, Cranmer had fully transformed the practice of pre-communion confession from a personal exchange between priest and penitent to a standardized utterance performed by the entire congregation."[17] Reinstated in 1559 after the Catholic Queen Mary's reign, the Elizabethan Book of Common Prayer continued the earlier Edwardian emphasis so that Holy Communion was "no longer a practice that require[d] an individualized act of auricular confession."[18] Taking into account Calvin and his vehement rejection of auricular confession, the 1563 Homily on Repentance walks a delicate line between approving confession to God or one's neighbor on the basis of 1 John 2: "If we confess our sin, God is faithful and righteous to forgive us our sins," and rejecting the institutional power of the keys: "Whereas the adversaries go about . . . to maintain their auriculer confession withall, they are greatly deceaved themselves, and do shamefully deceave others. For . . . priests are as much bound to confesse themselves unto the laypeople . . . then the laytie . . . hath as great authoritye to absolve [as] the priestes."[19] When the 39 Articles, inscribing the central tenets of the Elizabethan Church, were promulgated the following year, penance was specifically denied sacramental status and auricular confession to a priest was, if not proscribed, no longer authorized as a practice or demand of the Church of England.[20]

Modes of confession and activities of repentance did not simply cease, of course, with the dissolution of the sacrament of penance and the loss of auricular confession to a priest. Christopher Marsh gestures to a number of spiritual forms that might be said to have siphoned off more conventional penitential energies: a rich variety of catechisms may have worked to "preserv[e] and enhance . . . the educational aspects of confession," while "the business of the church courts expanded as these institutions took on more of the work of moral policing."[21] A stream of reformed primers and handbooks, like the Harim White treatise, directed readers in the proper ways to examine their consciences, recognize their sins, and make restitution. Such handbooks and manuals differed from their Catholic counterparts not only in terms of their rejection of the priesthood, but also, and perhaps more significantly, in terms of the way they described the causal logic of forgiveness. For the penitent Catholic, faith in the possibility of absolution was affirmed after penitential practice as its effect; for the penitent Protestant, faith in the possibility of absolution preceded—indeed, was required for—penitential practice as its cause. As Tentler summarizes, the contrite Protestant "need do only one thing: believe the promise of forgiveness, for that belief constitutes forgiveness itself."[22] The effect of this logic was, ironically, to make Protestant confession self-willed. As Marsh explains, "the Elizabethan clergy were officially required to 'exhort' those with troubled consciences to come forward and confess," so that "crucially, [confession and penance] became a voluntary responsibility."[23] Luther insisted, of course, that such a program released the Protestant worshiper from the potentially paralyzing demands of the complete confession; as the historian Henry Lea says, the Reformers believed that they "had so improved the benefits of absolution and the power of the keys that many afflicted consciences gained consolation; they believed in the gratuitous remission of sin through Christ, and felt themselves fully reconciled to God through faith, while formerly all the strength of absolution was weakened by the doctrine of works."[24]

Despite these optimistic accounts, the documents of religious history bear out the kinds of spiritual and psychic torment that the requirements of justifying faith—and the absence of sacramental penance—engendered. Marsh points out that the impact of the loss of the sacrament "should clearly not be underestimated," and he quotes Patrick Collinson in seeing "the abolition of compulsory, auricular confession as a disastrous error on the part of the reformed church."[25] The dramatic position of the Renaissance revenger represents the kind of experiential as well as epistemological crisis occasioned by the shifting grounds and practices of repentance. In a world that demanded voluntary contrition by people already convinced of the certainty of forgiveness, the Renaissance revenger, who dedicates himself to the course of vengeance—who promises to "wipe away all trivial fond records, / All saws of books, all forms, all pressures past / That youth and observation copied there"—puts himself in an untenable position in relation to the possibility of the remission of his sins. Although his avenging activities may represent, as Michael Neill has suggested, an effective means of memorializing a loved one in the post-Reformation absence of Catholic rituals for the dead,[26] his revenge commitment, which fills him so completely that "the chamber of [his] breast is even thronged/With firm attendance that forswears to flinch," alienates him—or proves his alienation—from available forms of restitution.[27] It is this alienation that the revenger attempts to resolve by overseeing the confession of the mother.

The confessing woman was, of course, not an invention of early modern revenge tragedy. Indeed, the model is deeply indebted to a long imaginative tradition—developed for both devotional as well as polemical purposes—of the woman at shrift or proclaiming her faith; and a long line of penitential manuals uniformly provided instructions, always ideologically fraught, for handling the sins of women.[28] What happens in revenge tragedies is that these models are transformed in a particular way, used neither, as their medieval genealogy would predict, as an authoritative example for devotional imitation nor as a caricature for mocking a corrupt clerisy. Rather, the confessing mother becomes an object of the specifically post-Reformation desire of the revenger: a desire to participate in—indeed to oversee—the purification of the maternal source of sin by means of the very ritual from which he has been alienated. This desire is indistinguishable from the overarching pursuit of vengeance; forcing the mother to confess, in other words, is one of the surest ways that the revenger avenges the crimes he suffers as well as those he is compelled to commit. Insofar as she serves these functions, the confessing mother is shorn of the compelling—even proto-feminist—influence and autonomy scholars such as Teresa Colleti have associated with figures of female penitence; there is no unequivocal equation here between this version of female piety and proof of female autonomy or authority.[29] The compromised vision of female piety offered here symbolizes more than the customary subordination of the world of the revenge play to the subjectivity of the revenger; rather, it marks a specifically gendered response to changes in the doctrines and practices governing the most psychically powerful notions of sin and repentance.

"That was motherly said"

Though there is no precedent for it in *The Spanish Tragedy* (1588), the play considered to be the pattern of the revenge genre in English,[30] a cluster of revenge plays, most explicitly *Hamlet* and *The Revenger's Tragedy*, feature mothers or maternal figures in a penitential pose. These figures answer demands not made by *The Spanish Tragedy*'s protagonist Hieronimo, whose position as father of a lost son distinguishes him from the bulk of other Renaissance revengers and their particular relations to issues of crime, and recompense. Insofar as avenging sons, in absorbing entirely the paternal command to revenge, emblematize a post-Reformation alienation from the possibilities of penance, they look specifically to the mother—the theological as well as psychic source of sin and its potential correction—to perform it for them: "for them" as a vicarious achievement and "for them" as a mode of revenge.

The most familiar version of this kind of performance is the closet scene in *Hamlet*, a scene that is both revised and intensified in Thomas Middleton's *The Revenger's Tragedy*, where the interactions between Vindice, the play's protagonist, and his mother, Gratiana, are orchestrated almost entirely in penitential terms—indeed, as opposed to Hamlet, Vindice has no other relation to Gratiana than that of scourge and minister. This focus is, of course, part of Middleton's hyperbolic parody of *Hamlet* and other revenge tragedies, but it also serves to hone down, and thereby clarify, the obsessive energies driving the stage convention and its concomitant misogyny.

Vindice enters the stage already dedicated to avenging his former lover, dead nine years, and his father. His manic pursuit is ostensibly directed at the duke and his son, Lussorioso, but it also fastens on his mother, whom first he tempts to, then excoriates for, then forgives of, sins of greed and concupiscence. This program begins in the second act, when, having disguised himself as "Piato," Vindice tries to seduce his mother into prostituting her daughter, Castiza, to Lussorioso. Vindice, again disguised, has already tried to seduce Castiza, but she proves invulnerable to his rhetoric. Vindice may be delighted by her rejection—"Oh I'm above my tongue! Most constant sister, / In this thou hast right honourable shown"—but his true investment is not in the chastity of his sister but the behavior of his mother, Gratiana.[31] Vindice lures Gratiana to prostitute the resistant daughter, and her initial refusal—"O fie, fie, the riches of the world cannot hire / A mother to such a most unnatural task"—only spurs on Vindice's seductive rhetoric. He thus engages Gratiana in the kind of temptation or testing scene so common to Renaissance drama, in which a man repeatedly invites a woman to participate in the kinds of activities he will then condemn her for:

> I would raise my state upon her [Castiza's] breast
> And call her eyes my tenants; I would count
> My yearly maintenance upon her cheeks,
> Take coach upon her lip, and all her parts
> Should keep men after men and I would ride
> In pleasure upon pleasure.
>
> (2.1.94–9)

Gratiana gives in at this point: "Oh heavens, this overcomes me!" she exclaims, admitting that Vindice's promises are "too strong for me. Men know, that know us, / We are so weak their words can overthrow us" (2.1.103–6). Gratiana's assumption here is that her tempter knows, and also wants, to "overthrow" her virtue: she suggests that the real design of Vindice's test is not to discover female purity but to elicit female betrayal. What really compels and satisfies this revenger, in other words, is the prospect of orchestrating female sin; the unimpeachable response of the sister makes more urgent the impeaching of the mother. Such a design stems from multiple concerns, not least of which is a need to control the threat of change represented in the female figure who is "both the sign of, and the cure for, the endless round of placements and displacements if the court."[32] But Vindice's obsessive treatment of his mother is also part of a revenge platform that allows for the orchestration of penitential ritual so as to reinforce a particularly hostile notion of femininity. The seduction of the mother into stereotypical sin thus accomplishes for Gratiana what Vindice, as dedicated revenger, cannot: she sins in a way that leaves open the possibility of sin's compensation.

Vindice oversees this kind of compensation in the fourth act, when, no longer disguised, he begins to accuse Gratiana of her failures. This is Vindice's particularly gendered fulfillment of the role of "scourge and minister": precipitating Gratiana's sexualized vices so that he can monitor her contrition, confession and, ultimately, her purification:

Vindice: O thou for whom no name is bad enough!
Gratiana: What means my sons? What, will you murder me?
Vindice: Wicked, unnatural parent!
. . .
Gratiana: Are you so barbarous, to set iron nipples

Upon the breast that gave you suck?
Vindice: That breast is turned to quarled poison.

(4.4.1–7)

Vindice plays the role of a particularly antagonistic confessor here, not
simply questioning or hinting at Gratiana's faults but identifying and
condemning them. When he reveals that he was the one who seduced her,
Gratiana begins to rue her lapse: "Oh hell unto my soul. . . . Oh sons / Forgive
me, to myself I'll prove more true; / You that should honour me—I kneel to
you" (4.4.37–9). Gratiana kneels and weeps, assuming the penitential pose
that sanctions both Vindice's forgiveness and her fresh infusion with grace:

> *Vindice*: I' faith 'tis a sweet shower, it does much good;
> The fruitful grounds and meadows of her soul
> Has been long dry. Pour down, thou blessed dew.
> Rise mother, troth this shower has made you higher.
> *Gratiana*: Oh you heavens,
> Take this infectious spot out of my soul!
> I'll rinse it in seven waters of mine eyes;
> Make my tears salt enough to taste of grace;
> To weep is to our sex naturally given
> But to weep truly—that's a gift from heaven!

Vindice celebrates this moment with a kiss and suggests that Gratiana is
responsible for his own spiritual unburdening. "Our hearts wear feathers
that before wore lead," he tells his brother (4.4.88), acknowledging that now
Gratiana's words are "motherly said" (4.4.94).

The benefit that Vindice records here could be seen as the result of a
substitutive economy: Gratiana's repentance, that is, takes the place of
Vindice's, the atonement of the mother serves to wash her child clean.
But the satisfaction the confessing mother offers is also part of the revenge
economy which structures the play and makes forgiveness a more certain
form of punishment. Gratiana's cycle of contrition, confession, and absolution is not only forced on her, it is forced on her by the very person
who stands for the impossibility of effective repentance. She thus becomes
the object of a specifically misogynist penitential fantasy: one in which the
mother suffers for and is absolved of sin, even as this absolution is called
into question. The deepest satisfaction of this revenger lies in inflicting upon
the mother such a compromised position.

Hamlet, of course, is not dedicated to revenge in the same way; indeed,
it was part of Middleton's parody to turn his own protagonist from the
vacillating, melancholic Danish prince into a manic Italian courtier.[33] But
Vindice's mania illuminates something important about Hamlet's more
complicated, ambivalent interest in Gertrude: that his fixation is rooted in

penitential longing, and that the paths it follows are simultaneously repar-
ative and revengeful. Hamlet is told by the Ghost to "leave her to heaven,"
but in a world so exceptionally "out of joint," it is unclear precisely what
such a command means for Hamlet's treatment of his mother.

Stephen Greenblatt has identified the Catholic resonances of Shakespeare's
play, chronicling the doctrinal instability of a text that places its protagonist in Wittenburg, seat of the Lutheran Reformation, while featuring
a Ghost whose uncertain moral status derives from his provenance in
Purgatory.[34] Such theological and ethical uncertainty also inheres in the
Ghost's demand that Hamlet, "Leave her to heaven, / And to those thorns
that in her bosom lodge / To prick and sting her" (1.5.86–8): in Hamlet's
haunted post-Reformation world such an order is deeply ambiguous, not
necessarily implying that Hamlet should ignore or let go of Gertrude, but
rather that he should instruct her precisely in order that she can be left
to heaven. Such instruction itself becomes a deeply ambivalent project for
Hamlet, a mixture of confessional as well as punitive energies. Leaving her
to heaven, in other words, becomes a way of directing Gertrude in a penitential display that satisfies both the spiritual and vengeful energies of both
father and son.[35]

These energies could be said to begin as early as the second scene, when
Hamlet, proclaiming that he has "that within which passeth show," incites
his mother to the kind of deep gazing associated with the experience of
contrition. They continue into the *Mousetrap* inset play, where Gertrude is
quite literally shown the scenes of what Hamlet imagines are her transgressions. And they climax in the closet scene, with Hamlet's showing Gertrude
first "a glass / Where you may see the [inmost] part of you" and then the
"counterfeit presentment of two brothers" (3.4.19–20, 54). What follows is
Hamlet's infamous, prurient screed against adult, maternal sexuality:

> Here is your husband, like a mildewed ear,
> Blasting his wholesome brother. Have you eyes?
> Could you on this fair mountain leave to feed,
> And batten on this moor? Ha, have you eyes?
> You cannot call it love, for at your age
> They heyday in the blood is tame, it's humble,
> And waits upon the judgment, and what judgment
> Would step from this to this?

> (3.4.64–71)

The model of repugnant female sexuality offered here, although colored by
Hamlet's personal revulsion, is also a conventional prompt to remorse; the
accusation of sexual sin, in other words, is knit up in a broader penitential
agenda. It is an agenda in which the Ghost himself participates, appearing
at this very moment "to whet thy almost blunted purpose" and to direct the

shriving: "O, step between her and her fighting soul. / Conceit in weakest bodies strongest works, / Speak to her, Hamlet" (3.4.111–13). Hamlet and his father become allies here, in Gertrude's closet, to purify her of the sexual "falling-off" by which they both have been plagued from the start of the play. Hamlet continues, in deliberate terms:

> Confess yourself to heaven,
> Repent what's past, avoid what is to come,
> And do not spread the compost on the weeds
> To make them ranker.

(3.4.149–52)

He finishes his exhortation with specific conditions for making satisfaction:

> Good night, but go not to my uncle's bed—
> Assume a virtue, if you have it not.
> That monster custom, who all sense doth eat,
> Of habits devil, is angel yet in this,
> That to the use of actions fair and good
> He likewise gives a frock or livery
> That aptly is put on.
> Refrain [to-]night,
> And that shall lend a kind of easiness
> To the next abstinence...

(3.4.159–67)

Hamlet and the Ghost jointly conduct Gertrude through her shrift, extolling first contrition, then confession, and finally the requirements for satisfaction. This is the process denied to both father and son: Hamlet senior has from the first act rued his murder "Unhous'led, disappointed, unanel'd," and Hamlet, having placed the Ghost's "commandment all alone... Within the book and volume of my brain" (1.5.77, 102–3), functions now as though also deprived of the possibility of forgiveness. The confession of the mother, then, affords an experience of repentance now unavailable to the father and son. In Hamlet, then, the mother, whose confessional status is never established beyond her admission that Hamlet has "cleft her soul in twain," practices a ritual lost to both father and son.

But it is not only the practice of penitence that Gertrude offers. In this play of continually dissolving binaries, repentance is never separable from its theological opposite, vengeance. Overseeing Gertrude's confession— "speaking daggers" to her—is also a form of revenge for Hamlet; he makes his bear the burden of a penitential practice whose efficacy the play both idealizes and challenges. Bearing this burden—and not simply enduring

Hamlet's tortuous imaginings of her betrayal—is Gertrude's punishment, a punishment that combines retribution and penitential practice.[36] As in *Revenger's Tragedy*, yet with the kind of hesitation and ambivalence characteristic of Hamlet, punishing the mother—by confessing her—represents the play's particular contribution to revenge tragedy misogyny. This misogyny has been diagnosed in various ways, but no diagnoses have taken into account the genre's specific use of the woman as an object for negotiating the psychic ramifications of lost or changing religious practices. The approach offered here, then, verges on what Eric Santner calls the psychotheological—the deliberate connecting of traditions of belief with the demands of the unconscious—in its effort to correct for precisely that gap in our thinking about the role of women—here the mother—on the stage of revenge.[37]

Notes

1. Harim White, *The Ready Way to True Repentance* (London, 1618), A3.
2. Eileen Allman, *Jacobean Revenge Tragedy and the Politics of Virtue* (Newark: University of Delaware Press, 1999).
3. Steven Mullaney, "Mourning and Misogyny: *Hamlet, The Revenger's Tragedy*, and the Final Progress of Elizabeth I, 1600–1607," *Shakespeare Quarterly* 45 (1994): 144.
4. See Jean Howard's seminal work, *The Stage and Social Struggle in Early Modern England* (London: Routledge, 1994).
5. John Marston, *The Malcontent*, ed. Bernard Harris (New York: W. W. Norton, 1967), 1.5.33–9.
6. Mullaney, "Mourning and Misogyny," 154.
7. Janet Adelman, *Suffocating Mothers: Fantasies of Maternal Origin in Shakespeare's Plays* (New York: Routledge, 1992).
8. Ibid.
9. Ibid.
10. The juxtaposition of revenge and repentance, usually figured in terms of Christ's ministry, is commonplace; see for instance Thomas Wager on Mary Magdalen: "Into this worlde God hath sent his owne, / Not to iudge the world, or to take vengeance, / But to preach forgeueness and pardon, / Through true faith in hym, and perfect repentance" (*A new enterlude . . . of the life and repentance of Marie Magdalene*, London, 1566), Fii.
11. Eamon Duffy, *The Stripping of the Altars: Traditional Religion in England, 1400–1580* (New Haven, CT: Yale University Press, 1992), 58-9.
12. Ronald Rittgers, *The Reformation of the Keys: Confession, Conscience, and Authority in Sixteenth-Century Germany* (Cambridge, MA: Harvard University Press, 2004), 3.
13. Martin Luther, "Sacrament of Penance," in *Luther's Works*, ed. E. Theodore Bachmann (Philadeplphia: Muhlenberg Press, 1960), 35: 20.
14. See *The Oxford Encyclopedia of the Reformation*, ed. Hans J. Hillerbrand (New York: Oxford University Press, 1996), 403.
15. *Reformed Confessions of the 16th Century*, ed. Arthur C. Cochrane (Philadelphia: Westminster Press, 1966), 42.
16. Diarmid MacCulloch, *Thomas Cranmer* (New Haven, CT: Yale University Press, 1996), 246.

17. Ramie Targoff, *Common Prayer: The Language of Public Devotion in Early Modern England* (Chicago: University of Chicago Press, 2001), 30.
18. Ibid., 33.
19. *The seconde tome of homelyes* (London, 1563), fol. 284.
20. The 25th article reads: "There are two Sacraments ordained of Christ our Lord in the Gospel, that is to say, Baptism and the Supper of the Lord. Those five, commonly called Sacraments, that is to say, Confirmation, Penance, Orders, Matrimony, and Extreme Unction, are not to be counted for Sacraments of the Gospel, being such as have grown partly of the corrupt following of the Apostles, partly are states of life allowed in the Scriptures; but yet have not the like nature of Sacraments with Baptism and the Lord's Supper, for that they have not any visible sign or ceremony ordained of God."
21. Christopher Marsh, *Popular Religion in Sixteenth-Century England* (New York: St. Martin's Press, 1999), 82.
22. Thomas Tentler, *Sin and Confession on the Eve of the Reformation* (Princeton, NJ: Princeton University Press, 1977), 354.
23. Marsh, *Popular Religion in Sixteenth-Century England*, 82.
24. Henry Lea, *A History of Auricular Confession and Indulgences in the Latin Church* (London, 1896), 1: 516.
25. Marsh, *Popular Religion in Sixteenth-Century England*, 81.
26. William Shakespeare, *Hamlet, The Riverside Shakespeare*, ed. G. Blakemore Evans (Boston: Houghton Mifflin, 1974), 1.5.99–101. Michael Neill, *Issues of Death: Mortality and Identity in English Renaissance Tragedy* (Oxford: Clarendon Press, 1997), 46.
27. John Marston, *Antonio's Revenge*, 2.3.11–12.
28. For an overview of the literary tradition in terms of the figure of Mary Magdalen, see Marjorie Malvern, *Venus in Sackcloth: The Magdalen's Origins and Metamorphoses* (Carbondale, IL: Southern Illinois Press, 1975). For an historical survey of medieval manuals and their gender ideology, see Jacqueline Murray, "Gendered Souls in Sexed Bodies: The Male Construction of Female Sexuality in Some Medieval Confessors' Manuals," *Handling Sin: Confession in the Middle Ages* (York: York Medieval Press, 1998), 79–94.
29. Teresa Colleti, *Mary Magdalen and the Drama of Saints* (Philadelphia: University of Pennsylvania Press, 2004). Lisa Severt King discusses the decline of such influence as it is dramatized in Shakespeare's *Antony and Cleopatra*: see "'Blessed when they were riggish': Shakespeare's Cleopatra and Christianity's Penitent Prostitutes," *Journal of Medieval and Renaissance Studies* 22 (1993): 429–49.
30. See Fredson Bowers, *Elizabethan Revenge Tragedy* (Princeton, NJ: Princeton University Press, 1940), 62–80.
31. *The Revenger's Tragedy*, ed. Brian Gibbons (New York: W. W. Norton, 1991), 2.1. 44–5. The authorship of *The Revenger's Tragedy* is a consistent source of debate. I follow Brian Corrigan among others in taking Middleton as the author. See Corrigan, "Middeton, *The Revenger's Tragedy*, and Crisis Literature," *SEL* 38 (1998): 281–95.
32. Peter Stallybrass, "Reading the Body: The Revenger's Tragedy and the Jacobean Theater of Consumption," *Renaissance Drama* 18 (1987): 129.
33. For a comprehensive discussion of the dramaturgic as well as philosophical differences between Shakespeare and Middleton, see Gary Taylor, "Forms of Opposition: Shakespeare and Middleton," *ELR* 24 (1994): 283–314.

34. Steven Greenblatt, *Hamlet in Purgatory* (Princeton, NJ: Princeton University Press, 2002).
35. There is considerable literature contesting the Ghost as definitively Hamlet's father or, rather "in the same figure like the King that's dead." (1.1.41). For my purposes here the important point is that Hamlet at least considers the Ghost his father.
36. Wreaking this kind of punishment can be seen as yet another form of Hamlet's work as scourge and minister. For the classic discussion of scourge versus minister as damned versus chosen agent of God's vengeance, see Fredson Bowers, "Hamlet as Minister and Scourge," *PMLA* 70 (1955): 740-49. See also R. W. Dent, "Hamlet: Scourge and Minister," *Shakespeare Quarterly* 29 (1978): 82–4.
37. Eric Santner, *The Psychotheology of Everyday Life* (Chicago: University of Chicago Press, 2001).

4

Feminist Criticism and the New Formalism: Early Modern Women and Literary Engagement

Sasha Roberts

> As figures be the instruments of ornament in every language, so be they also in a sort abuses or rather trespasses in speech, because they pass the ordinary limits of common utterance.... Figurative speech is a novelty of language evidently (and yet not absurdly) estranged from the ordinary habit and manner of our daily talk and writing.
>
> George Puttenham, *Arte of English Poesie* (1589): I: 7
> (repr. in Vickers, 231–2 and 236)

> The technique of art is to make objects "unfamiliar", to make forms difficult, to increase the difficulty and length of perception because the process of perception is an aesthetic end in itself and must be prolonged. *Art is a way of experiencing the artfulness of an object; the object is not important.*
>
> Victor Shklovsky, 'Art as Technique' (1917), repr. *in Russian Formalist Criticism: Four Essays*, ed. Lee T. Lemon and Marion J. Reis (Lincoln and London: University of Nebraska Press, 1965): 12

This is the compelling question: can formalist literary analysis be reconciled with feminist literary criticism? Of course, it was not always so: questions about form have only recently begun to excite scholars again, at least at an explicit and confrontational level. For in the wake of new historicist and materialist feminist criticism, formalist approaches to literature have long been tainted by their ahistoricism and apoliticism; stained by their failure to engage with the real world of social inequality and the complexities of cultural discourse. Skepticism has prevailed. What can form tell us, really, about the central categories of literary criticism that have been privileged in the last decades: politics, history, gender, race, class? What possible contribution can formalist analysis make to the wider project of understanding the place of literature in the minute particulars of an unjust world?

It is no use beating about the bush: the disjunction between formalist and feminist criticism is gloriously profound. It all turns on gender, of course. For Shklovsky, "the object is not important," while the tacit assumption of so much materialist feminist criticism (which has dominated feminist approaches to early modern literature) is precisely the opposite: that not only the objects of art but the objectifications and, indeed, subjects of art are vitally important, constitutive even. We abandon content and context at our peril, for it is precisely in terms of content and context that notions of difference—notions which underpin critical discussion of gender, race, and class—can best (fundamentally?) be articulated. Thus in *Major Women Writers of the Seventeenth Century* James Fitzmaurice et al. argue that "feminist criticism must first be described according to its intent, that is, to acknowledge that men and women, because of their different positions and activities in a culture, approach writing and reading from different directions, directions that must be acknowledged in order for a literary analysis to have both theoretical and historical validity" (9). Formalism, however, does not readily (if at all) accommodate a difference that resides ultimately in identity. Even given the diversity of its practices, formalism is distinguished by a different set of critical interests: language, rhetorical figures, tropes, meter, versification, narrative structure, genre, etc.

It is not that feminist criticism has no use for these terms: on the contrary, feminist criticism has been deeply attuned to the gendered operations of language, tropes, genre, poetic and narrative structures. It is rather that formalism has not, historically at least, attempted to address issues of gender. As recently as 1992 Joe Andrew, presenting the work of the British Neo-Formalist Circle, posited that "we Neo-Formalists have insufficiently taken on board the more politically orientated branches of literary criticism," and "feminism" in particular: "very few papers reflect this vital (and no longer so new) current."[1] But this insufficiency is not wholly a function of lamentable gender-blindness; a political myopia that unwittingly plagued previous and current generations of scholars. No, this neglect of cultural context is critically deliberate. And as such it demands to be taken seriously.

By this I do not mean revisiting the mid-twentieth century to dismantle the latent gender politics of I. A. Richards' practical criticism, the American New Criticism, or the still fascinating work of Russian Formalist critics writing in the first decades of the twentieth century. In this essay my concern lies with "new formalism" or "new formalisms"—a tendentious label for a recent and disparate critical trend—and more particularly with the possibilities of reconciliation and resistance between new formalism and feminist criticism in the field of early modern literary studies. The case for new formalism has been variously argued in a special issue of *Modern Language Quarterly* (61: 1, 2000): "forms matter not just as local articulations, or even as local articulations radiating into and unsettling the ground on which they stand, but as constitutive of the works at large" (Wolfson, 11); "the loss of form threatens both literary and cultural studies, not only at the level of methodology, where reading becomes impossible without it, but also at the level of disciplinarity" (Rooney, 20).[2] For scholars of early modern literature, however, the most pertinent recent exploration of new formalism comes in the 2003 volume edited by Mark David Rasmussen, *Renaissance Literature and Its Formal Engagements*.[3] Rasmussen posits that "a freshly theorized formalism might be expected to take two main directions, either inflected toward the historical/cultural or toward the literary/aesthetic" (3). In the same volume, Douglas Bruster suggests that "new formalism could be defined as follows: a critical genre dedicated to examining the social, cultural, and historical aspects of literary form, and the function of form for those who produce and consume literary texts" (44), and points to recent studies focused on "words, tropes, figures, or genres" (ranging from Annabel Patterson's *Pastoral and Ideology*, 1988, to Lynne Magnusson's *Shakespeare and Social Dialogue*, 1999) that understand form "as possessing significant agency before, during, and after literary composition" and often stress "the social and political implications of literary form" (45). Indeed, as Lynne Magnusson points out in her insightful study, "it is time to negotiate some common ground between close reading and cultural poetics and, in particular, to propose taxonomies for verbal analysis that can address the place of collective invention in the production of Shakespeare's complex texts" and, I would add, the work of early modern writers at large (7).[4]

Even so, the position of feminist criticism in relation to new formalism remains problematic. As Rasmussen admits, "most conspicuous in its absence" in *Renaissance Literature and its Formal Engagements* "is any sustained reflection on how formalist approaches might be broadened by reckoning with the achievements of feminist scholarship in the field, and particularly the recovery of Renaissance literary texts written by women" (9). This "absence" reflects the wider conceptual problem: while formalist analysis has not recognized gender difference, feminist analysis is predicated on it. In the same volume, Heather Dubrow points out that "if we need to realize that the study of form can be reconciled with a commitment to, say, the study of ideology or gender [we] need as well to confront and argue about tensions that will remain" (85), a confrontation which Dubrow does not have the space to develop but which I want to pursue here. And where best to begin than with bare inconsistencies in the basic tenets of criticism? For one tension is undeniable, even insurmountable: a feminist criticism that takes gender to be a central category of analysis and a formalist criticism that does *not* will remain, at this fundamental level, exquisitely incompatible.

But this does not preclude dialogue. From the perspective of literary history, and more precisely early modern women's literary history, there are not only productive but *necessary* grounds for reconciliation between new formalism and feminist criticism. It is not just a matter of understanding that *access* to forms and formal play has a gendered history. As I have argued in relation to women's engagement with Shakespeare in the seventeenth century, and as I shall argue here first in the context of Renaissance literary criticism addressed to women—particularly by George Puttenham and Dudley North—and second, in Katherine Philips' discussion of her own writing practices, if we neglect early modern women's interest in questions of literary form, we fail to do justice to their work as readers and writers. In this respect I want to take up Rasmussen's challenge of reckoning formalist and feminist approaches precisely in the context of "the recovery of Renaissance literary texts written by women" (9).

The rub comes when we move from literary history to literary criticism; from the study of literary culture to specific literary works. Of course, I have to flag my provisos: neither literary history and literary criticism, nor literary culture and literary works, are neatly divisible—the waters are always muddy (and therefore more interesting). What I have in mind here are not differences of kind but of *emphasis*. It is in the close reading of the formal properties of literary works that the interests and agendas of new formalism and feminist criticism really begin to collide. I want to explore that collision by taking what may seem the most uncompromising material for anything but a feminist analysis—misogynist verses "Upon women" discovered in a woman's manuscript miscellany—and subject them to a formalist close reading inspired by Puttenham's critical lexicon. I want to see where reading against the grain of our current critical climate might lead.

Of course, the invocation of "feminist analysis" as an apparently stable entity is itself problematic. Further, in *Gender Trouble* (1990), Judith Butler makes the point that the very categories of analysis of "gender" and "women" are not stable but performative: "the postulation of a true gender identity" is "as a regulatory fiction," for "gender reality is created through sustained social performances" (180).[5] This in turn impacts on our conception of feminism: "if a stable notion of gender no longer proves to be the foundational premise of feminist politics, perhaps a new sort of feminist politics is now desirable to contest the very reifications of gender and identity" (9). In this respect pitting formalism against a feminism that assumes "gender" or "women" to be a stable category of analysis may appear to evade the ways in which feminism, at least in the field of literary theory, is changing.

But history works its magic, and the feminist politics of today may not always be the best tool for reading the position of women or men in the past. I am struck by the disjunction between Butler's innovative and often liberating emphasis upon gender as performative and the repetitious and restrictive performances of gender that were readily available to early modern women and men. Even as we may chart the performative operations of "gender" in the period—perhaps especially in the field of drama and sexuality where Butler appears to have been most useful to Renaissance scholars— it is hard to conceive of a feminist criticism of Renaissance literature that does not make recourse to "gender and identity" and their material effects;

indeed, their reifications. Which is not quite Butler's point, but nonetheless we should remain alert to the (productive) points of tension between "performative," historicist and materialist conceptions of gender.

Materialist feminist criticism has rightly dominated feminist analysis of Renaissance literature because it is materialism that teaches us most about men's and women's lives and their work in literary culture. There is no substitute for materialism. But it is precisely the points of resistance between materialist and formalist approaches to literature that may encourage us to think more expansively.[6] We can learn much from the conjunctions and agreements between new formalism and feminist criticism, but we can learn more from their disjunctions and discords. If the reconciliation between new formalism and feminist criticism should prompt us to think in more nuanced ways about the conditions of early modern women's literary engagement, then the resistance between new formalism and feminist criticism should inspire us to think about what it is we really mean by literature, by literariness or, as Puttenham would put it, by *poesy*.

Poesie, formal engagement, and the woman reader

Perhaps one reason why the fledgling canon of Renaissance literary criticism has proved of comparatively little interest to feminist criticism of Renaissance literature is precisely that it appears to have so little to say on the subject of gender or women, or more widely on the content and contexts of specific literary works. As such it has, in our current critical climate, all the semblance of irrelevance. Of course we are not obliged to adopt the critical frameworks, assumptions, and occlusions of past generations: how else could literary criticism continue to be relevant for readers? But precisely because the gap between early modern and modern critical modes runs so wide and deep, it is worth probing in terms of the investment we choose to make in questions of form, content, and context. While Renaissance literary criticism—beyond the broader project of mounting a defense of vernacular literature (Sidney, Heywood)—is obsessed by versification, rhetoric, rhyme, and decorum (Wilson, Puttenham, Daniel, Jonson, North), modern critical discourse has little time for such matters. In this respect modern critical discourse, for all its talk of historicizing and contextualizing, is brilliantly, beguilingly anachronistic.

George Puttenham's compendious *Arte of English Poesie* (1589) has proved emblematic for New Historicist criticism of the political maneuvers and instrumentality of Renaissance poetry.[7] In part this is enabled by Puttenham's dedication of the volume to Queen Elizabeth, whose portrait appears so prominently in the volume's frontispiece. Puttenham was not merely aiming at a royal figurehead; the dedication to Elizabeth was especially apt given her own aptitude at writing poetry:

But you (madam) my most honoured and gracious, if I should seem to offer you this my device for a discipline and not a delight, I might well be reputed of all others the most arrogant and injurious, yourself being already, of any that I know in our time, the most excellent poet. . .

> (Book I, chapter I: "What a poet and poesy is, and
> who may be worthily said the most excellent poet
> of our time"; repr. in Vickers, 193)

All well and good in the rhetoric of flattery. But I want to move beyond both political instrumentality and the patriarchal master narrative as a lens through which to read Puttenham's *Arte of English Poesie*. In a feminist reading of the *Arte of Poesie* (1990) that deploys deconstruction and psycho-analysis, Jacques Lezra notes "the insistence with which Puttenham returns to the issue of sexual difference—principally in stories of rape, seduction, or instruction, but also of generation and/or infanticide" when attempting to persuade the reader or explicate a point (55). In this way the *Arte of Poesie* may be read in terms of its indelibly gendered tropes that serve to reduce women to their sexuality or, alternatively, to limit their rhetorical discrimination—as in Puttenham's example of a "lady [who] was a little peruerse, and not disposed to reforme her selfe by hearing reason" (153; cited in Lezra, 58). This critical narrative may be characterized as one of exclusion; however, the *Arte of Poesie* remains an ambivalent and conflicted text in relation to women, articulating their exclusion from humanist literary culture while assuming their participation and interest in it as writers and readers. It is this emphasis upon participation that especially interests me. Here I want to go beyond Robert Matz's persuasive recent reading of the role of poetry in Puttenham "as a form of linguistic cultural capital" in the context of courtly speech and humanist literacy (196). For the *Arte of English Poesie* functions in part as an exercise in the promotion of *women's* literary capital; a literary competence that is exemplified precisely through the manipulation of poetic form.

Puttenham not only dedicates the *Arte of English Poesie* to a woman "excellent" in poetry and monarchy; he continues to address gentlewomen readers in the most substantive Book of the treatise, *The Third Book: Of Ornament*—a brilliant and expansive taxonomy of rhetorical figures from allegoria to zeugma.[8] The mastery of rhetorical figures was a fundamental element of humanist literary practice, understood to enhance eloquence and thus persuade: hence the attention devoted to taxonomies of *figurae* in rhetoric manuals from Aristotle, Quintilian, and Longinus through to Peacham, Puttenham, and Hoskyns.[9] Puttenham contributed to this distinctive and highly codified literary discourse by defining poesy in terms of figurative speech: as "the instrument of ornament" (231) rhetorical figures *constitute* ornamental language, "a novelty of language . . . estranged from the ordinary habit and manner of our daily talk and writing" (236). Hence Puttenham's analysis of rhetorical figures dominates his discussion of the five elements of poetic language: staff (stanza), measure (meter), concord (rhyme), situation (positioning of verse in a stanza), and figure (figurative speech).

What makes it all the more compelling is that Puttenham should single out women as the "chief" audience of the *The Third Book: Of Ornament*— and in so doing assume women's interest in the formal details of rhetorical figures, both as "good makers" of poetry themselves and as a discerning "judge" of others' work:

> *Chapter X. A Division of figures, and how they serve in exornation of language*
> And because our chief purpose herein is for the learning of ladies and young gentlewomen, or idle courtiers, desirous to become skilful in their own mother tongue, and for their private recreation to make now and then ditties of pleasure, thinking for our part none other science so fit for them and the place as that which teacheth *beau semblant*, the chief profession as well of courting as of poesy . . . we have in our own conceit devised a new and strange model of this art, fitter to please the court than the school, and yet not unnecessary for all such as be willing themselves to become good makers in the vulgar, or to be able to judge of other men's makings.
>
> (repr. in Vickers, 235)

"The chief praise and cunning of our Poet is in the discreet using of his figures" (3.1, 221); hence Puttenham's innovation of giving English adaptations for the Latin names of rhetorical figures speaks precisely to his chief audience, since in the vernacular they are "pleasanter to beare in memory: specially for our Ladies and pretie mistresses in Court, for whose learning I write".[10] Yet if, on the one hand, Puttenham credits gentlewomen with the aptitude to make and judge poetry, albeit as a private and courtly "recreation," he goes on to assume their lack of knowledge in even the "plainest" "school points":

> *Chapter XIII. Of your figures auricular working by disorder*
> *PARENTHESIS; or, the insertor.*
> . . . The figure is so common that it needeth none example; nevertheless, because we are to teach ladies and gentlewomen to know their school points and terms appertaining to the art, we may not refuse to yield examples even in the plainest cases . . .
>
> (repr. in Vickers, 240–2)

But even (especially) in the hands of an unschooled lady a little wit is a dangerous thing; thus, at least, Puttenham perpetuates the ubiquitous stereotype of women's shrewish wit:

> *Chapter XXI. Of the vices or deformities in speech and writing principally noted by ancient potes*

... So as every surplusage, or preposterous placing, or undue iteration, or dark word, or doubtful speech are not so narrowly to be looked upon in a large poem, nor specially in the pretty poesies and devices of ladies and gentlewomen makers, whom we would not have too precise poets lest with their shrewd wits, when they were married, they might become a little too fantastical wives.

(repr. in Vickers, 280)

Perpetuates or plays upon? For it is not unfeasible, especially given Puttenham's dedication of the volume to Elizabeth, his repeated addresses to women throughout the volume, and his condemnation of anti-feminist Latin verse as the injurious writing of "some old malicious Monke" that Puttenham is being ironic here; teasing his female readers as much as pandering to the projected prejudices of his male readers.[11] As Puttenham writes of "IRONIA: or, the dry mock," "ye do likewise dissemble when ye speak in derision or mockery, and that may be many ways: as sometimes in sport, sometimes in earnest" (repr. in Vickers, 249). After all, he never loses sight of his (albeit unmarried) dedicatee, addressing his "most excellent Queen" in the final chapter of the Book (III: 25, repr. in Vickers 290) and in the volume's conclusion: "I write to the pleasure of a Lady and a most gratious Queene, and neither to Priestes nor to Prophetes or Philosophers" (The Conclusion, WW 308).

Questions of content and context are not entirely lost in the *Arte of Poesie*: Puttenham briefly attends to "the subject or matter of poesy" and its modes from "rejoicings" to "lamentations" (I: 10, 23–4), while the (Aristotelian) notion of *decorum*—of fitting "style" to "the nature of his subject: that is, if his matter be high and lofty that the style be so too" (III: 5, 228)—implies an engagement with "subject" and "matter": with "the person who speaks; another, of his to whom it is spoken; another, of whom we speak; another, to what we speak" (III: 23, 287). For Derek Attridge, decorum is central to Puttenham's principle of "naturalness" in poesy: "the ideal is to be natural, by being yourself as nature is. But if you cannot—and the entire manual is built on the premise that you cannot—you need to supplement your own natural inadequacies by the exercise of decorum, that 'natural' art" (43). Further, "nature" and "art" serve to frame the distinction between non-literary and literary (artificial) language (8); an unstable distinction that, in Puttenham and beyond, is beset by contradiction (45). In this context, however, I want to take Puttenham's methods literally. It is the painstaking articulation of the formal properties of verse that dominate the *Arte of Poesie* and especially Book III, "for the learning of young ladies and gentle-women" (235).

Likewise questions of form dominate another work of Renaissance literary criticism dedicated to a woman, Dudley North's "Preludium" addressed to Lady Mary Wroth (*c*.1610), first published in North's *A Forest of Varieties*

(1645). Arguing against poets who "affect to shew more wit than love," North mounts a critique of contemporary poetry that centers on the undisciplined deployment of rhetorical figures:

> Like ill-ranging spaniels they spring figures, and, ravished with their extra-vagant fancies, pursue them in long excursions. . . . The poetry of these times abounds in wit, high conceit, figure, and proportions; thin, light, and empty in matter and substance; like fine-coloured airy bubbles or quelque-choses, much ostentation and little food. Conceits, similes, and allegories are good, so the matter be carried along in them, and not inter-rupted by them.
>
> (Vickers, 505)

It is not that North rejects figurative language; it is "over-crushed" conceits, "lines of a far-fetched and laboured fancy" that he objects to (509, 511). Thus his "Preludium" continues with a careful analysis of diction in "versi-fying" (506), of "cadence and sound" (508), of "pithy and tough lines" (509) and "terms well chosen" (510). What the poet should aim at is "well-wrought" verse:

> [a] fineness of conceit, and conclusions so designed, wrought, limned and coloured, touches so bold, covert allegories and subtleties so neat, trans-itions so easy, epithets so material, metaphors and ambiguities so doubly fine, as shall be more master-like than sententious, sublime, abstruse, and strong-appearing lines.
>
> (510)

North's emphasis, like Puttenham's, not only on the varieties of poetic discourse (allegory, epithet, metaphor, ambiguity) but also the *craft* of poetry (designed, wrought, limned, colored), demonstrates his passionate interest in questions of literary form. That he anticipates these interests will be shared by Mary Wroth–not only as a practicing writer but as Sidney's niece ("your unimitable uncle's extant works"; 507) and a and as a literary patron in her own right ("I wish your Ladyship's authority would so abate the price [of second-rate poetry] that our poorer abilities might hold trade without straining"; 509)—should alert us to the contemporary *expectation* of early modern women's engagement with the formal properties of literature. Or, more precisely, privileged, educated, literary gentlewomen: as so often, inequalities of class cut deeper than those of gender.

Expectation engenders engagement (though not always). (Elite) women's literary engagement and rhetorical mastery—an engagement that runs counter to the weary adage of women's axiomatic silence—has precedent in both the print culture of poetry (Gascoigne's *Adventures of master F.J.* (1573), for instance, pivots upon the exchange of poems between men and women) and the manifold poetic forms women deployed in manuscript culture (as the 2001 Oxford anthology of *Early Modern Women Poets: 1520–1700*, edited by Jane Stevenson and Peter Davidson demonstrates). We need further to grasp that the formal conventions, experiments and innovations of early modern women's writing were made in the context of a literary and critical culture that placed high value on form; hence the emphasis in so much Renaissance literary criticism on rhetorical forms, imitation (that is, understanding formal models), and decorum (adapting form and style to subject matter). Or, more succinctly, early modern women's writing is *predicated* on their engagement with literary form.[12] This statement is elementary in formulation—tautological even—but expansive in implication: to ignore the formal engagements of early modern women's writing is to ignore what constitutes their literary practice and their literary capital.[13]

Katherine Philips and the intricacies of form

One of the difficulties, and delights, of studying early modern women's writing is that we are forced to work in the dark. So rarely do the specific conditions and contexts of the production, transmission, or reception of early modern women's writing come to light, particularly by comparison with later periods; so rarely is early modern women's writing, in all its activity and range, fully visible. Among the sources that we lack for early modern women's literary production, as indeed for men's, are records of the *process* of writing—although manuscript culture represents a vital medium for thinking about the processes of transmission. Without wishing to generalize (and thus proceeding to do so), while scholars of later periods of literature may sometimes consult a writer's working drafts and papers or supporting correspondence and accounts of the writing process, scholars of Renaissance literature inevitably work at an ontological disadvantage—and hence an imaginative advantage.

But the ontological cupboard is not entirely bare. Katherine Philips' letters to Sir Charles Cotterell, posthumously published by Bernard Lintott as *Letters from Orinda to Poliarchus* (1705), offer a glimpse into one woman's writing practices. The *Letters* are commonly cited as evidence that Philips' did not seek publicity, especially in her response to the piratical publication of her poetry by Richard Mariott in 1664—"[I] never writ a Line in my life with the Intention to have it printed" (Letter XLV, January 29, 1663)—but rather than offering evidence of a restrictive gender ideology the *Letters* demonstrate Philips' proprietary *control* over her work, her authorial ambition, and her collaboration with powerful male allies (especially Cotterell and Lord Orrery in Dublin) in the progress of her literary career. This is especially clear in letters that discuss her translation of Corneille's *Pompey*—the first play written in rhymed couplets and written by a woman to be produced on the public stage in Britain (Dublin, 1663, and later London), and which Philips took pains to see published not once but twice (in fact, she died before the reprint went to press). For Philips the rub lies in versification. For instance, she finds the couplet "And lending his Despair a kinde Effort, / It should the staggering Universe support" (1.1.27–8) particularly problematic:

> I am oblig'd to you [Cotterell] for examining POMPEY with so much care, as to have found one Fault, though I believe you might still find many: I had it once in my Mind to tell you, that I was loath to use the word *Effort*, but not having Language enough to find any other Rhyme without losing all the Spirit and Force of the next Line, and knowing that it has been naturaliz'd at least these twelve Years; besides, that it was not us'd in that place in the *French*, I ventur'd to let it pass: But I know you are better able to correct that Passage than my self, and I hope you will yet do it.
>
> (Philips to Cotterell, Letter XXI, December 11,
1662, 98–9, sigs. H1v–H2r)

Evidently Philips was dissatisfied with the rhyme of "Effort" with "support" and perhaps with its disruption of the regular meter of iambic pentameter ("support" functions as a regular iamb, / _, but "Effort" is a trochee, _ /). As Puttenham might put it, when "rime is strained" and "sound[s] not nor be written alike" it is "a signe that such a maker is not copious in his owne language" (2.5). Cotterell responded with a "Turn" of "Expression" to alter "the Word *Effort*" (Letter XXIII, January 10, 1663), but Philips resolved to keep the original since "my Lord Orrerry would absolutely have it continu'd" (Letter XXVI, April 8, 1663). The exchange demonstrates Philips pulling the sleight of hand of deferring to Cotterell's expertise with conventional modesty while asserting her own authorial judgment over the necessary "Spirit and Force" in a line of verse.

Philips was equally exercised over "the words *Heaven* and *Power*" in Cleopatra's lament for Pompey's widow, Cornelia:

> *To mourn your fortune, Madam, and to swear,*
> *You'd still enjoy, a Man so justly Dear*
> *If Heaven, which does persecute me still,*
> *Had made my Power equal to my Will.*

(5.2.5–8)

Apparently responding to Cotterell's reservations about "Heaven" and "Power" as bi-syllables, Philips argues that "Heaven" "may, I think, be some-times so plac'd, as not to offend the Ear, when it is us'd in two Syllables" (in fact, she used both words both as monosyllables and bisyllables; Greer and Little, 3: 78 n. 2; Letter XXIII, January 10, 1662/3, 112, sig. H8v). But heaven and power cannot be so readily resolved, in line or in life, and by January

31, 1662/3 Philips had apparently changed her mind. Sending Cotterell "a Packet of printed POMPEY'S", one intended for the king to "Place in his Closet," Philips asks Cotterell "before you part with any [copy], pray mend" the offending lines: "My Objection to them is, that the words *Heaven* and *Power* are us'd as two Syllables each; but to find fault with them is much easier to me, than to correct them" (Letter XXV, January 31, 1662/3, 122–3, sigs. I5v–I6r). And yet correct she must. When arranging for the "reprint" of *Pompey* ("there being in all but five hundred [copies] printed" of the first edition), Philips requests that Cotterell should "correct it before it goes to the Press, particularly the two Lines I writ to you of last Post, and those where the word *Effort* was us'd, which I desire may be alter'd as you once advis'd. And unless you will take the trouble upon you of correcting the Proofs, I am sure it will be as false printed as was my Copy of Verses to the Queen" (Letter XXVII, April 15, 1663, 127, sig. I8r; in fact, the early printings of the play do not emend "Heaven" and "Power," although the 1667 edition substitutes "did" for "does").

The scansion of three little words in lines of iambic pentameter is hardly the stuff of ambitious literary criticism today. Philips' concern appears to lie with particulars too minute to be consequential: the broader picture is entirely lost in her partial account of the writing process. Where are the big ideas? Where is the relevance? It is not as if the work is unpromising in terms of its content. *Pompey*, as one can imagine from a play with Cleopatra as a central figure, makes for productive reading in terms not only of the portrayal of female sexuality, stoicism, and heroism, but of the retrospective nostalgia for an age when women's literary capital rose to prominence in the court of Henrietta Maria; further, its exploration of friendship, clemency, and reconciliation had active political connotations in the Restoration, as Sophie Tomlinson points out.[14] But for Philips the challenge of writing *Pompey*, at least as recorded in her letters to Cotterell, lay not in questions of content but of form. By the same token, to study Philips' work without engaging with their formal maneuvers is to ignore a vital context of its production and, indeed, reception. Now, to an extent we can submit those formal interests to a gendered analysis in terms of access and appropriation: for instance, by observing Philips' rhetorical deference to Cotterell's literary authority in the correction of "Lines" or, conversely, her active engagement with male literary associates (Cotterell, Orrery, Cowley) on points of language. But the devil lies in the detail, and the details of scansion and meter offer little mileage for gender as a category of analysis. It is thus. We cannot squeeze gender out of the syllables of Heaven.

"Upon women" and Puttenham's rhetorical figures

At one level our critical choices can be simply conceived: they are about where we look and what we want to look for. Despite appearances this is not an altogether redundant truism or a prelude to a politically impotent relativism. Sometimes simple observations can serve us well; the shame would be if, in the context of a critical culture that (for many good reasons) values complexity, simplicity should strike us as wholly surprising, irrelevant, or irresponsible.

And so I want to look for different things in the same material, by exploring the confrontation between a critical reading of a misogynist poem that attends to gender and one that examines its rhetorical figures as outlined in Puttenham's *Third Book: Of Ornament*. Conventional wisdom in the field of feminist criticism is, intriguingly, often incredulous in expression: how can gender possibly be ignored in the context of a profoundly patriarchal culture, let alone in a poem "Upon women" which resolutely, relentlessly, turns on gendered stereotypes? But what of rhetorical ignorance? Brian Vickers is typically strident on this point:

> We cannot understand the goals and preoccupations of writers in the sixteenth and seventeenth centuries without a knowledge of their use of rhetoric.... Most modern critics have yet to acquire the basic knowledge of rhetoric that would allow them to identify the verbal devices used by Renaissance poets, the necessary first stage in evaluating how they have been used, according to the coherent rationale given by rhetoricians like Puttenham or Peacham ('for a figure is ever used to some purpose').
>
> (Vickers, 21–2)

Of course, we are not obliged to agree with Vickers; and it would be a strange critical world if we did (as Vickers might be the first to admit). But I think it does behove us—and by us I include feminist literary critics of early modern literature—to engage with the modes of Renaissance literary criticism more thoughtfully. It is not simply about reading Renaissance literature in its critical context, but about reading it more expansively; of seeing more.

"Upon women" appears amidst the pages of a *c.*1630s manuscript miscellany (British Library Add MS 10309) autographed by one Margaret Bellasis: probably the daughter of Sir George Selby (Co. Durham), later the wife of Sir William Bellasis, mayor of Newcastle and supporter of anti-Royalist forces, and through this marriage to the prestigious Bellasis family of the North Riding. Bellasis's miscellany presents many of the methodological problems of interpretation that are germane to manuscript studies: we do not know the circumstances of the volume's compilation (although it appears to be transcribed in the single and neat italic hand of an amanuensis) and what role Margaret Bellasis may have played as compiler or even as reader of the volume. Certainly it includes a lot of material readily associated with men's miscellanies from the universities or inns of court—romantic, erotic, misogynist, bawdy, and topical verse, ranging from "Gnash: his Valentine" to satires on Buckingham—but this does not rule out Bellasis as a reader of the volume; rather, this range should challenge us to think again about the possibilities of early modern women's engagement with homosocial manuscript culture. Among the plentiful material that relates to women in the volume are these unashamedly mediocre verses:

> "Upon women"
> Are women fayre? I wondrous fayre to see to,
> Are women sweet? yea passing sweet they be to,
> Most fayre & sweet, to them that inly loue them
> Chast and discreet to all saue those that proue them.
>
> Are women wise? not wise, but they be wittie
> Are women wittie? yea the more's the pittie.
> They are so witty, and in wit so wilye,
> That be yee ne're so wise, they will beguile you.
>
> Are women fooles? not fooles but fondlings many
> Can women fond be faithful unto any?
> when snow-white swan co[n]verts to colour sable
> Then women fond, will be both firme & stable.
>
> Are women saints? no saints, nor yet no deuills
> Are women good? not good, but needfull euills.
> So angell like, that deuills I ne're doubt them,
> So needfull ills, that few can liue w[i]thout them.
>
> Are women proud? yea passing proud [that] praise 'em
> Are women kind? I wondrous kind [that] please 'em
> Euen so imperious, as no man can endure them
> Or so kind harted, any may procure them.
>
> (British Library Add MS 10309, 175–6, fols. 89r–v)

It is hard not to submit this poem to a feminist analysis: there is little resistance in the material on this count. The poem trots out one gendered stereotype after another of women's sexual proclivity, infidelity, and mutability, and is dismissive in its conclusions: that women are "needfull euils," unendurably "imperious" (the bossy woman never goes away), indiscriminately available to "any." We could then go on to argue whether the poem participates in the perpetuation of these gendered stereotypes—contributing in its own small, mediocre way to the wider suppression of early modern women—or whether it attempts to unpiece them. This is in part a question of tone and humor. If, for instance, we read the tone of the poem as straight-faced or sarcastic, it might be said to feed a perniciously misogynist agenda; if we read it as vitriol or satiric rant, it might be said to undermine such an agenda. Similarly, we can think of the humor of the piece (and I am conscious that not all readers will find "Upon women" humorous) as

speaking principally *to* a male readership (perhaps an adolescent homosocial readership centered on the universities and inns of court) or *beyond*
that readership—in which case the target of the poem's humor shifts significantly. In other words, is the poem attacking women or the ubiquitous
putting down of women, especially by unimaginative ranting men? At this
point other criteria might enter the field: the poem, it could be argued, is not
sufficiently subtle or skillful to operate at the level of nuanced, self-reflexive
irony; it lacks complexity. Alternatively, we might consider the poem in
the field of reception: in the hands of its erstwhile reader Margaret Bellasis,
the poem may have functioned to enforce her sense of exclusion from a
misogynistic discursive tradition; to confirm her sense of superiority over
the rank and file of fickle women; to endorse her critical dismissal of the
tired spent tropes of misogynist rhetoric; to confirm her assessment of the
limited creative ability of its author; to make her laugh.

All well and good. But a reading of the poem inspired by Puttenham's
rhetorical figures leads us both away from the operations of gender and
back towards a more nuanced understanding of how the very forms of the
poem may speak to gendered interests. Like Philips' scansion of Heaven,
it is hard to locate gender in the poem's tight rhyming scheme (aabb)
and metrical structure (an eleven-syllable line beginning with four stressed
syllables, proceeding to iambs)—although we can notice the coincidence
between its subject matter and the feminine (unstressed) ending of each
line. Then there are those rhetorical figures in which gender as a category of
analysis appears, frankly, irrelevant. With its refrain "Are women . . . ?" the
poem turns on the use of *Anaphora*, or the "Figure of Report" or "Repetition
in the first degree . . . when we make one word begin, and as they are wont
to say, lead the daunce to many verses in sute, as thus. *To thinke on death it
is a miserie, / To thinke on life it is a vanitie"* (*Arte of Poesie*, 3: 19, WW, 198).

But it also makes use of the *"Ploche*, or the Doubler"*: "a speedie iteration
of one word, but with some little intermission by inserting one or two
words betweene" (*Arte of Poesie*, 3: 19, WW, 201), as in "sweet? yea passing
sweet," "wise? not wise." The poem's deployment of *Ploche* works hand in
glove with *"Antistophe*, or the Counter turne" that ends "many clauses in
the middest of your verses or dittie . . . [called] the *counter-turne*, because he
turnes counter in the middest of euery meetre," signaled most obviously in
"Upon women" by the use of question marks (*Arte of Poesie*, 3: 19, WW,
198–9). Indeed, the poem is structured around questions or *"Antipophora*, or
Figure of response . . . when we will seeme to aske a question to th' intent we
will aunswere it our selues, [a] figure of argument and also of amplification"
(*Arte of Poesie*, 3: 19, WW, 204).

To understand these figures is, in part, to understand how the poem is
constructed—yet it yields little if any insight into the poem's construction of gender. Hence perhaps the impatience that modern criticism has
with such formal analysis: it does not seem to further our understanding

of a poem beyond anything but a superficial level. Syllables and repetition: so what? But I suggest that this is partly down to the impatience of the critic, not the creative writer; if you or I tried to write across eleven syllables and deploy rhyme and repetition (*anaphora, ploche*) and counter-turns (*antistophe*) and response (*antiphopora*), these formal challenges might become more engaging. Indeed I think this is, in part, the point about such poems as "Upon women" circulating in manuscript: among an interpretive community of readers who are themselves writers or, at the very least, emenders of verse in transmission, a poem is intriguing not least for its formal conventions and challenges. And this is what emerges so powerfully from a sustained reading of manuscript miscellanies from the period: their accumulative shifts of genre, voice, and viewpoint force an attention to the formal dimensions of verse; to literary experiment; to literary play. In the context of Margaret Bellasis' miscellany, not only are the misogynist sentiments of "Upon women" swiftly undercut by the poem following praising women's wit; amid the range of material encompassed by the miscellany the misogynist rhetoric of "Upon women" begins to look even less like authentic or authoritative expression and more like formal performance; a play upon words.

But I am being misleading here because the great thing about Puttenham's taxonomy of rhetorical figures is that he goes far beyond metrics, rhyme and repetition. In this way Puttenham's explication "Of sensable figures altering and affecting the mynde by alteration of sense or inte[n]dements in whole clauses of speeches" (3: 18) can be used to generate a nuanced analysis of tone ("sense or intendements") and its impact upon our understanding of a literary work ("affecting the mynde"). Reading "Upon women" in terms of "*Sarcasmus*. or the Bitter taunt ... when we deride with a certaine seueritie" we might argue that its conclusions should be viewed with a degree of seriousness, a severity born out of knowledge, or that those conclusions are merely the bitter taunts of the disrespectful (*Arte of Poesie*, 3: 18, WW, 189). In this respect the poem's deployment of "*Meiosis*, or the Disabler"— to "diminish and abbase a thing by way of spight or mallice, as it were to depraue it", as in "*A great mountaine as bigge as a molehill*" or, in "Upon women," the line that women are "Chast and discreet to all saue those that proue them"—arguably diminishes the authority of the speaker by marking their remarks as spightful and malicious (185). Moving from spite to mockery again alters the sense of the poem. For instance, reading the poem in terms of "*Micterismus*. or the Fleering frumpe ... when we giue a mocke with a scornefull countenance as in some smiling sort looking aside or by drawing the lippe awry, or shrinking vp the nose" (191) entails less emphasis on malice and, consequently, on the (arguably) diminished authority of the spiteful speaker, while yoking the poem into the remit of "*Ironia*, or the dry mock" arguably allows for a more authoritative construction of the speaker— precisely because we do not have to take those tired old taunts against women seriously—and opens up the possibility of a more playful relationship with the reader. In Puttenham's "sensable figures" that alter and affect the mind "by altering the sense . . . of speeches," there is, then, great scope for altering our understanding the construction and range of meaning in poetry.

But in this context perhaps the most intriguing of Puttenham's figures comes in the field of argument: "Of Figures sententious, otherwise called Rhetoricall" (3:19); figures which serve precisely to emphasize the adversarial mode of the poem. A key figure of "Upon women" is "*Orismus*, or the Definer of difference," a "maner of definition, thus: Is this wisedome? no it is a certaine subtill knauish craftie wit, it is no industrie as ye call it, but a certaine buside brainsicknesse" (*Arte of Poesie*, 3: 19, WW, 231). Not only does the poem proceed by one such definition of "difference" after another ("Are women wise?; not wise but they be wittie"), but in so doing it arguably evokes the adversarial stance that Puttenham characterizes for *Orismus*: it serves "many times to great purpose to preuent our aduersaries arguments, and take vpon vs to know before what our iudge or aduersary or hearer thinketh, and that we will seeme to vtter it before it be spoken or alleaged by them" (*Arte of Poesie*, 3: 19, WW, 231). Likewise the poem's deployment of *Paragon*, "the figure of comparison . . . [setting] the lesse by the greater, or the greater to the lesse, the equall to his equall, and by such confronting of them together, driues out the true od[d]s that is betwixt them, and makes it better appeare," as in the lines "Are women saints? no saints, nor yet no deuills / Are women good? not good, but needfull euills" (*Arte of Poesie*, 3: 19, WW, 234). Puttenham incorporates *Paragon* into the figure of "*Expeditio*, or the speedie dispatcher," when "our maker [poet] as an oratour, or perswader, or pleader should go roundly to worke, and by a quick and swift argument dispatch his perswasion," briefly setting down "all our best reasons seruing the purpose, and reiect[ing] all of them sauing one, which we accept to satisfie the cause: as he that in a litigious case for land would prooue it not the aduersaries, but his clients" (*Arte of Poesie*, 3: 19, WW, 233). Of course, the allusion to law suits is not incidental: not only is *Paragon* common to both lawyer and poet "as an oratour," but the legal reference is relevant to the social contexts out of which such poetry was so commonly circulated, the inns of court.

Even more keenly relevant is the poem's use of "*Antitheton*, or the rencounter," a "figure very pleasant fit for amplification," which answers one point with a contrary one, as in "Are women wise? not wise, but they be wittie." Puttenham notes that "following the Latine name by reason of his contentious nature, we may call him [*Antitheton*] the Quareller, for so be al such persons as delight in taking the contrary part of whatsouer shalbe spoken: when I was a scholler in Oxford they called euery such one *Iohannes ad oppositum* . . . . In this quarrelling figure we once plaid this merry Epigrame of an importune and shrew wife, thus: '*My neighbour hath a wife, not fit to make him thriue, / But good to kill a quicke man, or make a dead reuiue*'" (Arte of Poesie,

3: 18, WW, 210–11). *Antitheton* not only takes us to the contentious nub of the poem but to a culture of "quarelling" at the universities which gives rise, among other things, to "merry" epigrams of shrewish wives. To be "quarel-ling," adversarial, and "litigious" "Upon women" is to be expected from a *Iohannes ad oppositum* at Oxford. The literary figure unfolds the dialogic nature both of literary composition and anti-feminist discourse.

And yet, if we probe further into *antitheton* we can glimpse one woman's purchase upon even this quarrelling figure. *Antitheton* is often known as *contentio* (opposition, strife, contrast) in rhetoric manuals: hence Thomas Wilson summarizes the figure as "contrariety . . . when our talk standeth by contrary words or sentences together" (*An English Rhetoric*, 1560), and John Hoskyns as "an opposition" of "terms disagreeing" (*Directions for Speech and Style*, c.1599). But Hoskyns goes further: "this figure Ascham told Sturmius that he taught the Queen of England, and that she excels in practice of it." Indeed, Roger Ascham, private tutor to Elizabeth (1548–50), remarked in a letter of April 4, 1550 that "she especially admires and strives for suitable metaphors and combinations of antitheses aptly matched and happily set in opposition."[15] *Contentio[n]* does not always preclude the woman writer.

And so an understanding of the rhetorical figure can lead us not only away from but precisely towards a more nuanced feminist analysis; towards a finely calibrated taxonomy for understanding the tone, "sense," argument, and oratory of poetry—and, where relevant, the gendered dynamics and disruptions of figurative speech. In this respect my attempt to read a Renais-sance poem against the grain of materialist feminist criticism has only been partially successful: gender returns as a point of reference. But this is not indicative of the inescapability of gender. Rather, it should yield a *contin-gent* understanding of literature: depending on rhetorical context, form may either speak or not speak to gender; thus formal analysis is *not necessarily* antithetical to feminist criticism. Sometimes the obvious is, in fact, right, and worth restating.

Towards a dialogic formalism

Of course, early modern writers and readers were not composing or reading poetry in earnest consultation with Puttenham's *Arte of Poesie*. My interest does not lie in train-spotting rhetorical figures, although I think that their proliferation and location embedded in verse may have appealed to the anoraks of early modern poetry. (How many figures can I use here? How many can I identify?) Indeed, such identification was of fundamental concern to the humanist curriculum: hence in *The Education of Children* (1588) William Kempe advises that pupils should learn, observe, and practice "every trope, every figure" of rhetorical ornament; in *Ludus Literarius or The grammar Schoole* (1612) John Brinsley recommends annotating "the several tropes and figures" in the right-hand margin of texts, "but in two or three

letters. As for metonymia, efficeintia, nor more but met, effic, or the like";
and, in his copy of Harington's *Orlando Furioso* (1591) the dutiful pupil John
Milton carefully marked out the use of rhetorical figures and metaphors (see
Brian Vickers, *In Defence of Rhetoric* [Oxford: Clarendon Press, 1988], 260–1).
Puttenham's emphasis on the importance of rhetorical figures was generic to
rhetoric manuals of the period and germane to the construction of literary
capital in the context of a humanist education (see my "Women's literary
capital in early modern England: formal composition, rhetorical display, and
the possibilities of manuscript miscellanies," in *Women's Writing*).

What especially interests me here, however, is that Puttenham's account of
rhetorical figures illuminates not only the gendered dimensions of figurative
language but the *dialogic* nature of literary culture in the period; quarrelling,
adversarial, provocative; anticipant of an answer, a rejoinder, a reposte. More
widely, the *Arte of Poesie* remains useful as a guide to thinking about form and
rhetoric more expansively and subtly. In a curious way, my own rhetorical
ignorance puts me in a situation analogous to Puttenham's projected readers
of Book III and to "the learning of ladies and young gentlewomen . . . such
as be willing themselves to become good makers in the vulgar, or to be able
to judge of other men's makings" (repr. in Vickers, 235). To judge other
men's and women's "makings" better, I need to engage not only with the
ideas and contexts that make literature but also with the very materials
that make literary writing: words, figures, tropes, rhythm, rhyme, rhetoric,
genre—and, still more expansively, the materials that make up the history
of the book such as marginalia, page layout, editorial apparatus. In this
respect we could, mischievously, refigure "materialism" to embrace *both*
an attention to literary and bibliographic materials (forms) *and* a (post-)
Marxist understanding of the economic and social conditions of literary
production.

To be sure, a conventionally materialist feminist analysis and a formalist
analysis of early modern literature will look different and look differently,
and despite their points of overlap will remain inconsistent on the centrality of gender as a category of analysis. But it seems a nonsense, especially
in the context of the formal engagements of Renaissance literary criticism,
to have to choose between them. We should instead be working across
them; working with and across literary form. As the examples of Philips
and Puttenham suggest, there are at least two modes in which feminist
criticism of Renaissance literature can work with formalist analysis: first, by
examining (where relevant) the gendered dimensions of rhetorical figures,
tropes, and genres; second, by examining the formal conventions, experiments, and innovations of writing by women—writing that was, if Renaissance literary criticism is to be believed, produced within the context of a
literary culture heavily invested in form and rhetoric as principal modes of
literary endeavor. Indeed, to understand and appreciate the work of Renaissance women's writing fully, we need to consider its formal engagements; "to

attend more closely," as Katherine King argues for poetry, "to such matters
as poetic models, poetic apprenticeships, manipulation of verse forms and
kinds, borrowings, and answerings" (57). As Margaret Ezell puts it, to fail to
read women's writing in the context of its formal traditions and appropriations is to "deny [women] their mastery of their chosen forms and impov-
erish our understanding of the abilities and influence of early women writers
in general."[16] And we can press the point further: formalist analysis can and
should serve the feminist project of promoting Renaissance women's writing
and ensuring its longevity in the (albeit ever-changing) literary canon. In
this respect formalism may indeed prove politically strategic.

But the tensions and conjunctions of formalist and feminist analysis are
also shaped by chronology. Moving from "early modern" to "modern" and,
especially, modernist literature yields different terrain for the crossed paths
of formalist and feminist analysis. Arguably, modernism may be regarded
both as historically "gendered masculine" (Scott, 1990) and "a way of seeing
pioneered by women" (Hanson, 1990); a way of seeing that finds expression, not least, in formal experiment (Emily Dickinson, Virginia Woolf,
Gertrude Stein, and Mina Loy, for instance, in an extended trajectory of
modernism). While formal experiment has been underplayed in the study
of Renaissance women's writing, the "primacy given to experimental form"
in modernist women's writing is a point of critical departure and contention
(Scott, 2003).[17] The relations between formalist and feminist analysis should,
then, be contingent on the material. There is no one-size-fits-all thesis that
can be applied across literary cultures.

In the field of Renaissance literary studies we are so spoilt by the riches
of the canon—by the dazzling work of Shakespeare, Donne or (in the revisionist canon) Mary Sidney—that it is all too easy to take formal innovation
for granted. And so we have allowed ourselves to become less sensitive to
the *work* of form. But form constitutes literariness; it makes poesy. This is the
fundamental point which links the work of Puttenham with Russian formalism (an otherwise anachronistic coupling). Moreover, both Puttenham
and Shklovsky understand literary writing as "*estranged* from the ordinary
habit and manner of our daily talk and writing" (*Arte of English Poesie*, I:
7; repr. in Vickers, 236); as characteristically "*unfamiliar*" (Shklovsky, 12)—a
conception of the literary that extends back to Aristotle ("a really distinguished style [uses] strange words and metaphor and lengthened words
and everything that goes beyond ordinary diction," *Poetics* 1458a; cited in
Attridge, 2). Of course, this principle applies more readily to poetry than
to prose or drama, and even in the field of poetry there are many ways of
arguing against defamiliarization: with poetry that deliberately mimics the
ordinary habits of speech; with poetic forms that have become so relentlessly familiar that they lack estrangement; with the political implications
of an aesthetic that distinguishes itself from the vernacular (this is, in part,
Raymond Williams' problem with modernism, and of Lunacarskij's with the

intellectual "decadence" of Russian Formalism).[18] But regardless of the wider functions and qualities we might choose to ascribe to literary form—whether ornament, estrangement, defamiliarization, unity, or mere technicality—we cannot ignore the *distinctiveness* of literary discourse.

This is all the more so in the wake of materialist modes of critical analysis that have dominated literary studies in the past decades. Let me be clear at the outset: materialism is necessary—necessary if we care about class, history, politics, gender, race. My objection is emphatically not with materialist feminist criticism—it has produced brilliant, insightful, impassioned critical readings that have changed the way we conceive early modern literary culture and energized the academy. My point is rather that amid the textuality of history and the history of textuality, materialist feminist criticism should not abandon the distinctiveness of literary writing. Actually, I would be more passionate: it should embrace what makes literature special. This appeal is not new, but the articulation of "new formalism" as a response to the new historicist turn is. In *Renaissance Literature and its Formal Engagements* Paul Alpers argues that an account of Renaissance lyric "that seeks to be both formalist and rhetorical must work through Burke, who alone among modernist critics made it a principle that human uses of language, including literary uses, are inevitably rhetorical," but the most (historically) relevant formalist precedents are precisely those from the early modern period: the work of Renaissance literary critics, if such they can be called, like Puttenham.[19] We need to read this body of work—especially its points of resistance with the interests of modern criticism—with more critical imagination: to confront, not ignore, the wider implications of the gaps between early modern and modern critical discourse. And Renaissance literary critics assumed literature's distinctiveness: thus in Sidney's hands poesy may be conceived on a continuum with history and philosophy but it remains vitally different from them.

What feminist criticism of early modern literature needs to engage with, then, is the literary as a category of critical analysis and distinction. Like all categories of analysis, the literary and literariness can be conceived in different ways; further, those conceptions may be political in scope: the literary is not immune to history, society, culture. On this point Derek Attridge's *Peculiar Language: Language as Difference from the Renaissance to James Joyce* (1988) remains a valuable and intelligent study. For Attridge, "the conception of the special language of literature which we inherit from the Western aesthetic tradition seems to be based on two mutually inconsistent demands—that the language of literature be recognizably different from the language we encounter in other contexts, and that it be recognizably the same"; further, "our notions of the 'literary,' and the functions of literature within our culture, depend on just this oscillating and unstable relationship" (3–4). More recently, Jonathan Culler observes the "general tendency in recent theory to locate the distinctive features of literature not in particular qualities of language or framings of language, but in the staging of agency and in the relation to otherness into which readers of literature are brought," prompted in part by Stephen Knapp's conception of "literary interest" as offering analogies of agency.[20] Or, to return to the early modern, rhetorical controversies in the period were "charged with ideological valence," as Deborah Shuger points out: "changes in what appears to be a formalist aesthetic in fact adumbrate the central tensions in Renaissance intellectual and political history."[21] As Barthes succinctly puts it, "a little formalism turns one away from History, but . . . a lot brings one back to it."[22]

And yet if we draw literariness, as I want to, into the wide green field of form, we must also acknowledge that politics, history, and culture cannot fully explain or explicate the work of literary form, especially at a local level; in a literary thick description. And although such categories of critical analysis as gender, history, politics, race, and class remain fundamental in many (most?) contexts of literary production and reception, we should be prepared to let go of their centrality for *every* analytical context. This is not as contentious as it may sound: critical master-narratives cannot be expected to treat all minute particulars; this is not their function. It does not matter that "the patriarchal master narrative" or, more widely, the operations of gender cannot *always* be discovered in form, in rhetoric, in literariness. This does not mean that feminist criticism is merely optional; one among many critical -isms to choose from on the literary shelf. Critical relativism is not my intent. Even in the field of form, gender remains crucial at the fundamental level of access and appropriation. But what is fundamental is not what is necessarily, or always, central. The trace of gender cannot be uncovered under every stone. The literary ground is inconsistent. That is the point.

Inconsistency has a troubled reputation in academic discourse, however; deemed almost as bad as the denial of history in early modern literary studies. Again, I find the battleground of Russian Formalism especially suggestive on this point—and pertinent to the incipient debate on the "tensions that will remain" (Dubrow) between feminism and new formalism. The first flush of Formalist thinking was swiftly denounced in the 1920s for its failure to engage with historical materialism. Trotsky, no less, articulated in *Literature and Revolution* (1923) one of the most insightful of contemporary Marxist counter-arguments to the work of "the formalists" (40), and Shklovsky in particular, by insisting upon the social embeddedness of literature:

> The form of art is, to a certain and very large degree, independent, but the artist who creates this form, and the spectator who is enjoying it, are not empty machines, one for creating form and the other for appreciating. They are living people . . .
>
> (32)

Although "materialism does not deny the significance of the element of form, either in logic, jurisprudence or art" (37) it does insist on "the social process" of art (31) and its historical contingency (37). Thus "the methods of formal analysis are necessary, but insufficient" to understanding what really matters: the "social conditions" of art, especially "its moving force [in] economics—in class contradictions" (38). Ultimately, the problem with Formalism is that it understands works of art synchronically not diachron- ically; it substitutes Kantian idealism for materialism (40). Persuasive stuff, despite other passages of reduction and now outmoded determinism, but Boris Eichenbaum's rejoinder was brilliantly instructive. Eichenbaum argued that Formalism and Marxism were "mutually irrelevant": "the former explained literature from the inside, the latter from the outside; because each had a different object of study, there could be no real conflict between them." Mikhail Bakhtin made the same point in *The Formal Method in Literary Scholar- ship* (1928): "Completely different things cannot contradict one another."[23] Transposed to the "tensions" between feminism and formalism, there is no intrinsic conflict between feminism and formalism because, as critical projects, they are inconsistent. Before assuming conflict we should, in fact, perceive intellectual differences more astutely.

I began with a different articulation of this same idea: that feminism and formalism are exquisitely incompatible. But this incompatibility, this incon- sistency, is a point of intellectual departure not an impasse. It is an invitation to dialogic analysis. (I would use the term dialectic if it had not, from Platonic discourse through to Kant, Hegel, and Marx, brought with it the burden of analytical *synthesis*. Indeed, the impulse to synthesize characterizes even Bakhtin's thesis of dialogic translinguistics in *The Formal Method in Literary Scholarship* (1928; see Holquist, 86). My point is rather that synthesis is a chimera in the confrontation between feminism and formalism, though not in all contexts: contingency remains inherent in the material.).

Dialogic thought is afraid of neither confrontation, inconsistency, nor agreement; it does not seek synthesis but remains open to it. What I am calling for, then, is what might be termed *dialogic formalism*. "New form- alism" is an umbrella term covering different practices and remains useful as such. Dialogic formalism at least has more economy of scope; a recognition that formalist analysis can work in conjunction with or disrupt other modes of analysis; that it is not the be all and end all; that it is not a critical master narrative. It might be countered that we are obliged to choose our central categories of critical analysis and choose between them; to do otherwise is to practice a critical pluralism or eclecticism that is without theoretical or methodological integrity. I cannot both practice and abandon feminist or formalist analysis at will; I cannot have my cake and eat it too. But there are (at least) three problems with this contention. The first is that it misunder- stands the dialogic for the eclectic; the two are distinct. The second is that it remains insensitive to the infinite varieties of literary contexts; to contin- gency. The third, and most important, is that such theoretical puritanism is experientially misplaced. Cake is for eating.

Notes

1. Joe Andrew, "Introduction," *Poetics of the Text: Essays to Celebrate Twenty Years of the Neo-Formalist Circle*, ed. Joe Andrew (Amsterdam and Atlanta, GA: Rodopi, 1992): iii–xx, viii–ix.
2. Susan J. Wolfson, "Reading for Form," *Modern Language Quarterly* 61: 1 (March 2000): 1–16; Ellen Rooney, "Form and Contentment," *Modern Language Quarterly* 61: 1 (March 2000): 17–40; see also Jim Hansen, "Formalism and its Malcontents: Benjamin and de Man on the Function of Allegory," in *New Literary History* 35: 4 (Autumn 2004): 663–84. For Hansen, "a new formalism must not concert that which it studies into objects of or for consumption . . . but rather [practice] a politically and historically inflected formalism" (680).
3. Mark David Rasmussen, *Renaissance Literature and Its Formal Engagements* (Basingstoke: Palgrave Macmillan, 2003), 9.
4. Lynne Magnusson, *Shakespeare and Social Dialogue: Dramatic Language and Elizabethan Letters* (Cambridge: Cambridge University Press, 1999), 7; see also Patricia Parker, *Shakespeare from the Margins: Language, Culture, Context* (Chicago and London: University of Chicago Press, 1996), 1–2 and 17–18.
5. It might be argued, via French feminist literary theory of the later twentieth century, that language itself collapses any disjunction between formalism and feminism since linguistic forms (grammar, the pronoun) are argued to enshrine and encode not merely gender but gender inequality. But the debate has moved on. Judith Butler's *Gender Trouble: Feminism and the Subversion of Identity* (New York and London: Routledge, 1990) plays Luce Irigaray's conception of language as fundamentally phallocentric against Monique Wittig's thesis that language is not misogynist in its structures but only in its applications (35) to argue that "there is no gender identity behind the expressions of gender; that identity is performatively constituted by the very 'expressions' that are said to be its results" (33).
6. William Morris's argument still holds true: that there is no art without resistance in the material. See Jerome McGann, *Black Riders: The Visible Language of Modernism* (Princeton, NJ: Princeton University Press, 1993), xiii..
7. See Robert Matz, "Poetry, Politics and Discursive Forms: The Case of Puttenham's *Arte of English Poesie*," *Genre* XXX (Fall 1997): 195–214, 195–6.
8. Puttenham, *Arte of English Poesie*, allegoria, "the figure of false semblant," III: 18, Vickers, 247; 'zeugma, "the single supplie," III: 12, 136.
9. See, for instance, Ann Moss, "Humanist Education," in Glyn P. Norton, ed., *The Cambridge History of Literary Criticism* (Cambridge: Cambridge University Press, 1999): 145–60; and Brian Vickers, *In Defence of Rhetoric* (Oxford: Clarendon Press, 1988), chapter 6.
10. Puttenham, *The Arte of English Poesie*, ed. Gladys Doidge Willcock and Alice Walker (Cambridge: Cambridge University Press, 1936), 173. Puttenham earlier characterizes women as "judges neither sour nor severe . . . being all for the most part either meek of nature or pleasant humour"; however, the judgment at stake here is not of the literary merit of specific works but of the status of figurative speech *per se*. By being favorable "judges" of figurative speech (unlike "the grave judges Areopagites" forbidding figurative speech in the court of law) women make apt judges of "the exercise of this art" of poetic discourse (3.7, Vickers, 232–3).
11. Ibid., 14. Puttenham's account of women is both conventional in its articulation of the feminine virtues of pity and shamefastness (249 and 267) and innovative

in the field of rhetoric manuals in its assumption of women's creative and critical literary interest, for instance by introducing tropes and figures as particularly "meete study for Ladies" (anagram, 108; see also the "hipallage. Or the Changeling", 173).

12. As Montefiore puts it: "no one can *write* poems without being enabled, however contradictorily, by knowledge of a tradition, even if their relation to that tradition may be marginal and awkward. To produce even straightforward forms like ballads, and to do it well, a poet must learn the skill of narrating a story by stanzas... the art of metrical competence and probably an ear for refrains" (Jan Montefiore, "Women and the English Poetic Tradition: The Oppressor's Language," in *Arguments of the Heart and Mind. Selected Essays 1977–2000* (Manchester: Manchester University Press, 2002: 33–47, 36)

13. See my "Women's Literary Capital in Early Modern England: Formal Composition and Rhetorical Display in Mnauscipt and Print," in *Women's Writing*.

14. Sophie Tomlinson, "Harking Back to Henrietta: The Sources of Female Greatness in Katherine Philips's *Pompey*," in Jo Wallwork and Paul Salzman (eds), *Women Writing 1550–1750*, special issue of *Meridian* 18: 1 (2001): 179–90, 181.

15. For Wilson, see Lee A. Sonnino, *A Handbook to Sixteenth-Century Rhetoric* (London: Routledge & Kegan Paul, 1968), 60; for Hoskyns and Ascham, see Vickers, *English Renaissance Literary Criticism*, 416.

16. Kathryn R. King, "Cowley Among the Women: or, Poetry in the Contact Zone," in Katherine Binhammer and Jeanne Wood (eds), *Women and Literary History: "For There She Was"* (Newark: University of Delaware Press, 2003): 43–63, 57; Margaret Ezell, *Writing Women's Literary History* (Baltimore, MD: Johns Hopkins University Press, 1993), 159.

17. Bonnie Kime Scott, *The Gender of Modernism* (Bloomington, IN: Indiana University Press, 1990), 2; Clare Hanson, in *The Gender of Modernism*, 303; Bonnie Kime Scott, "Beyond (?) Feminist Recuperative Study," in *Women and Literary History: "For There She Was"* eds. Katherine Binhammer and Jeanne Wood (Newark: University of Delaware Press, 2003): 220–34, 228.

18. Victor Erlich, *Riussian Formalism: History, Doctrine* (1965; New Haven, CT and London: Yale University Press, 1981): 106.

19. Paul Alpers, "Learning from the New Criticism: The Example of Shakespeare's Sonnets," in Mark David Rasmussen, ed., *Renaissance Literature and Its Formal Engagements* (Basingstoke: Palgrave Macmillan, 2003): 115–38, 131.

20. Jonathan Culler, "The Literary in Theory," in Judith Butler, John Guillory, and Kendall Thomas, eds., *What's Left of Theory? New Work on the Politics of Literary Theory* (London and New York: Routledge, 2000): 273–92, 281–2. Culler's analysis is centered on Stephen Knapp's conception of "literary interest" as "linguistically embodied representation that tends to attract a certain kind of interest to itself" and which "offers an unusually precise and concentrated analogue of what it is like to be an agent." Stephen Knapp, *Literary Interest: The Limits of Anti-Formalism* (London and Cambridge, MA: Harvard University Press, 1993): 2 and 139. On literariness in Russian Formalism, see Tony Bennett, *Formalism and Marxism* (London: Methuen, 1979): 59–60.

21. Deborah Shuger, "Conceptions of Style," in Glyn P. Norton, ed., *The Cambridge History of Literary Criticism. Volume 3: The Renaissance* (Cambridge: Cambridge University Press, 1999): 176–86, 177.

22. Roland Barthes, "Myth Today" (1957), trans. Annette Lavers, in *Mythologies* (New York: Hill and Wang, 1972), 111–12.

23. Boris Eichenbaum, in *The Press and the Revolution*, 1924, paraphrased by L. T. Lemon and Marion J. Reis in their introduction to Eichenbaum's "The Theory of the 'Formal Method'," in Lemon and Reis (trans.), *Russian Formalist Criticism: Four Essays* (Lincoln, NB and London: University of Nebraska Press, 1865): 99–139, 100; Eichenbaum's *The Press and the Revolution* still awaits translation. Erlich gives an alternative paraphrase in *Russian Formalism*, 108). Mikhail Bakhtin makes the same point in *The Formal Method in Literary Scholarship* (1928): "Completely different things cannot contradict one another," trans. A. T. Wehrle (Baltimore, MD: Johns Hopkins University Press, 1978), 146.

5
Ophelia's Sisters

R. S. White

> Her speech is nothing,
> Yet the unshaped use of it doth move
> The hearers to collection. They aim at it,
> And botch the words up fit to their own thoughts.
>
> $(4.5.7–10)^1$

For an apparently empty vessel ("her speech is nothing"), and one who is given the acquiescent line, "I do not know, my lord, what I should think" (1.4.104), Ophelia has unexpectedly generated a richer, more varied, and even perverse afterlife than almost any literary figure. It is the very "unshaped" fragmentariness of her words and songs in Act 4 which has coaxed not only critics, whether feminist or otherwise, to "botch [her] words up fit to their own thoughts," interpreting them in a variety of ways. Nowadays "botch" is used only in the pejorative context of repairing clumsily or imperfectly; but the *Oxford English Dictionary* assures us that the original meaning was "To make good or repair (a defect, damage, damaged article); to patch, mend." Horatio (or a "Gentleman," depending on which text is consulted) uses the word in a sense paralleled in 1530:[2] "I botche or patche an olde garment . . . I have botched my hosen at the heles," and in 1561: "Augustines booke of repentance . . . botched of good and bad by some scraper together."[3] The phrase sounds like a wry, metadramatically prophetic observation by Shakespeare about the way his texts—often absurdly meddled with, or "botched up" in the modern sense—will in centuries to come be "botched" in the Elizabethan sense, patched, repaired, in the service of a unitary meaning of the editor's choosing, which may or may not "move the hearers to collection."

Botching was clearly women's work, and the etymological degeneration of the word into "clumsy" patching mirrors societal disregard for women's work. In a couple of different ways this chapter is about the process of botching, but with its origin recuperated and valued. It may be an image especially chosen for Ophelia:

> My lord, as I was sewing in my chamber,
> Lord Hamlet, with his doublet all unbraced,
> No hat upon his head, his stockings foul'd,
> Ungartered, and down-gyved to his ankle;
> Pale as his shirt, his knees knocking each other,
> And with a look so piteous in purport
> As if he had been loosed out of hell
> To speak of horrors, he comes before me.
>
> (2.1.78–85)

Shakespeare's typically visual imagination takes us from Ophelia's "sewing" to her perceptions of Hamlet's "foul'd" stockings and pale shirt: it is clear that she sees him not only literally, but also metaphorically, in terms of his outward garb, discouraged and in urgent need of botching.

Ophelia's function in the narrative of the play is as disconcerting and disruptive as the effect of her words on the play's audience, and her impact is out of all proportion to the number of scenes she appears in and the number of lines she speaks. Initially, and with reluctance, she is manipulated into complicity with the plots against Hamlet, as she allows herself to be used as "bait" in Lacan's unkind term of reference. However, when she later sings in ballad fragments and hands flowers to those at court, she literally "loses the plot" for all the puzzled characters around her and for audiences. Her interpolation is as much a play-within-a-play as "The Mousetrap," and the changes of language and emotional register are just as striking. The play *Hamlet* is for a time forgotten as Ophelia in reverie provides a distraction into some other, quite spellbinding dimension, a different narrative that nobody can ignore or incorporate, "botch" or repair to fit the history of "the Prince of Denmark." The critic Lucy Potter, by "placing Ophelia on centre stage," suggests that it is she, not Hamlet, who attains a free and active agency through a suicide, which is "an escape from the patriarchal supervision that subjects her while she is alive and an action that allows her to rewrite the meanings that the play has assigned to her as a passive woman."[4] Ophelia has bequeathed images for successive generations of women specifically, down through the centuries, not only in the pregnancy of her words but also in the ability to provide an alternative plot, an enigmatic but self-sufficient value system that is parallel to and never meshes with the "men's story." This essay rapidly traces her reception into "women's stories" up to 1990, then focuses in more detail on the surprises she has sprung since then with the transformations wrought in women's movements. In many ways, her changing destiny has matched changes in feminist thought.

This kind of appropriation of Ophelia to a cause has been happening for two centuries at least. There is, of course, a plausible argument that Shakespeare's works contain no genuine female characters because they were written to be acted by males and they were conceived by a male writer.[5] At best, they are peopled by female impersonators, at worst, by creations of male fantasies. Against that, some critical accounts, for very similar reasons concerning the imaginative power of the particular creator, suggest that Shakespeare more or less created modern stereotypes of femininity by depicting persuasive images that have entered subsequent cultures. Other critics focus on the mind that created the dramatic personages, seeing the writer as either misogynistic or as containing both masculine and feminine sides to his psyche, as either terrified of women's sexuality or one of the rare males who can acknowledge female sexual desire; and so on through a conflicting spectrum. What the debate reflects, perhaps, is that a male writer, whether accidentally or from observation, particularly in the medium of drama which shifts between points of view, can sometimes reflect women's predicaments and women's desires, juxtaposed with those of men. Equally, he may be able to inscribe memorably, whether from the stance of ideological insider or outsider, the oppressions which his own patriarchal society manifestly imposed upon women.[6]

Analysis of Shakespeare's "women" as gendered beings seems to have started in 1788 with William Richardson's *On Shakespeare's Imitation of Female Characters (addressed to a friend)*. Richardson, who at this surprisingly early date before Mary Wollstonecraft espoused the rights of women, concedes that at least some wives are "domestic slaves," and recognizes that just because the range of employment undertaken by women is limited, that this does not mean they are more limited than men as human beings. His main aim is to answer specifically the charge that Shakespeare shows no flexibility in his female characters "because female players were in his time unknown." To prove otherwise, he trawls through the virtuous heroines (but not unsympathetic figures like Lady Macbeth and Volumnia), showing their diversity. Miranda is "more inclined to ingenuous confidence than to shy or reserved suspicion"; Isabella is distinguished by "intellectual ability" and good sense, driven by indignation and strong feeling; Beatrice uses wit as the tool of intelligence, affecting "to be mirthful when she is most in earnest," and employing her wit "when she is most afraid." When Richardson comes to Ophelia, he is less positive, and concentrates only on the character in the early stages of the play. He sees her "sisterly and filial affections" as uppermost and as morally ambiguous, "leading her to such deference for a father, as to practise deceit at his suggestion on a generous lover, and [striving] to entangle him in the toils of political cunning."

Anna Jameson, writing in the 1830s, may have been recalling the plangent line "Lord, we know what we are but we know not what we may be" in making the acute observation that Ophelia, like Miranda, is a character "in whom all intellectual and moral energy is in a manner latent, if existing . . ."[7] Just as her later, disordered words are "unshaped," so are her personality and destiny in life. In the "morn and liquid dew of life," Ophelia, early in *Hamlet*, is a figure of unrealized potential, and the dismaying events depicted in the play push her, willy-nilly, over the shadow line of adolescence into the shadow itself of a tragic confrontation with adult experience. Jameson's tone is idealizing and reverential of Ophelia's "elemental feminine qualities, modesty, grace, tenderness," but she is not, in fact, sentimentalizing but rather clinical in her analysis. In an image from her own observation, Jameson sees Ophelia as "a dove caught in a tempest": "She is so young, that neither her mind nor her person have attained maturity: she is not aware of the nature of her own feelings; they are prematurely developed in their full force before she has strength to bear them . . ." She is, after all, faced with a situation that includes not only being rejected by her lover, but also his going mad and murdering her own father. One could barely imagine a worse scenario, most of all for a woman who is defined insistently as "young." Jameson sees Ophelia's disordered speech as a symptom of her age and inexperience: "She says very little, and what she does say seems rather intended to hide than to reveal the emotions of her heart." She is, in short, an adolescent caught in an adult predicament, and, predictably, unable to communicate coherently her confused and overwhelming emotional state. The comment could have been generalized to include Hamlet, who initially is a young philosophy student pushed similarly out of his depth, which would open up a significant and original way of reading the play, and one which to some extent is developed by Barbara Everett, who sees *Hamlet* as a play about "growing."[8] For our purposes, however, Jameson has anticipated the reception of the Ophelia figure into a wider culture of the 1990s and toward the present. In doing so, she confirms Judith Johnston's assessment that Jameson, "by giving Shakespeare's female characters independent structures, and by valuing and emphasising the female roles . . . constructs a particular form of feminism that celebrates difference, or otherness . . ."[9]

In surprising ways, nineteenth-century writers anticipated some of the approaches adopted by feminist critics in the movement, or movements, which we usually date as post-1970s. The Victorian actress Helena Faucit, writing in the 1880s, tells us how "misunderstood" Ophelia was in her stage representations: "It hurts me to hear her spoken of, as she often is, as a weak creature, wanting in truthfulness, in purpose, in force of character, and only interesting when she loses the little wits she had."[10] Faucit speaks of Ophelia being "one of the pet dreams" of her own lonely girlhood, "partly, perhaps, from the mystery of her madness." As an actress she was not asked to play Ophelia, a role reserved at the time for an accomplished singer, until invited to do so by Charles Macready. The rather closet performance was in

Paris and, to her apprehension, she realized that famous Italian singers were in the audience. However, she felt her performance was sympathetically received, and she was even visited backstage by, among others, Georges Sand. Her "English shyness" caused her nerves but may also have been a key to her success that night. Macready praised her, saying she "had thrown a new light on the part, and that he had never seen the mad scenes even approached before." Faucit's conception of the character, she readily confesses, had been shaped in her "youthful dream." And this dream is a mini-biography of a motherless child brought up amongst country-folk, which accounts for Ophelia's knowledge of the rustic lore of wildflowers, her apparent streak of an aspect "tended only by roughly-mannered and uncultured natures" (her bawdiness, that is), and the practice of strewing a grave with flowers ("Larded with sweet flowers"). Brought to court by her father to "become a court lady," Ophelia remains lonely and is drawn to the equally solitary figure of romantic prince and to his idealized mother, Gertrude, who encourages the budding love affair. (Faucit will have none of Gertrude's collusion in the murder of old Hamlet.) Faucit does not blame Ophelia for spurning Hamlet, because she finds Polonius's explanation plausible, that the prince's madness is caused by love for her, and that her returning his gifts is a test of his affection. The rest, leading to the murder of her father, becomes a sequence of tragic misunderstandings in which Hamlet does not "[come] out well in his relations with Ophelia" since he loves with his head and not his heart, his claims of love being "a string of euphemisms" not given substance by trusting actions. A part of Faucit's "new light" on the role lies, she thinks, in Ophelia's ambiguous gestures towards her brother, Laertes, whom she fears and who has selfishly misunderstood the nature of her grief even more drastically than Hamlet. By this stage the "unobtrusive calm" of a "thoughtful, reticent, gentle Ophelia" has been "changed to waywardness" through what we might call adolescent trauma. Faucit does not believe that Ophelia's death by drowning is suicide, but "the accidental watery death of this fragile bud," whom "the kindly stream embraces." Female-centered if hardly feminist, Faucit's reading is not the last time that a fictional but personally inflected reconstruction of Ophelia's past, her "girlhood" (of which the most fanciful had been Mary Cowden Clarke's in 1851–2), will be used to make convincing the character's role in the play. The habit is surely related to Victorian readers' familiarity with their preferred form, the novel, with its generic expectation that all will be revealed about a character's formation in early "life."[11]

Other female writers, given license (if they should need it) by Richardson to impute gender characteristics to the dramatic characters, find even more diversity, and Ophelia becomes one of their favorites, since they focus on the circumstances that drive her to insanity, and see her symptoms of madness to be uniquely female. It is quite possible that Sigmund Freud, not above being parasitic on Shakespeare and literary critics alike, may well have been persuaded by received opinion stemming from Ophelia, when he came to analyze (or create) female hysteria.[12] Just as the "oedipal conflict" was developed with explicit reference to Hamlet, so do Freud's "Anna O." and "Dora" bear comparison in certain aspects with Ophelia, as trauma caused by her father's death triggers the repressed unconscious to reveal itself in largely sexual imagery. In some ways Bradley's much derided reverse theory—that madness is a protection mercifully adopted by the traumatized Ophelia—has a refreshing innocence. Elaine Showalter touches on this buried link between Ophelia and the history of madness in an essay which argues that visual representations of Ophelia through the centuries mirror changing paradigms of female insanity.[13] She suggests that Ophelia's full story lies not in Shakespeare's text but in the history of her reception, especially in art history and psychoanalysis. Conveniently, Showalter's account allows me to glide through two centuries of appropriations without the need to rehearse detail. Her words in the mid-1980s, "the madwoman is a heroine," were marked by protest and rebellion not only against patriarchal systems like families and social systems, but also against male attempts to control female sexuality by pathologizing and attempting to "cure" it as Freudian hysteria. At that stage in the history of feminisms, Ophelia's madness was seen in a celebratory and liberating light. Schizophrenia, mental breakdown, and hysteria could be seen, in the wake of R. D. Laing's writings, not as female maladies but as female weapons, intelligible responses to the internal contradictions and coercions of patriarchy, not afflictions to be pitied and cured but rousing calls to women's liberation. What has happened since then, however, has pulled against this comforting tide in ways that would then have seemed surprising.

A book which equally conveniently allows us to summarize a whole cultural reception of Ophelia, if not a specifically feminist line, is James M. Vest's *The French Face of Ophelia from Belleforest to Baudelaire*.[14] The French took to Ophelia as one of their own, and in fact claimed her as originally French, pointing out that Belleforest translated the story in an analogue (deftly upgraded by patriotic scholars to "source") for *Hamlet*. Belleforest's episode involving the character is brief compared to Shakespeare's, but he anticipates one future feminist strand by making Ophelia a willing collaborator in Hamlet's campaign; in fact, she was in this version his foster sister, as Helen is to Bertram in *All's Well*, and an assertive figure in her own right. Vest takes us through a series of French Ophelias. Enlightenment writers such as Voltaire and Diderot make her role crucial to the plot, sometimes as "l'héroïne," Hamlet's "Maîtresse," or "amante," and certainly a "princesse" rather than a commoner. She is strong-willed, sane, and certainly deserved a better fate than that consigned her by Shakespeare. In the eighteenth century, on both sides of the Channel, rules of poetic justice were regarded as too important to flout so easily by killing off a heroine with such cavalier abandon. "Ophélie" became "one of the most attractive and memorable heroines on the French stage,"[15] something she has never quite been on the English. During the Romantic era, while English poets gravitated to the "lyrically affecting" verse of her dementia, French writers like Stendhal perpetuated a strong Ophelia, a proto-romantic rebel even in her madness or "folie." Victor Hugo's "Fantômes" created her as a figure of "lovely derangement and threatened innocence," "victim of deception, rage, and violence, rather than love," an "exploited, moribund beauty."[16] It was in her role as Ophelia at the Odéon Théâtre, Paris that the Irish actress Harriet Smithson attracted the attention of Hector Berlioz (along with all the rest of the French Romantics, apparently). Berlioz subsequently married her, after writing *Symphonie Fantastique* under her influence, so it was indirectly Shakespeare's character that generated a French work of art. Smithson in turn has inspired a ficto-biography by an Australian author, Christine Balint, who wrote *Ophelia's Fan: A Story about Dreams, Shakespeare and Love.*[17] French Symbolists assimilated Ophelia to their turbulent vision of the world, reflected in Delacroix's lithographic series, Gautier's theme of "existential chaos and despair,"[18] encapsulated in death by water,[19] and Baudelaire's association of Ophelia with moral sadness that combines acceptance and resistance to adverse experience. In *Les Fleurs du Mal*, Baudelaire evokes dichotomies: "The Hamlet–Ophelia couple represents a basic and vital reflection of the duality of human existence: body-spirit, poet-muse, reality-ideal."[20] The main point of confluence is that the French were much more continuously able to accept Ophelia's part in the play as virtually equal to Hamlet's, and certainly important in its own right. Once again, the English tradition of acting and interpreting her has had less confidence in believing in her centrality, and it is this centrality which must be taken for granted in mounting any feminist argument about her significance as both textual creation and cultural icon.

My own contribution, *Innocent Victims: Poetic Injustice in Shakespearean Tragedy*,[21] shows its genesis in the feminism of the late 1970s and early 1980s, analyzing the roles of children and women in the tragedies where their final fate violates expectations of poetic justice. It was written during a topical debate about victimology in criminal law, particularly noting the way courts and the public blamed rape victims. Ophelia's plight was seen as analogous to Lavinia's, the genuine victim of rape, and Desdemona and Cordelia whom critics tended to construct as women who had invited the treatment they receive in their plays, through docility, lying, or obstinacy. My argument was that these are virtuous and assertive characters who die through no fault of their own, and can more properly be seen as emblems of martyrdom, victims of societies created and perpetuated by warmongering males and shaped by patriarchal institutions. The plays are seen as humanist in their educative mission—injustices are made conspicuous so that they will, in Aristotelian fashion, stir consciences and activate social change. The two books most influential at the time in showing "women as victims" and expressing outraged appeals for reform, had both been published in 1970: Germaine Greer's *The Female Eunuch*, and Kate Millett's *Sexual Politics*. Given that Greer had completed her PhD on Shakespeare's comedies (her phrase "female eunuch" may have been conceived as fitting the Elizabethan boy-actors as well as disempowered women) and that Millett's book is liberally sprinkled with quotations from Shakespeare, it is arguable that the dramatist significantly contributed to the growth of feminist theory. This would have been ironic since in the 1980s he was derided as hopelessly enmeshed in patriarchal assumptions and complicit with the forces degrading women—wheels have turned several times since then.[22] In my book, I tried carefully to define "innocence" in a quasi-legal framework—the women and children are "not guilty"—rather than innocent in a sexual or sentimental sense. Ophelia and Desdemona, for example, are certainly aware of sexuality, the former able to understand Hamlet's "country matters" and to sing songs about male fickleness, the latter capable of sexual banter with Iago and publicly insisting that she has married Othello for a full physical relationship. Again, the feminist advances made in the 1970s in the wake of the introduction of the contraceptive pill in the 1960s, was to assert female desire in a positive sense. However, although my book was written with these cultural influences consciously present, it is strange that sometimes books take on new significances in changing times. *Innocent Victims* now seems to me to be just as morally applicable to the deaths of civilians in wartime, and the human consequences of such cataclysms as the one on September 11, 2001 in New York. Again, although Shakespeare did not invent feminism or anti-terrorism, four centuries on, responses inscribed in his plays can be re-focused to clarify moral issues underlying contemporary events.

The wider cultural context appears to leave Shakespeare as text and literary influence far behind, and takes us into the world of such doves caught in tempests as young females who may have no knowledge of Shakespeare, but who face the saddest and most age- and gender-specific situations of all. As feminism changed in the 1990s, so did Ophelia. In the 1960s she could be a worldly wise "drop-out" played by Marianne Faithfull in Tony Richardson's *Hamlet* in 1969, the year in which she wrote "Sister Morphine" and attempted suicide in Australia. Faithfull claims that during the stage version of this production she was taking heroin in the intermissions: "[The heroin] cut me off from the other actors," she said. But in the 1990s, Ophelia became the patron saint of more vulnerable kinds of victims, young women afflicted with anorexia and who contemplate teenage suicide not from drug addiction but other afflictions. A book published in 1985, *The Owl was a Baker's Daughter* by Marion Woodman, may have been the first to associate her words with eating disorders. It is not entirely clear why this association has evolved, although it is equally not difficult to see a connection between the acknowledged roots of anorexia nervosa as lying in an internalization of society's prioritizing of some female body shapes over others, with the ways in which Ophelia in the play is constructed by the court in terms of her gender. It is easier to see the link with teenage suicide, though this presupposes the answer to the very debate conducted by the gravediggers, controversially instructed to dig her grave inside hallowed ground, as to whether she came to the water or the water came to her.[23] More generally she has become associated with tribulations of adolescent females in the modern world. This is a different evolution from feminism—gone is the anger and zealous social reformism, to be replaced by compassion for the individual and a willingness to build supportive and protective networks. We may no longer live in a world which requires passionate gestures like bra-burning, or railing against conservative bureaucracies. At least some battles have achieved recognition (if not full implementation) of issues such as the need for childcare, and equal working conditions for men and women. It is at least arguable that we no longer live in a benighted and uncaring society, and that the senior echelons of western public service agencies are staffed by the very people who had sought to change the system, and some at least remain steady to their principles. We have seen, since the days of Thatcher and Reagan, the rise of preventative medicine, risk management, behavior management, safety nets, and benevolent social engineering. Ophelia has played her part even in those movements. The link seems to have started in 1994 with the publication of Mary Pipher's *Reviving Ophelia: Saving the Selves of Adolescent Girls*. The writer is an American psychologist who worries about the "girl poisoning" culture of media images, "lookism" (being valued by appearances alone), precocious sexual display, consumerism, drug avail-ability, and pressure to reject parents, blaming these cultural forces for identity crises in adolescent females which in turn lead to tragedies like anorexia, depression, and suicide. In an interview, Pipher explained the literary allusion:

> The book's title comes from *Hamlet*. Ophelia was mentally intact and happy until she fell in love with Hamlet. She was torn between her desire to please him and to please her father.
> She grows confused, depressed, and eventually, she kills herself. Her experience is a good metaphor for what happens to many girls in early adolescence. They become confused by others' expectations and their true selves are lost.[24]

This may not be entirely adequate as an interpretation of Shakespeare's play, but one can readily see it as a plausible construction of Ophelia, one of the many "botchings" available. It emerges from Pipher's clinical account that sadly little has changed for young women since Shakespeare's time. Instilled with "rigorous training for the female role" which comes down to developing "false selves," they discover "that it is impossible to be both feminine and adult," in fact, "impossible to score as both a healthy adult and a healthy woman" (39) in a "game" whose rules are confusing but compulsory.

The bleak message has been tempered in a way that shows adolescents are not such unknowing dupes as Pipher's adult account implies, and that though they are still caught in a mesh of contradictions, they may be more self-aware than expected. For Pipher's book in its turn generated another—Sara Shandler's *Ophelia Speaks: Adolescent Girls Write about their Search for Self*, published in 1999.[25] When she was sixteen, Shandler read Pipher's book, felt dissatisfied with it because she was spoken *"for"* rather than *"to,"* and called on American teenage girls themselves to talk about their lives, which they did in their thousands. The result is a remarkably mature and recognizably authentic account of adolescent females' own frank accounts of their attitudes and experiences, on subjects ranging from eating disorders, abuse, parents and siblings, divorce, pregnancy, death, friendship, self-laceration, sex, education, and therapy. Even with the painful honesty of the accounts, the overall impression is not grim but inspiring. It seems to represent a kind of feminism which is confident enough not to use that word at all, and one which above all stresses shared communication. One assumption may be that if Shakespeare's Ophelia, who is defined by her loneliness and by the absence of female peer companionship, had been able to share her confusions and predicaments with others going through adolescence, her fate may have been avoided. Another implicit illumination of Shakespeare's play emerging from Shandler's book is the insistent yearning for stability, reliability, and listening skills in adults, and an end to hypocrisy. Given that Shakespeare's Ophelia is never listened *to* but her words are listened *for* and "botched" to suit a range of adult preconceptions and presuppositions, and given that she must act in an adult world of spying, murder, plotting, and manipulation, even within her own family, the insight seems pertinent. Certainly one gains from Shandler a strong respect for the understanding and wisdom of the many contributors aged from twelve to seventeen, and a sense of genuine hope for the future of society when it comes to be inherited by this generation. As is the inevitable fate for all best-sellers, this book in turn spawned another, and significantly it refers to the one thing missing in Shakespeare's play, Ophelia's natural mother. Cheryl Dellasega's *Surviving Ophelia: Mothers Share Their Wisdom in Navigating the Tumultuous Teenage Years*.[26] Well-meaning though it is, the book seems one sequel too many, the complacent title suggesting that after the wide-eyed honesty of their juniors, mothers are always right, even when they are wrong. The latest in the sequence of spin-offs is forthcoming as *Move over Ophelia*, on the psychology of young men.

The most recent manifestation of this Ophelia is "The Ophelia Project,"[27] a worldwide Internet support system for young women suffering eating disorders and a range of other personality and mental conditions such as "relational aggression" (behavior that harms one's peers, like spreading rumors, purposely ignoring somebody, using social relationships as a weapon).

The Ophelia Project is. . .
dedicated to creating a culture that is emotionally, physically and socially safe. We serve youth, families, schools and communities with an expertise in covert peer aggression and issues unique to girls. We promote healthy character development and mentoring relationships through awareness, education and advocacy.

. . .

It's Coming!!
Ophelia is growing up. Now that we're maturing, we're giving "Ophelia" a new look. Just like your own daughter, one moment she's a twirling girl, the next she's a sophisticated young woman. Keep your eyes on this site to watch the transformation!

The aim of the network is to create a culture in which girls can be respected and nurtured in emotional, physical, and social acceptance—everything, indeed, that Shakespeare's Ophelia is deprived of.[28]

Various turns in the increasingly complex map of evolving feminisms have allowed Ophelia to be reconstructed in quite different ways that reveal still more depths in her textual origin. Drawing inspiration perhaps from punk rock in the 1980s, "grrl power" in the 1990s, and media images of assertively sexualized women in advertising and the music industry, Ophelia, the once limply docile emblem of victimhood, has in some quarters taken on a completely different identity. Justine Ettler's novel *The River Ophelia: an Uncompromising Love Story* (1995) consciously draws on both Shakespeare and de Sade, placing Ophelia in a "grunge" world of drug-taking, violence, and sexual obsession in an Australian city. Meanwhile, *Hamlet II: Ophelia's Revenge* by David Bergantino (2003), judging from its menacing cover and inscription ("Something is *rotting* in the state of Denmark"), appears to be in the horror genre or a "slasher flick." The book blurb ominously states: "Too bad nobody counted on the ghost of a drowned girl rising from her watery grave with vengeance on her mind!" Its usefulness in a scholarly article on Shakespeare may lie in the simple reminder that in a play usually seen as a revenge tragedy, Hamlet is not the only one who has justification for revenge, and that Ophelia's revenge, though less gory than Hamlet's, may in the long run have been more effective. As Margaret Attwood named her lecture at the Stratford Festival in 1997, "Ophelia Has a Lot to Answer For."[29]

Michael Almereyda's Hamlet (Ethan Hawke) and Ophelia (Julia Stiles) are presented as misunderstood, manipulated, and traumatized by their respective families, though their families regard them, as the Bushes and Reagans have seen their wayward offspring, as disreputable embarrassments. Hamlet embodies potential youth revolution, Che Guavara on his wall and Mayakovsky on his bookshelf, adept at using modern technology and a clever but stymied student, at once guilelessly romantic and warily circumspect. Ophelia is sullenly resistant from the start, and it is made clear that she is unwillingly compelled into the plot to spy on her lover. Wearing street-cred baggy clothing and living in a rambling bed-sit which is lit bordello-red, and listening to new age music, she stands against her prematurely reactionary collaborator of a brother and wily politician of a father. Her positioning as "bait" finds no co-operation from her and is a product of the sinister males' conspiring. Her madness after the death of her father is played out in the public forum of the Guggenheim Museum of Modern Art, her words echoing for all to hear. The symbolic flowers she distributes are photographs, simulacra typical of the technological environment in which she is forced to live. Her suicide is anticipated from the beginning in her vision of falling headlong in the swimming pool, as Polonius and Claudius hatch their plots in her hearing. Even her apparently docile line, "I know not, my lord, what to think," is spoken with petulant defiance. Both Ophelia and Hamlet, in their different ways, are victims from the same mould as Luhrmann's *Romeo + Juliet*, representatives of a neglected "generation X," but treated with caution by the worldly-wise political forces that run the "Denmark Corporation," which in turn is a political microcosm of the United States. The differences between them, in social status and gender empowerment, are regarded as significant by their elders, but apparently not by them. They seem to treat each other as equals, and they feel equally disempowered in this uncaring and corrupted society.

A recent novel, *Dating Hamlet,* by Lisa Fiedler (2002) tells the story from Ophelia's point of view, and it is marketed as presenting a feminist heroine for teenage readers. It would be fairly incomprehensible to such readers if they did not know the play *Hamlet*, which is interesting in itself as a symptom of how deeply Shakespeare has impregnated American society through school syllabuses and popular films, like the one starring Mel Gibson (1991). *Dating Hamlet* certainly springs some surprises, and they are ones designed to "botch" perceived holes in the text. For example, to get around the unlikelihood of such an unpleasant character as the disposable Polonius siring the intelligent Ophelia, he emerges as her adoptive father, which shifts her motivation away from grief for his death—in fact, she could not care less. Her real father turns out to be—wait for it—the gravedigger, who has lived as a reclusive, wise, and loving hermit ever since Ophelia's mother died. An omnipresent if ghostly figure in the novel is Ophelia's mother, who, like Hamlet's father, returns to communicate with her child. She was an expert in herbal lore, which explains Ophelia's fascination with and knowledge of the subject. Both Barnardo and Claudius lust after Ophelia and sexually abuse her, but at least she is given the bonus that Shakespeare withholds, a friend and confidante, Anne, who is in love with Horatio. In another patching of the play's abrupt shift to the madness of Ophelia, the novel traces it in more detail. Ophelia begins as a feminist of sorts, demanding an equal and collaborative part in Hamlet's life, and if anything she is more assertive on his behalf than he is in plotting the revenge killing of Claudius. Together, they hatch the plan of both putting on a shared "antic disposition," feigning madness. For most of the time, they knowingly maintain the mutual pretence, signaled by winks and later comparing of notes, and even in her full "mad" scenes, Ophelia is knowing and calculated. Her snatches in these two scenes are mediated by her narrative voice, and they are fueled, she explains, by her hatred of Claudius, her suspicions about Gertrude (who, though once regarded as a surrogate mother now is tarred with Claudius's brush); and her knowledge of bawdy songs which comes from childhood memories of her brother Laertes's locker-room singing sessions with his male cronies. However, in the "serious" insets to the novel, Ophelia does reveal through diary-like internal monologues that she is becoming genuinely disturbed and deranged, in a way that Hamlet does not.

> I must shake off this state that tempts me—for there is no freedom in true madness.
>   Only freedom in the game of it.

The "game" of madness is exercised in feigning grief for her step-father, while "true madness" is triggered by Hamlet's absence in England, and her phrase "he is gone" refers to her lover. Fielder supplies a reason for another of Shakespeare's unexplained gaps, the mystery of how Gertrude can show such detailed visual knowledge of Ophelia's drowning ("there is a willow..."). In the novel it is because it is reported to her by the fictional Anne, and furthermore the drowning is part of the feigned behavior since she plans not to die but to mimic death with the kind of sleeping potion taken by Juliet. In a moment evoking the "misunderstood teenager," she speculates on how people will mourn her, even as she plans to escape after her awakening to live with her natural father. Unlike *Hamlet*, the novel ends happily, with Ophelia and Hamlet setting off on their honeymoon to Verona, to consult an apothecary whom her mother knew... and thereby, can we deduce, lies a sequel? Although the heroine of *Dating Hamlet* has been publicized as a witty feminist—and at least she is certainly not a passive but an active agent—yet the novel, if anything, demonstrates that Shakespeare's play holds a cultural dominance that makes it ripe for pastiche and parody. If its core is a version of feminist thought, it is, for its time, not taking itself seriously. I presume this also is parody, the conclusion of an article published in the feminist journal *Hecate*, but it playfully makes the point that Shakespeare's enigmatic character can constantly be transformed to fit contemporary preoccupations:

Ophelia was a florist in a former life. Ophelia had endometriosis. Ophelia wore too many clothes for her own good. Ophelia slipped and fell. Ophelia was a slut. Ophelia considered becoming a nun. Ophelia was a junkie. Ophelia was bright. Ophelia had potential, her grade five teacher said so. Ophelia was an angel. Ophelia drowned.

If Ophelia came back from the grave, she would say, "I have a *theory . . .*"[30]

She can be all things (or at least many things) to all women.

Truth, however, may be even stranger than fiction or parody, and may open up the most startling of all revelations of a "new" Ophelia who belongs in the Ophelia Project. Consider the italicized herbs and flowers in her actual words, when she addresses the court in the scene with which this essay opens:

Ophelia: There's *rosemary*, that's for remembrance. Pray, love, remember. And there is *pansies*; that's for thoughts.
Laertes: A document in madness—thoughts and remembrance fitted.
Ophelia: There's *fennel* for you, and *columbines*. There's *rue* for you, and here's some for me. We may call it herb-grace o' Sundays. O, you must wear your rue with a difference. There's a *daisy*. I would give you some *violets*, but they withered all when my father died. They say he made a good end.
(Song)
  For bonny sweet Robin is all my joy.

(4.5.173–82; my emphasis)

The multiple significances of each flower in schemes of herbal symbolism have invariably been attributed to each receiver as Ophelia distributes them. (The reasoning is often tortuously circular, since we don't know from stage directions who receives which plant: another neat example of critical "botching.") However, there is in fact a deep center to the special plants she chooses, and it may say more about Ophelia than about her stunned audience. This information comes unexpectedly from the World Health Organization Indigenous Fertility Regulating Methods Project in the late 1970s, as reported by Lucile F. Newman in the journal (of course, where else?) *Economic Botany.*[31] Newman has scoured herbals and *materia medica* from Hippocrates, Theophrastus, Dioscorides, and Pliny, to the present day in the US, and has discovered a "two thousand year tradition of plants used for the particular purposes of fertility regulation." The plants which recur are exactly Ophelia's. Rosemary, fennel, rue, pansies, and violets, in various combinations with each other, are read "as a shocking enumeration of well-known abortifacients and emmenagues . . . effective in provoking abortion or inducing menses." This was known in Shakespeare's day. Newman does not mention columbines and daisies, the odd ones out, but daisies were associated with graveyards, from "the prettiest daisied plot" chosen by the brothers in *Cymbeline* to bury the body they think is Imogen's, to John Keats's dying hours when he felt daises growing over him. Columbine, if it were *Verbena officinalis*, was described by Nicholas Culpeper as helping to alleviate the "swellings and pains in the secret parts," and was described by Chapman in *All* Fools as a "thankless flower" and sometimes associated with sexual infidelity. Newman does not go so far, but given the speculative nature of many accounts in the current chapter, it sounds quite plausible to suggest that Ophelia has aborted Hamlet's child, that it had poignantly already been named after the song of the day, "bonny sweet Robin," and that it is this trauma, coming at the same time as the murder of her father by her child's father, which has quite understandably thrown her into the state of deep and barely articulate shock. Or, with more pathos, she may have been trying to start a potentially missed menstrual period, and if she is pregnant, then the baby dies in the water with her. Even the author of *Dating Hamlet*, with the invention of a dead herbalist as Ophelia's mother, did not seem to spot this mine of secret "women's business" in the play. Such thoughts, however whimsical, give an entirely different emotional dimension to the scene and the character, and give added justification for the way in which Ophelia, now fully victim of the royal court, at this moment steals the show from that very court. As Laertes suggests, she does indeed have her revenge.

Laertes: Hadst thou thy wits and didst persuade revenge,
It could not move thus.

(4.5.167)

Gertrude expresses solicitude for Ophelia, which makes it useful to examine her role, in addressing more general questions raised by feminist critics. Is there a "women's play" in *Hamlet*? Presumably Jacqueline Rose would answer with a resounding "no," given her conclusion that the play is irretrievably patriarchal in its authorial viewpoint, that the female characters are merely male fantasies, and that they are scapegoated not only by the male characters but by the structure of the play itself.[32] However, we have observed that Ophelia has not only been appropriated to feminist concerns but also that the oddity of her theatrical intrusions into the dominant plot give the potential for arguing that she tries to assert herself against the prevailing "men's play." Her death may indicate failure, but this in itself can imply an attitude towards her courage in resistance, a pyrrhic victory highlighting surrounding injustices. And if we do some "botching" of our own, by stitching together the concerns of Ophelia and Gertrude, then we may find a subterranean potential for a "women's play" of the kind traced by Dympna Callaghan in "Looking well to linens: women and cultural production in *Othello* and Shakespeare's England."[33]

Gertrude is given an intriguing connection with sewing and mending, Ophelia's occupation, by Hamlet. His phrase, "the rank sweat of an enseamed bed" has baffled editors. The *Oxford English Dictionary* gives as the primary meaning of "enseam": "To cleanse (a hawk, later also a horse) of superfluous fat," and cites Hamlet's line as an example ("perh. The fig. use") of "greased (cloth)." Critics take this on trust, sometimes implying an association with semen stains welling from Hamlet's sexually morbid mind. However, it would not be the only occasion where the OED and critics give priority to men's work—hawking—over women's work—sewing. Another meaning given is "To sew or stitch up in" and "To mark as with a seam." The enseamed bed can mean literally a bed with a seam down the middle. To "housewives," for example, a bed, or rather sheet, with a seam down the middle has always meant something quite specific in domestic economy. "Sides to the middle" has down the centuries been a sensible and traditional "thrift" measure for prolonging the usable life of bed-linen.[34] When the middle of the sheet is worn, crumpled, and discolored, it is cut down the middle and the two edges sewn together to make a fresh middle—an "enseamed bed." A neutral if puzzling detail, one might think. But taken a little further, it reveals surprisingly rich aspects of the emotional worlds in collision during this scene and the play. Hamlet has already derided the "thrift" economy of recycling funeral baked meats for an untimely wedding, and this adds another dimension to his attitude. He is implicitly expressing contempt for his mother who is acting in a "housewifely" rather than regal way, trying to save a few pence by mending sheets. It can be a derogatory, class statement. Moreover, to Hamlet's mind, she is betraying her first husband who conferred on her through marriage her exalted status, and now reverting to the ways of a commoner. Recycling, of course, is quite specifically his complaint against his mother for replacing a husband who has been conveniently disposed of, with a second-hand one, a crude job of botching "a thing of shreds and patches" onto the memory of a greater figure. And the fact that this usurper, an uncle, has always attracted suspicious critical discussion about the laws of incest reinforces the sense of a family in the process of being recycled. The middle of the bed, the site of Hamlet's own conception, is now rudely pushed to the sides and the new middle is invaded by his enemy. The seam down the middle of a marriage bed creates other significances. It may cause minor discomfort analogous to the major frustrations of a sword, for example, and beyond that it signifies not unity in marriage but separateness, two sides joined, rather than an inviolate sheet. By contemplating this one word, and giving it the full significance of an aspect of "women's work," we open up a whole new "seam" in Shakespeare's play, which had seemed so hackneyed. Applying the familiar domestic practice defamiliarizes the play, but the reference, now largely lost in a disposable and consumerist society, has become so unfamiliar that it must itself be "unseamed" to be recognized.

Hamlet is, among other things, a tragedy of two families and of generational rebellion, and central to one family is an adolescent woman and to the other a mature, remarried widow. Where those two families could have been linked is through the marriage of Hamlet and Ophelia. One of the dynastic questions raised by the play is whether Gertrude is post-menopausal or whether she is fertile to produce an heir to Claudius, which would have confused the succession, which seems in Denmark not to be inevitably based on primogeniture. Gertrude's fertility seems unlikely when Hamlet is thirty by the graveside, but at the beginning of the play he behaves as though he is so much younger and more callow that a gap of anything up to twelve years might separate the two parts of the play.[35] Marriage between Hamlet and Ophelia would give the prince a stronger footing in the subject which is explicitly discussed: "election" to the throne. (Hamlet is particularly anxious to persuade Gertrude not to have sex with Claudius, and the motive may be more political than prurient or oedipal. He is equally anxious to prevent Ophelia conceiving another man's child.) Although Ophelia's father dismisses such a liaison as inappropriate on class grounds, she is to the Second Gravedigger a "gentlewoman" and Hamlet's mother takes the prospect seriously:

> Sweets to the sweet. Farewell.
> I hoped thou shouldst have been my Hamlet's wife.
> I thought thy bride-bed to have decked, sweet maid,
> And not t' have strew'd thy grave.

> (5.1.226–9)

It is Gertrude also who, admittedly after initially refusing to speak with Ophelia, shows genuine concern in her language: "Alas, sweet lady, what imports this song?" "alas, look here, my lord"; "Sweets to the sweet: farewell!" And it is she who gives the spellbinding description, a dismayed and mesmerized dirge, presumably not eye-witnessed but either reported or reconstructed, which has led to the most famous image, in Millais's painting:

> There is a willow grows aslant a brook
> That shows his hoar leaves in the glassy stream.
> Therewith fantastic garlands did she make
> Of crow-flowers, nettles, daisies, and long purples,
> That liberal shepherds give a grosser name,
> But our cold maids do dead men's fingers call them.
> There on the pendent boughs her coronet weeds
> Clamb'ring to hang, an envious sliver broke,
> When down the weedy trophies and herself
> Fell in the weeping brook. Her clothes spread wide,
> And mermaid-like a while they bore her up:
> Which time she chanted snatches of old tunes,
> As one incapable of her own distress,

> Or like a creature native and endued
> Unto that element. But long it could not be
> Till that her garments, heavy with their drink,
> Pull'd the poor wretch from her melodious lay
> To muddy death.

(4.7.137–54)

Unlike most critics, Gertrude through her imagery gives a lateral inclusiveness that comments through empathy on the young woman's capacity for "new age" innocence and a "grosser" knowingness about sexual matters.[36] At least a part of the tragedy for both Ophelia and Gertrude is their gender solitude and separation from each other. Even Lady Macbeth has an offstage "cry of women" to lament her death,[37] but these two are alone. Ophelia's death, like her living interventions, wrenches the play once more outside the male frame, and out of the action, to a space of lyrical nature evoked by Gertrude's words, but it is a place of the fancy and away from the stage. Gertrude takes wine in the general male frenzy, not knowing it is poisoned, and her death is a mistake based on a shabby trick that goes wrong. It is perfunctory, her realization comes too late, and this death causes barely a ripple on the dominant narrative:

Osric: Look to the queen there, ho!
Horatio: They bleed on both sides. [*To* HAMLET] How is't, my lord?
Osric: How is't, Laertes?
Laertes: Why, as a woodcock to mine own springe, Osric.
I am justly kill'd with mine own treachery.
Hamlet: How does the Queen?
King Claudius: She swoons to see them bleed.
Queen Gertrude: No, no, the drink, the drink! O my dear Hamlet,
The drink, the drink?—I am poisoned.
[*She dies*]
Hamlet: O villainy! Ho! Let the door be lock'd!
Treachery! Seek it out.
Laertes: It is here, Hamlet. Hamlet, thou art slain.
No med'cine in the world can do thee good.
In thee there is not half an hour of life.
The treacherous instrument is in thy hand,
Unbated and envenom'd. The foul practice
Hath turned itself on me. Lo, here I lie,
Never to rise again. Thy mother's poison'd.
I can no more. The King, the King's to blame.

(5.2.247–63)

What runs through all the different accounts of Ophelia is a pastel coloring of regret, the kind of futile speculation about an unlived future—"Lord we know what we are but we know not what we may be."[38] Blake's sunflower follows the sun, always wishing and seeking but never reaching, and finally pining away with unfulfilled desire. A grammar linking Ophelia with a strain implicit in many different feminisms which can inflect it angrily or wistfully, lies in the phrase "if only ... ". If only she could have had a mother, or a female confidante. If only Gertrude had not remarried. If only society had treated Ophelia as an adult and an equal. If only her lover had trusted her. Her situation evokes precisely the poignancy of wasted youth which has marked her many cultural transformations, and the fertility of these representations and constructions is in part a reflection of the character's unfinished plasticity. At the same time she becomes a wider emblem of human transformation and a plasticity of the personality. Change the conditions and we change the fate of the individual, allowing either communication and fulfillment or their opposite. But in the court of Denmark, where "the king's to blame" for muddying the waters of justice, the woman's story, undeniably present and sometimes disruptive, is always coerced back into shadows of silence and tears. When the tears stop flowing, so does the women's story.

Laertes: Too much of water hast thou, poor Ophelia.
And therefore I forbid my tears. But yet
It is our trick; nature her custom holds,
Let shame say what it will.
      [*He weeps*]
                  When these are gone,
The woman will be out.

(4.7. 157–61)

Notes

1. Horatio. References from *The Norton Shakespeare: Based on the Oxford Edition*, ed. Stephen Greenblatt et al. (New York, 1997).
2. 'Palgrave. 461/1 [OED ref.].
3. 'Thomas. Norton, *Calvin's Inst.* III. v. (1634) 319 [OED ref.].
4. Lucy Potter, "Ophelia Centre Stage," in *extensions*, ed. Sue Hosking and Dianne Schwerdt (Adelaide: Wakefield Press, 1999), 25–41, 39.
5. Dympna Callaghan, *Shakespeare without Women: Representing Gender and Race on the Renaissance Stage* (London and New York: Routledge, 2000).
6. For a trenchant account of the patriarchal oppressions imposed on Ophelia, see Emi Hamana, "Let Women's Voices be Heard: A Feminist Re-Vision of Ophelia," *Shakespeare Studies* (Shakespeare Society of Japan), 26 (1987–8), 21–40.
7. Mrs Jameson, *Shakespeare's Heroines: Characteristics of Women, Moral, Poetical and Historical* (London: George Bell and Sons, 1891), 153–70. First published 1832.

8. Barbara Everett, "*Hamlet*: Growing," *London Review of Books* (March 31, 1988); repr. *Young Hamlet: Essays on Shakespeare's Tragedies* (Oxford: Clarendon Press, 1989), 11–34.

9. Judith Johnston, *Anna Jameson: Victorian, Feminist, Woman of Letters* (Aldershot: Scolar Press, 1997), 78.

10. Helena Faucit, Lady Martin, *On Some of Shakespeare's Female Characters* (6th edn., Edinburgh: William Blackwood and Sons, 1899) p. 3; 1st edn., 1885, the Ophelia section substantially the same as in a "letter" published as part of a series in *Blackwood's Magazine* on August 10, 1880.

11. For some thoughts on this, see John Bayley, *The Characters of Love: A Study in the Literature of Personality* (London: Chatto and Windus, 1990), 34ff.

12. A brief and rather shallow "clinical case study" is given by Derek Russell Davis in *Scenes of Madness: A Psychiatrist at the Theatre* (London: Routledge, 1992), 39–41. Davis's most interesting proposal is that Ophelia's later "unsuitable, out-of-character display of sexual preoccupations" suggests something like a transference from her brother through the pressure he puts on her earlier. No thorough study of Freud's indebtedness to Shakespeare has, to my knowledge, been written, though there are suggestive comments by Marjorie Garber in *Shakespeare's Ghost Writers* (New York and London: Methuen, 1987).

13. Elaine Showalter, "Representing Ophelia: Women, Madness, and the Responsibilities of Feminist Criticism," in *Shakespeare and the Question of Theory*, ed. Patricia Parker and Geoffrey Hartman (New York and London: Methuen, 1985), 77–94.

14. James M. Vest, *The French Face of Ophelia from Belleforest to Baudelaire* (Lanham, MD: University Press of America, 1989).

15. Ibid., 107.

16. Ibid., 132–3.

17. Christine Balint, *Ophelia's Fan: A Story about Dreams, Shakespeare and Love* (Sydney: Allen and Unwin, 2004).

18. Vest, *The French Face of Ophelia*, 157.

19. For a view that "underwater women have long been a symbol of social oppression in Western literature..." from Homer's *Iliad* to Jane Campion's film, *The Piano*, see Charles Ross, "Underwater Women in Shakespeare Films," in *CLCWeb: Comparative Literature and Culture: A WWWeb Journal* 6 (2004) at: http://clcwebjournal.lib.purdue.edu/index.html.

20. Vest, *The French Face of Ophelia*, 171.

21. R. S. White, *Innocent Victims: Poetic Injustice in Shakespearean Tragedy* (London: Athlone Press, 1986, repr. of 1982 edn.). The first version of the chapter on Ophelia was published in *Ariel* 9 (1978): 41–53, and a different essay appeared as "Jephtha's Daughter: Men's Constructions of Women in *Hamlet*," in *Constructing Gender: Feminism in Literary Studies*, ed. Hilary Fraser and R. S. White (Nedlands: University of Western Australia Press, 1994), 73–89. The fact that the present essay is quite different again supports the thesis that the character is continually being culturally revised and metamorphosing. There is an excellent and comprehensive bibliography that supports the argument, prepared by Thomas Larque (updated June 22, 2004) at http://shakespearean.org.uk/ophbib1.htm. By following links one can find several of the older and more inaccessible critical sources. I acknowledge my indebtedness to Larque's invaluable and thorough resources. He includes references to some twenty original plays on Ophelia, half a dozen works of prose fiction, and numerous poems, as well as dozens of scholarly essays.

22. *The Woman's Part: Feminist Criticism of Shakespeare,* ed. Carolyn Ruth Swift Lenz, Gayle Greene, and Carol Thomas Neely (Urbana, IL: University of Illinois Press, 1980); Philip C. Kolin, *Shakespeare and Feminist Criticism: an Annotated Bibliography and Commentary* (New York: Garland, 1991), *The Matter of Difference: Materialist Feminist Criticism of Shakespeare,* ed. Valerie Wayne (New York: Harvester-Wheatsheaf, 1991).

23. For an extremely thorough discussion of the 'maimed rites' given Ophelia because of her suspected suicide, see James V. Holleran, "Mained Funeral Rites in Hamlet," *English Literary Renaissance,* 19 (1989), 65–93.

24. http://www.committment.com/ophelia.html.

25. Sara Shandler, *Ophelia Speaks: Adolescent Girls Write about their Search for Self* (New York: HarperCollins 1999).

26. Cheryl Dellasega, *Surviving Ophelia: Mothers Share Their Wisdom in Navigating the Tumultuous Teenage Year* (Boulder, CO: Perseus Publishing, 2001).

27. http://www.opheliaproject.org/index.shtml.

28. The Internet is a rich source of Ophelia sites, in varying degrees of wholesomeness—there are Ophelia clubs, Ophelia camps, and the Ophelia Muse (containing erotica).

29. Reproduced at http://www.web.net/owtoad/ophelia.html.

30. T. M. Peiris, "Ophelia: A Theory," *Hecate* 22 (1996), 140.

31. Lucile F. Newman, "Ophelia's Herbal," *Economic Botany* 33 (1979), 227–32.

32. Jacqueline Rose, "Sexuality in the Reading of Shakespeare: *Hamlet* and *Measure for Measure,*" in *Alternative Shakespeares,* ed. John Drakakis (London and New York: Methuen, 1985).

33. Dympna Callaghan, "Looking Well to Linens: Women and Cultural Production in *Othello* and Shakespeare's England," in *Marxist Shakespeares,* ed. Jean Howard and Scott Cutler Shershow (London and New York: Routledge, 2001), 53–81.

34. I learned this from Jane Whiteley, textile artist.

35. Such problems are rarely if ever raised by critics, presumably because they smack of the "how many children had Lady Macbeth" type. But they are in fact raised by the narrative, since succession to the throne is the most central issue facing Hamlet and the court.

36. One critic who does justice to Ophelia's contradictions, which he sees as transcended in "self-awareness and self-integration," is Ranjini Philip, "The Shattered Glass: The Story of (Ophelia)," *Thirty-One New Essays on "Hamlet"* [extracted from *Hamlet Studies* Vols. 1–21], ed. R. W. Desai (Delhi: Doaba House, 2000), 244–54.

37. See R. S. White, "'The Cry of Women' – Offstage Macbeth," *Shakespeare Jahrbuch* (1992): 70–9.

38. In searching for this phrase, I noticed one of those apparently meaningless statistics, but one that surely reinforces a pattern in a play about imperfect knowledge, that the phrase 'know not' recurs no fewer than seven times. In the world of *Othello,* where honest doubt would have been a healthy intrusion, it is not used once.

Part II
Women

6

Sex and the Early Modern City: Staging the Bawdy Houses of London

Jean E. Howard

Bawdy houses are ubiquitous in early modern London comedies, that is, comedies that explicitly take contemporary London as their setting. No such plays were written before 1598. However, within a few short years of the genre's inception, whores and their places of work had become a standard feature of this new urban drama. For example, *Westward Ho* (1604) depicts an enterprising urban bawd, Birdlime, who runs a busy "hothouse" within the city walls; *Northward Ho* (1605) shows an equally industrious sexual entrepreneur, Doll, moving her place of trade about to suit the season, sometimes working in suburban locations, sometimes setting up within the city limits; *The Dutch Courtesan* (1604) stages a high-status alien sex worker who plies her trade in London; *Michaelmas Term* (1606) shows a country wench coming to London and setting up as a courtesan. Many other examples could be mustered.

This vogue for representing whores and whorehouses is not surprising, given the city play's general preoccupation with London as a site of commerce and the whore as a well-established figure for representing the penetration of a market economy into all areas of life.[1] Whore plays and other popular texts are quite explicit, and often quite self-consciously funny, in presenting prostitution as a business parallel to other forms of urban commerce. In Robert Greene's *A Disputation Between a Hee Conny-catcher, and a Shee Conny-Catcher*, for example, the whore who is the chief "she conny-catcher" is fittingly named Nan a Traffique. Like others who engage in "the buying or selling or exchange of goods for profit,"[2] Nan is a merchant of sorts, her commodity being her own flesh. She has endless schemes for cozening her clients to increase her revenues. But not all whores, or their bawds and pimps, are presented as cozening or illegitimate "traffickers." In *The Dutch Courtesan* the bawd's trade is said be the "most worshipful of all the twelve companies" (I.ii.30),[3] that is, the twelve major guilds of the city,

117

because the bawd sells the best commodities on offer in the urban market. Here prostitution is equated, however ironically, with legitimate forms of business, including the "most worshipful."

In what follows, then, I take for granted that while whore plays partly reference the actual social problem of prostitution in early modern London, they also use the whorehouse and its central actor, the whore, to examine troubling or novel aspects of urban life, such as the quickening and expansion of the market economy, for which the prostitute often stands as a convenient figure, a character through whom a penumbra of related social problems is negotiated. How the drama employs this figure requires a reading practice that resists binary interpretation of the sort that insists that stage prostitution must either be "about" real-life prostitution or about something else like the market, disease, or cosmopolitanism. I want to suggest instead that whores and their places of work are capable of bearing several significations at once or, to put it another way, are simultaneously part of more than one discursive struggle.

The reading practice I will employ in this chapter reveals, I hope, the ever-deepening engagements between feminist and historicist critics over the last few decades, engagements so profound that to speak of them as separable is in many cases misleading. What I trace in this essay is a discursive thread focused on the urban prostitute as she materializes, in particular, on the Renaissance stage. This figure, I will claim, has her own specificity and historical interest, but not because she reflects the condition of actual prostitutes or because she illustrates moral positions drawn from prescriptive literature. Rather, created in relationship both to the demands of comic form and to the historical conditions of urban life amid which the commercial theater emerged, theatrical whores are pivotal figures in dramatic narratives that attempt to come to terms with the contradictions and tensions of their historical moment. If feminism leads me to ask why this particular female icon appears so often in the London plays of the period, it also prompts me now to seek out answers that go beyond a preoccupation with subversion and containment or victimhood and empowerment to examine how discourses of the feminine, whether or not they directly address the condition of historical women, can speak to the stress points of the age in which they were produced.

In what follows I will examine several recurring features of whore plots, arguing that these conventions offer the best evidence of how the drama responded to and shaped the social world of which it was a part. The first is the distinctive way in which prostitute plays treat the location and legibility both of bawdy houses and those who traffic in illicit sex. While these plays often evoke the city/suburb opposition, locating bawdy houses in the extramural wards or suburbs, more frequently they refuse to assign prostitution its own, singular, clearly legible place. It is a movable feast, and, I will argue, the more anxiety-provoking as a result. Both the ubiquity of bawdy houses and their frequent illegibility not only registers the corrosive effects of market forces on cultural boundaries and distinctions, but also the expansion of illicit sexuality's terrain and the proliferation of social actors who sometimes are, or are rendered indistinguishable from, whores. Second, I will explore the trope of conversion that animates many whore plots, a conversion often accompanied by a quasi-ritualized ceremony involving the casting away or the putting on of a new social self. I will argue that these conversion narratives link the prostitute to instabilities in the urban gender system, challenging the prescriptive literature's neat categories of women as maids, wives, widows, and illicit others. But let me begin by turning, if only briefly, to that illusive thing, "actual" prostitution in early modern London.

In the Middle Ages, the majority of brothels were concentrated on the south bank of the Thames where they had existed since Roman times.[4] Cock Lane in Smithfield was the only *allowed* area of prostitution north of the Thames, though it is clear that many forms of private and clandestine prostitution also flourished in and around the city. The Bankside brothels were regulated by ordinances dating back to the reign of Henry II in the twelfth century, and were under the control of the Bishop of Winchester (one result of which was that "Winchester geese" became a common slang term for prostitutes).[5] In 1546 Henry VIII ordered the officially licensed Bankside brothels ("stews") to be closed, supposedly to check the spread of vice and disease. Like most morality campaigns, it was unsuccessful. Within a few years, brothels had sprung up throughout the city and regrouped on the Bankside. John Taylor's *A Common Whore* jauntily records the change.

> The Stewes in England bore a beastly sway,
> Till the eight Henry banish'd them away
> And since those common Whores were quite put downe,
> A damned crew of private Whores are growne.

> (B6v)

(Common whores were those that inhabited the licensed and regulated stews; private whores, by contrast, plied their trade anywhere and in a variety of circumstances.)

Ian Archer, in *The Pursuit of Stability: Social Relations in Elizabethan London*, includes a map showing the location of bawdy houses in London in 1575–78, his data largely derived from the Bridewell records that have survived from that period.[6] He does not include the Bankside, and we know that many brothels were still located there. The scatterplot is very revealing, however, about the rest of London. Bawdy houses cluster at predictable places outside the city walls: Whitefriars in the west, Clerkenwell and Long Lane in the north-west, Whitecross Street in the north, Shoreditch in the north-east,

Aldgate, East Smithfield, and St. Katherine's to the east. In effect, the walled city was ringed by the equivalent of red light districts. But there were also a number of brothels *inside* the walls, especially toward the east. Rather than being confined to one or two areas, places of prostitution littered the urban landscape.[7]

Nonetheless, suburban regions and the liberties within the walled city became especially associated with prostitution, vice, and vagrancy in the popular imagination. Soon after ascending the English throne in 1603, James ordered the emptying out and pulling down of suburban tenements which had become the haunt of "excessive numbers of idle, indigent, dissolute and dangerous persons."[8] The immediate purpose was to halt the spread of the plague then raging in London, but it formed part of a larger campaign on the new king's part to clean up the city, restrict in-migration, and impose uniform standards on new buildings. Needless to say, the attempts failed. The population of London was growing too explosively to observe for long the ban on the proliferation of low-cost housing, and prostitution and other kinds of suburban (and urban) vice were never successfully suppressed. It was James's early attempts to tame the suburbs, however, to which Shakespeare famously refers in *Measure for Measure* (1604) when Pompey laments the proclamation ordering that "All houses in the suburbs of Vienna must be plucked down" (I.ii.78).[9] Incredulously, Mistress Overdone asks: "But shall all our houses of resort in the suburbs be pulled down?" To which Pompey replies: "To the ground, mistress" (I.ii.82–4).

The outpouring of urban plays featuring prostitutes between 1603 and 1606 is undoubtedly related to the notoriety that James's actions brought to what was a recurring preoccupation with controlling the sale of sex in and around the city.[10] Some of these dramas play with the lascivious reputation of suburban locations. *Westward Ho*, like many plays of the period, makes the village of Brainford the destination for the London wives who travel up the Thames with their gallants to spend the night in a tavern there.[11] In *Northward Ho* the destination for elicit adventure is Ware, with its infamous great bed. In *Eastward Ho* Cuckold's Haven marks one of the spots where husbands' horns begin to sprout. West, north, or east, the suburbs all signify sexual sin. But, so does the city proper. In *Westward Ho* the enterprising bawd Birdlime has her actual brothel, where several scenes are set, inside the city walls. In the play's first speech she claims to keep a "Hothouse in Gunpowder Ally (neere Crouched Fryers),"[12] and at the end of the play she returns to her city establishment, proudly proclaiming, "I scorne the Sinfulnesse of any suburbes in Christendom: tis wel knowne I have up-rizers and downe-lyers within the Citty, night by night"(V.iv.251–3). There is no simple opposition between vice-ridden suburbs and an orderly city.

Northward Ho is especially suggestive about the mobile nature of prostitution and the commercial and social conditions that govern its spread. The play opens with two gentlemen discussing, among other things, why a

Chamberlain named Innocence has moved from Dunstable to Ware. Innocence serves as a pimp in his spare time, and is known to the gentlemen because at Dunstable he had twenty times arranged a meeting between one of the gentleman and "two Butchers Daughters" (I.i.17),[13] a suggestive detail in itself since these women, while not identified as whores, clearly served the gentlemen's need for sexual services. Innocence left Dunstable when peace broke out in Ireland. Before then, legions of army captains bade farewell to their London wenches in Dunstable; with peace, there were fewer opportunities to barter flesh. Endlessly adaptable, however, Innocence has moved to the tavern in Ware on the York road to the north. As a principal stopping point for travellers, Ware too is a flourishing site for pimping and whoring. Prostitution here follows money and groups of men on the move, away from home.

Mistress Doll, the one prostitute with a face and a name in *Northward Ho*, shows a canny eye for the professional possibilities made available by the post-1546 decentralization of prostitution and the subsequent uptick in London's population and in its market economy. Doll is a thoroughly mobile whore with an eye to the main chance. Once attached to a young gentleman who is arrested for debt in the play's second scene, Doll immediately thinks about where to find new clients. With term time beginning, she determines to shift house and move to Charing Cross for "we that had warrants to lie without the liberties, come now dropping into the freedome by Owle-light sneakingly" (I.ii.74–6). She says she will seek out a

> faire house in the Citty: no matter tho it be a Taverne that has blowne up his Maister: it shall be in trade still, for I know diverse Tavernes ith Towne, that have but a Wall betweene them and a hotte-house. It shall then bee given out, that I'me a Gentlewoman of such a birth, such a wealth, have had such a breeding, and so foorth:... to set it off the better, old Jack Hornet shall take uppon him to bee my Father
>
> (I.ii.85–92)

Doll assumes that several lines of distinction can be blurred. She can pass over from her warranted place outside the city to the "freedom" within (playing, obviously, on the freedom citizens acquire to ply their trades lawfully within a guild structure); she can inhabit a tavern that in truth is barely distinguishable from a hot house, like the tavern to which Elbow's wife resorts in *Measure for Measure*; and she herself can successfully perform the codes of respectable femininity, making her "true" nature impossible to read. Later, we see Doll and her fake father and fake servants exulting in the pleasurable theatricality of their game of dressing up. Money allows a punk to purchase the trappings of rank and respectability, and Doll is quite successful in attracting men of quality.

Northward Ho is particularly forthright about depicting what other plays also assume: that London prostitution had become an opportunistic practice that could not be eradicated or confined to a single locale. There is evidence that before 1546 the licensed bawdy houses on the Bankside had been painted white to make them readily legible, and Ruth Karras argues that in many medieval towns—though not apparently in Southwark—prostitutes had had to wear distinctive clothing, such as a striped hood.[14] Stallybrass and Jones have argued that even in the Renaissance, clothing still constituted identity by defining one's social place, occupation, gender, and status.[15] But many popular texts from the late sixteenth century stress this idea of the automatic or easy legibility of whores or whorehouses. While women standing in taffeta dresses in the doors of buildings often advertised the whereabouts of suburban brothels, not all whores thrived on legibility. Doll depends on the fact that with the right props she *cannot* be distinguished from a respectable city lady nor a bawdy house from a tavern. In *Northward Ho*, any house might be a covert whorehouse, a place where loose women perform versions of respectable femininity in order to conduct their trade. In such a world the place of prostitution is potentially everywhere.

This fantasy occurs repeatedly in popular pamphlets and in numerous city comedies. It emerged in tandem with specific changes in the city in the later sixteenth century that facilitated the spread of prostitution and fostered fears that ordinary women might become involved. London's population doubled between 1550 and 1600; migration from the provinces exploded, and many of the migrants were women. In straitened times—and the 1590s were just that—many of these women lost or never found positions in service. They drifted in and out of legitimate employment, in and out of thieving and prostitution.[16] They had neither a "fixed" social identity nor a fixed and certain line of work, especially since they were excluded from most forms of labor in the guilds. Clients were plentiful. London had a ratio of 113 men to 100 women.[17] Many of the men were young and unmarried, serving apprenticeships; some were merchants away from home; and some were country gentlemen in town for term time or some other business. As John McMullan has argued, the city at the end of the sixteenth century offered a "structure of illegitimate opportunities,"[18] and if Archer is right that morality campaigns against sexual offenders were at their height in the 1560s and 1570s, he also makes clear that the kind of sexual disorder represented by the sex trade continued to be a source of concern in subsequent decades. The virulence of the plague in 1603 prompted Dekker and others to rail with renewed vigor against the disorderly suburbs, and James's proclamation targeting overcrowded tenements simply stirred the pot. The fantasy, then, of a city of whorehouses had a partial basis in reality. Plays about London life highlighted whore plots in part because prostitution had taken a new form after the 1546 dissolution of the stews, had spread widely and been nurtured by the very social changes that were making London into a much bigger and more cosmopolitan environment. Prostitution was part of London life, and theater practitioners knew it. Theaters on the Bankside and in the northern suburbs, in particular, including Shakespeare's Globe, stood in the middle of well-known brothel districts;[19] theater manager Philip Henslowe made money from a quartet of Bankside whorehouses; and Edward Alleyn, the famous Elizabethan tragic actor, also owned brothels.[20]

The omnipresence of bawdy houses in the city drama and their frequent indistinguishability from other kinds of buildings thus speaks simultaneously to the changing nature of prostitution in post-Reformation London and to the penetration of commercial exchanges into every aspect of life. John Wheeler's 1601 defense of The Merchant Adventurers, *A Treatise of Commerce*, contains a famous description of a world in which all men "contract, truck, merchandise, and traffic one with another."[21] Wheeler lists all those—children, princes, soldiers, ordinary men and women—who dote on commerce:

> and in a word, all the world choppeth and changeth, runneth and raveth after marts, markets, and merchandising. So that all things come into commerce, and pass into traffice (in a manner) in all times, and in all places: not only that which Nature bringeth forth, as the fruits of the earth, the beasts and living creatures with their spoils, skins, and cases, the metals, minerals, and such like things, but further also, this man maketh merchandise of the works of his own hands, this man of another man's labor, one selleth words, another maketh traffic of the skins and blood of other men; yea there are some found so subtle and cunning merchants that they persuade and induce men to suffer themselves to be bought and sold, and we have seen in our time enow and too many, which have made merchandise of men's souls.[22]

Wheeler progresses from what seems to belong inevitably to the realm of commerce—the riches of the natural world—to what he clearly finds repugnant—traffic in human bodies and even in their souls. The prostitute goes unmentioned, yet she is among those who "suffer themselves to be bought and sold," not once and for all, but repeatedly, their bodies being the merchandise they bring to market. In the many London whore plays presented on stage after 1598, the ubiquitous prostitute, passing from place to place, taking one guise and then another, figures a market economy that can feel like it knows no boundaries. All men "runneth and raveth after marts, markets, and merchandising." In London city plays, whorehouses are no particular place because they are (nearly) everywhere: within the walls and without, in Eastcheap and the Bankside, Clerkenwell and St. Katherine's. Potentially, they exist wherever a scrivener, a merchant, or a shopkeeper dwells, his legitimate trade serving as cover for the illegitimate operations of his boarder or wife. The place of prostitution is sometimes home.

That ordinary dwellings and places of business are often indistinguishable from bawdy houses suggests that whore plots also are involved in negotiating one of the central social relations of the domestic sphere, that between husbands and wives. Historians have shown that living in London impacted the daily lives of both men and women in numerous ways, heightening and often refiguring anxieties about proper gender roles. Consumption, whether for necessities or luxury items, became a newly important part of the lives of urban women, whether artisan or merchant wives, gentry or aristocrat.[23] As consumers, women were often equated with unregulated desire, especially sexual desire.[24] Retail work also grew rapidly for middling-sort wives and for unmarried women as the surge in London's population caused rapid growth in the number of retail shops, inns, taverns, and cookshops within the city,[25] all venues in which women played important roles. Those who sold goods could be suspected of also selling themselves, and the city gave women numerous opportunities to lead public lives that made them highly visible, including to strangers.[26] Poorer women came to the city to find work as household servants, and this could involve them in marketing, accompanying their mistresses on errands outside the house, or fetching water from the parish pump or conduit. Wives of shopkeepers not only sold the goods, but were themselves displayed at shop fronts to draw in customers.

Foreign visitors often remarked on the freedom enjoyed by London women, who did not seem as strictly kept as the women of Spain and Italy, but who went about the streets of the city their heads uncovered, consorted with their gossips, and did their marketing at will.[27] Hugh Alley's *A Caveatt for the Citty of London* (1598) a series of sketches of London markets, shows many images of women selling goods or walking freely through the major markets, baskets on their arms in which to place their purchases.[28] Of London women Ian Archer writes:

> Women probably enjoyed more independence in the capital because of the nature of their work, participating at the front of the shop, running an alehouse, buying provisions in the market. But certain demographic peculiarities of the metropolitan scene help to account for the intensity of anxieties about women. High mortality in London meant that many households, not less than 16 percent in Southwark in the 1620s, were headed by women; it also meant that remarriage in the capital was common; no less than 25 percent of the marriages of London tradesmen were to widows, running counter to the recommendations of the moralists that the husband should always be older, and thereby giving women greater leverage within the household. The lack of confinement of women in the capital impressed foreign visitors who commented on their drinking in taverns and engaging in unsupervised sports with members of the opposite sex.[29]

In short, the city was a distinctive social and demographic place, raising new questions about women's conduct, chastity, and proper subordination.

The drama's pervasive prostitution plots pick up on such anxieties and give a cultural form to their expression and reiteration as they obsessively stage the dangers (and scary pleasures) of women's urban existence, particularly the possibility that chaste women and whores could readily swap places or be converted into one another within the urban milieu. Many London plays, for example, comment on the potentially dangerous practice of placing respectable women at shop fronts to attract customers. Such scenes always involve sexual danger or illicit sexual opportunity for the woman and invite her passage into whoredom. In Heywood's *Wise Woman of Hodgson*, a shopkeeper's daughter, Luce, wishes that her father would not expose her to public view in a shop front as it violates her modesty.[30] She shows herself to be a wise girl, for there are strong semiotic parallels between a chaste woman placed at the door of a shop to attract trade and the equally widely reported practice of positioning whores at the thresholds of brothels for the same purpose. Jane Shore, in Heywood's *Edward IV*, for example, is seduced by the monarch himself while she is on duty in her husband's shop,[31] and in *The Roaring Girl* the gallants who cruise the shops of London are in constant dalliance with the shopkeepers' wives.[32] Most of the time in comic London plays, wives don't sleep with the gallants who pursue them in their shops, but part of the titillation provided by the genre is the ever-present possibility that their position within the shops of London will transform wives into unchaste women.

A subset of whore plays, however, make that threat a reality. They highlight the conversion of chaste women into whores, and vice versa. In these plays, narratives in which a possible fall is averted give way to the uneasy thrill of watching a seemingly absolute alteration in a woman's sexual status. Either a chaste woman gives in to a life of debauchery or an unchaste woman eschews whoredom for a newly found probity. In the last several years critics have drawn our attention to plays, mostly set in the Mediterranean, in which European heroes, inevitably male heroes, "Turn Turk," cast off their respectable English and Christian identities and become infidels, renegades, lost to both Christianity and their homelands.[33] The domestic counterpart to such narratives, I would argue, is provided by prostitute plays in which it is women who undergo comparable transformations of identity, particularly as their position in the city is imagined to allow easy passage across the supposedly unbridgeable gap separating chaste wives and maids from unchaste whores. To some extent, London is a woman's foreign land, the place where utter transformations are possible. However, while men's conversions in Turk plays usually result in tragedy, women's conversions in city drama are shaped by comic conventions, and as I will argue, this works over time to query the conceptual categories of prescriptive literature and to offer alternatives that stress the fluid, contingent, and commercially embedded nature of women's urban lives.

A recurring feature of whore plots involves women coming to the city from the country, the encounter with urbanity being what precipitates a crisis in identity, much as arriving in Tunis or Malta can precipitate a crisis for the male protagonist of the adventure genre. On stage the transformation of country maid into city whore could be materially registered by the manipulation of clothing, in particular, to emphasize the utter transformations of the female self under the influence of the city and its market culture. In Middleton's *Michaelmas Term*, for example, a country girl is quickly taught that "Virginity is no city trade, / You're out o' th' freedom, when you're a maid."[34] Given no name except the generic one of "Country Wench," this young woman is brought to London by a Pander, Dick Hellgill. As always, Middleton delights in crafting delicious names for his urban cast, and Country Wench is not only a generic appellation but a sexy one. It is a constant punning reminder that in the city this woman still pursues "cuntry matters," but of a new sort. Hellgill works for Lethe, a villainous "upstart adventurer" who has forgotten his simple country background (he was the son of a toothdrawer) and aspires to marry the daughter of Quomodo, a wealthy London woolen draper. Lethe, however, wants a little action on the side, and so he sends Hellgill to the country to fetch him a woman Hellgill subsequently describes as "Young, beautiful, and plump, a delicate piece of sin" (II.i.136). In I.ii, this girl arrives with Hellgill, who attempts to persuade her of the benefits of turning whore. He promotes this option as a form of advancement over country life, one that will strip away her "servile habiliments" (I.ii. 5) and introduce her to a world of "wires and tires, bents and bums, felts and falls" (13–14). In her new attire she can "deceive the world, that gentlewomen indeed shall not be known from others" (14–15), the others presumably being women of lower rank or of questionable virtue. The intricacies of fashionable dress elide distinctions between the chaste and the unchaste, common women and merchant wives or gentry ladies. Tellingly, it is when Hellgill tempts Country Wench with a satin gown that she agrees to comply. Rich clothing both seduces her and is the means of effecting her passage into another social milieu. In an aside, Hellgill comments: "So farewell wholesome weeds, where treasure pants, / And welcome silks, where lies disease and wants" (I.ii.51–2), acknowledging the link between a whore's rich dress and her eventual infection with sexual disease and slide into poverty. But with the Country Wench he is less forthright, saying only: "Come, wench, now flow thy fortunes in to bless thee; / I'll bring thee where thou shalt be taught to dress thee" (54–5).

The scene where the audience actually sees the Country Wench transformed into a whore is placed squarely in the structural center of the play (III.i). She is surrounded on stage by a tailor and a tirewoman, the agents of her sartorial makeover. The stage directions read: *"Enter Lethe's pander,* Hellgill, *the* Country Wench *coming in with a new fashion gown, dress'd gentlewoman-like, the* Tailor *points it, and* [Mistress Comings] *a tirewoman, busy about her head."* Predictably, the scene is packed with sexual innuendo and lewd jokes. Mistress Comings suggests, for example, that the Country Wench adopt a hair style "still like a mock-face behind; 'tis such an Italian world, many men know not before from behind" (III.i.17–18), alluding knowingly to the supposedly Italian vice of anal intercourse. The Country Wench enters fully into the banter and seems as transformed in manner as in appearance. When Hellgill ribs her about her country origins, she roundly replies: "Out, you saucy, pestiferous pander! I scorn that, i' faith," to which he rejoins "Excellent, already the true phrase and style of a strumpet" (III.i.24–5). The passage from country to city has in this case meant the conversion of a maid into a harlot, a simply dressed woman into a fashion-plate complete with satin gown, elaborate hairstyle, and employees hired to maintain her new façade. She is literally unrecognizable; the city has made her what she was not. For proof, Middleton has the Country Wench take her own disguised father for a servant, and the father does not recognize his daughter.[35]

Here, as elsewhere, the city seems capable of making almost alchemical changes in women's social and sexual status, partly by their entrance into a thoroughly commercial world with its structures of illicit opportunity. *Michaelmas Term* not only foregrounds the spectacle of the Country Wench's transformation, but eventually makes her the spokesperson for a cynical, but not inaccurate, reading of the commercial logic governing the behavior of most of the play's main London characters. Defending her behavior, she asks:

> Do not all trades live by their ware, and yet call'd honest livers? Do they not thrive best when they utter most, and make it away by the great? Is not wholesale the chiefest merchandise? Do you think some merchants could keep their wives so brave, but for their wholesale? You're foully deceiv'd and you think so.

(IV.i.10–16)

It is hard to say whether the wicked pun on wholesale and hole sale does more to discredit merchants or to elevate the whore's trade, here explicitly rendered as a selling of holes, a product much sought after and yet eerily empty, the "no thing" of other Renaissance puns.[36] Moreover, in their "(w)holesaling," Country Wench and merchant wife are made one as the merchant wife adds to family income by the calculated use of her nether end.

With high-spirited irony, Middleton's plot undermines the sanctity of marriage and blurs the line separating prostitutes from honest women. Eventually, Lethe, despite his pretensions to Quomodo's daughter, is forced by the court to marry the Country Wench, and she is thus legally, if not morally, transported back across the bar into respectability. There is, however, no corresponding transformation in her dress, no scene in which she eschews her satin garments and returns to the country homespun that was the original mark of female innocence. In the play's final scene (V.iii), the Country Wife is a wife in whore's attire, though the audience has already been shown that the fashion industry makes it hard to distinguish the one from the other. Middleton's plot underscores the point, and the theater renders it materially visible through its use of costume.

The play is as concerned, however, with the possible transformation of wives as of country maids. Throughout the action, Quomodo's respectable wife, Thomasine, has had her eye on the country gentleman, Easy, whose land her husband is trying treacherously to acquire. When Quomodo pretends to be dead, Thomasine promptly marries Easy (V.i.14–15), thus rendering ridiculous Quomodo's self-satisfied prattling about how his wife is so modest and loyal that she will mourn him for many a long month (V.i.58–73). City wives do not mourn anyone for long; they choose a new husband and move on. In the end the same court that makes Lethe marry his Country Wench returns Thomasine to Quomodo. But there is no longer any possibility of his believing that she is the kind of wife who defines herself through marriage to him alone. She returns to Quomodo after having slept, we assume, with her new "husband," Easy. By pretending to be dead, Quomodo in effect gave his wife the opportunity to cuckold him without knowingly committing adultery. The play leaves the audience with the spectacle of a Country Wench who was transformed into a whore being transformed into a wife; while a wife, unwittingly transformed into an adultress, is reconverted to her former status as wife, though now as shop-soiled goods. This anti-idealizing play certainly takes the bloom off marriage, and it seems to delight in underscoring the various passages a city woman can make across the line separating the chaste from unchaste, the wife from the whore, the once-married from the twice-married. In this play there is no formal whorehouse with its attendant bawd, just the unspecified lodgings where the Country Wench sets herself up to meet Lethe and his friends, and Quomodo's house where Thomasine installs Easy in her husband's place. Illicit sexuality needs no designated brothel; as I have argued, in these urban fantasies it can occur in common and unremarkable places, a lodging house or a home, wherever wives and maids can embrace the opportunity for illicit sex.

The fantasy of conversion, of course, can move in the other direction. If *Michaelmas Term* turns maids and wives into whores, in Dekker's *The Honest Whore* a prostitute crosses over to respectability, but with unsettling results. In her first stage appearance Bellafront, the whore, sits at a dressing table surrounded by the cosmetics, brushes, and articles of clothing that allow her to make herself, with the market's help, into an object of desire. She has a servant, a bawd, and regular clients whom she milks for money. But after she reforms and is married to the man who first slept with her, her life becomes hellish. A rake and a gambler, Matheo is also abusive. In a climactic scene he strips off his wife's one remaining satin dress, the last vestiges of her life as a whore, so that he can sell it to buy clothes and rapiers for himself (*Part II*, 3.2). He also urges his wife to return to her former trade to underwrite his desire for a gentleman's lifestyle. The scene strongly recalls the stories of patient Griselda, whom Bellafront resembles.[37] When Griselda is first brought to the court of the duke who marries her, her humble clothes are taken from her and she is attired in rich robes. When the duke later sends her away, she is made to resume her cast-off clothing. In *The Honest Whore*, being stripped to her petticoat is, for Bellafront, the equivalent of Griselda's humiliation. Ironically, it associates the conversion from whore to wife with a devastating loss of power. As a virtuous wife who refuses to do any more "(w)holesaling" to support her husband's desired lifestyle, Bellafront nearly starves. The reformed prostitute has put herself so outside the commercial logic of the city that she can only be dramatized as a secular saint, an exception to the culture's common sense. The overt moral of Dekker's play—that one should leave a life of sin and embrace virtue—is thus powerfully undercut by the terrible things that happen to a woman who does just that. However unintentionally, *The Honest Whore* suggests that in the urban context, a woman who refuses to blur the line between the chaste and the unchaste, the wife and the whore, is a throwback to another time and place—a holy fool, or maybe just a fool.

In the majority of conversion plots, however, the woman's transformation is seldom as absolute or as permanent as in *The Honest Whore*. Rather, the transition from chastity to unchastity, from wife to adulteress, from maid to whore can happen several times. Working from the evidence of social history, rather than as I do from an archive of plays, Faramerz Dabhoiwale argues that historians have taken a too polarized view of sexual behavior in early modern London, and that in reality there was a fluid spectrum of sexually immoral acts in which a range of women engaged, not simply a subgroup of professional prostitutes. "Whore," he reminds us, was the common term for any unchaste woman;[38] and Laura Gowing suggests how often that term was bandied about, by women themselves as well as by men.[39] Gowing argues that many women defamed by being called "whore" were probably not taking money in exchange for sex, but might be committing adultery or flaunting themselves in public in a way offensive to their neighbors. Moreover, as Dabhoiwale shows, when women did take some form of payment for sex, that did not make them professional or life-long prostitutes. It may have represented an economically motivated form of casual employment or a one-off opportunity. As with whores, bawdy houses were similarly hard to separate off from homes or legitimate places of business. Illicit rendezvous, he argues, could happen in "a private home or a tavern or a brothel, of greater or lesser sophistication and expense."[40] The city, with its ever-growing number of places to eat and lodge, made illicit opportunity omnipresent. Moreover, the standard practice of having shops in the front rooms of the same houses where the shopkeepers lived, further confused and imbricated the realms of commerce and of domestic life.[41] For a long time feminist critics have focused attention on the distinction among maids, wives, widows, and whores so common in the prescriptive literature. But we need to remember that these categories were just that—prescriptive injunctions that did not necessarily describe women's actual social experience, perhaps especially in London. City prostitute drama certainly revels in putting pressure on the absolute or fixed nature of these distinctions.

Nowhere is this more true than in the final "conversion" play I shall discuss: Middleton's *A Chaste Maid in Cheapside* (1613). It is no coincidence that the setting should be the very heart of one of London's oldest centers of commerce, Cheapside. Stretching from the Pissing Conduit on the west near St Paul's to the Great Conduit to the east, Cheapside was in the Tudor-Stuart period one of the great thoroughfares and commercial centers of London. It formed part of the ceremonial route used by monarchs in their inaugural processions and by lord mayors in the annual lord mayor's day pageants;[42] and it was lined with rich shops. In 1599 Thomas Platter wrote: "In one very long street called Cheapside dwell almost only goldsmiths and moneychangers on either hand so that inexpressibly great treasure and vast amount of money may be seen here."[43] At the very center of Cheapside, between Cheap Cross to the west and Bread Street to the east, was a section known as Goldsmiths Row, an area famous for the beauty and elegance of its buildings. Stow recounts:

> Next to be noted, the most beautiful frame of fayre houses and shoppes, that bee within the Walles of London, or elsewhere in England, commonly called Goldsmithes Rowe, betwixt Bredstreet end and the Crosse in Cheape... It contayneth in number tenne fayre dwelling houses, and fourteene shoppes, all in one frame, uniformly builded foure stories high, bewtified towardes the street with the Goldsmithes armes... [44]

This elegant and wealthy commercial stretch, refurbished in 1594, is the center of action in Middleton's play, the "chaste maid" of the title being the daughter of a goldsmith named Yellowhammer who has a shop in the Row. The choice of location can hardly be accidental. It invites the audience to locate the play's multiple plots of sex and marriage in what everyone would recognize as a notable center of trade.

By the second decade of the seventeenth century Goldsmith Row was not quite what it had been in earlier days. In 1619 it became the subject of a renovation campaign that was to last for at least twenty-five years. In 1619 the Goldsmiths Company spoke before the Court of Aldermen of the need to push out the "mean" traders and stranger merchants diluting the traditional community of goldsmiths who had long inhabited the Row, some of whom were now renting shops in the fashionable West End, instead. The perceived decay of Goldsmith Row partly signaled the Company's loss of control over the sale of jewels and gold and silver plate within the city due to competition from strangers and the illegal sale of high-value goods by criminals; it was also part of an almost inexorable drift to the West End. James I and Charles I both made the decline of the Row a matter of personal interest and called repeatedly for the return of guild members to their traditional shops in Cheapside. Most declined, claiming that rents on the Row were too high, and clearly seeing that many of their preferred clients might now have West End addresses.[45]

A Chaste Maid in Cheapside (1613) carries with it the faint whiff of decay, though it is not as concerned with the flight of goldsmiths from the Row as with the astonishing degree to which the commercial values of this center of commerce have percolated through the domestic realm, leading to an impossible confusion of the terms through which both men and women are defined in the traditional gender system. There *is* a designated whore in this play, known simply as The Welsh Gentlewoman, a punk formerly employed by Sir Walter Whorehound, who now brings her to London in order to marry her off, his own marriage to the chaste maid of cheapside, Moll Yellowhammer, being in prospect. This scenario ironically reverses the pattern with which Middleton had experimented in *Michaelmas Term* in which a country wench is inducted into the prostitution trade on her arrival in London. Here, London also effects an alchemical transformation in a country girl: this time from whore to wife. Whorehound brings the Welsh woman to Cheapside in order to marry her to Tim Yellowhammer, brother of Moll, his own bride. As Whorehound says to the Welsh gentlewoman, "I bring thee up to turn thee into gold, wench, and make thy fortune shine like your bright trade" (I.i.99–100). If he can contrive for her to marry Tim, she will inherit part of Yellowhammer's estate, and he, presumably, the rest. From whore and whoremaster, they will be converted into sister-in-law and brother-in-law. But Whorehound's statement does not separate the Welsh woman's marriage from her former trade; rather, he presents it is the perfect culmination of that trade. Tim is simply the most lucrative of all her clients, and one lent permanence through marriage.

The plan works, of course, only because the Yellowhammers are willing to use their children in the marriage market to acquire Whorehound's wealth and the cultural cachet that Mrs Yellowhammer, in particular, craves. She wants an alliance with a knight and so is quite willing to barter away both her unwilling son and unwilling daughter to Whorehound and his "niece." In the Yellowhammers the spirit of the pimp and bawd shine brightly. Mr Yellowhammer does not bat an eye when he learns his daughter is going to marry a whoremaster, being one himself. As he confesses, "I have kept a whore myself, and had a bastard" (IV.i.272); "The knight is rich, he shall be my son-in-law" (IV.i.277). So much for family values in Cheapside.

The Yellowhammer family is only one of several in the play in which the commercial and the sexual have become so intertwined that fathers and pimps, wives, whores, and bawds are not easily separated. What everyone remembers about *Chaste Maid* is the Allwit family. Their address is not given, but they live within easy distance of the Yellowhammers because there are several scenes in which members of one household are quickly summoned to the other. For the Allwits, the household *is* the place of prostitution. There Mrs Allwit sells her sexual favors to a "benefactor," Whorehound, who impregnates her repeatedly. In exchange for sex, he supports Mrs Allwit, her husband, and all the illegitimate children. Mr Allwit is satisfied with this arrangement because it relieves him of having to work for his living or even to perform sexual labor. One might say that Mrs Allwit simply engages in an unusual form of household production. Rather than producing a petty commodity such as lace, she produces sexual pleasure and children for Sir Walter, using her "hole" rather than her needle as her tool of labor. For that, she garners all the wealth that has maintained her household for ten profitable years (I.ii.16). No particular scandal surrounds her actions. The "fall" from wife to whore is not represented as a tragedy or even a sin; it is what is expected in a world in which the strong pull of gold is the lodestone governing everyone's actions.

Chaste Maid in Cheapside eschews obvious moralizing. Within the play, the only character seriously punished is Sir Walter Whorehound, who has the audacity to repent of his sinful ways. Ironically, he alone loses everything: Welsh mistress, prospective bride, land. He ends up in debtors' prison. By contrast, the other characters, eschewing both guilt and self-reform, escape punishment. Instead, they improvise, forming alternative social structures and every sort of idiosyncratic, non-normative family. Having lost their benefactor, the Allwits gather up their favorite possessions, including a velvet close stool, and set off to open a high-class brothel on the fashionable Strand. Like the smarter goldsmiths, they are following the money to the West End. And while Moll Yellowhammer marries the man she loves, Tim is not so lucky. Married to the Welsh Gentlewoman before anyone discovers her true identity, he makes the best of a bad situation, arguing that "Uxor non est meretrix" (V.iv.114) ("A wife is not a whore"). But the moral of the play seems to be just the opposite: wives can quite easily be prostitutes. Tim is a boob in love with useless Latin learning; Cheapside demands the vernacular and the street smarts that come with it. Without them, the university man is likely to find that "Meretrix est uxor." Yet Middleton, more than most of his contemporaries, refuses the usual alibi of gender whereby women alone bear the blame for the excesses and dangers of a changing economic order. In *Chaste Maid*, the men are just as implicated in the sex trade, pandering daughters and wives, making themselves fawning figures like Allwit who wishes only to avoid displeasing the "benefactor," however unpleasant he may be.

Middleton seems to have decided that the best way to reveal the under-lying logic of a commercial city was to treat its blurring of gender norms not as scandal, but as fact. *Chaste Maid in Cheapside* pushes the amoral logic of the market deep into the households of London's famous commercial district, making Cheapside households the site where a wife's "hole" is the chief commodity her husband sells and where children are simply bargaining chips on the way to greater wealth or new forms of cultural capital. In such an environment, the four prescriptive categories supposedly dividing one woman from another—the categories of maid, wife, widow, and whore—become unstable and fungible as the pursuit of gold leads to a whore's conversion into a wife and a wife's conversion into a whore. If the pervasive anxiety of the adventure drama is that a man will "turn Turk," the comparable fantasy of London comedies is that the wife or chaste maid will "turn whore." The city drama restaged variants of this fantasy in ingenious and remarkably obsessive ways. The reasons are multiple, but they have to do with the growing commercialization of London life and the material conditions that made gender relations in the city a special source of concern. And yet, city drama does not moralize the behavior of urban women so much as turn it into the stuff of comedy. Watching these prostitution plays, the audience sees prescriptions flouted and sexual transgressions repeatedly rehearsed in comic plots in which men marry whores and live to praise the fact, and in which women who make calculated decisions about the value of turning tricks still get a husband in the end. If Turk plays imagine the fragmentation of male identity under the pressure of foreign encounters, London comedies most often represent urban women's "conversions" as sometimes reversible, often economically rational, and frequently quite unremarkable. In so doing, they lay down discursive templates for a new age.

Notes

1. Thomas Leggatt, *Citizen Comedy in the Age of Shakespeare* (Toronto: University of Toronto Press, 1973), 99–124, esp. 103–5.
2. *The Oxford English Dictionary Online*, entry 2.a. for *traffic, n.* The word was in use after 1500, often in contexts involving overseas trade.
3. John Marston, *The Dutch Courtesan*, ed. M.L. Wine (Lincoln, NB: University of Nebraska Press, 1965). All quotations from the play will be taken from this edition.
4. See E. J. Burford, *Bawds and Lodgings: A History of the Bankside Brothels c. 100–1675* (London: Peter Owen, 1976). This book, while unreliable in details and often maddeningly under-documented, still provides the closest thing we have to a continuous historical account of prostitution in the area south of London. See also Ruth Mazzo Karras, "The Regulation of Brothels in Later Medieval England," *Signs: Journal of Women in Culture and Society.* 14:2 (1989): 399–433; Wallace Shugg, "Prostitution in Shakespeare's London," *Shakespeare Studies* 10 (1977): 291–313; and Paul Griffiths, "The Structure of Prostitution in Elizabethan London," *Continuity and Change* (1993): 36–63.
5. Gordon Williams. *A Dictionary of Sexual Language and Imagery in Shakespearean and Stuart Literature.* Vol. III (London: The Athlone Press, 1994), 1538–9.
6. Ian Archer, *The Pursuit of Stability: Social Relations in Elizabethan London* (Cambridge: Cambridge University Press, 1999), 212.

7. See also John L. McMullan, *The Canting Crew: London's Criminal Underworld 1550–1700* (New Brunswick: Rutgers University Press, 1984), especially chapter 4, "Criminal Areas," in which he discusses the many areas in which prostitution and other forms of vice could be found; and Walter Shugg, "Prostitution in Shakespeare's London," esp. pp. 296–301.

8. James F. Larkin and Paul L. Hughes, *Stuart Royal Proclamations*, Vol. I (Oxford: Clarendon Press, 1973), 47. This is part of the September 16, 1603 proclamation entitled "A Proclamation against Inmates and multitudes of dwellers in strait Roomes and places in and about the Citie of London: And for the rasing and pulling downe of certaine new erected buildings."

9. *The Norton Shakespeare*, ed. Stephen Greenblatt, Katharine Eisaman Maus, Walter Cohen, and Jean E. Howard (New York: Norton, 1997), 2033. All references to Shakespeare's plays will be to this edition. For the link between the play and the proclamation, see Shugg, "Prostitution in Shakespeare's London," 303.

10. Ian Archer argues (from admittedly limited Bridewell records) that by the end of the sixteenth century vagrancy was perceived as a more pressing problem than sexual vice. While the mid-century reformers had dreamed of creating a godly commonwealth, civic leaders in 1600 focused on the problem of the growing legions of poor who had to be brought to conform to the strictures of the new Elizabethan Poor Laws (*The Pursuit of Stability*, 255–6). Nonetheless, the control of prostitution remained a preoccupation of both the Bridewell officials and the ecclesiastical bawdy courts throughout the Stuart period.

11. For a fuller discussion of this play, and the significance of its opposition between Brainford and London proper, see my "Women, Foreigners, and Urban Space in *Westward Ho*," in *Material London, ca. 1600*, ed. Lena Orlin (Philadelphia: University of Pennsylvania Press, 2000), 150–73.

12. Thomas Dekker and John Webster, *Westward Ho*, ed. Fredson Bowers, *The Dramatic Works of Thomas Dekker*, Vol. 2 (Cambridge: Cambridge University Press, 1955), 319. All reference to this play will be to this edition.

13. Thomas Dekker and John Webster, *Northward Ho* in *The Dramatic Works of Thomas Dekker*, ed. Fredson Bowers (Cambridge: Cambridge University Press, 1955), 411. All references will be to this edition of the play.

14. See Burford, *Bawds and Lodgings*, 125, for evidence that the stews were painted white; and Karras, "The Regulation of Brothels in Late Medieval England," 421, for a discussion of the distinctive clothing that whores were required to wear in some cities.

15. Ann Rosalind Jones and Peter Stallybrass, *Renaissance Clothing and the Materials of Memory* (Cambridge: Cambridge University Press, 2001), passim.

16. John L. McMullan, *The Canting Crew: London's Criminal Underworld 1550–1700* (New Brunswick: Rutgers University Press, 1984), p. 33. See also Jyotsna Singh's convincing argument that early modern prostitution was materially connected to women's poverty. "The Interventions of History: Narratives of Sexuality," in *The Weyward Sisters: Shakespeare and Feminist Politics* (Oxford: Blackwell, 1994), 7–58.

17. Laura Gowing, *Domestic Dangers: Women, Words, and Sex in Early Modern London* (Oxford: Clarendon Press, 1996), 17.

18. McMullan, *The Canting Crew*, 24.

19. Shugg, "Prostitution in Shakespeare's London," 296.

20. McMullan, *The Canting Crew*, 139.

21. John Wheeler, *A Treatise of Commerce*, ed. George Hotchkiss (New York: New York University Press, 1931), 316.
22. Ibid., 316–17.
23. F. J. Fisher, "The Development of London as a Centre of Conspicuous Consumption in the Sixteenth and Seventeenth Centuries," in *London and the Economy, 1500–1700*, ed. P. J. Corfield and N. B. Harte (London and Ronceverte: Hambledon, 1990), 105–18.
24. See Karen Newman, *Fashioning Femininity and English Renaissance Drama* (Chicago: University of Chicago Press, 1991), pp. 111–43; and Jean E. Howard, "The Evidence of Fiction: Women's Relationship to Goods in London City Drama," *Culture and Change: Attending to Early Modern Women*, ed. Margaret Mikesell and Adele Seeff (Newark: University of Delaware Press, 2003), 161–76.
25. For a discussion of women's role in retailing and in the provisioning industries, see Sara Mendelson and Patricia Crawford, *Women in Early Modern England 1550–1720* (Oxford: Clarendon, 1998), 333–6. For more on the provisioning trades, see Sara Pennell, "'Great quantities of goosberry pye and baked clod of beef': Victualling and Eating out in Early Modern London," *Londinopolis: Essays in the Cultural and Social History of Early Modern London*, ed. Paul Griffiths and Mark S. R. Jenner (Manchester: Manchester University Press, 2000), 228.
26. See Gowing, *Domestic Dangers: Women, Words, and Sex in Early Modern London*, p. 15.
27. Emanuel Van Meteren, "Pictures of the English in Queen Elizabeth's Reign," in *England as Seen by Foreigners*, ed. William Brenchley Rye (London: John Russell Smith, 1865), 72–3.
28. *Hugh Alley's Caveat: The Markets of London in 1598*, Folger Ms V.a.318, ed. Ian Archer, Caroline Barron, and Vanessa Harding (London: Topographical Society Publication No. 137, 1988).
29. Ian Archer, "Material Londoners?" in *Material London, ca. 1600*, ed. Lena Orlin (Philadelphia: University of Pennsylvania Press, 2000), 174–92; 184–5.
30. Thomas Heywood, *The Wise Woman of Hogsdon* in *The Dramatic Works of Thomas Heywood*, Vol. 5 (London: John Pearson, 1874), I.ii, p. 285 (no lineation given). All references to the play will be to this edition and will be given by Act, scene, and page numbers.
31. Thomas Heywood, *The First Part of King Edward the Fourth* in *The Dramatic Works of Thomas Heywood*, Vol. 1, 64–6. All references to the play will be to this edition and will be given by page numbers only.
32. See, for example, II.i in which the gallants circulate among the shops of Mr and Mrs Tiltyard, Openwork, and Gallipot. Thomas Middleton and Thomas Dekker, *The Roaring Girl*, ed. Andor Gomme (London: Ernst Benn, 1976), 26–45. All references to the play will be this edition.
33. Critics who address this topic include Dan Vitkus, "Turning Turk in *Othello*: The Conversion and Damnation of the Moor," *Shakespeare Quarterly* 48 (1997): 145–76; Nabil Matar, *Islam in Britain 1558–1685* (Cambridge: Cambridge University Press, 1998); and *Turks, Moors, and Englishmen in the Age of Discovery* (New York: Columbia University Press, 1999); Barbara Fuchs, *Mimesis and Empire: The New World, Islam, and European Identities* (Cambridge: Cambridge University Press, 2001); and Ania Loomba, " 'Delicious Traffic': Racial and Religious Differences on Early Modern Stages," in Catherine M. S. Alexander and Stanley Wells (eds.) *Shakespeare and Race* (Cambridge: Cambridge University Press, 2000), 203–24.

34. Thomas Middleton, *Michaelmas Term*. ed. Richard Levin (Lincoln, NB: University of Nebraska Press, 1966), 24, I.ii.43–4.

35. Alexander Leggatt, in *Citizen Comedy in the Age of Shakespeare*, p. 117, shrewdly notes that while mistakes of identity are common in city plays, *Michalmas Term* is unusual in that the play ends with the father and his daughter still unknown to each other.

36. Gordon Williams, in *A Dictionary of Sexual Language and Imagery in Shakespearean and Stuart Literature*, Vol. III, 1525–6, says that the "wholesale" pun is particularly apt for describing mercenary sex, and lists *Michaelmas Term* as one of a number of dramas that play with its possibilities.

37. For a brilliant discussion of the role of clothing in the many renditions of the Griselda story, see Jones and Stallybrass, *Renaissance Clothing and the Materials of Memory*, pp. 220–44.

38. Faramerz Dabhoiwala, "The Pattern of Sexual Immorality in Seventeenth- and Eighteenth-century London," in Paul Griffiths and Mark S. R. Jenner, eds., *Londinopolis*, pp. 86–106; 88.

39. Laura Gowing, *Domestic Dangers: Women, Words, and Sex in Early Modern London* (Oxford: Clarendon Press, 1996), esp. chapter 3, "The Language of Insult," 59–110.

40. Dabhoiwala, "The Pattern of Sexual Immorality in Seventeenth- and Eighteenth-century London," 93.

41. See John Schofield, *The Building of London from the Conquest to the Great Fire*. 3rd edn. (Phoenix Mill: Sutton Publishing, 1999), esp. chapter 7, "To the Great Fire 1600–1666," 157–77.

42. Steven Mullaney, *The Place of the Stage: License, Play, and Power in Renaissance England* (Chicago: University of Chicago Press, 1988), 1–25, discusses what he calls the "ceremonial city" defined by events such as the monarch's or the lord mayor's carefully choreographed procession through London on ritual occasions. Both the monarch's entry and the lord mayor's pageant invariably moved along Cheapside.

43. Thomas Platter, *Travels in England*. Rpt. in *London in the Age of Shakespeare: An Anthology*, ed. Lawrence Manley (University Park: Pennsylvania State University Press, 1986), 38–9.

44. John Stow, *A Survey of London*, 2 vols. ed. Charles Kingsford (Oxford: Clarendon Press, 1908), Vol. I, 345–6.

45. Paul Griffiths, "Politics Made Visible: Order, Residence and Uniformity in Cheapside, 1600–45," in *Londinopolis: Essays in the Cultural and Social History of Early Modern London*, 176–96.

7

Women, Gender, and the Politics of Location

Kate Chedgzoy

What did the politics of location mean to women in the changing world of early modern Britain? Dwelling in and traveling through Wales, Ireland, Scotland, New England, the Chesapeake, and the Caribbean as well as England, women wrote in several languages of landscapes that were changing even as they inhabited and traversed them. In an uncertain time, the act of writing—in prose and verse, in prayers and commonplace books, seeking print publication or familial manuscript circulation—enabled women to express a sense of home, to describe the experience of travel, and to articulate the dynamics of belonging and displacement. Local, regional, and national identities and cultures, as well as popular understandings of what it meant to belong to a particular place, were constituted and expressed under pressure from international and internecine conflicts, revolutionary political processes, and massive social and economic change.

Such matters, and their effects on how people live their lives, are primarily the stuff of the discipline of geography. Yet they have immense implications for the extent to which scholars in other fields, such as literature, can hope to understand the refractions of such geo-historical processes in their objects of study. This essay brings insights enabled by recent work in feminist cultural and historical geography to bear on the ways in which women's writing gives expression to the everyday, intimate consequences of the major geopolitical changes that took place in the British Isles in the seventeenth century. By examining within a gendered analytic framework the specificities of the experience of place and movement, belonging and dislocation, as expressed in women's writing, we can both elicit a specifically female perspective, and gain richer and more complex understandings of the local and particular consequences of large-scale national and transnational events.

Historiographies of the early modern period have increasingly revealed the complex interrelations of domestic processes of state formation within the British Isles with the simultaneous tentative beginnings of the first, transatlantic, British empire—processes that transformed this archipelago's place in a wider world. This is a period in which the British state was frequently engaged in international or civil conflict, from the Nine Years' War in Ireland, through the wars in which all parts of the British Isles were involved in the period 1638–60, to King Philip's War in Massachusetts in 1674–6, among other instances. It was a time of cataclysmic change in the relations between the state and religious institutions. And it was a period of social and topographical transformation, brought about by influences including enclosure, urbanization, and colonial ventures overseas. The interrelation of all these pressures changed the material conditions of daily life and the quotidian experience of space and place, for many women, whether, like Magdalen Lloyd, they followed the drovers' roads from Wales to London in search of work (discussed below); reimagined their role in the household in time of civil conflict in order not merely to endure sieges, but to lead the defense of their homes, like Charlotte de la Trémouille in Lancashire or Lettice Fitzgerald in County Kildare; participated with their families in the Puritan Great Migration to Massachusetts in the 1630s, like Anne Bradstreet; or, like Mary Fisher and Anne Austin, voyaged in couples as Quaker preachers to Barbados.[1] Many critical questions about how these conflicts and changes affected women have yet to be adequately addressed by scholars. How did women experience these large transitions within their immediate localities? How did their sense of home and belonging enable them to understand and represent what was happening on the world's stage? How did they contribute to the remapping of familiar localities within a geographically and politically volatile world? If location is a matter of "places defined and places taken up through experience, identity and power,"[2] then in order to answer these questions we need to learn from the ways in which "cultural geographers have concerned themselves with . . . the intimate practices of emplacement, embodiment, and location through which subjects, communities and nations are bounded and bound together."[3] But we also need to attend to the processes of remapping that delineated the boundaries of communities and nations, and thus inflected the meanings of location in the early modern period. This chapter explores some methods for making sense of the transformations of women's lives effected by those changes in the meaning of location, at the local, regional, national, and transnational levels, that shaped the early modern period, and in doing so altered women's capacity to understand themselves as geopolitical subjects.

The diverse ways in which the production and experience of location are charged with social meaning have been richly and suggestively theorized in recent years, and the emergence of geographical ways of understanding the world in the early modern period has been a subject of considerable scholarly interest. The convergence of these intellectual agendas with feminist critique has begun to open up new ways of understanding how women's experience, and gender as a category of analysis, played key roles in shaping the meanings of place and space and the way they were experienced in early modern Britain, thereby illuminating the intimate consequences for people's lives of large-scale historical processes. The inception of feminist geography as both a sub-disciplinary area of study and a mode of politically committed intellectual inquiry can be dated to the early 1980s, making it roughly coeval with the revival of interest in the study of Renaissance women's writing. There are significant differences between these fields, which often occupy quite distinct institutional locations and employ widely divergent methodologies: as Mona Domosh and Karen M. Morin concede, "much of feminist geography remains resolutely non-historical,"[4] while feminist studies of Renaissance literature have not consistently benefited from the methodological sophistication and self-reflexiveness characteristic of work in social science disciplines such as geography.

Nevertheless, feminist historians, literary critics, and art historians are turning increasingly to interpreting the experiences and the cultural productions of early modern women in relation to key geographical concepts. For example, in studies of the material sites of women's textual production such as the aristocratic household, the convent, or the urban locus of commercial print activity known as Grub Street,[5] feminist geography's understanding of the social production of the spatial can give methodological density and flexibility to literary scholars' descriptive accounts of communities and places. Such perspectives are particularly valuable insofar as they emphasize that "[p]laces ...are open and porous,"[6] defined not by spatial boundaries that demarcate and contain them, but by their interactions with other places and other kinds of social forces existing in space and time. This is not to deny the significance of the material location in space and time, but women's writing about place demonstrates vividly how their apprehension and experience of it is molded by a range of social forces. As a young widow in the 1660s, Katherine Austen fought a long legal battle to keep her husband's estate, a struggle which, like Anne Clifford's earlier fight for the right to inherit her family's property, underscores the connections between an emotional attachment to a place and the economic and social importance of the ownership of land.[7] Austen's poem "On the Situation of Highbury" is both a discreet celebration of her success in the court case and a revision of the powerful genre of the country-house poem from the unusual perspective of a female property-owner. As if to anticipate Virginia Woolf's recommendation that in order to write a woman should secure a room of her own and an adequate income, Austen celebrates Highbury not least as the ground that enables her writing:

> Amidst its beauty, if a streame did rise
> To clear my mudy braine, and misty Eyes
> And find a Hellicon t'enlarge my muse
> Then I, no better place then this wud choose
> In such a laber and on this bright Hill
> I wish Parnassus to adorne my quill.[8]

The ways in which familiar geographies are brought into question under political and military pressure—an all too common concern for geographers concerned with the changing world of the early twenty-first century—are made powerfully clear in the letters of Brilliana Harley, who defended her home at Brampton Bryan, Herefordshire against a siege by Royalist forces in 1642. The violent transformations of the domestic effected by the war are poignantly recorded in a letter to her son Ned, written in a primitive code in March 1642. The crucial passages directed to him record hunger, shortage of supplies, and the fear of defeat, whereas the "nonsense" that surrounds them and is designed to confuse unauthorized readers evokes domestic comfort and plenty, referring to 'fisch good store', new gloves, and the pleasures of tobacco.[9] In Brilliana Harley's letters, the meaning of "home," a central subject of debate in interdisciplinary feminist studies, is reconstructed as it changes from a place of feminine domestic duties and power, a haven of familial pleasure and solidarity, into a site of entrapment, violence, and danger. As these examples make plain, the materiality of location takes on a variety of social meanings when place is conceptualized as "an intersection of a number of social relations, each with their own geographies."[10] Factors including gender, the terms of ownership, rural/urban location, historical context, political commitment, and religious affiliation, among others, all interact to ensure that "[t]he identities of place are always unfixed, contested and multiple" (Massey, p. 5). I now offer two case studies which explore how "the identities of place" are at issue in two texts by seventeenth-century women: Magdalen Lloyd, a Welshwoman who wrote a number of letters home from domestic service in London in the 1670s and 1680s; and a Quaker, Elizabeth Hooton, who addressed to members of her religious community powerful accounts of her travels in New England.

*   *   *

Magdalen Lloyd grew up in the countryside near Wrexham in north Wales, and like many young women from rural Britain, she set off to London in search of domestic work. Between July 1674 and March 1682, she wrote regular letters to her cousin Thomas Edwards, a senior member of the household staff at Chirk Castle, detailing her experiences in service and reflecting on the impact of her work on her life.[11] She moved between "places"—to use the contemporary, and highly over-determined, term for a job of domestic work—in London and in Tooting (at that time a small village a few miles south of London), though in November 1675 she was in Wrexham, apparently between places, and in the summer of 1680 she again returned to Wales, this time for a more extended stay. Magdalen Lloyd's movements over those eight years reveal the extent to which the history of domestic service is an aspect of the history of internal rural–urban migration and international migration.[12] In the seventeenth century, servants—most of them female migrants from the country—formed a very large part of the population of London. Though service could, as Theresa McBride argues, be a modernizing influence facilitating the movement of the rural poor into a world able to offer them upward social and economic mobility, Magdalen's story reveals a more complex, and often more precarious, set of relations between rural and urban, place of origin and migratory destination.[13] Endlessly anxious about the precariousness of her employment and the risks of being without a place, Magdalen is sharply conscious of the material and social factors that affect her job prospects, remarking at different moments both that "This contry is soe proud yt wan shall not have a good place except ye have good close," and that "one Must Make good frinds afore ye can have a place."[14] Yet her possession of marketable skills and territorial knowledge make her confident about her employability—"I doe not fear but yt I may have anufe of places being yt I am wunst in seris and am acquainted with this contry"[15]—and that in turn gives her sufficient economic confidence to contemplate borrowing money in order to cement her ties to north Wales by purchasing agricultural land there. Her story thus foregrounds the extent to which women's lives are lived at the site of complex intersections between gender, paid work, migration, social status, and personal life—issues that remain of crucial concern for feminist geographers and historians.[16]

Magdalen Lloyd's letters complicate Leonore Davidoff's claim that most ordinary women in the pre-modern era experienced "a lifetime of personal subordination in private homes,"[17] moving from childhood in the paternal home, via service, to the marital home. The letters suggest that Magdalen perceived herself not as subordinate to a series of others, but rather as bound to them by a range of ties of mutual obligation and care, relationships which could both foster and hinder autonomy. The pains of displacement from the familial home and the migrant's nostalgia for the place left behind are frequently articulated, though it is the webs of emotional relationship rather than the places themselves that are the focus of Magdalen's yearning for home. Her parents lived separately, and her father, far from being a dominant patriarch, is a shadowy figure. Her strongest emotional ties are to her mother, and she repeatedly expresses her distress at her inability to make the considerable journey from London to north Wales: "My dayly prayers is That my god will Bee plest to Lett me she my mother afore she dyes."[18] The letters give a fascinating insight into the gendered difficulties of managing spatial separation: when Magdalen wants to send a small parcel to a Welsh relative, she is frustrated by multiple material obstacles: "my mrs gave mee a loan to goe to London with her as for a nigh but I had noe acquainttans for to enquire for ye drovers if I might hear from Wals."[19] As places of work and of personal life, the London households where Magdalen experienced herself both as subordinate to her employer and as subject to her quasi-familial care mixed kin and others, raising concerns about intimacy and separateness that are negotiated in her writing. The painful intertwining of the psychic and the economic in situations of domestic work where "control is bound up with relations of obligation . . ., responsibility, love and desire"[20] are powerfully articulated when Magdalen, concerned about her future in the face of her employer's illness, remarks, "if I stay tell my mrs is ded I am sure I shall not gett 10 pound by it for I know see loves mee better then any servant yt ever see had: but I canot live by love."[21] Such an awareness of the tensions between the emotional and financial realities of her life made Magdalen acutely aware of her dependence on others, and the need to sustain and nurture her relationship with her primary patron, Mr Thomas, who was a friend of her cousin and occupied a senior role in service in a London household, is a recurrent theme in the letters: "I have not any body yels to provid a place for me but him he promis faithfull to doe any thing that lise in his power for me but a word from you when you writ to him wod doe noe harm onely yt he may enquire sum time after mee being I have noe acquainttans."[22] But she is also pleased to be able to reciprocate, when time and experience have established her in the London networks of patronage and mutual aid which were crucial to domestic workers: "I have a bove 6 yt promis mee faithfully to doe ther indevour and ye furst Place yt falls out in most part of whit hall your frind shall bee sure of it."[23]

Despite her anxieties about the difficulty of getting away and the hazards of travel, over the eight years spanned by the corpus of letters, Magdalen moves several times between Wales and London, and while dwelling in each place employs the exchange of letters and oral gossip to maintain human connections despite geographical separation. She also sustains a distinct sense of Welsh identity: her social contacts in London are primarily with other Welsh migrants, and her always implicit desire to return is made explicit in her efforts to purchase land in Wales. Expressing to Thomas her views about the domestic arrangements of acquaintances in their home region, she says: "it had Bin Better for him to mary one in his one contry I wod not goe to live A mongs them if ye wod give mee 20 pound."[24] Here we glimpse a strong sense of local or regional identity which is a recurrent feature of Magdalen's letters, and of her sense not merely of Welshness, but of belonging to a very specific location within Wales, which grounds the value system in terms of which she assesses her own and her acquaintances' behavior. The extent to which this identification as Welsh serves as a source of strength among the vulnerabilities of a young migrant woman's life is vividly illustrated in the single letter not addressed to Thomas. In September 1680, Magdalen wrote to one Mr Tompson care of a London lawyer, rejecting in no uncertain terms a proposal he had recently made to her, and insisting that she preferred the relative independence of work to the dependence that would be her inevitable lot if she married: "I have noe whear to goe but to serviss and I like yt soe well yt I will not Bee kept by you."[25] She concludes with a postscript: "if you intent to make A dying of it be sure to leave A nuff for both your doughters to mourn for you: if you wod dye for An engliss woman you wod have credit: But not for A wells woman." Wittily turning the relative cultural and economic inferiority of the Welsh to good advantage, Magdalen improvises an alternative cultural geography that allows her to assert a distinctive and unexpected voice and set of values.

* * *

The tension between personal identifications and values and larger social structures is also central to my second case-study, based on the accounts which English Quaker Elizabeth Hooton composed of traumatic experiences of captivity and travel in New England and the Caribbean. Intertwining religious faith with distinctive understandings of place and community to represent the experience of travel in New England in complex ways, Elizabeth Hooton writes of ordeals in which her identity as an Englishwoman and Christian was brought into question and reaffirmed. Women's travel writing has been an important source for feminist historical geography.[26] Like many other contributors to the genre, Hooton makes sense of her encounters with unfamiliar places and the people who inhabit them through volatile, unstable processes of othering, in which a number of factors, among which religion is pre-eminent, interact.[27]

Hooton does not write with a geographical sensibility: her account of her travels frames them less as a journey than as a narrative of the endurance of trauma and the accomplishment of a communitarian spiritual obligation. Frequently, she passes over her epic journeys almost without comment, blithely noting what must have been weeks if not months of arduous voyaging: "So we tooke shipping & went to Barbados & afterwards was moved to returne to New Engl^d againe" (p. 32). The experience and mode of travel itself become of interest only when they are shaped by the religious purpose of the journey, and by the political and spiritual meanings engendered by the hostility of the Quakers' enemies. For example, Hooton relates that because any ship that carries a Quaker from Old to New England would incur a £100 fine, she and her traveling companion, Joan Broksopp, had to sail to Virginia and then travel to Boston overland, "which was a dangerous voyage" entailing "a hard passage" (31). Similarly, a familiar trope of travel writing, the traveler's reliance on hospitality and its celebration as a value that enables transcultural solidarities, is addressed in a highly politicized manner. Hospitality is both threatened by the persecution of Quakers, so that on arrival at Boston "there was no house to receive us as we knew of by reason of their fines," and vindicated by means of solidarity among Friends, as one woman does take them in under cover of darkness (31). The term Quakers themselves prefer as a designation of their community, "Friends," itself inscribes the value of hospitality, and encounters with Friends in this particular strong sense serve to chart Hooton's travels in New England. In Boston she laments that "the Jaylour & his wife being filled full of cruelty, they would not let us come neare to the prison to see our friends" (31); in fact, instead of succoring their colleagues, the two women are brought before the Governor and threatened with imprisonment, for they are in a territory where merely to be a Quaker "was crime enough to commit us to prison without any just offence of lawe" (31).

On two occasions, Hooton was violently expelled from a Puritan settlement, describing these experiences in terms which precisely parallel many key motifs of the influential early American genre of the Indian captivity narrative. Hooton describes being

> driven out of their Jurisdiction by men & horses armed with swords and staffes & weapons of warre who went alonge with us neire two dayes journey in the willderness, & there they left us towards the night amongst the great rivers & many wilde beasts yt useth to devoure & yt night we lay in the woods without any victuals, but a fewe biskets yt we brought with us which we soaked in the water, so did the Lord help & deliver us & one caried another through the waters & we escaped their hands.
>
> (32)

This account closely resembles Mary Rowlandson's repeated references to being forced into the wilderness by Native Americans and sustained there by God in her immensely influential and widely read captivity narrative *The Soveraignty and Goodness of God . . . Being a Narrative of the Captivity and Restauration of Mrs. Mary Rowlandson.*[28] Similar tropes were used by radical Protestants in the British Isles to express a sense of spiritual exile or alienation from the worldly location where they found themselves: Scottish Covenantor Katherine Collace lamented that for "want of public ordinances and fellowship" her marital home at Ross, in the north of Scotland in the 1650s, "was nothing but a vast howling wilderness."[29] Thus the American landscape is saturated with European meaning in these examples. The notion of wilderness at such moments does not connote unspoiled nature; rather it evokes biblical precedents such as the wanderings of the Israelites and the temptation of Jesus, in order to map a literal and spiritual site of desolation and struggle. The forest likewise is a place of danger and otherness in the early modern European cultural imaginary. These two threatening zones are the terrain that Indian captives must invariably traverse, and the dangerous animals, rivers to be crossed, sleeplessness, and inadequate food evoked by Hooton are all tropes that recur frequently in captivity narratives. There is one key difference here though, which is that the Quakers are being expelled from English jurisdiction within which they are already positioned as disruptive strangers, rather than being led from their homes into Indian territory. This refocusing of the journey's direction and motive gives a different form and meaning to the whole account, which instead of finding its happy ending in return, as captivity narratives characteristically do, concludes with deliverance achieved through exodus, symbolized by the triumphant crossing of the waters in which the Quakers assist each other, showing the value of the community of the same in defiance of the other, and echoing a central trope of liberation in Christian tradition.[30]

Hooton is vulnerable to these experiences because she has un-settled herself, voluntarily embracing the Quaker ethos of travel and elective nomadism for the sake of her religious commitment. On several occasions Hooton is "whip[ped] for a wandring vagabond Quaker," including, in a vividly realized moment, a whipping with "a handful of willow rods at Watertown on a cold frosty morning" (41). In the classically paradoxical tactic used by settled societies everywhere to expel the disturbing presence of the nomad, each time the wandering vagabond Quakers come into conflict with the colonial authorities, they are moved on—forced into further mobility, but deprived of control over the direction and mode of movement. The conventional relations between English settlers and Native Americans are destabilized in Hooton's text, perhaps in part because this mobility gives her a certain equivalence or resemblance to Indians in the eyes of her New England Christian adversaries. Hooton herself does not have an interpretive framework that would enable her to disentangle the relations of otherness that shape these dynamics: thus she celebrates Indian hospitality extended to her in the face of European persecution, without fully realizing that the shared experience of such persecution might motivate the nomadic Indians' generosity to her:

thus have they [i.e. the Puritans] used us English people, as Vagabond Rogues & wandring Quak[rs] wch had not a dwelling place wch were true borne English people of their own Nation, yet had ye Indians wch were barbarous savage people, wch neither knew God nor Christ in any profession have been willing to receive us into their Wigwams, or houses, when these professo[rs] would murther us.

(44–5)

Early modern writings about cultural difference obsessively position the contrast between settled and nomadic peoples as a crucial boundary between civility and barbarism. The travel writings of Elizabeth Hooton trouble this boundary between civility and barbarism, culture and nature. Indeed, they trouble the notion that such a boundary could be securely installed. Rather than being a frontier across which civilization can be steadily rolled out, the wilderness in the writings of Hooton and other European women in early America, such as Mary Rowlandson or Sister Marie de l'Incarnation,[31] might more usefully be understood as a different kind of liminal zone, a borderland in the sense influentially elaborated by Gloria Anzaldúa, "a vague and undetermined place created by the emotional residue of an unnatural boundary, [which] is in a constant state of transition."[32] Thinking of seventeenth-century New England—or other zones of the early modern British Atlantic world—as a borderland in this sense can enable us to replace the notions of frontier and wilderness traditionally beloved of certain traditional kinds of American studies with more volatile and complex understandings of geopolitical and emotional territories as debatable lands, which the travel writings Elizabeth Hooton can help us to achieve. As Sara Ahmed emphasizes, all places may be liminal. The borderland is not necessarily a spatially specific and delimited zone; rather, any place can be made into a space of transition and instability through the practices of the people who inhabit it and move through it.[33]

As the example of Elizabeth Hooton demonstrates, the critical possibilities opened up by these new cultural geographies complement and extend the lessons of postcolonial theory, and the study of early modern Europeans' journeys to strange places and encounters with cultural others, which have for some time been teaching us to be sensitive to the power relations encoded in travel and the encounters it begets.[34] Under the influence of such work, the critical use of spatial metaphors to delineate patriarchal territories and map social and literary margins has begun to enable new analyses of women's cultural participation and production in various times and places. An awareness of the over-determined cultural politics of travel leads in turn to reflection on the factors that shape the meanings of space and place for those who remain at home, and the circumstances that variously produce either stasis or displacement. The choice between staying and going is never simple, and feminist geographers have done much to reveal the complex inter-implication of here and there, of home and away, of this place and that, as Alison Blunt and Ann Varley argue in relation to the category and space—just as crucial to feminist geography as it is to women's history and the study of women's writing—of the home:

> Rather than view the home as a fixed, bounded and confining location, geographies of home traverse scales from the domestic to the global in both material and symbolic ways. The everyday practices, material cultures and social relations that shape home on a domestic scale resonate far beyond the household. Geographical research on subjects as diverse as imperial domesticity, anti-colonial nationalism, diasporic resettlement, domestic architecture and design, and work within the global domestic economy, shows how household geographies are intimately bound up with national and transnational geographies.[35]

The production of knowledge about places, spaces, and the people who inhabit them is evidently not a neutral matter, as Andrew MacRae succinctly reminds us in summarizing the transformation of geographical knowledge that took place in the early modern period: "mapping the land brings power with knowledge."[36]

This chapter has suggested some ways in which the study of early modern women's writing might benefit from being situated in relation to more expansive, detailed, and complex cultural geographies of the period, enabling its scholars to draw new maps of a world we are still coming to know. Studying early modern women's writing as a textual inscription of the fractured, unstable cultural geographies of the period allows us to glimpse the interplay between gendered experiences in particular locations and in the wider, interconnected Atlantic world. Ironically, however, the insights thus generated reveal the need to complicate the spatialized vocabulary, influenced by geographical ways of making sense of the world, of centers and margins or peripheries, that has characterized much writing about processes of geo-cultural transformation and nation-building in the early modern British Atlantic world. Women's writing about place, belonging, and dislocation cannot be adequately analyzed within existing state-centered models for making sense of the geopolitical and geo-cultural changes that reshaped the early modern English-speaking Atlantic world in which its citizens participated in a wide variety of ways, not limited to their interpellation by the emergent British state. Feminist scholars need to sketch a richer picture, showing both what is distinctive about women's experience and their writing of it, and how that distinctiveness gives us a different sense of what the landscape as a whole is like—a difference of view on an all too familiar landscape that has the potential to enable revisionary scholarship in the broader field of Renaissance literature. As the resurgence of geographical metaphors in this last claim indicates, the languages and practices of critical geography have much to offer Renaissance studies.

Feminist geographies and feminist studies are, separately and conjointly, finding ways of articulating more complex and multifaceted understandings of the relations between space and time, places and histories. To invoke a politics of location is to insist on the consequentiality of such relations, but also their contingency, as Adrienne Rich does when she remarks, in the essay from which my title is derived, that "a place on the map is also a place in history"—one in which a woman is "created and trying to create."[37] The politics of location in Rich's account is powerfully formative but not wholly determining: though profoundly shaped by the historical and geographical place in which they find themselves, women do have some scope to choose to take up different positions in those changing landscapes. And in doing so, they reveal the limits and imperfections of the too familiar maps of the terrains we thought we knew, and insist on the need to re-examine and redraw them.

Notes

1. Katharine A. Walker, "The Military Activities of Charlotte de la Trémouille, Countess of Derby, during the Civil War and Interregnum," *Northern History* 38:1 (March 2001): 47–64; Angela Bourke, Siobhán Kilfeather, Maria Luddy, Margaret

Mac Curtain, Gerardine Meaney, Máirín Ní Dhonnchadha, Mary O'Dowd, and Clair Wills, eds., *The Field Day Anthology of Irish Writing, V, Women's Writings and Traditions* (Cork: Cork University Press in association with Field Day, 2002), 25–7; Elizabeth Wade White, *Anne Bradstreet: "The Tenth Muse"* (New York: Oxford University Press, 1971); Moira Ferguson, "Seventeenth-century Quaker Women: Displacement, Colonialism, and Anti-slavery Discourse," in Gerald Maclean, ed., *Culture and Society in the Stuart Restoration: Literature, Drama, History* (Cambridge: Cambridge University Press, 1995), 221–40, 228.

2. Steve Pile, "Introduction: Opposition, Political Identities, and Spaces of Resistance," in Steve Pile and Michael Keith, eds., *Geographies of Resistance* (London: Routledge, 1997), 1–32.

3. Sara Blair, "Cultural Geography and the Place of the Literary," *American Literary History* 10:3 (Fall 1998): 544-67; 547.

4. Mona Domosh and Karen M. Morin, "Travels with Feminist Historical Geography," *Gender, Place and Culture* 10:3 (2003: 257–64; 260.

5. On the household, see Marion Wynne-Davies, "'My Seeled Chamber and Dark Parlour Room': the English Country House and Renaissance Women Dramatists," in S. P. Cerasano and Marion Wynne-Davies, eds., *Readings in Renaissance Women's Drama: Criticism, History and Performance, 1594–1998* (London: Routledge, 1998), 60–8; on the convent, see my "'For virgin buildings oft brought forth': Fantasies of Convent Sexuality," in Nicole Pohl and Rebecca D'Monté, eds., *Female Communities 1600–1800: Literary Visions and Cultural Realities* (Basingstoke: Macmillan, 2000); and on urban literary culture, Paula McDowell, *The Women of Grub Street: Press, Politics and Gender in the London Literary Marketplace, 1678–1730* (Oxford: Oxford University Press, 1998).

6. Doreen Massey, "General Introduction," *Space, Place and Gender* (Cambridge: Polity Press, 1994), pp. 1–16, 5.

7. On Clifford's spatial politics, see Elizabeth V. Chew, "Si(gh)ting the Mistress of the House: Anne Clifford and Architectural Space," in Susan Shifrin, ed., *Women as Sites of Culture: Women's Roles in Cultural Formation from the Renaissance to the Twentieth Century* (Burlington, VT: Ashgate, 2002).

8. Katherine Austen, "On the Situation of Highbury," in BL Add. MS 4454, cited here from *The Oxford Book of Early Modern Women's Verse*, ed. Jane Stevenson and Peter Davidson; contributing eds. Meg Bateman, Kate Chedgzoy, and Julie Sanders (Oxford: Oxford University Press, 2001), 315–16.

9. Quoted from Suzanne Trill, Kate Chedgzoy, and Melanie Osborne, eds., *Lay by Your Needles, Ladies, Take the Pen: English Women's Writing, 1500–1700* (London: Edward Arnold, 1997), 144.

10. Gillian Rose, Nicky Gregson, Jo Foord, Sophie Bowlby, Claire Dwyer, Sarah Holloway, Nina Laurie, Avril Maddrell, and Tracy Skelton, "Introduction," in *Women and Geography Study Group, Feminist Geographies: Explorations in Diversity and Difference* (London: Longman, 1997), 1–13; 8.

11. National Library of Wales, Chirk Castle MSS and Documents, Group E.

12. Bridget Hill, *Servants: English Domestics in the Eighteenth Century* (Oxford: Clarendon Press, 1996), 3.

13. Theresa McBride, *The Domestic Revolution: The Modernization of Household Service in England and France 1820–1920* (New York: Holmes and Meier, 1976).

14. Tooting, September 23, 1676, E3352; Tooting, December 2, 1678, E3730.

15. Tooting, September 23, 1676, E3352.

16. Barbara Ehrenreich and Arlie Russell Hochschild, eds., *Global Woman: Nannies, Maids and Sex Workers in the New Economy* (New York: Metropolitan Books, 2003).
17. Leonore Davidoff, "Mastered for Life: Servant and Wife in Victorian and Edwardian England," in Davidoff, *Worlds Between: Historical Perspectives on Gender and Class* (Cambridge: Polity, 1995), 18–40; 21.
18. E4140, Tooting April 7, 1678.
19. E6211, Tooting November 6, 1676.
20. Linda McDowell and Joanne P. Sharp, "Gendering Work: Editors' Introduction," in McDowell and Sharp, *Space, Gender, Knowledge: Feminist Readings* (London: Arnold, 1997), 319–25; 323.
21. E3714, Tooting July 24, 1679.
22. E6211, Tooting November 6, 1676.
23. 3730, Tooting December 1678.
24. N.pl., n.d., E914.
25. E5010.
26. Alison Blunt, *Travel, Gender, and Imperialism: Mary Kingsley and West Africa* (New York: Guilford, 1994).
27. On the importance of "othering" as an analytical category in the new cultural geographies, see Women and Geography Study Group, *Feminist Geographies*, pp. 9–10, 78–9.
28. First published in 1682, Rowlandson's narrative is widely reprinted; see, for example, Carla Mulford, ed., with Angela Vietto and Amy E. Winans, *Early American Writings* (New York: Oxford University Press, 2002), 307–28.
29. Katherine Collace, *Memoirs or Spiritual Exercises of Mistress Ross. Written with her Own Hand* (Edinburgh, 1753), in David George Mullan, *Women's Life Writing in Early Modern Scotland: Writing the Evangelical Self, c. 1670–c.1730* (Burlington, VT: Ashgate, 2003), 45.
30. See my discussion of the liberatory symbolism of crossing Jordan in "Region, Religion, and Sexuality: 'Pilgrim through this barren land',", in Richard Phillips, David Shuttleworth, and Diane Watt, eds., *Decentering Sexualities* (London: Routledge, 2000).
31. Natalie Zemon Davis, "New Worlds: Marie de l'Incarnation," in Davis, *Women on the Margins: Three Seventeenth-Century Lives* (Cambridge, MA: Harvard University Press, 1995), 63–139.
32. *Borderlands/La Frontera: The New Mestiza* (San Francisco: Aunt Lute Books, 1987), 3.
33. Sara Ahmed, *Strange Encounters: Embodied Others in Post-Coloniality* (London: Routledge, 2000).
34. Ivo Kamps and Jyotsna G. Singh, eds., *Travel Knowledges: European "Discoveries" in the Early Modern Period* (New York: Palgrave, 2001).
35. Alison Blunt and Ann Varley, "Geographies of Home," *Cultural Geographies* 11 (2004): 3–6; 3.
36. Andrew McRae, "Female Mobility and National Space in Restoration England: The Travel Journals of Celia Fiennes," in Paul Salzman and Jo Wallwork, eds., *Women Writing 1550–1750*, special book issue of *Meridian*, 18(1) (2001): 105–14; 107.
37. Adrienne Rich, "Notes toward a Politics of Location," *Blood, Bread and Poetry: Selected Prose 1979–1985* (London: Virago, 1986), 212.

8

The "diffrence... in degree":[1] Social Rank and Gendered Expression

Kimberly Anne Coles

> It is... the deconstructive view that keeps me resisting an essen-
> tialist freezing of the concepts of gender, race, and class. I look
> rather at the repeated agenda of the situational production of those
> concepts and our complicity in such a production.
>
> Gayatri Spivak, "Feminism and Critical Theory"

The epigraph to this chapter indicates the extent to which feminists have
never been single-axis thinkers. But it is not—or not only—deconstruction
that prevents the essentialist freeze in current feminist inquiry concerned
with the early modern period. The archival project in which feminist critics
have been engaged over the course of twenty-five years has produced an
increased awareness of the material contexts of printing and publishing, a
more complex understanding of how texts were produced and circulated,
and a greater sensitivity to the political potential of textual editing.[2] Such
attention to the production of written culture has also renewed interest
in how the texts themselves were generated—what women read and how
they remodeled this material in their own writing. Further, in revisiting
questions of intertextuality, current feminist criticism has resisted an atom-
ized approach. It has therefore examined women's works in terms of a
wider transmission—attending as much to the ways in which women's texts
mediate and circulate cultural discourse as to the relationship between individual writer and work.[3]

This shift in emphasis is appropriate in the context of a period in which
imitation is an index of literary value, and where literary gestures of this kind
participate within a network of cultural meanings. The shift also underscores
an historicist practice that seeks to situate women's writing within the local
and particular context that produced it. Such an approach demands that we
read women's works in juxtaposition to other contemporary (male) writings
in order to analyze the tensions that act on their composition and material

production.[4] It also insists that we look at "woman" not only as a social actor, but also as a discursive sign—one that could be deployed by members of either sex.[5] One of the benefits of an intertextual method that considers women's writing in the context of a cultural circulation of ideas is that it registers female voice in terms of its representation. It understands gender in women's texts—as in men's—as constructed; perhaps more importantly, in the relay between the texts of men and women, it captures a moment of construction.

While a good deal of critical work has been done on how women were represented— in literature, conduct books, and on the English stage—there has been less analysis applied to how they represented themselves.[6] Danielle Clarke suggests that this is because "the particular investments and aims of feminist criticism are such that there is little interest in assuming the reversibility or flexibility of [the] paradigm" that the gender of a text does not (or not necessarily) correspond to the author's biological sex.[7] Gynocriticism initiated a tendency to read women's texts for gender-inflected markings that affirm personal biography and biology, and while this strategy has proved its value in both critical and political terms, it has also proved hard to overthrow.[8] This deposition seems even more difficult when dealing with texts that appear particularly pliable to gynocritical readings—where the sex of the author coheres with the speaker's gender. But in falling susceptible to such readings, we overlook the extent to which gender is performed within the text—part of a rhetorical strategy—for purposes other than self-expression.

The critical work which depicts Aemilia Lanyer as a "Seventeenth-Century Feminist Voice" is positively abundant.[9] I am not trying to disparage this body of criticism (from which I have benefited so much); nor am I suggesting that gender has gone untreated in relation to Lanyer's long poem, *Salve Deus Rex Judæorum*.[10] But while a number of articles have considered the gendered inscriptions of Lanyer's text, the gendered performance within the work itself in the context of poetic circulation and competition has remained, for the most part, unexplored.[11] While the proto-feminist appeals of *Salve Deus* are compelling to modern feminist readers, we need to be alert to the artifice of the voice that emerges from the poem. We cannot regard the proto-feminist voice of *Salve Deus* as authentic—a reliable index of "real" expression—but must instead understand its constructed nature in terms of the commercial economy in which it was developed and circulated.[12] While it is true that the argument of the poem stands in opposition to patriarchy, and that it is seductive to view this poetic positioning as representative of a personal stance, we must allow that the simulated nature of poetic composition at least suggests a verbal pose. My reading sees the pro-feminine expression of Lanyer's poetic text as a rhetorical tactic—one developed in contradistinction to male poets with whom she was in direct financial competition—that amounts to a marketing device.

It would be wrong to argue that in the case of the *Salve Deus* the biolo-gical subject asserts no claims on the text. But there are other pressures—market forces—that drive its formulations. There is some considerable yield to reading Lanyer's work in the context of the marketplace—and against the poets with whom she was competing. The practice locates rather precisely the strains of cultural discourse that Lanyer's text responds to; it reminds us of the sorts of imitative gestures that were a stock of literary circulation; and in measuring the gap between the poem and its paradigm (or source text), it allows us to view a specific instance of transmission and transform-ation. Concrete examples of such transference reveal a good deal about the fashioning of the gendered voice itself, for the creation of that voice occurs within the space between source (male) and text (female). Further, they provide object lessons in how the realities of financial need—or, put differ-ently, the circumstances of class position—actually compel the performance of gender within a text.

The dedicatory apparatus of *Salve Deus*, if one includes its appended country house poem "The Description of Cooke-ham" (which is a homage to Margaret Clifford and her daughter Anne), consumes over two-thirds of the text. Lanyer's insertion of herself into the patronage system is not subtle. But the sorority that she depicts in the collection of poems to aris-tocratic women that preface the work is fictitious. What is more, Lanyer is acutely aware of the social divisions that the poems themselves elide.[13] The ideal female community that she imagines is, rather, a clever means of self-promotion. As Lorna Hutson rightly argues, "patron–client relations cannot be forged without the competitive self-advertising that an open market of intellectual ability demands."[14] One way that Lanyer carves out her own space within this market is (obviously) to invoke a network of female patronage. But in order to garner the favor of rich women, she must prove that her own poetic services are indispensable. The nature of her service and the way that she represents it are the subjects that will take up the rest of this chapter. But we need first to look at how she situates her work commercially.

Lanyer's market savvy can be fully appreciated when we notice how she positions herself against other devotional poets similarly engaged in the pursuit of patronage. In spite of her claim that it was uncommon to read "A Womans writing of diuinest things" (a3r), the most unusual feature of her literary engagement is not her subject (divine things were the most common subjects of literary treatment by women in the early modern period), but her subject-position. Her pursuit of a professional writing career was contingent on her class status, and enabled by a standard of educa-tional training that was unusual for a woman of her social position.[15] The circumstance left her with only male competitors, and the two most obvious were Nicholas Breton and Abraham Fraunce.[16] Breton was perhaps the most popular contemporary poet of the late sixteenth and early seventeenth centuries—and certainly was the most prolific.[17] Fifteen of his religious works were printed, and of these, ten are versified.[18] Of the eight poetic works that bear dedications, four are dedicated to noble women and two to women of upper rank.[19] Breton clearly saw women as his most viable audience for devotional verse, and noble women his most likely patrons. With nine prefatory dedications to noble women, and one to "vertuous Ladies in generall," Lanyer exceeds Breton's example. But the generic form in which she was writing—devotional poetry—was female-identified in terms of the marketplace. The dedications of Breton and Fraunce make this clear.[20] The excessive nature of Lanyer's self-promotion, then, highlights the possible advantage that she felt she had as a woman writing in the service of other women.

While Fraunce and Giles Fletcher both composed verse narratives on the subject of the Passion, the poem with which Lanyer is most obviously engaged is Breton's *Countesse of Penbrookes passion*.[21] If Lanyer's *ottava rima* does not duplicate Breton's stanzaic pattern (six iambic pentameter lines rhymed ababcc) it certainly follows this structure more closely than that of other contemporary textual models that treat the subject of the Passion (Fletcher, for example, uses an *ottava rima* stanza, but the rhyme scheme, abacccdd, is very different). The space afforded here does not allow for a detailed exposition of the stylistic patterns and verbal echoes that suggest poetic imitation. But it is the correspondence between how the two works handle their subject that is most indicative of Breton's influence. Breton's poem is part of a group of texts ranging across genres, from printed sermons to literary works, that demonstrate a debt to Calvin's reading of the Passion in his *Harmony of the Evangelists* (1584).[22] *The Countesse of Penbrookes passion*, therefore, provides the segue to other Calvinist passion narratives which *Salve Deus*, as Barbara Bowen observes, "is in dialogue with."[23] The rhetoric of identification, in which the trials of the elect are conflated with the sufferings of Christ—in much the same way that Margaret Clifford, Lanyer's chief patron, is invited to commune with Christ in the poem—is also a feature of the narratives that are explicitly informed by Calvin's representation of the Passion in his biblical exegesis. Of course, this is classic Protestant typology. But the passion narratives that draw on Calvin depict a difficult relationship between suffering and responsibility. The reader/author, who is situated in the text as a form of Christ, also participates in his torture.

[T]he texts make it clear that if the torturer is the demonic other, he is also the reader. The reader must *identify* with the torturer. The notion that since Christ died for our sins we are all responsible for the Crucifixion originates early in Christian thought, but the Calvinist passion narratives intensify this complicity by merging the position of the reader with that of the torturer. Our sins become not simply the antecedent cause of Christ's sacrifice; rather, we find ourselves sucked into the scene as participants in the acts of cruelty.[24]

Identification becomes self-flagellation. One can immediately perceive the psychomachia of Donne's Holy Sonnet 7 ("Spit in my face you Jewes") in such a reading. But Breton's poem participates in this psychology as well:

> I saw [Christ] faultlesse, yet I did offend him,
> I saw him wrong'd and yet did not excuse him,
> I sawe his foes, yet sought not to defend him,
> I had his blessinges, yet I did abuse him.
>> but was it myne, or my forefathers deade?
>> whose ere it was, it makes my hart to bleede.
>
> (fol. 62r)[25]

The allocation of blame is the locus of Lanyer's radical reinterpretation of the Passion. She takes the central question of the Calvinist narratives ("was it myne, or my forefathers deade?") and answers it squarely: the responsibility lies with men. As Bowen notes, Lanyer's text is "in dialogue with" the Passion narratives, not in concert with them; which is to say that Lanyer both co-opts the form—culled from Breton and other sources—and corrupts it.

In the *Harmony of the Evangelists*, Calvin is absorbed by the psychosis that produced Christ's torments.[26] He focuses on the irrationality of the crime: the participants in the Crucifixion are "more stupid than brute beasts," having been gripped by the "giddiness with which God intoxicates the reprobate, after having long contended with their malice."[27] Consequently, Christ's enemies are rendered in inhuman terms, as animals overcome by fury: they are in the "darkness of . . . rage," "bewitched," and "intoxicated."[28] They are "filled with a malicious hatred," "seized with astonishing madness," and consumed by an "insatiable cruelty."[29] This depiction is imported into Breton's poem:

> Shall I not curse those hatefull hellishe feindes,
> that led the world to worke such wickednesse?
> and hate all them that had not bene his freindes,
> but followed on that worke of wretchednesse?
>
> (fol. 65v)

But the terminology also pervades Lanyer's representation of Christ's trial and execution.

> The Iewish wolues, that did our Sauiour bite;
> For now they vse all meanes they can deuise

To beat downe truth, and goe against all right.

. . .

The chiefest Hel-hounds of this hatefull crew,
Rose vp to aske what answere he could make.

(C3v)[30]

Calvin focuses on the insane malevolence of Christ's persecutors because he wants to underscore that they *knew* who Christ was—they recognized him as the Savior—and crucified him anyway.[31] "The circumstances of *an armed multitude* having been sent by *the chief priests*," Calvin writes, "and of *a captain and band* having been obtained by request from Pilate, make it evident that an evil conscience wounded and tormented them, so that they did every thing in a state of terror."[32] The emphasis on the collusion of the Jews in a sin against God serves Calvin in his displacement of responsibility. The depictions of a reprobate rabble whose "minds were darkened [by Satan], so that, *seeing they did not see*" are transposed by Calvin onto present-day Christians: "for this will excite in us deeper horror at our sins."[33] The implication is that this spiritual blindness possesses us all, and our sins make us complicit in Christ's death: "All sins resolve into reenactments of the Passion's sadistic violence."[34] As Breton claims: "my deede was cawser of his deathe" (fol. 65r). Lanyer obviously complicates this theory of shared responsibility, but what is equally clear is the extent to which her text is informed by it.

The Calvinist narratives, as Debora Shuger observes, "dwell repeatedly on the shamefulness of Christ's sufferings."[35] In Calvin, the image of Christ's agony becomes the locus of our shame and guilt—literally the picture of our sin.

> For if we are desirous to profit aright by meditating on the death of Christ, we ought to begin with cherishing abhorrence of our sins, *in proportion to the severity of the punishment which he endured.* This will cause us not only to feel displeasure and shame of ourselves, but to be penetrated with deep grief, and therefore to seek the medicine with becoming ardour, and at the same time to experience confusion and trembling.[36]

Consequently, the humiliation of Christ is emphasized in those works informed by Calvin's interpretation. These texts render Christ's degradation through both a loss of actual control over his body and a breakdown of his physical integrity. They therefore tend to focus on bodily fluids, which serve as symbols of Christ's shame.[37] Lanyer highlights the "whipping spurning, tearing of [the] haire" of Christ, and the "bloody sweat" of his dying body (D4v; C3v). Breton emphasizes his subjection, his bleeding injuries, and the tears on his face (fol. 65r [stanza 51], and below). The concentration upon

wounds and gore produces grotesque images that the poems nonetheless
compulsively fix on.

> To see the feete, that trauayled for our goode,
> to see the Handes, that brake that liulye breade,
> to see the Heade, whereon our honor stoode,
> to see the fruite, whereon our spyrite fedd,
>> feete pearc'd, handes bored, and his Heade all bleeding,
>> who doth not dye with such a sorrowe readinge.

> .   .   .   .

> His faultlesse members nayled to the crosse,
> his holye heade was crowned all with thornes,
> his garmentes giuen by lotts to gayne or losse,
> his power derided all with scoffes and scornes,
>> his bodye wounded and his spyrite vexed,
>> to thinke on this, what soule is not perplexed[?]

> (fol. 62r; 63v)

> His joynts dis-joynted, and his legges hang downe,
> His alablaster breast, his bloody side,
> His members torne, and on his Head a Crowne
> Of sharpest Thorns, to satisfie for pride:
> Anguish and Paine doe all his Sences drowne,
> While they his holy garments do divide:
>> His bowells drie, his heart full fraught with grief,
>> Crying to him that yeelds him no reliefe.

> (E3r)

But the degeneration of Christ's body to flesh and fluid is the necessary circumstance for our renewal. Understanding Christ on the cross as
the site of our salvation is of course Christian history and not particular
to Calvin. What is specific to Calvin is the proximity of the images. The
representation of the abject body gives way to the description of our own
transformation:

> The object of all these expressions of contempt [spitting in Christ's face]
> was, to show that nothing was more unlikely than that he should be
> a prince of prophets, who ... was not able even to ward off *blows*. But
> this insolence was turned by the providence of God to a very different
> purpose; for the face of Christ, dishonoured by *spitting* and *blows*, has
> restored to us that image which had been disfigured, and almost effaced,
> by sin.[38]

The face of Christ—bruised, bloodied, and spat on—is reconfigured here as the restoration of God's image in us. It is because of this construction (which is employed repeatedly in the *Harmony of the Evangelists*) that the narratives modeled on Calvin tend to closely juxtapose the radically different images of the man of sorrows and the lover of the Canticles.[39] Like the migration in Calvin's passage from mutilation to splendor, "by mapping the erotic body onto the disfigured one, [these texts] . . . fuse the two images."[40] They also fuse, by extension, the two ideas. In Breton's *Passion*, therefore, Christ's broken body is displaced by a lover's looks:

> Meethinkes I see, and seeinge sighe to see,
> how in his passion patience play'd his parte,
> and in his death, what life he gave to me,
> in my loues sorrowe to releiue my harte.
>
> .   .   .   .   .   .
>
> And lett me see how sweetelye yet he lookes,
> even while the teares are tricklinge downe his face,
> and for my life how well his death he brookes,
> while my deserte was cause of his disgrace.

> (fol. 64v; 65r)

Lanyer also represents the scene at Calvary in "A . . . description of [Christ's] beautie upon the Canticles."

> This is that Bridegroome that appeares so faire,
> So sweet, so louely in his Spouses sight,
> That vnto Snowe we may his face compare,
> His cheeks like skarlet, and his eyes so bright
> As purest Doues that in the riuers are,
> Washed with milke, to giue the more delight;
> His head is likened to the finest gold,
> His curled lockes so beauteous to beholde.

> (F1v)

The similarities between Breton's poem and *Salve Deus*, however, cannot be entirely accounted for with reference to Calvin. While both works respond to Calvin's interpretation of the Crucifixion, the internal parallels between the poems appear to be the result of Lanyer's use of Breton's *Passion* as a paradigm for her own.[41] Of all of the contemporary Passion narratives, in fact, none even remotely bears the likeness to *Salve Deus* as does Breton's passion for the Countess of Pembroke.

As Shuger notes, there are relatively few poetic narratives which concentrate on the Passion produced in England from the mid-sixteenth century to the civil war, and even fewer which employ a Calvinist reading.[42] The problems concerning religious poetry aside, Protestant devotional practice privileged introspection over visualization. Breton is therefore unusual in his repeated treatment of the topic.[43] In adopting his example, then, Lanyer is engaging this specific set of devotional narratives. Obviously, this circumvents the rivalry of secular poets, but it also puts her in direct competition with Nicholas Breton. The similarities between *Salve Deus* and the *Countesse of Penbrookes passion* are sufficiently pronounced not to go unnoticed by noble patrons familiar with Breton's work (such as Pembroke herself). In fact, the resemblance between the two poems invites the comparison— which is to say that it was quite possibly deliberately drawn. By signaling her connection to Breton's work, Lanyer indicates the point of departure for her own.

What she is offering the female patrons who support the endeavors of devotional poets (particularly the Countess of Pembroke, and her primary dedicatee, the Countess of Cumberland) is a response to the religious writing of men. *Salve Deus* reconsiders the evaluation of women within the Calvinist passion narratives. The male descriptions of the Passion tend to write women out of the story; Lanyer's service to her female audience is that she includes them as part of it. In fact, she privileges the female perspective in her revision. The elevation of women as witnesses of Christ in Lanyer's poem goes to the heart of her self-construction as a professional religious poet. The different moral vision of men and women is a theme developed within the *Salve Deus*, and becomes the argument for its value. The poem is premised on the superior capacity of women to perceive Christ.[44] But by advocating the devotional faculties of women, Lanyer also promotes the abilities of the female poet in the genre that she is currently activating. Understanding *Salve Deus* in the context of the Calvinist Passion narratives provides a different inflection from our current apprehension of how Lanyer interprets Christian history.[45] This is because it specifically notices the way in which the poem remodels contemporary discourse on the Passion with an eye toward poetic competition. This throws the motivation behind the gendered constructions in *Salve Deus* into sharp relief.

Lanyer is organizing her work as a counter to male-authored narratives. Breton's *Passion*, like other poems that employ a Calvinist interpretation, is consumed by a sense of shared responsibility with the past ("was it myne, or my forefathers deade?").[46] Lanyer's revision of these stories of crime and punishment similarly focuses on this question, but yields a very different answer. The arrest, trial, and execution of Christ are enacted in *Salve Deus* as a series of mistakes, misnomers, and misreadings of the event. But what is particular about Lanyer's depiction is that it is only the men who misapprehend the scene. The women recognize Jesus as Christ. It is Pontius Pilate's wife who has a dream (Matt. 27: 19), and it is she who sues to Pilate for "her Sauiours life" (C4v). When Christ is led through the streets of Jerusalem:

> First went the Crier with open mouth proclayming
> The heauy sentence of Iniquitie,
> The Hangman next, by his base office clayming
> His right in Hell, where sinners neuer die,
> Carrying the nayles, the people still blaspheming
> Their maker, vsing all impiety;
>> The Thieues attending him on either side,
>> The Serjeants watching, while the women cri'd.

(D4r)

The names of the offices of men give way in the stanza to the only human voices—the cries of distressed women.[47] While the men exhibit incomprehension, the women experience the full horror of the sin that is taking place.

Pilate's wife "speakes for all" women (D2r). She constructs Christ's death as a crime of men, not as a crime of humanity. Rather, she says that Eve's first Fall was a minor stumble in comparison to the second Fall of man which is about to occur. If Eve's action purchased the subordination of women to men,

> Then let vs haue our Libertie againe,
> And challendge to your selues no Sou'raigntie;
> You came not in the world without our paine,
> Make that a barre against your crueltie;
> Your fault beeing greater, why should you disdaine
> Our beeing your equals, free from tyranny?
>> If one weake woman simply did offend,
>> This sinne of yours, hath no excuse, nor end.

(D2r)

The killing of Christ releases women from their subordinate position. Her argument is that men were granted power over women, but have proved inadequate in their use of it. Their moral blindness in this instance is a case in point.[48] She identifies the execution of Christ as an exclusively male activity. If introducing knowledge into the world was women's fault, the Crucifixion is men's—one sin erases the other. But the indeterminacy of the narrative voice is such that it is difficult to tell if it is Pilate's wife who delivers the brief for the end of male domination or if it is Lanyer as omniscient author. (Difficult enough that more than one critical analysis of the poem has suggested that it is Lanyer's voice.[49]) In fact, this collapse is part of the poetic effect.[50] Lanyer claims that Pilate's wife speaks on behalf of all women; by leaving the voice that petitions Pilate so undefined, she opens the possibility of other female voices—or all female voices—arguing in unison.

This produces the effect of all women, regardless of specific time and place (except insofar as it is Christian), suing for their release on the basis of men's greater sin.[51] It further makes the demarcation between past and present unstable. The collapse between the torturers of Christ and present sinners is a feature of the Calvinist passion narratives. The consequence of sin is seen up close—our complicity in Christ's death is emphasized by our actual involvement. As Shuger states, "[a]ll sins resolve into reenactments of the Passion's sadistic violence." In Lanyer's diction as well, the sins of the past are ongoing. But while she does not place contemporary men at the foot of the cross, Lanyer nonetheless suggests that they "Crucify [Christ] daily" by other means.[52] The case for the role of men in the crime of Christ's execution is revisited precisely because the need to argue for women's delivery still persists. Lanyer further implies that the political violence that men practiced upon Christ continues to be exercised upon women.

Throughout *Salve Deus*, women have a special affiliation with Christ.

> To speake one word, nor once to lift his eyes
> Vnto proud *Pilate*, no nor *Herod*, king,
> By all the Questions that they could deuise,
> Could make him answere to no manner of thing;
> Yet these poore women, by their pitious cries
> Did mooue their Lord, their Louer, and their King,
>   To take compassion, turne about, and speake
>   To them whose hearts were ready now to breake.
>
>   (D4r)

Christ is depicted in feminized terms. Elaine Beilin argues that "in her direct praise of Christ, Lanyer actually reveals Him as the true source of feminine virtue."[53] His "owne profession" is described in terms of scripted feminine ideals: "patience, grace, loue, [and] piety" (D4r). His demeanor during interrogation has a feminized aspect: "[Lanyer's] Christ, like the ideal woman of the Puritan manuals, is silent except when induced to speak, and modest and taciturn when he does."[54] He has a special society with women because his relation to male authority is similarly constructed as submissive. He is an impoverished, marginalized, and subordinate figure, and as such shares an experience common to women. The suggestion in Lanyer's poem is that women are able to recognize Christ because his earthly circumstance resonates with their own.[55]

The role of women in Lanyer's Passion narrative is emphasized by the rubrics of its title-page. By contrast, Calvin's exegesis mentions women only once as Christ is led to the site of his execution.[56] But even in Calvin, these women exhibit some signs of faith:

And though [their] faith ... was weak, yet it is probable that there was a hidden seed of piety, which afterwards in due time produced fruit. Yet their *lamentation* served to condemn the wicked and shocking cruelty of the men, who had conspired with the scribes and priests to put Christ to death.[57]

He goes on, however, to use them to presage the destruction of Jerusalem. Consequently, women tend to be ignored in the treatments of the Passion which follow Calvin, or they serve only to highlight God's retribution. But Lanyer turns this passing mention in Calvin into an extended episode (in fact, the implication here that women resisted the deadly operations of men forms the basis of her argument). The manner in which the voices of women overcome the administrative noise of men has already been noticed. But Lanyer further develops Calvin's hint of a superior spiritual insight.

> Most blessed daughters of Ierusalem,
> Who found such fauour in your Sauiors sight,
> To turne his face when you did pitie him;
> Your tearefull eyes, beheld his eies more bright;
> Your Faith and Loue vnto such grace did clime,
> To haue reflection from this Heau'nly Light:
>   Your Eagles eyes did gaze against this Sunne.

>   (D4v)

The "Eagles eyes" of the women stand in contrast to the "Owly eies" of Caiphas (C4r) and the blindness of the men. Women not only possess a clearer moral vision, but also unfailingly recognize who and what Christ is. Such certain sight is inevitably given through faith.

Obviously, this acuity holds special privileges for the female poet. Like the voice of Pilate's wife which "speakes for all" women, knowledge of Christ is not confined to a historical time and place. If the logic of Lanyer's poem insists on the superior spiritual awareness of women, then she, as a woman, is able to perceive (and depict) the Passion of Christ with greater clarity than her male counterparts. This is not simply a conclusion inferred by logical extension; it is one explicitly drawn in the body of the text. Lanyer offers Christ's emblematic body to the female readership of her poem. "This," she tells the Countess of Cumberland, "with the eie of Faith thou maist behold," and proceeds to unveil the scene (E3r).

> Blacke as a Raven in her blackest hew;
> His lips like skarlet threeds, yet much more sweet
> Than is the sweetest hony dropping dew,
> Or hony combes, where all the Bees doe meet;
> Yea, he is constant, and his words are true,

His cheeks are beds of spices, flowers sweet;
His lips like Lillies, dropping downe pure mirrhe,
Whose loue, before all worlds we doe preferre.

(F1v)

Given the emphasis throughout poem on the different capacity of men and women to behold Christ, the requisite "eie of Faith" seems to omit the male gaze. In her address "To all vertuous Ladies in generall," Lanyer instructs them to "Put on your wedding garments euery one, / The Bridegroome stayes to entertaine you all" (b3r). Such erotic messages, modeled on the Song of Songs, were a common feature in Passion narratives (whether produced by Calvinist piety or not). It was also not uncommon to imagine Christ as a handsome young man (as is evident from Breton's depiction). But it is the feminized body of Christ that is made available here.[58] Lanyer's *ottava rima* stanza renders Christ in the mode of a Petrarchan beloved. Wendy Wall was first to notice Lanyer's use of the conventional female blazon to display the broken figure of Christ's Passion. Understanding the blazon as a means of inscribing authority and control, Wall asserts that Lanyer's employment of it serves as "a tool . . . to proclaim, to publish, to unfold to view."[59] But what she is publishing is not simply the erotic body of Christ as a desired subject, but also her own desires for authorial recognition and patronage. Lanyer assumes the Petrarchan mode of commodification and display in order to circulate the body of Christ to other Christian women.

But the feminized nature of that body complicates the access. The text's insistence on a female gaze provides acceptable channels for female desire, but as Jonathan Goldberg points out, the figure of the Passion that Lanyer constructs participates within a female–female exchange.[60] Breton also imagines a scene of execution in which the religious passion of the penitent speaker coincides with same-sex eroticism, but in dedicating his poem to Mary Sidney Herbert, he suggests that the female reader participates in the erotics of the moment as well.[61] By contrast, in Lanyer's poem, the body of Christ is inscribed as female and is witnessed—at least within the text itself—by an audience of women. In other words, the reconceptualization of the blazon is, in some sense, an act of literary enclosure: Christ is imagined as a woman for women. Of course, this fits with the particular network of female patronage that Lanyer is trying to serve. But it also effectively cordons off male intrusion. I am not suggesting that Lanyer is creating herself as a kind of pander within a female Christian community; but she is, on some level, establishing herself as a purveyor of Christ's favors.

This self-construction pervades the poem. In her dedication to Queen Anne, Lanyer (in diction that suggests domestic service) asks her to sit down and "feed upon" the "Paschal Lamb" that the poet has "prepar'd" (a4v). She instructs the Countess of Kent to "Receive [her] Love" whom she had "sought

so farre" and who "presents himselfe within [her] view" in the pages of
the poem (c2v). Such articulations of presentation and display are standard
in the dedicatory address; what is remarkable about Lanyer's expression is
that she claims to be offering Christ to her readership. Such offerings are
notably absent in the addresses of male poets. One could argue that the
implication of such a gift is tacit in the dedication of a devotional poem.
But, at most, Fletcher will only commend his "broken lines" to the reader,
and the dedicatee himself to "the best Physitian, IESUS CHRIST."[62] Breton
(in a different poem) will claim only "to acquaint the honest mindes of
vertuous dispositions, with the heauenly Meditations," of the Countess of
Pembroke.[63] The dedications of devotional works by men do not contain
bald assertions that their representations of Christ are authentic. But Lanyer's
poem itself opens space for such assertions. If the virtuous sight of her female
readership is able to penetrate Christ's earthly guise, then

> it [is] no disparagement to you,
> To see your Sauiour in a Shepheards weed,
>
> . . .
>
> Receiue him here by my vnworthy hand.
>
> (d3v)

While she appears to denigrate her work, what she is showing her female
audience is a faithful depiction of the good shepherd of the gospels.[64] Lanyer
herself makes the suggestion that her representation is more genuine because
she is a woman:

> And pardon me . . . though I presume,
> To doe that which so many better can;
> Not that I Learning to my selfe assume,
> Or that I would compare with any man:
> But as they are Scholers, and by Art do write,
> So Nature yeelds my Soule a sad delight.
>
> (b1v)

Here again, what at first appears pejorative is actually preferred. Lanyer seems
to claim that her poetic efforts are inferior to men's due to the limits of
her education. But by underscoring the artifice by which men achieve their
poetic effects, she renders the apprehension of Christ in their poems suspect.
By contrast, the perfection of her art is derived from her own nature—and the
syntax implies that men have moved away from this impulse as a result of
rhetorical training. Of course, this emphasis on her education has a gendered
inflection: Lanyer did not have the benefit of university training—nor did

her female readership—and it is this distinction that she is highlighting. The artfulness which arrests the ability of men to fully render Christ in their poems was presumably learned within the walls of higher institutions that shut women out.

The performance of gender within Lanyer's poem is central to its formulations. The argument of *Salve Deus* suggests that women are better able to receive Christ; but this converts to a claim for the enhanced ability of the female poet to present the Christian story. The valorization of women's virtue, then, is the foundation on which Lanyer constructs her own professional standing. Her self-presentation as a superior conduit of Christian revelation is premised on the gendered distinctions that are generated within her poem. Just as the "eie of Faith" allows women to perceive Christ regardless of his outward form, it is the "hand" of a female poet (the poem maintains) that is able to make Him legible. By reading *Salve Deus* against *The Countesse of Penbrookes passion* we can begin to see what strain of contemporary discourse Lanyer's text opposes. The central features of her poetic argument—the allocation of blame, the conflation of past and present crimes, the lamentation of women (the daughters of Jerusalem) at the site of the crucifixion, and the painful depiction of Christ's death that transforms into a spectacle to please the soul—are harvested from Breton's poem and Calvin's interpretation of the Passion. Understanding Lanyer's revision of the biblical story in the context of these models allows us to view the precise way that she is troubling existing textual paradigms. Rather than the more general observation that she is interrogating contemporary constructions of gender, we can see the strategies by which she challenges the norms and ideals that govern the generic form that she is engaging. Perhaps more importantly, we can perceive the economic motive behind her formal innovations.

The way that Lanyer remodels her poetic material directly counters the patriarchal assumptions that organize Breton's text. (Even the patrilineal diction of Breton's central question—"was it myne, or my forefathers deade?"—serves her counterargument.) But noticing how the points of Lanyer's argument contradict Breton's formulations underscores the calculated nature of her poetic presentation. Breton was the most prolific religious poet of his time; Lanyer offers her own Passion narrative as an alternative to female patrons of religious material. But the substitution turns on the matter of difference: it requires that she render the normative values in the poetic works by men fully visible; that she develop new models of evaluation; and, most importantly, that she distinguish her service as a poet by virtue of her sex. What emerges from Lanyer's text, under the pressure of an intertextual comparison, is a self-conscious performance of gender that the competition for patronage actually compels.

Salve Deus is, as are most poems of the period, an exercise in literary imitation. But rather than any sincere form of flattery, the imitative gestures of the poem call attention to the limits of Breton's work. Lanyer tries to dissolve the links between male poet and female patrons by emphasizing his sexual difference. The moral perspective of men is as inadequate in its assessment of female virtue as it is in the evaluation of Christ on earth. It is instead the female poet who is better equipped to administer devotional verse to a communion of female patrons. But the activities by which this inversion is achieved make the deliberate construction of the gendered voice in the poem transparent. If we are to understand what is unique about this construction, we must first accept that it is premised on the expectation of financial reward.

Given that Lanyer is arguably "the first woman writing in English who clearly sought professional standing as a poet," nearly all her critics have tried to understand the dynamics of the proto-feminist statements in her work.[65] It is legitimate to wonder what is added by the observation that these statements are the result of a poetic stratagem rather than the expression of a poet invigorated by a feminist energy.[66] But once we locate the expression in the context of competitive circulation, we begin to see its origin and impulses—how it is developed and why. What becomes clear is that Lanyer's terms are forged in opposition—not to patriarchy *per se*, but to male poets of the middling sort who experience similar financial need. If the terms of Lanyer's poetic project are formed by market pressures, however, it becomes an open question whether this expression would have been conceived absent the financial imperative that forces its claims. Situating *Salve Deus* in relation to Breton's passion narrative allows us also to situate our observations about the author's traces in the work. It helps to disentangle knotty questions of gender and class position—specifically, how social status inflects the gendered inscriptions of a text. At the very least, it provides an instance where the relationship of the individual to mechanisms of social power and wealth affects the gendered markings of her textual production.

Notes

1. *Salve Devs Rex Ivdæorvm* (STC 15227), H3v. All quotations are from this edition.
2. For a discussion of how feminist inquiry is inflected by the history of the book, see M. Bell, "Women Writing and Women Written," *Cambridge History of the Book in Britain, 1557–1695*, ed. J. Barnard and D. F. McKenzie (Cambridge: Cambridge University Press, 2002), 431–51. For the importance of a critical practice—particularly a feminist one—that does not produce a dichotomy between manuscript and print culture see, in particular, M. Ezell, "The Myth of Judith Shakespeare: Creating the Canon of Women's Writing," *New Literary History* 21 (1990), 579–92; and *Writing Women's Literary History* (Baltimore, MD: Johns Hopkins University Press, 1993). For an examination of the effect of editing practices upon texts, see S. Roberts, "Editing Sexuality, Narrative and Authorship: The Altered Texts of Shakespeare's *Lucrece*," *Texts and Cultural Change in Early Modern England*, ed. C. Brown and A. Marotti (Basingstoke: Macmillan, 1997), 124–52; and for a discussion of feminist editing practices, see V. Wayne, "The Sexual Politics of Textual Transmission," *Textual Formations and Reformations*,

ed. L. E. Maguire and T. L. Berger (Newark: Delaware University Press, 1998), 179–210.

3. D. Clarke, *The Politics of Early Modern Women's Writing* (Harlow: Pearson Education, 2001), 4. Clarke calls for precisely such an approach in the study of early modern women's writing, and examines the pitfalls of attempting to recover the autobiographical subject in women's texts.

4. The early appeals for this approach—that we read women's writing in terms of generation, not simply gender and class—came in the late 1990s: see, in particular, J. Mueller, "Complications of Intertextuality: John Fisher, Katherine Parr and 'The Book of the Crucifix'," *Texts and Cultural Change in Early Modern England*, ed. C. Brown and A. Marotti (London: Macmillan, 1997), 15–36; and M. Quilligan, "Completing the Conversation," *Shakespeare Studies* 25 (1997): 42–9.

5. For an examination of how gender stigmas attached to print venues, see W. Wall, *The Imprint of Gender: Authorship and Publication in the English Renaissance* (Ithaca, NY: Cornell University Press, 1993); and for an investigation of how the figure of "woman" operated within the commerce of the book trade, see Bell, "Women Writing and Women Written."

6. A notable exception to this are two recent anthologies: *Representing Women in Renaissance England*, ed. C. J. Summers and T. Pebworth (Columbia: Missouri University Press, 1997); and *"This Double Voice": Gendered Writing in Early Modern England*, ed. D. Clarke and E. Clarke (Basingstoke: Macmillan, 2000). But even the appearance of these anthologies—and how the editors represent their project—speaks to the absence of such critical work on women's writing in the early modern period.

7. D. Clarke, Introduction, *"This Double Voice,"* 6. See also, E. Grosz, "Sexual Signatures: Feminism after the Death of the Author," in her *Space, Time, and Perversion: Essays on the Politics of Bodies* (London: Routledge, 1995), 9–24.

8. Ibid., 2.

9. L. McGrath, "'Let Us Have Our Libertie Againe': Amelia Lanier's 17th-Century Feminist Voice," *Women's Studies* 20 (1992): 331–48. Other critical analyses of Lanyer's feminism include McGrath, "Metaphoric Subversions: Feasts and Mirrors in Amelia Lanier's *Salve Deus Rex Judaeorum*," *Literature, Interpretation, Theory* 3 (1991): 101–13; Wall, *The Imprint of Gender*, 319–30; and J. Mueller, "The Feminist Poetics of 'Salve Deus Rex Judaeorum'," *Aemilia Lanyer: Gender, Genre, and the Canon*, ed. M. Grossman (Lexington, KY: Kentucky University Press, 1998), 99–127. Early works that analyze Lanyer's opposition to patriarchy (without the feminist appellation) include: B. Lewalski, "Of God and Good Women: The Poems of Aemilia Lanyer," *Silent but for the Word: Tudor Women as Patrons, Translators, and Writers of Religious Works*, ed. M. Hannay (Kent, OH: Kent State University Press, 1985), 203–24; E. Beilin, *Redeeming Eve: Women Writers of the English Renaissance* (Princeton, NJ: Princeton University Press, 1987), 177–207; and T. Krontiris, *Oppositional Voices: Women as Writers and Translators of Literature in the English Renaissance* (London: Routledge, 1992), 103–20. The interrogation of Lanyer's oppositional voice has been the subject of many other subsequent investigations of her work: see, in particular, Lewalski, "Re-writing Patriarchy and Patronage: Margaret Clifford, Anne Clifford, and Aemilia Lanyer," *The Yearbook of English Studies* 21 (1991): 87–106; *Writing Women in Jacobean England*

(Cambridge: Cambridge University Press, 1993), 213–41; and "Seizing Discourses and Reinventing Genres," *Aemilia Lanyer: Gender, Genre, and the Canon,* 49–59; and in the same volume, S. Woods, "Vocation and Authority: Born to Write," 83–98; and N. Miller, "(M)other Tongues: Maternity and Subjectivity," 143–66.

10. Janel Mueller's "The Feminist Poetics of 'Salve Deus Rex Judaeorum'," is a case in point. My debt to her analysis of *Salve Deus* throughout this argument is obvious and great. Other notable examples of the analysis of gender—or of gender and class—in Lanyer's poem are: A. Coiro, "Writing in Service: Sexual Politics and Class Position in the Poetry of Aemilia Lanyer and Ben Jonson," *Criticism* 35 (1993): 357–76; M. Schoenfeldt, "The Gender of Religious Devotion: Amelia Lanyer and John Donne," *Relgion and Culture in Renaissance England,* ed. C. McEachern and D. Shuger (Cambridge: Cambridge University Press, 1997), 209–33; and H. Wilcox, "'Whom the Lord with love affecteth': Gender and the Religious Poet, 1590–1633," *"This Double Voice,"* 185–207.

11. Mueller touches on the issue, but makes "no pretense of offering...a full treatment" of what she herself notes is a "scarcely opened question" in critical terms ("The Feminist Poetics of 'Salve Deus'," 107).

12. The analysis that best situates Lanyer's work within a market economy—one that exerts pressure on the formulations of the text itself—is Lorna Hutson's fine article "Why the Lady's Eyes are Nothing like the Sun," *Women, Texts, and Histories 1575–1760,* ed. C. Brent and D. Purkiss (London: Routledge, 1992), 13–38. But a more recent article by Mary Ellen Lamb decries the fact that so many discussions of *Salve Deus* "have bracketed off financial motives as somehow extraneous to the work" (see "Patronage and Class in Aemilia Lanyer's *Salve Deus Rex Judaeorum*," *Women, Writing, and the Reproduction of Culture in Tudor and Stuart Britain,* ed. M. Burke, J. Donawerth, L. Dove, and K. Nelson [Syracuse: Syracuse University Press, 2000], 38–57).

13. In "Writing in Service" Anne Baynes Coiro emphasizes the context of Lanyer's class position, and argues that the "politics of current literary criticism in Renaissance studies and feminist studies in particular" has imagined a female community around Aemilia Lanyer, and failed to notice the more disruptive class tensions in Lanyer's work (358). Coiro is responding to something of a critical tradition, in many ways begun by the prominent, and truly valuable, work of Barbara Lewalski. In *Writing Women in Jacobean England,* Lewalski sees the dedications of Lanyer's poem as a rewriting of "the institution of patronage in female terms, transforming the relationships assumed in the male patronage system into an ideal female community" (221). The influence of Coiro's important corrective can be immediately felt in the arguments of, for example, Lisa Schnell ("'So Great a Difference is There in Degree': Aemilia Lanyer and the Aims of Feminist Criticism," *Modern Language Quarterly* 57 [1996]: 23–35; and "Breaking 'the rule of Cortezia': Aemilia Lanyer's Dedications to *Salve Deus Rex Judaeorum*," *Journal of Medieval and Early Modern Studies* 27 [1997]: 77–101); and Su Fang Ng ("Aemilia Lanyer and the Politics of Praise," *ELH* 67 [2000]: 433–51).

14. Hutson, "Why the Lady's Eyes are Nothing like the Sun," 23.

15. Exactly how Lanyer acquired her education is something of a vexed question. Lanyer calls Susan Bertie, the dowager Countess of Kent, "the Mistris of [her] youth" in a dedicatory poem addressed to her. This phrase has caused a good deal of conjecture as to how the Countess of Kent featured in Lanyer's tuition. Susanne Woods speculates that Lanyer, then Bassano, might have entered the service of Susan Bertie when her father, Baptista Bassano, died in 1576 (see

Lanyer: A Renaissance Woman Poet [Oxford: Oxford University Press, 1999], 9).
Leeds Barroll raises a number of objections to the theory (see "Looking for
Patrons," in *Aemilia Lanyer: Gender, Genre, and the Cannon*, 29–48), but an entry
in one of Simon Forman's diaries, whose astrological advice Lanyer sought,
does appear to support the claim that Lanyer was brought up "w the contes of
Kent." If this, in fact, occurred, very likely Lanyer would have been educated in
the Countess's nursery between the years 1576 and 1581 when Susan Bertie is
presumed to have lived at Elizabeth's court.

16. Both were also devotional poets in the service of noble patrons. Henry Lok would
be another example of a writer in this model (but he was deceased by this time).

17. See Mark Bland, "The London Book-Trade in 1600," *A Companion to Shakespeare*,
ed. D. S. Kastan (Oxford: Blackwell, 1999), 461, for a discussion of how evidence
of the London book trade can help us to reorient our assumptions of the literary
values of early modern English culture.

18. Breton's *The soules heavenly exercise* (STC 3700.5) is a composition that is written
in both verse and prose—and is dedicated to William Rider, the mayor of London.

19. The two exceptions are *An excellent poeme upon the longing of a blessed heart*
(STC 3649), dedicated to Lord Dudley North; and *The soules immortall crowne* (STC
3701), dedicated to James I. While *The Countesse of Penbrookes passion* (which will
be the subject of much of the discussion that follows) was printed by Thomas East
under the title *The Passions of the Spirit* (STC 3682.5), and dedicated to Mrs. Mary
Houghton, there is no indication that Breton was responsible for this change in
presentation (see M. Brennan, "Nicholas Breton's *The Passions of the Spirit* and
the Countess of Pembroke," *RES* 38 [1987]: 221–5). East printed the work without
attribution, and attached his own dedication.

20. Abraham Fraunce wrote one long devotional poem, dedicated to Mary Sidney
Herbert, the Countess of Pembroke.

21. See G. Fletcher, *Christs Victorie, and Truimph in Heauen, and Earth* (STC 11058);
and A. Fraunce, *The Countesse of Pembrokes Emanuel* (STC 11338.5). Although
Barbara Lewalski does not name *The Countesse of Penbrookes passion* (see n. 19,
above) as a source for Lanyer's work, she does include Breton's *The Rauisht Soule,
The Blessed Weeper, The Pilgrimage to Paradise*, and *The Countesse of Penbrookes
loue* in a list of suggestive Protestant analogues for Lanyer's work. Lewalski also
cites Fletcher and Fraunce as possible models (see *Writing Women in Jacobean
England*, 227).

22. Debora Shuger has identified and analysed this group of texts in chapter 3 of
The Renaissance Bible: Scholarship, Sacrifice, and Subjectivity (Berkeley: California
University Press, 1994), 89–127. The argument that follows concerning the
passion narratives relies heavily on Shuger's analysis.

23. B. Bowen, "The Rape of Jesus: Aemilia Lanyer's *Lucrece*," *Marxist Shakespeares*, ed.
J. Howard and S. C. Shershow (London: Routledge, 2001), 108. While Bowen
makes the observation, she does not examine the grounds for the claim. Erica
Longfellow has recently published a study that does trace the influence of
the Calvinist passion narratives on *Salve Deus*. While my own argument was
developed independently, Longfellow's research offers welcome support to my
findings. It is also a further example of current feminist critical work that tries to
understand women's writing in the context of a cultural circulation (see *Women
and Religious Writing in Early Modern England* [Cambridge: Cambridge University
Press, 2004], chapter 2).

24. Shuger, *The Renaissance Bible*, 92–3.

25. All quotations are from Sloane MS 1303.

26. See Shuger, *The Renaissance Bible*, 91.

27. J. Calvin, *Commentary on a Harmony of the Evangelists: Matthew Mark, and Luke*, trans. William Pringle (Grand Rapids, MI: Eerdmans Publishing, 1956), 3: 317.

28. Ibid., 3: 253; 278.

29. Ibid., 3: 256; 281.

30. Cf. *Salve Devs Rex Ivdæorum*, B4v (stanza 63).

31. Shuger, *The Renaissance Bible*, 91.

32. Calvin, *Commentary on a Harmony of the Evangelists*, 3: 240.

33. Ibid., 3: 317.

34. Shuger, *The Renaissance Bible*, 93. This transfer of responsibility and its effect on subjectivity in these texts are carefully analyzed by Shuger (91–104).

35. Ibid., 96.

36. Calvin, *Commentary on a Harmony of the Evangelists*, 3: 290 (my emphasis).

37. Shuger, *The Renaissance Bible*, 96.

38. Calvin, *Commentary on a Harmony of the Evangelists*, 3: 259.

39. Shuger, *The Renaissance Bible*, 97–8.

40. Ibid., 98.

41. Compare, for example, the similar progression within Breton's stanza 37 (fol. 63v) and Lanyer's stanza 146 (E3r) quoted above.

42. Shuger, *The Renaissance Bible*, 89.

43. See, for example, *A Diuine Poeme, diuided into two Partes: The Rauisht Soule, and the Blessed Weeper* (STC 3648); and the prose work *Marie Magdalens Loue* (STC 3665). Aside from Breton's poems, the other literary work based on the Passion and dedicated to a female patron, Mary Sidney Herbert, is Fraunce's *The Countesse of Pembrokes Emanuel*.

44. While various critics have made this point, I am concentrating upon how this formulation is driven by Lanyer's self-representation as a female poet in contradistinction to male competitors. See, in particular, Wall, *The Imprint of Gender*, 320–1; and Mueller, "The Feminist Poetics of 'Salve Deus'," 109–16.

45. Lanyer's modification of scripture has been the subject of a number of studies of her work. See in particular, A. Guibbory, "The Gospel According to Aemilia: Women and the Sacred," 191–211; and C. Keohane, "'That blindest weakenesse be not over-bold': Aemilia Lanyer's Radical Unfolding of the Passion," *ELH* 64 (1997): 359–89.

46. While Mary Ellen Lamb has made a case that the speaker of Breton's *Passion* is represented as the Countess of Pembroke, I do not agree with her reading (see *Gender and Authorship in the Sidney Circle* [Madison, WI: Wisconsin University Press, 1990], 49). In other verse narratives where Breton *does* represent Pembroke's voice, he figures himself in the text as overhearing her private meditations (see, for example, *The Countesse of Penbrookes loue* [STC 3683]).

47. Wendy Wall was the first critic to notice this construction; see *The Imprint of Gender*, 320.

48. The fact that Pilate is informed that Christ is the Savior is consistent with the moral blindness that Calvin describes. Christ's persecutors know him for who and what he is, but a kind of insanity grips them: "their minds were darkened, so that, *seeing they did not see*."

49. See, for example, Lewalski, "Re-writing Patriarchy and Patronage," 103; Hutson, "Why the Lady's Eyes are Nothing like the Sun," 32; and McGrath, "'Let Us Have

Our Libertie Againe'," 331–48 (which gives extended attention to "Eves Apologie" without acknowledging Pilate's wife as the speaker).
50. Mueller, "The Feminist Poetics of 'Salve Deus'," 123.
51. Ibid.
52. J. Donne, "Holy Sonnet 7," *John Donne: A Critical Edition of the Major Works*, ed. J. Carey (Oxford: Oxford University Press, 1990), 176.
53. E. Beilin, *Redeeming Eve*, 183.
54. Mueller, "The Feminist Poetics of 'Salve Deus'," 112.
55. Ibid.
56. Calvin does praise their fortitude in staying with Christ until the end (*Commentary on a Harmony of the Evangelists*, 3: 328).
57. Ibid., 3: 292.
58. See, in particular, Wall, *The Imprint of Gender*, 328; and J. Goldberg, *Desiring Women Writing: English Renaissance Examples* (Stanford, CA: Stanford University Press, 1997), 34–8.
59. Wall, "Our Bodies / Our Texts? Renaissance Women and the Trials of Authorship," *Anxious Power: Reading, Writing, and Ambivalence in Narrative*, ed. C. J. Singley and S. E. Sweeney (Albany, NY: State University of New York Press, 1993), 64.
60. Goldberg, *Desiring Women Writing*, 34.
61. See n. 46.
62. Fletcher, *Christs Victorie*, ¶2v.
63. Breton, *The Pilgrimage to Paradise, ioyned with the Countess of Penbrookes loue* (STC 3683), ¶3r.
64. Longfellow notices that Margaret Clifford is able to discern Christ on earth even when he comes to her disguised (*Salve Deus*, F2r). Clifford's "[t]rue interpretation" in this passage "is a sign of [her] election" (see *Women and Religious Writing*, 80–1).
65. Woods, *Lanyer: A Renaissance Woman Poet*, vii. Isabella Whitney's venture into print troubles this claim. While Whitney does not work within patronage systems, there is certainly evidence that she wrote for payment (see *The copy of a letter, lately written in meeter, by a yonge gentilwoman: to her vnconstant louer* [STC 25439] and *A sweet nosgay* [STC 25440]). Other previous instances of women's poetic work in circulation—in print and manuscript—do not exhibit signs of expectation for financial remuneration.
66. As Elizabeth Grosz claims, these classifications are so contingent that "at best a text is feminist or patriarchal only provisionally" (see "Sexual Signatures," 23–4).

9

A New Fable of the Belly: Vulgar Curiosity and the Persian Lady's Loose Bodies

Pamela Allen Brown

> She is more glorious, who unites two states,
> Than she, who like the Vulgar generate.
>
> John Owen, "The Offspring of the Virgin Queen"[1]

One question this volume seeks to answer is whether feminist work on early modern culture has been diluted into inconsequentiality by its absorption into other disciplines, becoming a nostalgic trace on the surface of cultural and literary studies. In at least one sector—the relatively new cross-discipline of visual studies—feminist work seems in little danger of losing its distinctive questing edge. Whether the topic is royal portraiture, the politics and aesthetics of racialization, courtly and popular performance, clothing, habit, and subjectivity, domesticity and household stuff, Ovidian imitation, issues of authorship, or lesbian erotics, feminists have emerged as leaders of the field in using visual evidence to explore "the other side of coin."[2]

Arguably a greater danger than assimilation comes from our understandable reluctance to bite the hands that teach us, in territories in which we're both guests and poachers. A concomitant hazard is gentility. As feminism has become institutionalized it has become more mannerly: indeed, it is a mark of distinction among certain academic feminists not to be "too feminist," meaning in your face. Unfortunately "not too feminist" work is often as quiet and unobjectionable as a flow of cream. Despite this behavioral mainstreaming, not all feminists have lost the ability to ask rude, unsettling, and at times enlightening questions at parties they have crashed. This essay will strive to demonstrate the value of sharp-eyed feminist curiosity in visual studies by looking at a portrait of a possibly pregnant gentlewoman by Marcus Gheeraerts the Younger, and its ingenious though unsatisfactory

171

explication by Sir Roy Strong. While the classical fable of the belly seems to bypass gender to explain the needful subordination of stomach and groin to the glorious head and haughty limbs, my version peeps insistently at the gendered body beneath, whose hidden presence breeds a wilder kind of discourse and a more slippery set of desires.

Pregnant with meaning

She is huge, public, unmissable. Almost seven feet tall, she stands waiting in the first room of the Renaissance collection at Hampton Court (Figure 9.1). Her billowing white gown studded with Tudor roses and phoenixes floats in the shadows of the forest, and it is only by coming closer that one can see that the animal at her right is a small stag, which wears a garland of flowers and pearls that trails from her white hand. Her auburn hair falls free under an elaborate turban with a long yellowish veil. She wears shoes of a startling shade of blue, criss-crossed with jewels and pearls. Calm and self-possessed, she greets our gaze with one arm cocked on her hip, the other reaching out to crown her tame stag. At her left we see a scrollwork frame, like a legend in old maps, which contains a lamenting sonnet painted in dull gold. Written on the tree behind her appear three inscriptions: *iniusti querla iusti* (a just complaint of injustice), *mea sic mihi* (thus mine to me), and *dolor est medicina a do[o]lori* (possibly "grief is medicine for grief").

She seems thoroughly aristocratic; but who is she? Frustratingly, the Hampton Court label refuses to provide any information beyond these words: "Portrait of an Unknown Lady, Marcus Gheeraerts the Younger, *c.* 1590–1600." Bland as it is, that label took over two hundred years to settle into its present state. From the early eighteenth to the early twentieth centuries, the painting was viewed as an allegorical portrait of Queen Elizabeth. Its provenance is murky: although Strong dates it to the late 1590s, no contemporary records have been found about who posed or paid for it. In 1734 George Vertue saw the portrait while making an inventory of the royal collection. He described it as "qu. Eliz in a strange fantastick habit" and noted it had "marks behind" proving it had belonged to Charles I. Like the king, the painting suffered a severe change of fortune, having been "sold as rubbish, to a painter in Moor fields" and then "recovered to the Crown" by Queen Anne's deputy, Sir John Stanley.[3]

For almost two hundred years, then, the Unknown Lady was one of the most known ladies in English history. In 1898 the author of *The Royal Gallery of Hampton Court Illustrated* called her "Elizabeth in Fancy Dress," chattily informing readers that the queen was deeply vain and loved dressing up in exotic gowns. While some believed that Spenser wrote the sonnet, this writer opined that they were tossed off by Elizabeth, "who, like everyone in those days, dabbled in poetry."[4] As for the artist, Vertue's guess that Zucchero was the man hardened into verity, but in 1914 Lionel Cust set that attribution

Figure 9.1 Portrait of an Unknown Lady. Marcus Gheeraerts the Younger, c. 1590–1600. The Royal Collection. Also known as "The Persian Lady."

aside. Relying on the work's distinctive style and inscriptions, Cust decided in favor of Marcus Gheeraerts the Younger, an artist from a Flemish émigré family who painted several famous royal portraits, including the Ditchley Portrait of Elizabeth. Cust believed that the sitter was not Elizabeth, but Arbella Stuart.[5]

At some point during the following decades, the label changed again. In a short article in 1959, Frances Yates mentioned the now unknown lady, noting her identity "remains a mystery now that the Lady Arbella Stuart theory has been abandoned."[6] She perceived a distinct stylistic likeness between the portrait and Gheeraerts' notorious bare-legged Portrait of Captain Thomas Lee—the nephew of Sir Henry Lee, Elizabeth's Champion and the proprietor of Ditchley. Yates cautiously speculated that "the allegories in the picture [of the Unknown Lady] may refer to elements in a masque in which the sitter was present" and that, if the comparison to Captain Thomas Lee was valid, the portrait referred "probably, to a masque at Ditchley."[7]

Yates was far more certain of her discovery that J. J. Boissard's *Habitus variarum orbis gentium* (1581) was used for the exotic hats in both the Unknown Lady and the famous Rainbow Portrait of Elizabeth. For the queen, the artist had copied the headdress of a Greek matron; for the Unknown Lady, a second artist had modeled her high turban on the "mitre-like cap with fringed hanging" of a Persian virgin.[8] Yates's discovery about the Boissard "Virgo Persica" also gave scholarly credibility to the longstanding perception that her "fantastick" garb is an Orientalizing fancy dress or masque costume, giving rise to her modern soubriquet, the "Persian Lady."[9]

A quarter-century later, Yates's student Roy Strong extended Yates's tentative speculations to develop a far more detailed argument, with Sir Henry Lee as linchpin. In "'My weepinge Stagg I crowne': The Persian Lady Reconsidered" (1993), Strong mines the painting's style and pictorial symbolism to assert that in all likelihood Henry Lee designed both allegory and sonnet, taking the same roles he had with the Ditchley Portrait, which shows Elizabeth standing on a map of England with Ditchley under her feet. The idea that the Ditchley Portrait and the Unknown Lady are related is immediately compelling. Both are gigantic, full-length portraits almost eight feet in height, both present challenging allegories featuring magical women in white, both have outdoor settings (a rarity in English portraiture at the time), and both have cryptic mottoes and sonnets, the latter inscribed in gold in strapwork cartouches at the lower right. Strong's thesis about the Persian Lady's identity proceeds from the claim of a Lee connection, despite any documentary evidence linking the painting to Lee or Ditchley. He proceeds from visual parallels to a literary one: both paintings have sonnets whose "rambling oblique style" is identical, with stanzas explicating in sequence "the symbolic contents" of each image. Taken together, he asserts, these two paintings "stand alone in Elizabethan painting, utterly unique, and I find it difficult not to believe that we are looking at expressions of the same mind, that of Sir Henry Lee."[10]

With bold aplomb, Strong then lifts the veil of anonymity from the portrait. Even more boldly, he decides that the Lady is pregnant. In a nutshell, he makes the case that she is Frances Walsingham, Lady Essex, widow of Philip Sidney and wife of Robert Devereux, who appears with her in the form of a stag, a motif in his family crest. Strong reads the Tudor roses on her gown, the pansies on her headdress, and the walnut tree above her as symbols of Elizabeth, meant to communicate an attitude of obedience and compliment.[11] Lee conceived and commissioned the painting in 1600 to stir the queen's sympathy on behalf of his friend Essex, who was often figured in courtly entertainments as Actaeon; that identity became especially fitting in 1599 when he fell from grace for rashly intruding on the Queen in her chamber. The old courtier hoped to accomplish a rapprochement by portraying the earl as a weeping stag alongside his wife Frances, who was pregnant with their child Dorothy in 1600. Both are in supplicant positions, hoping for mercy from their estranged queen.[12] Although Strong couches this reading as a hypothesis, he goes on to conclude triumphantly: "the Persian Lady, or may we say Lady Essex, remains a haunting and moving image, frank and direct in its coded message in spite of all its rambling conceits.... One day further scholarship will discover more, but I have no doubt that its context if not its eventual identity will remain the same" (124). Time will reveal a truth which is, like Elizabeth herself, *semper eadem*.

In making these claims Strong finds the Lady's loose robe consonant with Lady Essex's "enceinte condition" at the time the painting was created. Strong treats the matter as self-evident, a matter accessible to ocular proof— even though it is finally ambiguous, as we shall see. He anxiously avoids vulgar nomination in his diction, which is hemmed in with conditional tenses and questions. Instead of saying she is pregnant, or "with child," or "big-bellied," common early modern terms, Strong uses a Gallic euphemism appealing to a prudish modern elite. In his words, hers is a delicate condition, and by implication conditional, not a physical bulge with a fetus growing under it and a sex act at its root.

Qui parle?

Strong bases his case on his own considerable cultural authority, going from one supposition to the next with the certainty born of being pre-eminent in his field. He has played a central role in bringing scholarly methods to the study of English Renaissance art in general and the National Portrait Gallery in particular, and he has dated and identified many hundreds of portraits. His rhetorical style is impressive, but inclines to crescendos. When he says that the Persian Lady is "the most complicated of all English allegorical paintings, including those of the Queen" (118), the matter is presumably closed. A deep-dyed Tory, Strong has played both sides in the creation of the field of early modern visual studies: a deconstructor of "Britishness" in art history, especially during his collaborations with Stephen Orgel, yet a defender of royal interests and traditional art history, before and after.[13] As the leading authority on English Renaissance courtly art and festivals, his opinions find their way, directly or indirectly, into nearly every judgment scholars make about those topics. Strong's findings on portraits of special interest to feminists are widely quoted but rarely questioned. Certainly they are not infallible.

A case in point is his unriddling of the Persian Lady. Leaving aside the unlikelihood of Elizabeth being moved to anything but rage at seeing Essex crowned and his wife pregnant again (the queen suspected he coveted her crown, after all, and in 1590 she punished Essex for impregnating Frances and secretly marrying her) Strong's argument is especially weak in its reading of the sonnet painted on the cartouche.

> *The restles swallow fits my restles mind*
> *In still revivinge still renewinge wronges;*
> *her Just complaintes of cruelty unkinde*
> *are all the Musique, that my life prolonges.*
>
> *With pensive thoughtes my weepinge Stagg I crowne*
> *Whose Melancholy teares my cares Expresse;*
> *hes Teares in sylence, and my sighes unknowne*
> *are all the physicke that my harmes redresse.*
>
> *My onely hope was in this goodly tree*
> *which I did plant in love, bringe up in care;*
> *but all in vanie, for now to late I see*
> *the shales be mine, the kernels others are.*
>
> *My Musique may be plaintes, my physique teares*
> *If this be all the fruite my love tree beares.*

Strong hears in these lines the remorseful voice of Essex instead of the pregnant lady who crowns him with flowers. Despite all appearances, the speaker is the Lady's husband, speaking over and through her: "we need to re-examine the verses and mottoes through his eyes . . . the sonnet can in one sense be read as spoken by Actaeon-Essex, for its contents would fit exactly his condition in the autumn of 1600."[14] In this rather wrenched reading, the Unknown Lady is an elaborate mouthpiece in a "static masque" which is also a "double portrait," masterminded by Essex and Lee.[15] Strangely, given his thesis, Strong chooses to title his essay with the very phrase that conjoins the Lady's loving words with her painted action. This phrase "my weepinge Stagg I crowne" also stresses her priority as speaker with power over the tame stag—an animal as likely to represent an adulterous lover as a husbandly lord and master.[16] Unless one were to argue that Essex is somehow both Lady and stag, and crowns himself, this sonnet inscribes the painted Lady's voice, whoever authored her words. Like many female laments, the sonnet is anonymous, and its anonymity seems a deliberate move to heighten the sense of the illicit that haunts the image.[17] Strong's desire to hear a male speaker/author is symptomatic of his more general elision of female presence, although the painting is replete with verbal and visual signals that the Lady is to be taken as speaker of the sonnet and lead player in the scene before us.

Some of the effort of elision requires recourse to fields such as ornithology and botany. The speaker in the sonnet states first that "restless swallows" and their music suit her "restless minde," brooding over wrongs that are "cruelly unkinde." With these lines the bird-sisters Philomela and Procne enter the picture demanding to be heard. In Ovid's tale, Philomela is turned into a nightingale and Procne a swallow after Tereus rapes and mutilates Philomela. The sisters retaliated by killing his son and serving him up in a pie—a grotesque and pitiful story, but one whose theme of violent revenge against rank tyranny (*iniusta querla iusti*, as the tree reminds us) seems singularly unsuited to the goal of pacifying Elizabeth.

Strong's solution is to dispose of the swallows. In the branches above the Persian Lady sit tawny-breasted birds which closely resemble barn swallows in my Audubon guide, but Strong is absolutely sure that they are "chaffinches, one of the most common of all European birds. Whether, however, they have any symbolic intent is doubtful" (115). To consider them swallows might require a rereading of the sonnet, and the portrait itself, from a female point of view. Both men and women writers of female laments frequently cited the tragic story of the bird-sisters, a practice ultimately traceable to Sappho's letter to Phaon in Ovid's *Heroides*, the classical fountainhead of female lament.[18] By showing a woman aligning her "restless mind" with that of Procne, "the restless swallow," the painting seems less static, more discomposed, and more female in its point of view and intended audience than in Strong's reading. As Ann Rosalind Jones has shown, the familiar Ovidian tale was treated in different ways by male and female poets: the men deployed them as ornaments of melancholy and "occasions for rhetorical virtuosity," while women, such as Gaspara Stampa and Tullia d'Aragona, explored their potential for voicing women's alliance, feelings of tragic loss, and angry satire.[19] For the viewers of this painting—and especially women—the possibly pregnant lady's specific invocation of swallows decrying "cruelly unkinde" treatment might well suggest a tragic story instead of decorative attitudinizing, and challenge them to decipher the plotwork of the lament and its chief actors.

By neglecting the Ovidian symbolism the problematic pregnancy of the Lady is sanitized in Strong's argument, made respectable, marital, and legitimate—not to mention verisimilar and sincere—rather than passionate, painful, ambiguous, or theatrical. In his mind it is a "safe" pregnancy, with no hint of the scandalous or the unruly, and he gives it less space than his long botanical discussion about the tree (he insists it is a royal walnut). I would argue that the tree's deeper import lies in its organs of generation, that is, in its tragic capacity to bear fruit. The poem's reference to the "goodly tree" which the Lady planted in love and raised in care ("the shales be mine, the kernels others are," "if this be all the fruit my love tree beares") points to a story of reproductive labors lost and to some trauma involving her own offspring, whether legitimate or illegitimate; the shells and kernels most likely allude to children or childbearing.[20] The painting's "dark conceit" frames the Lady with emblems of her own state: the melancholy stag weeping from love's wound, the swallows' sad plaint, and the love-tree's Latin and Italian inscriptions echo her sonnet lament. Painted in autumnal colors, these emblems are tonal foils to her loose white embroidered gown, which is slightly convex, and shaped by folds and converging lines that direct attention to her invisible belly and groin.

In combination, these elements lead me to infer (not unreasonably though not definitively) that this Lady appears to lament an absent lover who has broken faith with her; she may be married or unmarried, but she is very probably pregnant (though she may be ruing a former pregnancy or miscarriage, or her own childlessness). Furthermore, her complaint about suffering "harmes" at the hand of someone who is "cruelly unkind" points to emotional or physical violence—a narrative element that invites "vulgar" readings to detect real bruises and real culprits, just as readers would have done in eagerly deciphering thinly veiled narratives of contemporary brutality in Lady Mary Wroth's *Urania*. Intending to breed that degraded verbal art, gossip, this hypothetical sexual scenario is far more culturally and generically coherent than Strong's. Certainly the female lament tradition resounds with the plaints of pregnant and abused maidens and abandoned wives. Some are crudely comic, like the fourteenth-century lyric in which a pregnant maid complains "Now wyll not my gyrdyll met—A, dere god, qwat xal I sayn?" Many more emphasize sexual, physical, and emotional violence, as in "The Complaint of a Woman Rauished, and also Mortally Wounded," and "A love-sick maid's song, lately beguil'd, by a run-away lover that left her with childe."[21]

In short, a pregnant woman alone in the forest, surrounded by laments and tags about injustice and grief, inevitably evokes the rather hackneyed sound of tears and groans.[22] And it is precisely the overtones of a troubled pregnancy that point up the inscription of scandal in this painting, particularly in the chastely lettered sonnet-lament. The anonymous female lament was an extremely popular genre in the sixteenth century, inspiring readerly efforts to identify the speaker, her lover, and her situation. Intending to inspire guesswork, such female laments often functioned as "miniature devices for generating interpretive instability," spurring readers on to what John Kerrigan calls "false decoding." In *Mirrour of Magistrates*, for example, a prime source of female lament, William Baldwin touts his work's appeal to everyone who enjoys the "indoor sport" of allegorical decipherment, discovering "the persons and situations reflected."[23] Replete with coded invitations to play, the Persian Lady painting attracts the eye and then the mind, challenging viewers to bandy around the names of real people whose situations might fit its copious riddles and self-evacuating visual and textual clues. Few desires are painted as more vulgar than the curiosity that feeds sexual gossip—yet this is partly what this image was created for. When the sex lives of the rich and famous enter the picture, so does the curiosity of the uninformed, which must include most of us, as well as some elite viewers of the day. Guesses at her identity include several court ladies whose careers featured scandalous pregnancies. In addition to Frances Walsingham (once the secret lover of Essex), these include Anne Vavasour (Henry Lee's married mistress), Elizabeth Vernon (Southampton's lover), and Mary Fitton (whom William Herbert impregnated but refused to marry).[24] In the 1590s, when Elizabeth's power over the younger courtiers' sexual lives was waning, scandals over rumored and real pregnancies multiplied, despite Elizabeth's sometimes violent methods of surveillance and punishment.[25] The late years of Elizabeth's court were especially rife with scandals over pregnancies among her ladies-in-waiting, resulting in prison and exile for some, so the possibilities for identification on this count would be numerous.

Vulgar curiosity

Gossip about pregnancy is peculiarly and intensely scopic—people ask "is she showing yet?" and note unkindly that so-and-so is "as big as a house," betraying an overwhelming curiosity mixed with unease as the swelling belly intrudes uninvited into discourse. For an early modern woman, being known as pregnant by "showing," unlacing, and growing to term bore heavily on her honor, social worth, and economic future. On the other hand, so did being barren. As a result, women past menarche were constantly observed for signs of pregnancy, as their status as maid, bride, wife, or widow was linked to fertility and childbearing as tightly as their honor was linked to publicly observed continence. A woman's sex life and reproductive status could become public far more cruelly, whether through neighbors' rude inquiries or formal state intervention, when the probing fingers of a jury of matrons sought out signs of pregnancy, most commonly by squeezing a suspected woman's breasts to see if she gave milk.[26]

Today our curiosity is tempered—but its demands do at least acknowledge female experience and interest (how often do men chat about whether a woman is "carrying high" or "low"?) and may even point the way to a more comprehensive view of the Persian Lady's elaborate mysteries. Like iron filings pointing toward a magnet, every other element, from the sonnet's meaning to the stag's crown, from the swallows overhead to the lady's volu-minous gown, wavers in meaning and realigns in relation to the question of her gravidity. Not the answer, but the question itself is vital to the painting's meaning. Put simply, it means to make us restless for an answer. We can be no more secure in the results than the women who prodded their neighbors' bodies four hundred years ago, as all evidence short of childbirth could be perceived, or narrated as, deeply ambiguous, as Laura Gowing has amply demonstrated.[27]

Our minds' eyes seek the body beneath, yet the more one looks at the painting, the less embodied the Unknown Lady seems. The visual field is dominated by the gigantic rhomboid of densely patterned cloth, topped with a conical turban. In contrast, the pale face and hands seem dispropor-tionately small, offering far less surface activity and texture than the richly embroidered gown to which they are rather arbitrarily attached. In a sense, as in contemporary prints of a jester playing Nobody, she has no body, only extremities. Her breasts are covered, and her gown is constructed so that no horizontal seams, stays, or fastenings give shape to the body it masks. Only the diagonal lines of the fabric, crossing over her torso down to the hem, suggest that her body is pear-shaped; but those folds might simply be the effect of the heavy layers of fabric. According to Janet Arnold, an authority on early modern clothing, the Persian Lady's attire is very odd. While it seems to be a costume, it is unsuited to masque dancing because its folds would disarrange at the slightest movement.[28] Though it looks simple, it actually has four layers, consisting of a white lace smock next to the skin, underneath a long embroidered jacket, and a length of embroidered cloth over that; this carefully arranged gown is covered with a transparent veil of spangled lace, often used to protect precious embroidery. Arnold does not state an opinion about whether the Lady is pregnant, though she does else-where that loose-bodied gowns may have been used to conceal pregnancy.[29]

The possibility of an answer tantalizes as we scrutinize the veiled, embroidered folds, asking ourselves whether an early modern would hesitate in forming a conclusion, perhaps by noting codes that may be lost to us. Here the artist's larger *oeuvre* is instructive because he had a unique specialty in addition to (and quite unlike) his allegorical portraits: what Karen Hearn, who recently curated the first solo exhibition of Gheeraert's work, calls "the pregnancy portrait."[30] While the names of some of Gheeraerts's preg-nant sitters have been lost, all the identified ones are married women whose husbands commissioned the artist to paint their wives at an advanced stage of pregnancy. In her book on Gheeraerts Hearn shows that some families arranged for these portraits for various reasons, some of them contradictory: to stress a man's virility, to display a family's wealth, to celebrate fertility, and to record the life of a mother who might not survive the birth. All Gheeraerts's pregnancy portraits show women in gowns that accentuate the large bulge under the breasts, whether using high seams, draped pearls, wide

Figure 9.2 Portrait of a Woman in Red. Marcus Gheeraerts the Younger, 1620. Tate Gallery, London.

unlaced bodices, or curving trim; sometimes women are shown with a hand resting protectively on the belly (see Figure 9.2). So it is significant, given her expertise in this rare genre, that Hearn does not place the Persian Lady in the chapter called "Pregnancy Portraits," but in "Portraits of Women." This editorial decision keeps the Lady's reproductive status in the realm of conjecture, though Hearn attempts to control speculation with a veiled warning about presentism and anachronism: "her loose robe might suggest to the modern viewer that the lady is pregnant."[31]

But evidence exists that a loose robe might suggest precisely that to a curious or hostile early modern eyes as well. Arnold places the dress in the general category of "loose-bodied gowns," kirtles and gowns without tight waists, which were considered both stylish and comfortable in the late Elizabethan court. Such gowns were often worn as night gowns and as maternity wear, though they were also worn in public and by women who were not pregnant. The Virgin Queen herself had such gowns in her wardrobe. However stylish, a loose gown might elicit gossip in courtly circles, where many liaisons were dangerous secrets that came to light when a woman's bump could no longer be hidden by her lacing. As Arnold points out, "Kirtles and gowns in this style may well have concealed pregnancy."[32] The satirist's prying eyes focused insistently on women's wombs, clothed by flesh and fabric; even the lack of pregnancy could invite scandal, as in Jonson's epigram "To Fine Lady Would-Be," in which the poet accuses a childless woman of having secret abortions: "What should the cause be? Oh, you live at court: / And there's both loss of time, and loss of sport, / In a great belly."[33]

Under such conditions it is not surprising that the courtly fashion for loose-bodied gowns, worn for comfort, modishness, or necessity, continued into the reign of James. Bosola certainly notices when the duchess changes from fitted gowns to loose ones in *The Duchess of Malfi*: "I observe our duchess / Is sick o' days; she pukes, her stomach seethes, / . . . She wanes i' the cheek, and waxes fat i' the flank / And . . . wears a loose-bodied gown – there's somewhat in' t" (2.1.72–7). While plotting how to get her to expose her pregnancy, Bosola turns aside to inveigh against female deception made possible by these ample folds:

> A whirlwind strike off these bawd farthingales,
> For, but for that and the loose-body'd gown,
> I should have discovered apparently
> The young springal cutting a caper in her belly.

> (2.1.155–8)[34]

As is true today, the word "loose" was pejorative when applied to a woman; but here (echoing the thesis of Jones and Stallybrass) not only her behavior, but her dress, seems to constitute unchaste subjectivity. A loose-bodied dress was one worn without the stiff bodice, or "bodies," which exposed and defined the female body.[35] A missing or loose "bodies" would free the body one way, but freight it in another. Fittingly for this study, tracking the emblematic and sexual meanings of "looseness" leads us straight back to Ditchley, lending some weight to Strong's theory that this painting is connected to Sir Henry Lee (though not, I believe, in the way Strong posits).

In the 1592 entertainments at Ditchley for Elizabeth under the direction of Lee, the queen watched a pageant about enchanted maids and youths who are placed in thrall to a Fairy Queen because of their inconstancy. Elizabeth is asked to interpret allegorical pictures to free them all from the spell. After Elizabeth duly overthrows the charm, two freed maids playing Liberty and Constancy praise her and present her with gifts. Liberty, "the Inconstant Maid," offers a loose embroidered garment, but Constancy follows with a garment (probably a bodice or girdle) that will discipline its looseness:

> Li[berty]... To your Ma[jes]tie by whom I was sett at liberty, in token of my thankfullnes, I offer this simple woorke of mine own handes, which you may weare as you please; but I made them to be worn, after my own minde, loose.
> Co[nstancy]... I do present you with as unwoorthie a wark of mine owne handes; which yett I hope you will better accept, because it serves to binde the loosenes of this inconstant Dames token.[36]

Faced with this rebuke Liberty caves in, and renounces her desire for "liberty without constancy," vowing henceforth to be, like Elizabeth, "semper eadem."

An elbow in the eye

Faced with curious eyes which seek to bind up her looseness, the Persian Lady seems unperturbed. It appears unlikely that her reputation was touched by her ambiguous costume and sonnet. Indeed, would a woman whose pregnancy was notorious sit for such an elaborate portrait, one that was later hung at court? Who would pay for it? And, just as perplexing, if she was immediately identifiable in her own lifetime (as seems all but certain), why is her demeanor so relaxed and even genial? This line of questioning unsettles any judgment about her sincerity: perhaps the lady is not troubled or ashamed because she is not to be taken as the person of the sonnet but its personator, like the figure in the masque who points to various emblems on display and beckons viewers to interpret them.

This would help explain why, at the basic level of emotional expressivity, an insuperable discontinuity between image and text has been staring us in the face. While Strong says she is deeply melancholy, her expression, her exotic costume, and especially her gestures imply the opposite. Her eyes meet ours us with a gaze that is tearless and disconcertingly direct. Instead of seeking our pity or imploring the gods for help, she seems rather pleased with herself, as if saying "How like you this?"[37] Moreover, her loose hair and pale skin are tokens of an eroticism echoed in her dress, which has no visible means of support and may have been seen as "undress" or bed wear rather than clothing for public view or courtly performance.[38] Her right hand crowns the stag in a gesture redolent of courtly romance, while the left is cocked on her hip in an assertive gesture more often associated with soldiers, gallants, and kings. According to Joaneath Spicer, who has written a fascinating study of Renaissance subjects posed with arms akimbo (one or both hands on hip), the gesture is almost exclusively masculine and expresses the "self-possession associated with authority" typical of a leader, who sometimes holds a scepter, baton, or whip in the other hand. The stance is often strutting, defiant, and aggressive, and the jutting elbow is "incompatible with humiliation or humility."[39] Indeed, a survey of the visual record shows just a few women sporting the gesture; they include an emblem of "Boldnesse"; a Venetian courtesan; a naked Pict covered with flower tattoos; a martial Penthesilea in *The Masque of Queens*; and the frontispiece portrait of Margaret Cavendish in her collected plays.[40] If this is the affective code in which the Lady is portrayed, it is difficult if not impossible to reconcile her confident stance with the sullen despair of the texts.[41] If we agree that she is not expressing "gloom" and "woes," as Strong puts it,[42] but rather a mix of bold pride and erotic playfulness, then the entire carapace of interpretation built on penitent lament collapses.

More doubts rush in, along with a fresh array of possibly relevant images and scenes. Perhaps this portrait is not painted to provoke questions about the subject's identity. Instead, she may be daring us to divine her role, as if in a parlor game. If so, the portrait may belong to a genre of portrait popular in Italy, with some notable examples in northern Europe and England: the great beauty dressed up as a woman famous in myth, literature, or history. Sonnets and poems are often incorporated into such "costume" portraits, just as they are in the Gheeraerts painting; in some cases these poems are written in the voice of the depicted subject. In all of them, women strike poses to create performative fictions, tableaux which summon the stage player acting out "a dream of passion." Italian examples include Raphael's and Giorgione's noted portraits of beautiful young women costumed as Salome and Lucretia and Artemisia Gentileschi's self-portrait as Judith slaying Holofernes. English examples include Van Dyck's elegant lady as Arminia arming herself for battle, and an unknown artist's stunning portrait of Elizabeth Throckmorton, Lady Ralegh, playing Cleopatra's final scene (see Figure 9.3). With her right arm raised and eyes cast resolutely to the asp, Lady Ralegh employs movement and expression suited to a scene of noble suicide.

A more frenzied gestural idiom was used to personate the abandoned maid. In John Fletcher's *The Maides Tragedy*, the jilted Aspatia berates her needlewomen for embroidering a scene of the abandoned Ariadne without enough "miserie." She acts out her own grief as a model:

> These colours are not dull and pale enough,
> To show a soul so full of miserie
> As this poore Ladies was. Doe it by me,
> Doe it againe, by me the lost Aspatia . . .
> Suppose I stand vpon the Sea breach now

Mine armes thus, and mine haire blowne with the wind,
Wilde as the place she was in; let all about me
Be hearers of my story; doe my face,
If thou hadst euer feeling of a sorrow,
Thus, thus, Antiphila; make me looke good girle
Like sorrows monument . . . [43]

Figure 9.3   Elizabeth Throckmorton, Lady Ralegh, as Cleopatra. Artist unknown. National
Portrait Gallery, London.

The Persian Lady's sonnet cries out for a similarly sorrowful pose—for example, the one shown in many early illustrations of a lamenting woman sitting out of doors, her hands clasped and eyes cast to heaven. Yet with her arms akimbo and her eyes calmly assessing us, Gheeraerts's subject surely embodies something other than "sorrow's monument."[44]

Given the dramatic disjunction between word and image in the Persian Lady, Yates's cautious comment on its copious overlays and laminations— "Perhaps the allegories in this picture may refer to elements in a masque at which [the sitter] was present"[45]—seems increasingly insightful. Whether it depicts an aristocratic masquer who danced while pregnant, like Queen Anna in *Masque of Blacknesse*; a gentlewoman posing *à la turque* for her portrait; an allegorical fiction employing masque-like costuming and scenery; or even a version of Elizabeth herself, it is theatrical in the extreme.[46] Compared with Strong's dramatic Eureka!, Yates's hesitancy has the virtue of granting a representational independence to the painted image, opening up rather than closing off hermeneutic possibility. But its usefulness is limited by her silence (possibly tactful) on the crux of the painting: the woman's suggested pregnancy and its relation to her emotional state. Only a boldness equal to the Lady's somatic challenge, and an alertness to the vocabulary of theatricality, allows us full access to the clashing fields of meaning in the portrait, with its admixture of mirth, scandal, seriousness, dressing up, eroticism, and complaint. Only performance invites the aestheticized rupture of identity, in which a person deliberately takes on a persona for effect, and then abandons it in an instant. Once one views the Persian Lady as a kind of female performer *in potentia* whose role is meant to be taken as temporary and artificial, the carefully placed emblems seem stage props in an elaborate show, rather than compensations for her painted muteness. In her gorgeous, loose-bodied gown, she colludes in making a spectacle of herself, presenting her body and its words as dark conceits written fair. We cannot know that this lady is deeply wronged or gloomy, because we cannot know if she is pregnant or abandoned; we can only be reasonably sure that she is in a kind of costume, and that she commands her props, and our gaze, like an actress sure of her hold on an audience.

If this is so, then the primal urge to name the Lady and stag and to define her sexual status sends us on a fool's errand, along with Strong and every other sleuth who has sought a name. The alluring sonnet-complaint only increases this fruitless desire, like others of its genre: "Plaint is often vulnerable to forced readings *à clef*. With its busy rhetoric pointing to ill-defined hurts, it offers the goad of urgency and uncertainty of a puzzle."[47] My view is that the painting invites, but successfully repels, such forced entries to its meaning. In the manner of Giorgione's *La Tempesta* or Botticelli's *Primavera*, the Unknown's Lady's pictorial allegories and textual elements ensure that no single answer is possible: artist, patron, sitter, and poet have rendered the quest moot through an embarrassment of clues, some contradictory.

For now obscure reasons they produced what James Elkins calls an Anti-Subject painting, or one lacking the hierarchalizing interpretive codes that characterize Subject paintings. Such a work may result when the artist deliberately layers codes so thickly that the Subject is partially erased, becoming a cipher: "Anti-Subject paintings show traces of the effort to efface them – they are palimpsestic, both literally and figuratively" (232).[48] While our curious painting seems to be a portrait, its *raison d'être* is far from obvious. Even for those who instantly recognized the sitter (years before her image was "sold as rubbish"), few could have synchronized the multiple meanings of her sonnet-lament and the tree's triple inscriptions, the Ovidian swallows and the embroidered impresas, the weird turban and the blue buskins, the eroticized stag and the map-like cartouche—at least not in such a way as to produce a credible linear narrative, a solution to the riddle.

The Persian Lady promises nothing of the kind. In a manner reminiscent of Spenser's dark conceits, the painting's verbal and visual codes clash and redouble teasingly, strangely combining emblems and narratives about sexual violence, familial rupture, pregnancy, and childbearing with contradictory signs of female performance, mirth, and mimetic creativity—from courtly masquing and singing and dancing, to the designing of impresas and emblems in needlework, to the writing of plays and sonnets, to the teasing play of lovemaking. If the sitter, artist, or patron had any game in mind, it involves the syncretic wit of the impresa, the glamour of disguise, and the kinetic hieroglyphics of the masque, not the verbal mechanics of the riddle. Her label remains "Unknown."

* * *

In their important volume *Early Modern Visual Culture*, Peter Erickson and Clark Hulse issue a "provocation" to traditional art historians to stop being so Italo-centric and obsessed with high art, and "a reciprocal challenge" to practitioners of literary and cultural studies to stop treating visual images as casual adjuncts to their weightier meditations on texts. Instead, we should

> attend in a critical way to the visual dimensions at the core of prevalent methodologies. These visual dimensions have often been unexamined and unexplained precisely to the extent that they have seemed to be easy tools for examining and explaining literary texts and explaining cultural phenomena as texts.
>
> (12)

The strength of visual studies lies in being committed to such labors via the "bottom-up, archivist cross-discipline of the intellectual shop floor" (13).

That idea of an "intellectual shop floor" is an attractive one, summoning up a noisy workshop of scrappy comrades sharing ideas; but feminists working in visual studies often discover this happy realm adjoins the chillier drawing rooms of art history, applied arts, and architecture, where a few authorities reign supreme and talk mainly to each other. One must be bold to gatecrash a discipline such as art history without an engraved invitation or specialized degree, as I have done here, but the sometimes tense encounter has the potential to produce some laudable results. Traditional art historians could capitalize on the work of "literary" feminists bringing to light a world of theatrical performance that includes some women as full-fledged players, and others as lively participants in arenas of writing, speech, and the emblematic arts. A few Englishwomen, such as Mary Wroth and Elizabeth I, for example, and many European ones, such as Tullia d'Aragona, wrote sonnet laments of the sort displayed in the Persian Lady painting; multitudes more on both sides of the Channel designed and sewed allegories, impresas, and devices like those on the gown she wears. The possibility that this portrait shows a poet-player in the mold of a Mary Stuart, Mary Wroth, Isabella Andreini, Veronica Franco, or Lucy Harington must also be discussed in any closer examination of voice, anonymity, and authorship inspired by its inscribed texts.

At the same time, feminist historians provide an important ballast and counter-weight to readings that consider only high politics and elite bodies. On the question of the Persian Lady's pregnancy, art historians would do well to acknowledge a specialized viewership for this painting: virtually all early modern women would have been schooled in reading other women's bodies for signs of pregnancy, and some would have served as matrons legally charged with determining this fact; the skill was marked as peculiarly female. This bias could not but affect the reception and meaning of this portrait when it was created. On the other hand, scholars in literary and cultural studies would benefit greatly from knowing far more about the history and economics of portraiture, the continual encoding and overlay of visual genres, and the allegorical obsessions of early modern English art. All would benefit from asking a few questions motivated by vulgar curiosity (is the stag a cuckold?) After all, discipline-crossers are by definition willing to risk being gauche, and to become novices again. With these kinds of collaborators, the intellectual shop floor might become a ruder, more vital, and far more interesting place.

Notes

1. The two states are Scotland and England, Elizabeth's "offspring," but these lines also neatly capture the allure of somatic undecidability that is my subject. From Thomas Pecke's translation of Owen's *Epigrammatum Ioannis Owen Cambro-Britanni Libri Tres* (1607).
2. Notable examples include Susan Frye, *Elizabeth I: The Competition for Representation* (New York: Oxford University Press, 1993); Kim F. Hall, *Things of Darkness: Economies of Race and Gender in Early Modern England* (Ithaca, NY and London: Cornell University Press, 1995); Clare McManus, *Women on the Renaissance Stage: Anna of Denmark and Female Masquing in the Stuart Court*

1590–1619 (Manchester: Manchester University Press, 2002); Ann Rosalind Jones and Peter Stallybrass, *Renaissance Clothing and the Materials of Memory* (Cambridge: Cambridge University Press, 2000); Lena Cowen Orlin, *Private Matters and Public Culture in Post-Reformation England* (Ithaca, NY and London: Cornell University Press, 1994); and Valerie Traub, *The Renaissance of Lesbianism in Early Modern England* (Cambridge: Cambridge University Press, 2002).

3. Sir Roy Strong, "'My weepinge Stagg I crowne': The Persian Lady Reconsidered," in *The Art of the Emblem: Essays in Honor of Karl Josef Höltgen,* ed. Michael Bath, John Manning, and Alan R. Young (New York: AMS Press, 1993), 103–41; 105.

4. Ernest Law, *Royal Guidebook of Hampton Court Illustrated* (London: George Bell, 1898), 139.

5. Lionel Cust, "Marcus Gheeraerts," *Third Annual Volume of the Walpole Society* (1913–14), 27.

6. Frances A. Yates, "Boissard's Costume-Book and Two Portraits" (1959), rpt in *Astraea: The Imperial Theme in the Sixteenth Century* (London: Routledge & Kegan Paul, 1975), 221.

7. Yates, *Astraea*, 222, n. 3.

8. Yates, *Astraea*, 221. Strong later found that Gheeraerts also used Boissard for *Thomas Lee* (Jones and Stallybrass, *Materials*, 289 n. 65). Some scholars attribute the Rainbow Portrait to Gheeraerts; others argue for Isaac Oliver or an unknown artist.

9. Nonetheless, there is little that is explicitly Persian about her, as Strong concedes, and Yates points out that "it does not necessarily follow that she appeared as a Persian character in the masque" (*Astraea*, 221). Early moderns generally called any exotically "Eastern" clothing Turkish dress, and costume books show women in Turkey, Greece, and Africa wearing quite similar robes and turbans; see the Sultana Roxelana wearing the tall pointed *kashbasti* with dress and overdress, and "a noblewoman of Karamania in Anatolia" in *Vecellio's Renaissance Costume Book* (New York: Dover, 1977), 114, 138. The scrolled embroidery of roses, pansies, and honeysuckle on the "Persian" Lady's dress is "uniquely English" (Hearn, 44), quite unlike that worn by Persian Ambassador Sir Anthony Shirley or his wife, Countess Teresia Shirley, in portraits by Van Dyck (see Jones and Stallybrass, 56–8, and D. W. Davies, *Elizabethans Errant* [Ithaca, NY: Cornell University Press, 1967], 172–4). One possible visual intertext, which unfortunately I do not have space to explore, is religio-political: what Yates calls a "mitre-like" tiered turban may have evoked in viewers the *Persian* miter worn by the Pope, the Whore of Babylon in anti-Catholic polemics, or even Spenser's Duessa in *Faerie Queene*.

10. Strong, "My weepinge Stagg," 110. The sonnets seem quite different, however. The Persian Lady laments her own frustrated will; the Ditchley sonnet praises Elizabeth for her climatic power over and leniency toward her people. Even more important, the latter poem cannot be deciphered completely: inches were cut off the painting at some point, causing the last words in each line to be lost.

11. Strong does not mention the phoenixes embroidered on her gown, which I noticed only after a return visit to Hampton Court. Of all Elizabeth's impresas the phoenix is probably most important; but it was also a favorite emblem deployed by Mary Stuart, Marie de Guise, Eleanour of Austria, and others. James I, too, used the symbol early on to link himself to Elizabeth.

12. Strong, "My weepinge Stagg," 112, 120. He theorizes that the Persian theme was in fashion because of the intense interest aroused by news of Sir Anthony Shirley, who had just presented himself to the Grand Sophy and would later become

Persian Ambassador. He does not explain what Lee and Essex hoped to gain by this association. He does mention in passing that Spenser calls Persia "the nourse of pompous pride," and that Duessa wears a Persian miter ("My weepinge Stagg," 112), though these are associations hard to square with his reading of the portrait as an appeal to a Protestant prince. For more on the painting's "Persianness" see note 9.

13. "Introduction," *Early Modern Visual Culture: Representation, Race, and Empire in Renaissance England*, ed. Peter Erickson and Clark Hulse (Philadelphia: University of Pennsylvania Press, 2000), 3–5.

14. Strong, "My weepinge Stagg," 123.

15. Ibid., 107, 123. His scenario resembles *Hamlet*'s nunnery scene, in which Ophelia is staged by Polonius and Claudius. Strong furnishes the Persian Lady with props of sonnet-speech and garland, just as Ophelia is furnished with hers (a book and love-gifts), and she speaks on cue yet without a script of her own.

16. In courtly love iconography a lady crowning a lover with a garland signifies her "formal acceptance of [his] love service" and "her complementary desire for the male"; see Chad Coerver, "Donna/Dono: Chivalry and Adulterous Exchange in the Quattrocento," in *Picturing Women in Renaissance and Baroque Italy*, ed. Geraldine A. Johnson and Sara Matthews-Grieco (Cambridge: Cambridge University Press, 1997), 196–293; 207.

17. For more on the association of anonymous female lament with shame and eroticism, see Marcy North, *The Anonymous Renaissance: Cultures of Discretion in Tudor-Stuart England* (Chicago: University of Chicago Press, 2003), 222–34. Such poems are commonly held to be "ventriloquized" by male writers, but North persuasively questions such assumptions, exploring the possibility that women also assumed female voices not their own in writing anonymously (212, 222).

18. "Only the bird of Daulis, that grief-stricken / mother who brought an awful revenge/to her lord, cries for Itys of Ismarus. / The pitiable bird sings of Itys, / while Sappho sings her song of love abandoned." Ovid, "Sappho to Phaon," *Heroides*, trans. and intro. Harold Isbell (London: Penguin, 1990), 138. An eerie echo of "complaints of cruelly unkind" appears in Whitney's *Emblemes*, which calls Procne a woman "of cruell kinde" (Geffrey Whitney, *A Choice of Emblemes* [Leyden: Plantin, 1586], 29).

19. Ann Rosalind Jones, "New Songs for the Swallow: Ovid's Philomela in Tullia d'Aragona and Gaspara Stampa," in *Refiguring Woman: Perspectives on Gender and the Italian Renaissance*, ed. Marilyn Migiel and Juliana Schiesari (Ithaca, NY: Cornell University Press, 1991), 263–7.

20. Compare the phrase in *Henry VI, Part Three*, when Henry rages at Gloucester, calling him "Not like the fruit of such a goodly tree" (5.6.52). For the use of "kernel" to signify a child, see *Winter's Tale*: "How like, methought, I then was to this kernel, / This squash, this gentleman" (1.2.155–6). Quotations from *The Riverside Shakespeare*, ed. G. Blakemore Evans et al. (Boston, MA: Houghton Mifflin, 1974).

21. John Kerrigan, *Motives of Woe: Shakespeare and "Female Complaint": A Critical Anthology* (Oxford: Clarendon, 1991), 89, 127, 14, n.1.

22. The triteness of the association is satirized in Rowley's *Birth of Merlin*, in which a clown mocks a pregnant maid moaning to the trees, saying she should have searched in town for a husband before combing the woods for a lover.

23. Kerrigan, *Motives*, 12, 19.

24. Those who have taken stabs at naming the Persian Lady include Hildegard Hammerschmidt-Hummel, doggedly arguing for Elizabeth Vernon, who turns out to be Shakespeare's Dark Lady; this identification enables her to show that both the sonnet and the unborn child are his (*Das Geheimnis um Shakespeares "Dark Lady": Documentation einer Enthullung* [Darmstadt: Primus Verlag, 1999]). I thank Dominique Nauheim for her generous kindness in translating chapters for me. Janet Arnold opts for Anne Vavasour or her sister ("Elizabethan and Jacobean Smocks and Shirts," *Waffen-und Kostumkunde* 19.2 [1977]: 89–110). A nameless anti-Stratfordian sees the portrait as "Elizabeth in a maternity dress, raising the distinct possibility that the 'Virgin Queen' bore children, namely Francis Bacon" (www.sirbacon.org/gallery/lizl.html).

25. For details about these and other courtly lovers punished in the 1590s by being tongue-lashed, beaten, banished, or sent to the Tower or Fleet, see Paul Hammer, "Sex and the Virgin Queen: Aristocratic Concupiscence and the Court of Elizabeth I," *Sixteenth Century Journal* 31. 1 (2000): 77–97; 6–7, 12.

26. Laura Gowing, "Secret Births and Infanticide in Seventeenth-Century England," *Past and Present* 156 (August 1997): 87–115; 90. Also see Richelle Munkhoff, "Reading Mothers and Matrons: Visual Literacy and Textuality of Womanhood," paper delivered at the Shakespeare Association of America meeting in 2001.

27. Gowing, "Secret," 90.

28. Arnold, "Elizabethan and Jacobean Smocks," 100–1.

29. Janet Arnold, *Queen Elizabeth's Wardrobe Unlock'd* (Leeds: Maney, 1988), 121.

30. Karen Hearn, *Marcus Gheeraerts II: Elizabethan Artist* (London: Tate Publishing, 2002), 40–51.

31. Hearn, *Marcus Gheeraerts II*, 36.

32. Arnold, *Queen Elizabeth's Wardrobe*, 121.

33. Ben Jonson, *The Complete Poems,* ed. George Parfitt (New Haven, CT: Yale University Press, 1982), 53.

34. John Webster, *The Duchess of Malfi, Drama of the English Renaissance*, ed. M. L. Wine (New York: Modern Library, 1969), 492–600.

35. As Jones and Stallybrass say in discussing *Hic Mulier*, "The 'bodice' is / are the materials which construct a body, as if the made bodies preceded any physical body and gave shape to it" (*Materials*, 85).

36. Jean Wilson, *Entertainments for Elizabeth* (Woodbridge, Suffolk: D. S. Brewer, 1980), 135.

37. "How like you this?" is a key line from Thomas Wyatt's "They fle from me," which layers erotic and performative codes remarkably similar to those in the Persian Lady portrait painted decades later. Most obviously, Wyatt's poem calls up an illicit encounter "after a pleasant gyse" with a lady in a provocatively loose gown ("thyn arraye"), while toying with Petrarchist wordplay on dear/deer and hart/heart.

38. See Arnold, "Elizabethan and Jacobean Smocks," 104–5. For a brilliant examination of the ambiguous erotics of undress in another "staged" portrait, see Ellen Chirelstein, "Lady Elizabeth Pope: The Heraldic Body," in *Renaissance Bodies: The Human Figure in English Culture c. 1540–1660*, ed. Lucy Gent and Nigel Llewellyn (London: Reaktion, 1990), 36–59.

39. Joaneath Spicer, "The Renaissance Elbow," in *A Cultural History of Gesture*, ed. Jan Bremmer and Herman Roodenburg (Ithaca, NY and London: Cornell University Press, 1991), 87–8. On the rarity of the pose in women's portraits, also see Zirka Z. Filipczak, "Poses and Passions: Mona Lisa's 'Closely Folded' Hands," in

Reading the Early Modern Passions, ed. Gail Kern Paster, Katherine Rowe, and Mary Floyd-Wilson (Philadelphia: University of Pennsylvania Press, 2004), 68–88. Even for men the thrust elbow was discouraged as prideful and aggressive by Erasmus and John Bulwer, among others, but soon took over as a favorite masculine stance, crossing class lines (Spicer, 83–5).

40. For "Boldnesse," see figure 4.1 in Paster, Rowe, and Floyd-Wilson, *Reading the Early Modern Passions*; for the Venetian courtesan, see Albert Racinet, *The Historical Encyclopedia of Costumes* (1888; rpt New York: Facts on File, 1988), figure 3.7. For the tattooed maid, see Le Moyne de Morgues, *A Young Daughter of the Picts*, Yale Center for British Art; for Penthesilea, see McManus, *Women on the Renaissance Stage*, figure 4; for Margaret Cavendish, see *Plays, Never before Printed, written by the Thrice Noble, Illustrious, and Excellent Princess, the Duchess of Newcastle* (London, 1668).

41. Clark Hulse makes a similar point about Holbein's grim portrait of Thomas Cromwell, which once bore a warmly laudatory inscription which seems "wildly inappropriate to the visual evidence" ("Reading Painting: Holbein, Cromwell, Wyatt," in *Early Modern Visual Culture: Representation, Race, and Empire in Renaissance England*, ed. Peter Erickson and Clark Hulse [Philadelphia: University of Pennsylvania Press, 2000], 148–77; 169).

42. Strong, "My weepinge Stagg," 113, 117.

43. Quoted and discussed in Kerrigan, *Motives*, 229.

44. For an example, see Kerrigan, *Motives*, figure 2.

45. Yates, *Astraea*, 221.

46. Perhaps the Unknown Lady is pictured at her ease after a play or masque. This begs the question about what scene and figures are indicated, of course. While Yates muses that it may indeed show a version of Elizabeth among allegories based on "elements from a masque" (*Astraea*, 220–1), the image echoes with scenes of both good and ill fame. Diana the huntress is often depicted with bow and arrows and a tame stag at her feet; certain saints' tales feature visions of tame stags as Christ; and emblems of Prudenza, Adulation, and Vita Longa are figured as women with stags in Ripa's *Iconologia*. More troubling associations include the Whore of Babylon with her distinctive Persian miter, the pregnant and shamed Calisto, the harlot-goddess Flora, Circe with a victim, the scandalous concubine/empress Roxelana, and the incestuous and pregnant Myrrha, punished by being turned to a tree (for the latter suggestion I am grateful to Elizabeth Harvey). Eve was also sometimes shown with a stag, signifying human lust.

47. Kerrigan, *Motives*, 18.

48. James Elkins, "On Monstrously Ambiguous Paintings," *History and Theory* 32.3 (October 1993): 227–47; 232. This portrait also shows signs of literal erasure and over-painting at the right, where shapes can be seen below the Lady's veil and under the brown hill rising behind her.

10
Construing Gender: Mastering Bianca in *The Taming of the Shrew*

Patricia Parker

At the beginning of Act 3 of *The Taming of the Shrew*, Lucentio (disguised as Cambio, master of "letters") and Hortensio (disguised as Litio, master of music) vie as rival "masters" for Bianca, the sister presented up to this point as exhibiting (in contrast to her sister the "shrew") the "Maid's mild behavior and sobriety" (I.i.71), which appears to guarantee that she will be a tractable, obedient, and subordinate wife. As the scene opens, Lucentio accuses Hortensio the "fiddler" of being too "forward" in putting music *before* letters or "philosophy" rather than the other way round, in lines that curiously echo the descriptions of the "forwardness" and forwardness of Kate the "shrew" herself:

> *Lucentio*: Fiddler, forbear, you grow too forward, sir,
> Have you so soon forgot the entertainment
> Her sister Katherine welcom'd you withal?
> *Hortensio*: But, wrangling pedant, this is
> The patroness of heavenly harmony.
> Then give me leave to have prerogative,
> And when in music we have spent an hour,
> Your lecture shall have leisure for as much.
> *Lucentio*: Preposterous ass, that never read so far
> To know the cause why music was ordain'd!
> Was it not to refresh the mind of man
> After his studies or his usual pain?
> Then give me leave to read philosophy,
> And while I pause, serve in your harmony.
>
> (III.i.4–14)

"Preposterous" here is usually glossed by editors of the play as "reversing the natural order of things" or putting "the cart before the horse," the form of *hysteron proteron* or preposterous placing that was routinely available in the period for the inversion of allegedly natural orders of all kinds.[1]

This inversion or exchange of place is introduced in a contest between two rival masters which appears, at least initially, to be simply wrangling over which of the arts should have "prerogative," or come first. There is, however, much more at stake in the staging here of competing arts, in a scene in which the "preposterous" becomes the marker of much broader issues of order at work within the play as a whole. This prominently includes the "cambio," or exchange, within the Lucentio–Bianca subplot itself, whereby Bianca becomes the master of both of her potential masters in this pivotal scene and finally emerges as an anything but a tamed wife by the play's post-marital end.

That the proper ordering of rival arts appears to be the subject of the debate in this scene is consistent with the emphasis on arts and learning that pervades *The Taming of the Shrew*—though it is has often been easy to forget this emphasis in a play so often characterized as simply an early Shakespearean farce. It might even be said that its combination of such traditionally elevated with lower (and lower bodily) registers is part of the cambio of preposterous inversions it foregrounds. Lucentio opens the taming play proper by speaking of "the great desire I had / To see Padua, nursery of arts" (I.i.2), a reminder that Padua's university was famous throughout Europe. As the subsequent rhyming of "arts" and "hearts" and the competition of rival suitors for Bianca makes clear, however, the *ars amatoria* is the principal *ars* it pursues, however loftily disguised. Even the following of an "art" or *ars* itself within the play becomes part of the preposterous bodily reversals it both echoes and compounds. In a play that features a "tongue" in a "tail," and in ways crucial for the Latin lesson used in this scene by Lucentio as a cover for his wooing of Bianca, Latin *ars* from the venerable *sermo patrius* or "father" tongue already came compounded with inverted, preposterous or lower bodily senses. Lyly's *Endymion* famously rhymes "I am all Mars and Ars" with "Nay, you are all mass and ass," but it is only one of the many translations from father to mother tongue that mingled high and low in the period. Nashe's lines on the "excrements of Arts" even more explicitly exploit the bodily and bawdy potential in any discussion of the learned *artes* or *ars*.[2] Within *The Taming of the Shrew*, Grumio's "O this woodcock, what an ass it is"—in response to Gremio's "O this learning, what a thing it is!" (I.ii.159)—is comically underwritten by such vernacular slippages, but so is Lucentio's "Preposterous ass" as an insult to a master of music who insists on the right of his particular *ars* to come first or before. Lucentio-Cambio's accusation against his "forward" rival—that he is "preposterous" for desiring to put *before* what should come behind—resonates with the scatalogy that from as early as Augustine identified the *ars musica* with the lower bodily or hindparts, as well as the literal sense of *preposterous* as arsy-versy which gives Hortensio's placing of music first the stigma of turning back-to-front. In a scene that will soon suggest the lower bodily counterparts of this "fiddler" teaching Bianca "fingering" and of the *re* (or "thing") as a double-meaning part of the musical gamut, it is impossible to separate the apparently high discourses of learning and the arts from the lower bodily and all it implies.[3] As modern readers or audiences, we are distanced from the full implications of such preposterous play in *The Taming of the Shrew* by what Norbert Elias has characterized as the historically intervening "civilizing process," or what Pierre Bourdieu has described as later developments of "distinction" between high and low. But as with the scatalogical overtones of apparently learned or mock-learned scenes of *Loves Labours Lost*, another early Shakespeare play, we need to take time to learn this historical vernacular in order to see what is at stake in the dramatic *mise-en-scène* of preposterous or arsy-versy exchanges of place and position in *The Taming of the Shrew*, not only in relation to gender but also for the other kinds of order and hierarchy it both stages and disrupts.[4]

* * *

The sense of reversal introduced into this subplot scene by Lucentio's "preposterous ass" soon involves subtle and not so subtle over-turnings at the level of gender, but ones that we are able to track only if we become aware of the gender and other hierarchies already at work within contemporary discussions of the arts and of what was at stake in the Latin texts used by Lucentio as Bianca's would-be "master," both pedagogically and maritally. Debate over the hierarchy of rival "arts" was a preoccupation not only in Castiglione's *The Courtier* (translated by Thomas Hoby in 1561 and published in no fewer than four London editions by 1603), but also in the spate of books directed at upwardly mobile bourgeois families like Bianca's (and Kate's) in *The Taming of the Shrew*, concerned with what their merchant father Baptista calls "good bringing-up" (I.i.99). Such manuals offered the aspiring merchant class the promise of access to the more gentle arts, while simultaneously foregrounding the cultural capital of such markers of distinction as something that (like clothing) could be acquired—as the tutoring of Bianca by hired masters suggests.

Maureen Quilligan (whose reading of the play is attentive to its emphasis on "class" as well as on hierarchies of gender) notes that the Induction to the play—where Sly is schooled in how to address his Lady ("SLY: Ali'ce madam, or Joan madam? / LORD: Madam, and nothing else: so lords call ladies")—draws "a quick conduct-book lesson in how to 'lord it,'" in a period when social identity itself was being shaped by these models of fashioning and "'self-fashioning,'" thus staging in the process "the same social premise that underlies the courtesy books," that "social behavior is not a natural, biologically determined fact" but "can be learned (and unlearned)."[5] As so much feminist work over the past two decades has taught us, this same vogue for conduct literature was simultaneously schooling young women on how to be "chaste, silent, and obedient," alongside a sprinkling of learning in music and other arts. The conduct book culture that the scene of rival "masters" and "arts" evokes in Shakespeare's *Shrew* should not, therefore, be unexpected in a play that repeatedly underscores the markers of upward mobility—or social hierarchies in a state of transition—including the double-meaning "titles" and "deeds" that hover between their older chivalric or aristocratic meanings and the new world of property transfers and marriage markets. In this sense, the "preposterous" (as a marker of the unnatural as well as the reversed), introduced into this scene of tutors hired by Bianca's upwardly mobile father, was itself a cultural keyword for all such "unnatural" acquisitions, as well as for social and gender reversals in the period.

In the scene that begins with the contest between Lucentio and Hortensio as supposed masters of arts who are simultaneously rival masters for Bianca on the marriage market, Lucentio's "Preposterous ass, that never read so far / To know the cause why music was ordain'd" directly evokes such contemporary reading. At the same time, the gendered invocation of "heavenly harmony" in these opening lines recalls contemporary debates over what should come *first* and what follow after, in a pivotal scene in which what seems to be simply a learned or mock-learned discussion of the priority of different arts has implications for the corresponding order of first and second, or subordinate, in the hierarchy of gender and social place. Hortensio (or Litio), in advancing music's "prerogative" or right to come *first*, invokes the Neoplatonic and Pythagorean tradition of "heavenly harmony," music as the cosmic *arche* or beginning of the world. Lucentio/Cambio, who reverses Hortensio's status and claim by denigrating this master of music, in social terms, as a mere "fiddler," champions the inverse tradition in which music itself was characterized as subordinate or second, upbraiding his rival for not having "read" enough to know that music was to come only *after* more exalted studies. His "Preposterous ass, that never read so far / To know the cause why music was ordain'd! / 'Was it not to refresh the mind of man / *After* his studies or his usual pain?" (III.i.12–15) thus recalls texts such as *The Courtier* itself, where music is cast in a subordinate or secondary role, as "a most sweete lightning of our travailes and vexations" or "a verie great refreshing of all worldlye paines and griefes." In Castiglione's influential text, which also had a major impact on conduct books for upwardly mobile or not yet gentle readers, the frequent or unsolicited performance of music by members of the aristocracy is rigorously condemned because such a pursuit would break down the distinctions between a nobleman and his music-performing servant (much less "fiddlers," or mechanical practictioners of the art).[6]

Sir Thomas Elyot's *The Boke named the Governour*—in its description of the "order" to be followed in "the bringing up of . . . children"—similarly counsels that music should come after more serious study, emphasizing that music "only serveth for recreation after tedious or laborious affairs."

In ways that make clear the multiple hierarchies at stake in texts that have
a noble audience in view, Elyot too warns that aristocratic practitioners of
music risk being held "in the similitude of a common servant or minstrel,"
a term of opprobrium not unlike Lucentio's depiction of the music master
as a "fiddler" here. But even Thomas Morley's *Plain and Easy Introduction to
Practical Music*—directed to a readership of the middling sort—makes clear
that music is meant to "recreate" scholars only *"after* [their] more serious
studies."[7]

Music in such guides to "good bringing up" was thus understood as a
diversion or form of recreation, not primary or first but subordinate or
second. By contrast, to put music *first*—as Hortensio seeks to do, before
he is called down by Lucentio as a "fiddler" as well as a "forward" and a
"preposterous ass"—would be simultaneously preposterous in other senses,
since it would involve a reversal of first and second, higher and lower on the
social hierarchy reflected by the hierarchy of the arts themselves. "Fiddler"
here evokes several of these subordinate positions at once. Contempt for
musicians as practitioners of a "mechanical" art ranged from complaints
such as Stephen Gosson's in *The Schoole of Abuse* against beggar companies
of "fiddlers," to the use of the term "fiddler" itself both for the player of the
violin (considered a rather vulgar instrument) and for the lower social status
of musicians in the period. John Ferne, in *The Blazon of Gentrie*, treats of
these "mechanicall practicioners" of "so base a profession" that the laws of
the "Countrey . . . have determined them for roages and vagabonds, enemies
to the publique good of our Countrey" and contrasts them to the "learned
professor of that Science" commended by Pythagoras, Plato, Aristotle, and
others, a social bias reflected in Thomas Morley's reference to "ignorant *Asses*,
who take upon them to lead others, being more blind than themselves."[8] As
is well known, derogatory references to such musical "roages and vagabonds"
in the period join contemporary sneers at players and other practitioners
of "mechanic" arts. Hortensio complains that even Katherine had branded
him with this class sneer when he attempted to teach her music in an earlier
scene. There, having had the "lute" broken on his head in her resistant
"frets," he complains that "she did call me rascal fiddler / And twangling
Jack, with twenty such vild terms, / As had she studied to misuse me so"
(II.i.157–9).

Lucentio's ridicule of his rival tutor as ignorant of the proper order of the
arts is thus a pedantic putdown grounded in one of the multiple indices of
upward mobility in the period, reflected in texts such as Castiglione's *Courtier*
and its bourgeois counterparts. Treatises such as Elyot's *The Governour* were
directed to the governing classes broadly conceived, but handbooks such as
Morley's joined the demand for tutors in the households of upwardly mobile
merchants like Baptista who "had made fortunes . . . and who modelled their
households on those of the social strata immediately above them."[9] At the
level of contested social hierarchies, *The Taming of the Shrew*—which already

calls such sustained attention to the marriage-market "cambio" or exchange between landed gentry and merchant money—simultaneously reflects in this contest between Bianca's rival masters the market for schooling in the "arts" of proper "bringing up."

Lucentio's "preposterous" is pronounced as a judgment on his rival's ignorance of this required reading. But even more importantly for the place of this Bianca scene within the larger taming plot, what appears to be simply a pedantic discussion of the priority and ordering of the arts comes with important implications for the hierarchy of gender, in a scene in which Bianca will soon preposterously overturn the hierarchy of mastery itself. The casting of music as a diversion or recreation—to follow only after more serious pursuits—had its parallel in the subordination of music, as handmaiden, to letters, philosophy and the *logos* of words, the patroness of "heavenly harmony" not as *arche* or first but as literally ancillary (the etymological resonance of its "handmaiden" status). In this respect, the subordination of music was frequently described in the period of *The Taming of the Shrew* in explicitly gendered terms. If Wagner, much later, could make music female in the scale of gender—noting that "Music is the handmaid of Poetry [and] in the wedding of the two arts, Poetry is the man, music the woman; Poetry leads and Music follows"—the more contemporary witness of early modern texts such as *The Passionate Pilgrim* (1599) invoked the gendering of music and poetry as "sister" and "brother" ("If Music and sweet Poetry agree, / As they must needs, the Sister and the Brother . . ."). Music is directly associated with women in *The Courtier*, which advises its readers that music is "meete to be practised in the presence of women" because their "sights sweeten the mindes of the hearers, and make them the more apt to bee pierced with the pleasantnesse of musicke, and also they quicken the spirits of the very doers" (Book II, 101). At the same time, music was feminized as something seductive that must be kept subordinate or under control. The same *Boke named the Governour* that counsels that male children should be "taken from the company of women" at age seven, lest they be imperiled by "sparks of voluptuosity which, nourished by any occasion or object, increase often times into so terrible a fire that therewith all virtue and reason is consumed" (Book I, ch. vi, 19), warns in its chapter on music that its "pleasant" diversion must not "allure" to "so much delectation" that it lead to "wantonness," "inordinate delight," or the "abandoning [of] gravity" and more serious pursuits (Book I, ch. vii, 21–2).

As a "thing to passe the time withall," music is simultaneously associated in *The Courtier* and other contemporary texts with the making of womanish or effeminate men, along with "other vanities" that are "meet for women, and peradventure for some also that have the likeness of men, but not for them that be men in deede: who ought not with such delicacies to womanish their mindes." Ascham writes that "The minstrelsie of lutes, pipes, harps, and all other that standeth by such nice, fine, minikin fingering is farre more fit for the wommanishnesse of it to dwell in the courte among ladies."[10] Music is thus not only associated *with* women but is cast as able to turn men *into* women, a transformation highlighted explicitly in *The Taming of the Shrew* in multiple forms, not only in the transvestism that makes its first apparently tractable wife the Induction's scripted transvestite page, but also in the later scene on the "sun" and the "moon" (already highly gendered figures), where the patriarch Vincentio is pronounced a "maid" and Hortensio comments "twould make a man mad to make a woman of him" (IV.v.36).

But there is an even more striking echo in the lines in which Lucentio claims that music should be not "forward" or first but subordinate or second, and that to invert this order would be "preposterous"—an echo that comes with direct implications for the gendering of this hierarchy through even more authoritative contemporary forms. The scene's invocation of the "preposterous" as a culturally loaded term that already foregrounds the issue of what should have "prerogative" or precedence thus simultaneously calls for even closer scrutiny in relation to the marriage market and the hierarchy of male and female within it. Lucentio's "Preposterous ass, that never read so far / To know *the cause why music was ordain'd*" directly echoes the "causes for which *Matrimonie* was ordeyned" from the marriage ceremony in the Boke of Common Prayer (1552), the text that enjoins the woman as the "weaker vessell" to be "subiect" unto her husband as a "milde and quiet wife" in "quietnes, sobrietie & peace," or in other words precisely what Bianca is assumed to be potentially when the play begins, in contrast to her sister, the "shrew."[11] This unmistakable echo of the Ceremony of Matrimony here—and with it the Pauline and other biblical assumptions of male prerogative and female subordination from the Genesis 2 order of Adam *before* Eve—has momentous implications for this pivotal scene in which Bianca will master both of her would-be "masters" in turn, extending the sense of preposterous overturning from the initial context of the ordering of the arts to a reconstructing at the level of gender.

Such a direct echo of the Ceremony of Matrimony sets up even further reverberations between this Bianca subplot scene and the larger shrew-taming play, which repeatedly recalls that ceremony (foundation of the Elizabethan homiletic tradition that counseled the subordination of women) and famously ends with Kate's apparent iteration of the Pauline figure of the man as "head" (V.ii.147). The Ceremony itself invokes the prescribed sequence of the genders among the "thinges set in ordre" in Genesis, and other biblical texts from which this order of priority was derived: man made in God's "owne ymage and similitude," and woman, secondarily and "out of man." If music as handmaiden or subordinate is "ordain'd" to "refresh the mind of man / *After* his studies or his usual pain"—in the hierarchy of primary and secondary in which its "harmony" is to be "serve[d] in" only *following* the "prerogative" of "philosophy" or "letters"—then in the order derived from Genesis 2, matrimony is "ordained" to be similarly refreshing ("for the mutuall societie, helpe & comfort, that ye one ought to have of the other, both in prosperitie and adversitie"), with the helpmeet wife, or "weaker vessel," a clearly subordinate second.[12]

That there should be an echo of the Ceremony of Matrimony in the very lines that evoke a "preposterous" reversal at the opening of Act 3 thus gives to the question of order in this first major Bianca scene a much greater resonance than mere wrangling over rival arts, one with implications not only for the play as a whole but also for the portrayal of the apparently tractable Bianca within it. By the end of the play, as already noted, Bianca herself will be anything but subordinate or submissive, but will be chastised instead, like Kate before her, for being too "forward" as well as "froward" (V.ii.119, a synonym for the "preposterous" that was routinely used for unruly wives). In this pivotal Act 3 scene, the echo of the Ceremony of Matrimony and with it, of the ordaining of matrimony in Genesis, is sounded in opening lines devoted ostensibly to a contest only between men, with Bianca the apparently passive object of their rivalry. But in this first major scene of the play to feature the supposedly submissive younger sister, this unmistakable echo invokes the Ceremony's strictures on the hierarchy of the genders at the very moment when Bianca will overturn it and manipulate it, becoming not a submissive female but director of both masters.

Textual editors from Theobald (1733) and Malone (1790) onwards have emended what they see in this opening as a truncated line—"this is / The patroness of heavenly harmony"—to a formulation that identifies this "patroness" of "harmony" as Bianca herself, as distinguished from the discordant "frets" of her shrewish sister, Kate. Bianca in this scene, however, far from providing a contrast to her elder sister, proves to be less tractable than her alignment with music as either handmaiden or heavenly harmony suggests. The scene's initial discussion of the proper order of the arts is cut short by Bianca herself. She refuses to be a "breeching scholar" (III.i.18) to either of her rival tutors, rejecting the master–pupil relationship of "following" or imitation prescribed in school texts such as Mulcaster's *Positions* and the following of appointed "hours" and "times," in ways that pointedly recall the earlier rejection of "appointed hours" (I.i.103) by Kate the *designated* shrew, in the scene that had contrasted Bianca's "mild behavior and sobriety" (I.i.71) to her more "froward" sister (I.i.69). Bianca puts an end to the wrangling of her would-be masters by reminding them of *her* prerogative:

> Why, gentlemen, you do me double wrong
> To strive for that which resteth in *my* choice.
> I am no breeching scholar in the schools,
> I'll not be tied to hours, nor 'pointed times,
> But learn the lessons *as I please myself...*

> (III.i.16-20; emphasis mine)

The scene that invokes the "preposterous" in relation to the appropriate sequence of the arts thus not only summons echoes of the proper order of the genders from the Ceremony of Matrimony (where women, like music, are to be secondary or subordinate), but already undercuts the taming plot's ostensible contrast between a "fretful" shrew and her apparently obedient younger sister, long before the final scene. This overturning is even clearer when this scene in Act 3 turns (after Bianca asks "Cambio" to "conster" or construe some Latin lines) into a lesson in translation—or what was known in early modern English as construing or construction. For this kind of linguistic construction was dominated by the very discipline of subordination, or obedient following of a "master," that Lucentio proceeds to assume.[13]

In a play that is literally filled with tags from grammar school texts—including the *Grammar* of Lilly and Colet whose "Masculine gender is more worthy than the Feminine" was already a watchword for more than simply grammatical gender in the period—the lesson offered by the would-be "master" Lucentio/Cambio to Bianca as his intended pupil is based on precisely this contemporary order of following after, the pedagogical counterpart to the later textual description of Bianca as a supposed wifely "appendix" (IV.iv.104) and the printing metaphors of the husband's' "ad imprimendum solum" or exclusive "right to print." This scene's actual staging, however, of the formula for such pedagogical construing or construction—a student's supposedly faithful following of a master's script—simultaneously evokes a "construction" that is exploited elsewhere in Shakespeare with different and much more suggestive implications: from the impossibility of reading the "mind's construction in the face" (*Macbeth*) and the ambiguous "merciful construction of old women" (*Henry VIII*) to the adulterously "shrewd construction" to be made of Mistress Ford, in the scene where her husband "prescribes" to himself "preposterously" (*Merry Wives* II.ii.223), and the "illegitimate construction" of women in *Much Ado About Nothing* (III.iv.50). "Illegitimate construction" itself turns as a *double entendre* on the connection between the infidelity of translations or constructions and the feared infidelity of women, the cultural anxiety evoked in *The Taming of the Shrew* when the Pedant responds: "Ay, sir, so his mother says, if I may believe her" to the question of whether Lucentio is his legitimate son (IV.v.34). Though it may be as foreign to us as modern readers as the multiple early modern implications of the "preposterous," this interconnection between the fidelity of translations and the fidelity of women was commonplace in Shakespeare and other contemporary texts. In *Merry Wives*, for example, Mistress Quickly translates into ever-more promiscuous vernacular constructions the Latin of the *sermo patrius* she fails to understand, in a play that makes clear that words, like wives, can be both diverting and unfaithful.[14]

In *The Taming of the Shrew*, the disguised Lucentio/Cambio, who argues for the "prerogative" of going *first*, begins by expecting that his Latin lesson will unfold according to his own agenda and construing:

> '*Hic ibat,*' as I told you before, '*Simois,*' I am Lucentio, '*hic est,*' son unto Vincentio of Pisa, '*[Sigeia] tellus,*' disguis'ed thus to get your love, '*Hic steterat,*' and that Lucentio that comes a-wooing, '*Priami,*' is my man Tranio, '*regia,*' bearing my port, '*celsa senis,*' that we might beguile the old pantaloon.
>
> (III.i.31–7)

But in contrast to the schoolboy or "breeching scholar" who might be expected to follow the construction of a "master," Bianca produces her own, very different construction, no more seconding or repeating his words than she consents to yield to "appointed times" or "hours." If from the perspective of the master's script, the role of the schoolboy is to follow after, this is precisely the subordinate or second position that Bianca here eschews. Instead of iterating the translation of her would-be master (in both the pedagogical and the marital sense), then, Bianca provides her own very different, and more ambiguous, construing:

> Now let me see if I can conster it: '*Hic ibat Simois,*' I know you not, '*hic est [Sigeia] tellus,*' I trust you not, '*Hic steterat Priami,*' take heed he hear us not, '*regia,*' presume not, '*celsa senis,*' despair not.
>
> (III.i.41–5)

Editors have argued that Bianca's very different translation here is simply a way of raising her price in the marriage market, by withholding immediate assent from a suitor at the same time as adding that he should not "despair." But the implications of this translation lesson—and of Bianca's more ambiguous as well as divergent construings—are actually much more subtle and far-reaching than any such culturally commonplace reading of her demurring might suggest. Bianca turns the tables here by providing a very different translation of the same Latin text that Lucentio or "Cambio" is attempting to make serve his turn with her. But strikingly, even feminist critics have missed the female complaint that provides the very basis of this Latin lesson—as well as the inter-textuality that makes Bianca's doubts about Lucentio's constructions both more resistant and more complex.[15]

Such intertextual markers frequently go unnoticed in *The Taming of the Shrew*, perhaps because of the longstanding critical fiction that it is part of a supposedly naive or simple "early Shakespeare." Once again, even feminist critics have concurred with Lucentio's constructions, or read Bianca as simply repeating the words of her "master" here, making this scene continuous with (rather than a striking departure from) the Bianca described by others earlier in the play as the tractably chaste, silent, and obedient woman of the conduct books. However, the actual text that provides the basis for this translation lesson—from Ovid's *Heroides*, familiar to schoolboys including Shakespeare in Latin, and already translated into English by Turberville in 1567—is Penelope's anything but submissive or silent complaint against her own husband and master for taking so long to return home, a complaint that Shakespeare puts into the mouth not of a mild and tractable but rather of a "shrewish" wife in *The Comedy of Errors*, another early play.[16] The particular Latin lines presented for translation in this scene are from Penelope's complaining that other wives have heard the Troy story directly from their already returned husbands, while she has had to get the story herself, and only at second hand, by sending her son to find his father. But Bianca's "Where left we last?" (I.iii.26) makes clear that Penelope's much longer female complaint—which initiates the entire series of female complaints that make up the *Heroides* and includes her anger at being left alone for twenty years as well as her justified suspicion that Ulysses has been unfaithful—had already provided the text for a lesson begun even before this scene. The choice of the particular lines for translation here—on the siege of Troy before the ultimate guileful breaching of its "walls" (or in Turberville's translation "walles which you by breach haue brought to utter spoyle and sacke")—may themselves be part of the sotto voce commentary here; for the disguised Lucentio has himself gained entry to Bianca's house only through guile and the wooers in the sources for this subplot of Lucentio's wooing use their disguised entry to breach the walls of the corresponding female figures, in a sexual sense.[17]

The text chosen by Shakespeare for Lucentio's supposed instruction of Bianca here thus provides a highly suggestive commentary indeed, though the implications of this striking choice have been passed over by feminist as well as other editors and critics. The implications of such well known subtexts for Bianca's resistance to Lucentio's instruction-construction in this scene become even more telling when the lesson moves on to the next line of the *Heroides* text, which Lucentio presents in a translation he offers as authoritative or "sure":

> *Bianca*: In time I may believe, yet I mistrust.
> *Lucentio*: Mistrust it not, for sure Aeacides
> Was Ajax, call'd so from his grandfather.
> *Bianca*: I must believe my master, else I promise you,
> I should be arguing still upon that doubt.
> But let it rest. Now, Litio, to you. . . .
>
> (III.i.51–6)

This next line of the *Heroides* text, which Lucentio's "sure Aeacides / Was Ajax" appears to be translating, is *"illic Aeacides, illic tendebat Ulixes."* But—contrary to the translation of "Aeacides" (or descendant of Aeacus) that Lucentio presses Bianca to believe is "Ajax"—both Turberville and modern translations of the *Heroides* agree that "Aeacides" in this line from Penelope's complaint is not Ajax at all, but Achilles. Turberville translates this as "There fierce Achylles pight his Tents, / there wise Vlysses lay," while the modern Loeb translation has no index entry for Ajax at all, since *Aeacides* designates Achilles every time this phrase appears, even in its other female complaints.[18]

In ways equally suggestive for a subplot in which closing the marriage-market deal with Bianca's father requires Lucentio's patrimony or inheritance from a "supposed" father is so crucial, Lucentio or "Cambio" here assures Bianca that his construction is "sure" by appealing to the male lineage for this connection ("for sure Aeacides / Was Ajax, call'd so *from his grandfather"*).[19] But his attempt to assure as well as instruct in answer to Bianca's "yet I mistrust" is even at the level of purely textual translation a construction that is simply not to be trusted. In mistrusting the assurance of her would-be "master," in the pedagogical as well as the wooing sense here, Bianca not only takes over the direction of that wooing but proves to be clearly the better scholar, since what he tells her to believe—on his assurance—is like other supposes in this play of supposes, only his own very doubtful construction. As part of an in-joke that those with grammar schooling might be expected to appreciate, there is already every reason to mistrust this master's translation from Penelope's well-known *Heroides* complaint. But even more tellingly, Lucentio/Cambio's insistence that "Aeacides" is "Ajax" here actually abandons the *Heroides* text of justifiably complaining women for a different text altogether, one where there are no women present but only rival men competing for possession of a property or prize that is both passive and inert, as before she intervened, Bianca herself might have been supposed to be. In this very different text—from the famous rivalry between Ajax and Ulysses over who will inherit Achilles' armor in *Metamorphoses* 13 (a debate that Shakespeare would later write large in *Troilus and Cressida* as well as echoing in *Hamlet*)—Ajax's claim that he is "Aeacides" or male kinsman to Achilles and hence legitimate heir to this prize, bases his dubious right to inherit it as his property on a patriarchal line of descent and "title," while arguing that his rival can only by a "forged pedigree" ally himself to the "Aeacyds" (as Golding translated it) because Ulysses himself is a bastard—not his supposed father Laertes' son but offspring of his mother's coupling with another.[20] The text that the wooing "Cambio" here exchanges or substitutes for Penelope's introduction to the litany of complaints against men that fill the *Heroides* is, in other words, not only a rivalry exclusively between men for possession of a purely passive object but a text that once again draws attention to the very issues of property, patrimony, supposed fathers, or "illegitimate constructions" that pervade *The Taming of the Shrew* itself.[21]

Ajax, of course, also famously loses the debate, with even his own claim to be "Aeacides" left open to question.

In a scene that begins with such a clear echo of the Ceremony of Matrimony and its supposed "weaker vessell" who is to be "subiect" to her husband, Bianca not only intervenes but takes over the lessons offered by both "masters." And there is in her bringing of an end to the lesson in translation or construction a comment that is even more suggestive for the apparent shrew-taming trajectory of the play as a whole. When Bianca moves from "In time I may believe, yet I mistrust" to "I *must* believe my master" (in a line that may at first *appear* to signal her tractability or submission), it is not because Lucentio's is a "sure" construction or one she actually accepts. As this anything but passive female quickly makes clear, it is only a practical way of putting an end to what otherwise might continue interminably here: "else I promise you / I should be arguing still upon that doubt. / But let it rest. Now, Litio, to you."

Bianca's bringing Lucentio's proffered "lesson" to an end—in ways that make good on her promise to "learn the lessons as I please myself"—thus conveys something very different from acceptance of the conclusion that Lucentio himself presents as "sure," in a scene that forecasts the much less tractable Bianca of the play's post-marital end. It may even provide a suggestive advance gloss on her sister Katherine's apparent seconding of *her* master's constructions, when she makes the decision to iterate but also to transform Petruchio's aberrant designations of the "sun" and "moon," and delivers what appears to be her apparently submissive final speech. In a play full of such dramatic cross-references, as well as such "counterfeit supposes" (V.i.117)—beginning with the *sotto voce* witness of the Induction, where the play's first and perhaps only tractably obedient wife is a transvestite page following his master's script—perhaps Katherine's own apparent iteration of a culturally proffered script or construction is simply a way of bringing an otherwise endless debate to an at least temporary end, and nothing so straightforward as assumed assent.

*   *   *

Whatever the larger implications of this pivotal subplot scene—which begins by invoking the "preposterous" in the context of what should come *first* and what subordinately *second*—it is crucial in relation to the trajectory of Bianca within the play. Both Bianca's putative masters here find the orthodox teacher–pupil relationship unexpectedly overturned. The evocation of Penelope not in her patient but in her complaining mode joins the echoing of the Ceremony of Matrimony from the lines on the preposterous overturning of other orders with which this scene begins, yielding not the simple subordinate Penelope, but one used elsewhere in early Shakespeare for the speeches of a "shrew." And Bianca herself—described at the opening of the taming play as the wifely ideal so often represented by the more submissive Penelope—emerges through her own constructions of the *sermo patrius* or Latin text as a much less tractable figure, even while she continues to be described by others, who see her from the outside as a wifely subordinate or "appendix" (IV.iv.104).

My reading of this pivotal subplot scene is thus that Bianca is revealed to be neither a submissive Penelope nor the subordinate "weaker vessel" of the biblical texts on which the Ceremony of Matrimony itself depended. Characterizations of Bianca as only much later turning into a surprisingly "froward" wife—in the play's final, post-marital scene—miss the implications of the "preposterous" overturning displayed in this much earlier scene of a putative master's construing. Even a feminist critic as prescient as Karen Newman falls into this conventional reading of Bianca when she asserts of this language lesson that "Far from the imaginative use of language and linguistic play we find in Kate, Bianca repeats verbatim the Latin words Lucentio 'construes' to reveal his identity and his love. Her revelation of her feelings through a repetition of the Latin lines he quotes from Ovid are as close as possible to the silence we have come to expect from her." What, on the contrary, we encounter in this scene of putative instruction is a very different Bianca from either the representations of her the play has already cast up, as the potentially chaste, silent, and obedient future wife, or the assumptions and constructions of otherwise astute feminist readings.

Notes

1. The edition used for quotations throughout is *The Riverside Shakespeare*, ed. G. Blakemore Evans (Boston, MA: Houghton Mifflin, 1975). For sample glosses on "preposterous" here, see G. R. Hibbard, ed., *The Taming of the Shrew* (Harmondsworth: Penguin, 1968), "one who inverts the natural order of things, one who puts the cart before the horse"; Brian Morris, ed. *The Taming of the Shrew* (London: Methuen, 1981): *Preposterous* literally, placing last that which should be first (OED, a.1)"; Ann Thompson, *The Taming of the Shrew* (Cambridge: Cambridge University Press, 1984): "*Preposterous*: Used literally to mean that Hortensio puts things first which should come later"; The Signet Classic Shakespeare, ed. Robert B. Heilman (New York: New American Library, 1966), "putting later things (*post-*) first (*pre-*)." As noted in H. J. Oliver, ed., *The Taming of the Shrew* (Oxford: Clarendon Press, 1982), "preposterous" is used by Lucentio here in "the literal meaning 'having last that which should be first', but the more general meaning 'perverse' or 'unreasonable' was already common" as well by the time of the play (57).

2. See Lyly's *Endymion* I.3; and Thomas Nashe *The Anatomie of Absurditie*, with chapter 1 of my *Shakespeare from the Margins* (Chicago: University of Chicago Press, 1996) on the posterior implications of the "preposterous" in the bodily sense, including what was known as "preposterous venery."

3. In the slang of the period, "fiddler" connoted among other things a "sexual partner," and "fiddle" and "fiddle-case" (Aretino's double-meaning "cassa de la viola") various kinds of sexual instruments, both back and front. In *A Young Man's Tryal* (1655), a later "Kate" is anxious "for one to play on her Fiddle,"

while in Fletcher's *The Woman's Prize* (*c*.1611), the play that rewrites *The Taming of the Shrew*, Petruchio comments on how some husbands are deprived of their conjugal rights while others "fall with too much stringing of the Fiddles." See Gordon Williams, *A Dictionary of Sexual Language and Imagery in Shakespearean and Stuart Literature* 3 vols. (London and Atlantic Highlands, NJ: Athlone Press, 1994), vol. 1 under "fiddle" for these citations as well as Aretino's *Ragionamenti* I.ii.48 ("cassa de la viola") and the "fiddlestick" and "consort" of *Romeo and Juliet* (3.1). Williams also cites *Comforts of Whoreing* (1694) 29 on a prostitute satisfying her client "with her various Motions and Activity, that his Breech Dances, Capers and Firks it in as good Time as if she had a Fidle in her Commodity." *Commodity*, in this sexually double-meaning sense, is the term that Sly substitutes for "comedy" in the Induction to *The Taming of the Shrew*. For more examples of the sexual senses of "fiddling," see *The Oxford English Dictionary* under "minikin."

4. I refer here to Norbert Elias, *The History of Manners* (1939), vol. 1 of *The Civilizing Process*, trans. Edmund Jephcott (New York: Pantheon, 1978); and Pierre Bourdieu, *Distinction: A Social Critique of the Judgement of Taste*, trans. Richard Nice (Cambridge, MA: Harvard University Press, 1984). See also Gail Kern Paster, *The Body Embarrassed: Drama and the Disciplines of Shame in Early Modern England* (Ithaca, NY: Cornell University Press, 1993), which draws on the opposition between the closed and the open grotesque body from Mikhail Bakhtin, *Rabelais and his World*, trans. Helene Iswolsky (Bloomington, IN: Indiana University Press, 1984). For an analysis of *Loves Labours Lost* in this regard, see my "Preposterous Reversals: *Loves Labours Lost*," *Modern Language Quarterly* 54.4 (December 1993): 435–82. For the whole of *The Taming of the Shrew* in relation to these broader cultural and historical contexts, see my *Preposterous Shakespeare*, forthcoming.

5. See Maureen Quilligan, "Staging Gender: William Shakespeare and Elizabeth Cary," in James Grantham Turner, ed., *Sexuality and Gender in Early Modern Europe* (Cambridge: Cambridge University Press, 1993), esp. 216 and 219. I put "class" in scare quotes here to underscore that both in Quilligan and here the term is used not in the classical Marxist sense but rather as a current critical shorthand for position within a social hierarchy.

6. On music as primary in creation, see Joseph Barnes's *The Praise of Musicke* (Oxford 1586): "time cannot say that hee was before [Music], or nature that she wrought without her. To prove this looke upon the frame & workmanship of the whole worlde, whether there be not above, an harmony between the spheres." For Castiglione's *Il Cortegiano* (published in Venice in 1528), see *The Courtier*, trans. Thomas Hoby, Book I, 75–7.

7. See Morley's *A Plain and Easy Introduction to Practical Music*, 2nd edition, ed. R. Alex Harman (New York: W. W. Norton, 1963) 298; Sir Thomas Elyot, *The Book named Governor* (New York: Dutton Everyman's Library, 1962), 15, 20, 22.

8. In addition to Morley, see Stephen Gosson, *The School of Abuse* (London, 1587); and John Ferne, *The Blazon of Gentrie* (London, 1586).

9. See the editor's introduction to Morley's *Practical Music*, p. viii. On the differentiation between music as heavenly harmony (or the music of the spheres) and practical music in the period, see John Hollander's classic study *The Untuning of the Sky* (Princeton, NJ: Princeton University Press, 1961).

10. See Castiglione's *The Courtier* (Hoby trans. Book I, 75) with Book II, p. 101 on music as ""meete to be practised in the presence of women"; Roger Ascham, *The Schoolmaster*, ed. John E. B. Mayor (1863; rpt. New York: AMS Press, 1967), Book I, which also includes the warning that "Moch Musick marreth mens maners."

Music in relation to gender is also the subject of the analysis of the play in Linda Phyllis Austern, "'Sing Againe Syren': The Female Musician and Sexual Enchantment in Elizabethan Life and Literature," *Renaissance Quarterly* 42 (1989): 420–48.

11. See Brian Morris's gloss in the Arden 2 edition, 218.

12. For the impact of this Genesis 2 creation story, combined with Aristotle on the female as a secondary or defective male, see the final chapter of my *Literary Fat Ladies: Rhetoric, Gender, Property* (London and New York: Methuen, 1987).

13. For the master–schoolboy form of translation from Latin to English and back again, see chapter 4 of my *Shakespeare from the Margins* on Ascham's *The Scholemaster* and the translation scene of *The Merry Wives of Windsor*.

14. See chapter 4 of my *Shakespeare from the Margins*, with the reading of this translation lesson in the opening chapter of *Literary Fat Ladies: Rhetoric, Gender, Property* (London and New York: Methuen, 1987).

15. Ann Thompson's New Cambridge edition of the play (p. 106) compares "Bianca's skill at 'holding off'" to that of "Cressida, who knows all about such techniques." Like other editors of the play, she does not pick up on the complaint of Penelope that forms the basis of the Latin lesson; curiously, she also supports Lucentio's "sure" translation of "Aeacides" as "Ajax," though, as other editors point out, this is a highly doubtful translation. Thompson's edition was first published in 1984, when it was rare to have a female editor in such a prestigious series. Since then, however, she has published pioneering work on feminist editing and become a General Editor of the Arden Shakespeare Third Series. On possibilities for feminist editing, see also Laurie Maguire in Dympna C. Callaghan, *A Feminist Companion to Shakespeare* (Malden, MA: Blackwell, 2000).

16. In *The Comedy of Errors*, the complaints of Adriana against her absent husband echo Penelope's in the first epistle of the *Heroides*, including the suspicion that her husband's delayed return means that he has been unfaithful; and are contrasted to her sister Luciana's iteration of the familiar Pauline counsel to wives. For the English translation of the *Heroides* already in print well before *The Taming of the Shrew*, see George Turberville, trans., *The Heroycall Epistles of the learned Poet Publius Ouidius Naso* (London, 1567). On the importance of the *Heroides* for Shakespeare and others, see Elizabeth D. Harvey, *Ventriloquized Voices: Feminist Theory and English Renaissance Texts* (New York: Routledge, 1992). Harvey (personal communication) notes that Turberville's text continues the Renaissance practice—and tradition ascribed to Aulus Sabinus, Ovid's contemporary and friend, but not reflected in Ovid's own text—of providing male responses to the charges in three of the female complaints: Ulysses to Penelope, Demophon to Phyllis, and Paris to Oenone.

17. Lucentio's counterpart in Gascoigne's *Supposes*, the immediate source for the Bianca subplot, uses his entry into the household as a tutor to lie with his pupil, not just instruct her. For the line of transmission through Ariosto's *I Suppositi* and the disguised lover of Terence's *Eunuch*, see Keir Elam, "The Fertile Eunuch: Twelfth Night, Early Modern Intercourse, and the Fruits of Castration," *Shakespeare Quarterly* 47: 1 (Spring 1996): 1–36. The breaching of walls identified by Shakespeare with "maiden walls" (as in *Henry V*) is similarly identified with entry into Troy through the disguise of the Trojan horse in *Cymbeline*, where Iachimo gains entry into Innogen's bedroom hidden inside a trunk.

18. In Ovid, *Heroides and Amores*, with an English translation by Grant Showerman (Cambridge, MA: Harvard University Press; London: W. Heinemann, 1977),

Aeacides is translated as "Achilles" every time it appears in the *Heroides* text (I.35; III.87; VIII.7, 33, 55). Turberville (1567) likewise renders *Aeacides* in Penelope's complaint as "Achylles," as he also does consistently elsewhere.

19. The provision of "assurance" for Lucentio's own required patrimony or male inheritance as a rival suitor for Bianca is stressed in relation to his "supposed" father in the scene just before this translation lesson, where the plot is hatched to invent a "supposed Vincentio" (II.i.408) to underwrite the patrimony or "assurance" promised to Bianca's father (II.i.387, 397) as part of the deal.

20. See *Ovid's Metamorphoses: The Arthur Golding Translation 1567*, ed. John Frederick Nims, with a new essay "Shakespeare's Ovid" by Jonathan Bate (Philadelphia: Paul Dry Books, 2000), 320, for Book 13, lines 27–41, where the Latin title *Aeacides* is claimed by Ajax, who also claims that Ulysses was fathered adulterously by Sisyphus rather than his supposed father Laertes. While it might be expected that Lucentio would present himself as the successful Ulysses—rather than the traditionally blockish Ajax (man of deeds not words)—it is ultimately Bianca who wins the debate. The original Arden edition, edited by R. Warwick Bond (London: Methuen and Co., 1904), 73, traces editorial awareness of this other Ovidian intertext back to Steevens' eighteenth-century glosses on Lucentio's "Aeacides" with Golding's translation of *Metamorphoses* XIII.27–8 ("The highest Jove of all / Acknowledgeth this AEacus, and dooth his sonne him call. / Thus am I Ajax third from Jove") and comments that "The application of the patronymic by Ovid to Peleus, Telamon, and Phocas, AEcus' sons; by Homer and Virgil to Achilles, another grandson; and by Virgil to Pyrrhus, his great-grandson, might justify Bianca's professed 'doubt,' line 55." Though this Bianca translation scene recalls other mock translation lessons cited in Bond's edition (71–2)—including one in Lyly's *Mother Bombie* (III.i.139), where "Candius translates Ovid to Livia while their fathers overhear, 'I am no Latinist, Candius, you must conster it. *Can.* So I will, and pace (parse) it too'." Bianca by contrast not only provides her own construing or translation, but proves a better Latinist than her tutor of "letters."

21. The complexity of the larger shrew-taming plot's presentation of women as only ostensibly passive objects is analyzed in relation to Petruchio's pun on "Kate" and "cates" (etymologically connected to "chattel" and the mercantile context of purchases or "achats") in Natasha Korda's "Household Kates: Domesticating Commodities in *The Taming of the Shrew*," *Shakespeare Quarterly*, vol. 47, no. 2 (Summer, 1996): 109–31.

Part III
Histories

11

Hermione's Ghost: Catholicism, the Feminine, and the Undead

Frances E. Dolan

Recent work on mourning, memory, and commemoration in early modern England dwells on survivors' grief and the various strategies by which the living manage their painful longing for those who have died by sustaining and performing their connection with them. What about less tender feelings? The living also feared the dead and strove to placate them and keep them at bay.[1] As Peter Marshall observes, "The impulse to assist the dead is not incompatible with a desire to propitiate them and guard against their precipitate return."[2] Until 1828, for instance, suicides were given burials that now sound disturbingly like those given to vampires in horror movies. As Michael MacDonald and Terence Murphy explain:

> The night following the inquest, officials of the parish, the churchwardens and their helpers, carried the corpse to a crossroads and threw it naked into a pit. A wooden stake was hammered through the body, pinioning it in the grave, and the hole was filled in. No prayers for the dead were repeated; the minister did not attend.[3]

Such a burial suggests not just horror at the sin and crime of suicide, but fear of the "unruly," "restless," "dangerous dead" who, if not rooted in the grave, might haunt the survivors.[4] Many practices associated with Catholicism had as their goal separating the dead from the living definitively; they worked to "lay" a ghost not to evoke it (as a seance might do). Although some writers claimed that ghosts had been a clerical delusion and disappeared with the Reformation, ghosts seem to have persisted as a post-Reformation problem because the dead and the claims they might make on the living continued to be a problem. Changing burial practices—sewing the corpse into a shroud, nailing it into a wooden coffin—suggest growing distaste for the corpse and a desire to confine it. These bodies, however carefully packaged, were everywhere in early modern cities: inside the walls of the city, inside the walls of churches.[5] Perhaps this is why the displacement of the dead that accompanied the dissolution of the monasteries provoked surprisingly little opposition, and even some displays of rage and ruthlessness, as reformers disinterred, intermingled, and dumped remains.[6] Requiring appeasement or provoking rage and desecration, the fearsome departed lingered on, not quite dead enough.

In this chapter I will argue that Catholicism was the undead of post-Reformation English culture. I will draw on the connection between Catholicism and the feminine in the early modern imagination, and the insights of feminism, to interrogate the complex responses this status as "undead" provoked in contemporaries and still provokes among scholars of the period. If the ghost is often called a revenant— "one who returns from the dead" (a term critics of *Hamlet* especially like)—then perhaps the presence of Catholicism in the plays might more properly be called, as widows were, a "relict"— "a survivor, the remains, remnant or residue" (OED). The relict activates what Steven Mullaney identifies in Hamlet's response to his mother's sexual vitality as "mourning before the fact, over a vitality that one wants to be or imagines or finally produces as past and dead . . . a response to what should be dead but isn't."[7] The relict is often also, as in Mullaney's example, feminized, since the woman who outlives her husband is still identified in relation to him as his leavings. In the two conceptually linked cases, of Catholicism and the widow, the remains pose "the problem of the leftover" Catherine Gallagher and Stephen Greenblatt discuss with regard to Eucharistic controversies.[8] This is a problem simultaneously material and imaginary.

The vanishing Catholic?

What I mean by Catholicism here is not a coherent theology but rather a cultural phenomenon, an eclectic ensemble of objects, images, stories, practices, and beliefs that might be drawn on indiscriminately and a field of projection for a range of anxieties about difference and, more alarmingly, identity. The association between Catholicism and the undead operates at two levels. First, Catholic belief is invested in a two-way traffic between living and dead, body and spirit, manifested in the real presence of Christ in the chewed and digested Eucharist, relics of saints and martyrs, a reverence for images and objects as part of worship, the imagined vitality and power of stones and bones. Because of these components of Catholic belief, both John Bale and Pierre Viret, a Swiss reformer, described Catholicism as "necrolatrie" or worship of the dead.[9] An accretion of leftovers, Catholicism is also the undead of European history. Latin is, according to Thomas Hobbes, "but the *Ghost* of the Old *Romane* Language" and thus appropriate to a pope who is "the *Ghost* of the deceased *Romane* Empire, sitting crowned upon the grave thereof."[10] Catholicism haunts the cultural imaginary of early modern England as the supposedly superseded and defeated that yet keeps adapting and re-conceiving itself in uncanny and disturbing, rather than welcome, ways.

As many scholars are now demonstrating, a neat division between pre- and post-Reformation, Protestant and Catholic, misconceives how gradual and uneven the Reformation was and how it confused rather than clarified relations between self and other, past and present, at least at first. While confessional identity may have achieved some stability at the extremes, most people occupied what Arthur Marotti has called the "muddled middle."[11] Ritual objects were sometimes melted down or burned, but often simply redistributed and assigned new places or functions wherein they often retained a vaguely magical significance.[12] As Anthony Milton points out, Protestants worshipped in the same spaces in which Catholics once did, and these spaces were only gradually and unevenly stripped of their ornamentation.[13] Beliefs and practices were even more lingering because less tangible, surviving in the compromise of the Elizabethan settlement, in the eclecticism and wavering that characterized many people's faith and worship, and in the adaptability and survival of Catholicism itself.[14]

By thinking about Catholicism in these terms, as a vibrant if sometimes disturbing presence in post-Reformation England, I want to trouble the presumed nostalgia for Catholicism that now challenges the once widespread presumption that Shakespeare's England was and ought to be unambivalently Protestant. My concern, then, is as much with how early modernists talk about Catholicism as it is with early modern people's own attitudes. Some scholars locate fond nostalgia in those who resisted the Reformation from the start. Eamon Duffy, for instance, describes a reluctant populace clinging to the accoutrements and affect of the old faith. Others locate nostalgia or longing in those who understood themselves to be "reformed," but who nonetheless missed certain practices or beliefs.[15] Keith Thomas argues, with regard to exorcism and other protections against bewitchment and possession, that with the Reformation "all the old mechanical protections were dismissed as empty symbols, lacking any efficacy in themselves." As a consequence, "it is not surprising that many old Catholic formulae retained their value in times of emergency for Protestants who found themselves disarmed in the face of the old enemy."[16] Michael Neill and Stephen Greenblatt have drawn our attention to how Protestants might have responded to changes in doctrine that withdrew means of intervening to help the dead in Purgatory and therefore left the living helpless against the dead's demands and reproaches. But if Catholicism was associated with lost resources for appeasing demons and the dead and protecting one's self against occult forces, it was also associated with the very uncanny forces to be feared. While I find it persuasive that some people might have clung to officially discredited beliefs and longed for lost rituals, I also believe that such longing requires faith not only in lost beliefs and practices but in the fact that they are indeed "lost." If, as Greenblatt argues, "Purgatory...enabled the dead to be not completely dead," then this might be disturbing as well as reassuring.[17] Longing for the dead requires a confident sense that they really are dead, securely buried, and unlikely to reanimate.

Like staking the corpse of the suicide, locating, binding, and burying a body helps to insure that the dead will not come back. We can see the importance of this in James I's careful management of his own accession. As Jennifer Woodward shows, there was some ambiguity regarding where sovereignty resided in the month between Elizabeth's death and James's arrival in London. Although James claimed that "at the very moment of the expiring of the king reigning, the nearest and lawful heire ent'reth his place," he did not enter the city until Elizabeth had been interred. In the meantime, her bewigged and brightly painted effigy represented the body royal.[18] James did not assume that role himself until his subjects could visit Elizabeth's tomb and reassure themselves that the queen was dead—long live the king.[19] Since Catholicism had no sepulcher, no rituals could mark the conclusion of its reign or the smooth transition into a new era. Perhaps the need to witness the reduction to ashes of some symbolic representative of Catholicism helps to explain the popularity of pope burning processions later in the seventeenth century.[20]

Imagining early modern responses to a resurrected Catholicism, or a female ghost, is a thought experiment in the limits on longing to speak with the dead. In this chapter, I will link two specters—undead Catholicism and undead women—because these alarming prospects were intertwined in the early modern period. As I have argued elsewhere, Catholicism was associated with actual women, such as the Stuart kings' wives and mistresses, and with men who were viewed as effeminized by their celibacy or exclusion from public life. The religion was also associated with the Virgin Mary and a large cast of female saints and martyrs who dominated stories and visual representations. More generally the Church itself was figured as the Whore of Babylon, and the association of the Church with disorderly women was condensed into the figure of Pope Joan, who was depicted as historical rather than apocryphal, and representative rather than exceptional. Remembering what we know about the complexity of early modern gender constructions should alert us to the complex responses a feminized Catholicism would express and provoke.[21] Like the feminine, Catholicism was associated with horror and longing, with rot and ornament, with anger and compassion. It was therefore more beautiful and desirable, least troublesome and ambiguous, if absolutely dead.

As has been widely observed, in Shakespeare's tragedies it is often easier to love dead women.[22] Desdemona, whose loquacity, appetite, and love of company provoke her husband's suspicion as much as his desire, becomes an object of his affection again when she is first asleep "smooth as monumental alabaster," and then dead, "cold, cold, my girl, / Even like thy chastity"

(5.2.282–3).[23] As Othello pledges, "I will kill thee and love thee after." Hamlet is finally able to express his love for Ophelia in the past tense and in the presence of her corpse.[24] Antony articulates preference for the dead particularly bluntly in *Antony and Cleopatra*. Learning of Fulvia's death, he remarks, "She's good being gone; The hand could pluck her back that shoved her on" (1.2.115–16). Of course, Antony has no intention of plucking her back, since she is only good in so far as she *is* gone.

In these tragic plots, the hero must reject or even kill the heroine so as to mourn her wholeheartedly; mourning requires the certainty that the woman, threatening when vigorous, is irremediably extinct.[25] What happens when the story is told at the national level, and when a group rather than an individual must be killed first and loved later? Perhaps it will be useful here to look at a well-documented sequence of events in which a nation removed a group of its inhabitants and then lamented their passing. Consider, for instance, the stories about and sightings of the supposedly "last" Indian in the United States in the nineteenth century. Many of those who drew attention as the last members of various tribes were old, childless women. This European fantasy is one of burying, not of being haunted, of valuing what is about to be utterly and reassuringly gone and one's own power both to obliterate and to remember. As Jill Lepore puts it, "For Indians' role in American history (even as wartime enemies) to be cherished, romanticized, and fetishized, Indians themselves must exist only in the past, mute memorials, silent as a rock."[26] Stripped of their lands and autonomy, Native Americans "have vanished into the minds of those who have dispossessed them."[27]

There have been successful genocidal programs, and the relationship of European settlers to Native Americans can be seen as one such. Yet, as Jean O'Brien and other scholars have shown, when Indians or other groups "vanish," this usually means that they have, in fact, intermarried and blended in.[28] The "vanishing" or "last" Indian depends on a fantasy of racial purity—of both self and other—that can be preserved by erasing and then mourning the other. Historians of Native Americans have redirected questioning from "what happened to the Indians" to "who or what is an Indian?" How does the practice, meaning, and location of such an identification shift so that it becomes less localized, less visible, but perhaps, thereby, more pervasive? These are also good questions to ask about Catholicism. What about Catholic survival?

Attempting to imagine what it might have been like had there been sightings of and stories about the "last Catholic" in England makes it easier to understand a grave problem at the heart of Catholic identity in the post-Reformation period: Catholics were everywhere, could be anyone, and were very difficult to spot. Although Catholicism was sometimes associated with foreignness, it could not consistently be construed as a stable, visible, and incontrovertible racial or ethnic identity because most people's ancestors were Catholics; penal laws emphasized conduct rather than lineage and therefore the possibility of avoiding penalties by acting, if not believing, differently; and people constantly converted back and forth. Although they were in the minority in post-Reformation England, Catholics were in the majority in powerful countries like Spain and France. The constant intermixture that fueled and was redressed in the fantasy of the "last Indian" defined Catholicism. The last Catholic was just too much to hope for.

The earliest and most influential new historicist essays often made such comparisons, drawing on Clifford Geertz's interpretation of a Balinese cockfight, for instance, in order to shed light on the Renaissance court. Such comparisons have long been an important part of feminist work as well, sometimes provoking the critique that too many feminist projects are transhistorical and therefore ahistorical. The limitations of such approaches have been anatomized in detail. Yet the assumption that we might learn from comparing widely various times and places invigorated early new historicism, as well as ground-breaking work in postcolonial, feminist, and queer studies of early modern English culture. Some of that wit and energy has been lost in the recent turn to the local, with its sharp focus on a particular place, time, and body of evidence. An unexamined juxtaposition cannot speak for itself, of course. Nor should we ignore crucial differences between the cultural moments we compare. In this case, for instance, I am not arguing that Catholics were the "natives" of post-Reformation England—although such a claim is usefully provocative. Furthermore, at least one contemporary made precisely this analogy. In *New Shreds of the Old Snare* (1624), John Gee's follow-up to *The Foot Out of the Snare*, his enormously popular exposé of Catholic corruption, he argues that both Indians and Catholics trade what they hold most dear for "rattle-baby toyes."

> Why doe we laugh at the barbarous *Indians* for imparting to us their richest commodities in exchange for glasse, beads, peny whittles, copper rings, &c? But the *Popes Benediction*, or any the least touch of Sainting Miracle-monging fiction is able to infuse the highest worth into the basest baggagely New-nothing to hang upon the sleeve of admiring adoring ghostly Children of the *Jesuites*. How doth his *Holines* exorcise and conjure *Beads* of wood, of stone, of Corall, and of all other stuffe, making besotted Ignaro's beleeve they have great power against sinne, the Devill, and Hell; whereas alas all is but cheating, and to gull them of their money.[29]

Interestingly, the connection between Indians (whatever group Gee so identifies) and Catholics also creates a parallel between those who exchange glass and beads for the Indians' "richest commodities" and the pope, who trades fictions for faith and "new-nothings" for salvation itself. Indians and Catholics are similarly barbarous and gullible. But the laughing cheats who prey on them are disturbingly similar, too. Gee's text suggests that there is early modern precedent for the connection I am exploring between Indians and Catholics.

In my analysis here, however, I am less interested in proving the early modern existence of this association than in making the methodological suggestion that considering the status of the Indian in nineteenth-century American culture—as it is now understood in revisionist historical accounts that interrogate both the assumption that Indians vanished and the professions of grief thereupon—helps us to see how a sequence of emotions characteristic of Shakespeare's tragic heroes—displacing and then mourning— might also operate at a larger cultural level. The grief that is now of interest to scholars followed *after* dissolving the monasteries, stripping the altars, fining and jailing recusants, executing priests. I draw attention to how violence precedes mourning, in national histories and in tragic plots, as a reminder that we should scrutinize the conditions that enable sorrow and approach expressions of grief critically as well as empathetically.

Several influential recent studies of lingering attachments to the Catholic past have focused on the ways in which the official rejection of Purgatory stripped survivors of the capacity to assist and appease the dead. In such accounts, the claims of the past are figured as ghosts, demanding a redress that it is not clear their survivors can offer. Ghosts are thus ambiguous figures for a transitional period—welcome, fascinating, horrifying. Similarly, Bergland argues that the Indians who were stripped of their lands and lives so as to be installed in the "national uncanny" of nineteenth-century America were imagined as ghosts, consigned to the past yet still demanding attention in the present, perhaps even cursing the future. In two very different contexts, then, guilt toward the dispossessed was explored through ghost stories. But how does gender operate in the post-Reformation stories? In the heterosexual plot writ large in ghost stories about Catholics and Indians the character who is more lovable when dead is a woman. What stories were told about women who returned from the dead? How do undead women figure in recent studies of death and grief in the early modern period?

Looking for female ghosts

Apparently, the desire to speak with the dead, then and now, focuses on some and not others. Extending his oft-cited claim that he wishes to speak with the dead to everyone in early modern England, Greenblatt argues that "Though the return of a dead person arouses terror, the collective impulse is not to flee from and not even simply to ward off the weird apparition, but rather to approach and find out what it is and what it wants." For Greenblatt the ghosts themselves have no choice but to make their demands for "they fear they are being forgotten."[30] In the many texts Greenblatt addresses in his book *Hamlet in Purgatory*, those who long to return from the dead, or to interact with those who do, are usually men. Why would that be?

A few female ghosts do turn up in Greenblatt's magisterial study. In Middle English versions of *Trental of St. Gregory*, which Greenblatt describes as "one of the foundational stories of Purgatory," a pope is haunted by his mother who had "committed lechery as a young woman and had murdered her child." Since shame had prevented her from admitting her sin in life, she confesses to her son, who then prays for her and releases her from both Purgatory and hideous ugliness (129). In Thomas More's *The Supplication of Souls*, according to Greenblatt, More "characteristically does not imagine dead wives looking on at their husbands' carousals, but only dead husbands returning . . . to see their wives" (146), "looking in horror" at their remarriage, "and shrieking to make themselves heard" (204). When More does imagine "dead wives speaking out" it is "not to lament their surviving husbands' pleasures but to regret their own past delight in gorgeous clothing, jewels, and cosmetics" (148). Thus, whether the wife or the husband returns, what is to be lamented is the wife's conduct. Female ghosts are driven by their sexual guilt, not by a sense of grievance; they seek to confess rather than accuse or demand. The only other female ghost in the book is a con, in John Gee's description of a Jesuit ruse that presented "impressionable" young women with the apparition of a woman in white who advises them that they can avoid the torments of Purgatory she suffers only if they are "nunnified" (255). Interestingly, the Jesuits' deceptive theatricality is figured in a female apparition of the sort we see so rarely on the stage. Given Greenblatt's convincing claim that Shakespeare's "ghosts are figures who exist in and as theater, figures in whom it is possible to believe precisely because they appear and speak only onstage" (195), it is telling that, despite the associations of theatricality and the feminine, ghosts are so rarely women in Shakespeare's plays and in early modern culture more generally.

Refutations of belief in Purgatory dwell on one female ghost who is conspicuous in her absence: St Augustine's mother, Monica. In his *An Exposition of the Catholike Faith*, Gervase Babington wonders why love does not compel all the dead to return, "since we must needs grant, that if of themselves they could, sure they would be often with us, they being not now deprived of love, and become cruell." Babington turns to St Augustine as his authority: "For surely, saith he [Augustine], my deare mother Monica, who in her life time followed me over the Sea and land, would never thus long have beene from me if there had beene any such walking of dead spirits as is talked of."[31] In *Shield of Our Safetie* (1581), Anderson also appeals to Augustine's argument from absence: "Augustine sayth that if the soules of the dead could walke wyth men on earth, his godly mother Monica, who travayled from sea to lande to be with him, would never nowe after her death be absent from him. No truely the soules of dead men cannot walk in this worlde."[32] Both Babington and Anderson seem to assume that the dead retain their own desires and affections—they are not now cruel—but cannot enact them. Augustine assumes that if his mother could return she would; surely her love would tether her to her son. There is something disturbing, then, in an epitaph such as this one for Elizabeth Leigh, who died in 1619: "What friends, what children, what blest Marriage, / Dead I forgette."[33] In death as in life, mothers and wives cannot win. It is disturbing to imagine that they might blithely forget the attachments through which they once defined themselves; it is disturbing to imagine that they might *not* leave one alone.

Other studies turn up only a few more female ghosts. Keith Thomas cites a Star Chamber case of 1613 in which one Southwark woman called another "a hag" whose "ghost doth continually haunt her and her husband that they cannot thrive," as well as popular accounts in 1679 of a midwife who returned to confess the murder of two illegitimate children. In addition, Thomas asserts that "many stories related to widowers, haunted by their wives for breaking their promise not to marry again, or for neglecting the children of their first marriage."[34] His source is Thomas Nashe's *The Terrors of the Night* (1594): "A number of men there be yet living, who have been haunted by their wives after their death, about forswearing themselves, and undoing their children, of whom they promised to be carefull fathers: whereof I gather no reason but this, that Women are borne to torment a man both alive and dead."[35] That last sentence suggests Nashe's snide perspective on such stories, which, for him, provide mundane rather than supernatural evidence of the ways in which women are woes to men. Nashe positions these ghostly wives after a story of hogs who pursue a man's coach from London to his country house and before accounts of those pursued by weasels, rats, squirrels, and hares, which he dismisses as "the exploytes and stratagems of witches" and an "old wives' tale of divells and urchins" that must be withstood by those stout of heart. Nashe thus links three kinds of female pests: wives (living and dead), witches, and old wives' tales.

In his sweeping study of changing beliefs about the dead, Peter Marshall recounts a story of a woman who haunted her husband and his children because her spouse broke his promise to bury her in the churchyard. He also tells the story of how the specter of a young woman haunted the household of Sir Thomas Wise, appearing first in the maids' bedchamber and then at the foot of Wise's own bed. A minister advised Wise that it must be a bad rather than a good spirit because the latter did not appear in woman's form. Finally, Marshall discusses sightings of "Old Mother Leakey" who purportedly returned in fulfillment of her threat to her daughter-in-law that she would do so.[36] Laura Gowing assesses a fascinating case in which a woman's ghost repeatedly visits her female servant.[37]

Hunting for female ghosts, then, turns up some but not many. My point is not that Greenblatt neglects them, but rather that their very paucity demands discussion. That is why I have not been sifting through early modern texts and archives, trying to dig up a few more female ghosts to include or celebrate. I assume that other scholars do not grossly under-represent female ghosts. Therefore, the feminist project in this case is not to recover female ghosts but rather to observe how few there are and to inquire why that might be the case. If, as Marshall claims, "in numerous accounts, purgatory was designated an 'old wives' tale,' an example of gendered (and generationed) discourse designed to stress its marginality and redundancy" then the old wives' tales of demanding, familiar revenants include surprisingly few old wives.[38] There is a dearth of female ghosts both before and after the Reformation, in continental Europe as well as in England. Jean-Claude Schmitt asserts that female ghosts were rare in the medieval period, despite the fact that men's and women's souls were considered equally valuable and as many women died untimely deaths as did men. Schmitt links the emphasis on female relict and male revenant to inherit-ance practices that invested men with the orderly and uninterrupted succes-sion of goods and power, and to widows' ambivalence about their status as survivors. Nancy Caciola concurs that female revenants were "rare among the individual, hostile variety of the undead," perhaps because of women's "relatively tenuous connections with violence: women did not lead the kinds of lives, nor die the kinds of death, associated with the evil undead."[39] Both Schmitt and Caciola link the gendering of ghosts to the gendering of investments in the world, to men's monopoly over property, power, violent action, and efficacy, a monopoly that, it was imagined, would be hard to surrender.

Female ghosts are even rarer on the sixteenth- and seventeenth-century stage than they were in recorded sightings. When they turn up, they tend to be silent. In Joshua Cooke's *How to Chuse a Good Wife from a Bad*, a man imagines that the ghost of his dead wife haunts him; he suddenly blurts her name in the middle of his own speech but her apparition says nothing. In *The Witch of Edmonton*, bigamist Frank Thorney murders his second wife; despite the fact that she seems content to die if it suits him, and forgives him as she dies, she appears silently at his bedside later in the play.[40] In *The Second Maiden's Tragedy*, a Lady kills herself rather than consent to marry a tyrant. He then steals her dead body, threatening to have his way with her now that she can no longer resist. Her apparition appears before her tomb to announce to her true love, Govianus, that she has been abducted and to spur him on to rescuing her corpse. While the Lady, like other ghosts, has a demand, she only lays claim to her own body, insisting that, even after death, it matters. Govianus then employs her dead body (painted with poison) to kill the tyrant. The Lady thus appears in the play as a living woman, a speaking ghost, and a manipulable, desirable, but lethal corpse.[41] Fletcher's *The Woman's Prize* imagines a Petruchio who hides "his breeches out of fear" that the ghost of his first wife (Katharine, in *The Taming of the Shrew*) "should walk and wear 'em yet" (1.1.35–6).[42] Sadly, this bellicose, cross-dressed ghost does not make an appearance.

The last acts of two tragedies with female protagonists are haunted by a thwarted desire for their return. Mariam, Queen of Jewry, and the Duchess of Malfi both die by the end of Act IV. The final act of both tragedies is devoted to lamentation. The first part of Elizabeth Cary's *The Tragedie of Mariam* revolves around responses to Herod's supposed death and anxiety "Should Herod's body leave the sepulchre / And entertain the severed ghost again" (2.1.81–2). It turns out that Herod's little-lamented death was a rumor. If Herod returns from the dead, why can't Mariam? Even before Herod has Mariam executed, he imagines that she might be revivable. Discussing how to kill her with his sister, Salome, Herod remarks that if he cannot live without the sight of Mariam, once dead, Salome will "find the means to make her breathe again" (4.7.31). Upon hearing Mariam is dead, Herod immediately wishes she had not died (5.1.115), addresses her "pure unspotted ghost" to ask pardon (l.1.82), and denies that she's really dead: "But sure she is not dead, you did but jest, / To put me in perplexity a while" (5.1.135–6). The Nuntio assures him that if she appears it will be "attired in robe of heaven" (l.2023). Before she dies, Mariam herself tells the Nuntius, "By three days hence if wishes could revive, / I know himself would make me oft alive" (5.1.77–8). Herod does wish her back again, but his wishes cannot make it so. Her head has been severed from her body. Although she is more loveable once dead and Herod longs for her, she has nothing more to say to him.

The Duchess of Malfi famously claims that she is flesh and blood, not the statue kneeling at her husband's tomb. But when her brothers kill her she is not given even this substantial commemoration; she lingers as an echo in the ruined abbey, where, we are left to suppose, her body has been unceremoniously stashed. After she is murdered, the Cardinal makes up a story about the ghost of an old, murdered woman to explain Ferdinand's madness (5.2.90f); Bosola says "the Duchess / Haunts me" (5.2.364–5). But she returns only as admonitory fragments of her husband's speech. She has no body and is not the origin of meaning. Her voice does not accuse or explain. In all these examples from the drama, dead wives appear or threaten to appear, or their husbands long for their return, but they either fail to materialize or, when they do, refrain from reproaching, menacing, or intervening. All these appearances leave open the perplexing question of what dead women want.

Ann Jones and Peter Stallybrass directly address the gendering of stage ghosts, querying why, while there was "a wave of female ghosts in narrative poetry" in the 1590s, there are so few on the stage. They argue that the ghosts of the stage "are materially and legally entitled. . . . Most stage ghosts have active stakes in inheritance, which is both about the ownership of the future and about the control of memory. Most of these ghosts are the revenants of men and of aristocratic men at that . . . They return to claim a future that they 'properly" own and that has been taken away from them."[43] Jones and Stallybrass argue that women were not understood to have the same sense of entitlement and therefore would not have the same claim to sympathy and redress for the loss of property, power, and even life.

In Shakespeare's plays, the women who are dead have often completed their most important task, which is to give birth and die, or at the very least to die, and so have no unfinished business. Nor do the plots need them to explain important back stories or to embody how the past impinges on the present. In an influential article, Mary Beth Rose draws our attention to the elimination of mothers from Shakespeare's plots: "Since the mother would remove one from what is conceived as the world of action—the public, socialized world—the best mother is a dead or absent mother."[44] Other female characters, too, contribute to the plot precisely by dying—not at the end but in the middle. Look at it this way: how often do male characters advance the plot by seeming or pretending to be dead, as Juliet, Hero, Hermione, and to a lesser extent, Imogen, do?[45] Why is it so often female characters who aid resolution by drugging themselves into a coma or turning to stone?

Hermione's ghosts

Although there is not a ghostly mother in Shakespeare's plays to rival the ghost of Hamlet's father, *The Winter's Tale* comes closest to imagining an undead mother. In the figure of Hermione and her ghostly refractions, the gendering of ghosts and the gendering of Catholicism conjoin. Tellingly, the play fractures the undead mother into three very different apparitions, and minimizes or displaces her rage in each manifestation. The three apparitions of Hermione all occur after her supposed death in Act III, scene ii. In the very next scene, Antigonus describes a dream in which Hermione appears to him. Antigonus, of course, has not heard the news that Hermione is dead, yet he introduces his description of his dream by remarking, "I have heard, but not believed, the spirits o' th' dead / May walk again."[46] He closes by concluding that, however "superstitiously," he will believe in and follow the instructions of this apparition as that of the dead Hermione. In between, he describes a figure "in pure white robes / Like very sanctity," bending its head from side to side, bowing three times, gasping, and weeping. When this specter finally finds words, she announces this as the place in which her baby should be abandoned, names the infant (a name that rather magically sticks, despite the fact that the only person to whom it is communicated dies), and pronounces the cost that Antigonus will pay as the "thrower-out" of her "poor babe": he will never see his own wife again. While she issues commands regarding the treatment of her child and makes a prediction about Antigonus's fate, she does not defend her innocence or express rage at her treatment; indeed, Antigonus seems to believe in Hermione's guilt more at this point than he had earlier, concluding that he is to leave the baby in Bohemia "upon the earth of its right father," i.e. Polixenes. The apparition does not attempt to intervene to prevent the baby's abandonment.

As has been much discussed, Antigonus's dream announces the play's movement out of tragedy and into comedy, out of the past and into the future. The Old Shepherd's remark that "Thou met'st with things dying, I with things new-born" (3.3.112–13) refers not only to the juxtaposition of Antigonus's gnawed remains and the abandoned infant, but to Hermione's body just after childbirth, which straddles death and birth. Indeed, Hermione's phantom body seems to linger in this post-partum Purgatory for years. Rose and Eggert both argue that the play announces loss as the condition of its own possibility; what is lost is the queen mother's youth and sexuality. When Hermione returns at the end of the play, she is less queenly and authoritative, less openly, fecundly sexual. She also lacks the vengeful power the Catholic tradition invests in the figure of the queen mother. The play occludes three layers of feminized rage—the retaliations of the spurned wife, the humiliated queen, and the avenging mother of heaven and earth.

The disturbing possibility of Hermione's return is again addressed in Act V, in a scene that reminds us that Paulina has been talking to Leontes for sixteen years, amplifying his regret, and restraining him from remarriage. In response to a discussion of Hermione as irreplaceable, Leontes curiously imagines that her ghost would return to haunt him should he remarry.

> No more such wives: therefore, no wife: one worse,
> And better us'd, would make her sainted spirit
> Again possess her corpse, and on this stage,
> (Were we offenders now) appear soul-vex'd,
> And begin, "Why to me?"
>
> (5.1.56–60)

Such a return is obviously to be feared, not desired. Paulina and Leontes then engage in a duet of horror. Paulina points out that such a "sainted spirit" would have "just cause" to haunt her husband, and Leontes imagines that the ghost "would incense me / To murder her I married" (5.1.61–2). Leontes here places himself in a revenge tragedy, where ghosts require redress, yet, despite the feverishness of his fantasy, does not imagine that what the ghost of Hermione might want is revenge against him rather than against his second wife. This fantasy is not about the past—Hermione's grievances against her husband for slandering and jailing her, for breaking her son's heart, for exposing her infant. Just as the play displaces punishment for the abandonment of Perdita from Leontes and onto Antigonus and the ship's crew, Leontes never imagines that he might be the target of his wife's ghost's murderous rage. When Paulina then inhabits the perspective of Hermione's ghost, she says

> Were I the ghost that walked I'd bid you mark
> Her eye, and tell me for what dull part in't
> You chose her. Then I'd shriek that even your ears
> Should rift to hear me: and the words that follow'd
> Should be, "Remember mine."

(5.1.63–7)

At this point, Leontes and Paulina share a fantasy that what would concern Hermione most is being replaced as Leontes' wife. Paulina promises him only such a second wife "As, walk'd your first queen's ghost, it should take joy / To see her in your arms" (5.1.80–1). Obviously, this emphasis serves Paulina's project of preventing Leontes from committing bigamy. What interests me most here is the contrast between the cry of Hamlet's father's ghost to "remember me"—which, as critics such as Michael Neill have pointed out, emerges as a more important and more challenging demand than "revenge me"—and "remember mine" that is "my eyes." Greenblatt remarks that "there is nothing notably Catholic or purgatorial about this vision," yet links it to Thomas More's depiction of dead husbands who shriek at the wives who have forgotten and replaced them.[47] It is crucial, I think, that Hermione does not actually shriek at anyone but is instead imagined doing so in a conditional future; and is a wife and not a husband. These differences suggest how disturbing the figure of a vengeful wife might be. Here, Leontes and Paulina invent that specter to keep *Leontes* suspended in limbo. Yet even this disciplinary fantasy stops short of imagining a wife who calls for the remembrance of her dead children rather than her eyes and who demands revenge.

Throughout, the play evokes revenge only to refuse it: when he first accuses and arrests her, Hermione warns Leontes "how will this grieve you / When you shall come to clearer knowledge, that / You thus have publish'd me!" (2.1.96–8). In her trial, she wishes that her father, the Emperor of Russia, were alive and a witness, seeing her misery "yet with eyes / Of pity, not revenge" (3.2.122–3). It is Paulina who undertakes to imagine that vengeance might be called for: "The Queen, the Queen, / The sweet'st, dear'st creature's dead: and vengeance for 't / Not dropped down yet" (3.2.200–2). The vengeance Paulina exacts requires Hermione's apparent death, a death that Leontes at first desires and then that Paulina persistently asserts. From Act II to Act V, Hermione is constantly imagined as dead. The prospect of killing a wife is presented in *The Winter's Tale* as a wish—"Say that she were gone, / Given to the fire, a moiety of my rest / Might come to me again" (2.3.7–9); as a false report that Paulina circulates and emphasizes, referring to Hermione as "she you killed" and provoking Leontes' concurrence and annoyance

"Killed! / She I killed! I did so: but thou strik'st me / Sorely, to say I did" (5.1.16–18); as Leontes' probable response to a second wife; and finally as an imminent danger when, in the last scene of reunion, Paulina urges Leontes to take Hermione's hand: "Do not shun her / Until you see her die again; for then / You kill her double" (5.3.105–7). Killing his wife occurs so often at the level of Leontes' dream that her second death is evoked even at the moment of her apparent resurrection. For, with Paulina presiding, Hermione is asserted to be dead in order to emerge as the undead. Paulina envisions a future that could resolve these conflicts as one in which the dead walk: she says it is as likely that Leontes' lost child should be found as for Antigonus "to break his grave / And come again to me" (5.1.42–3); she responds to the praise for Perdita by invoking Hermione whose grave must "give way to what's seen now" (5.1.97–8).

Whatever the mysterious processes by which Paulina and Hermione conspire to keep the queen outside Leontes' awareness and the play's staged action, Hermione seems to die in Act III. As many critics have pointed out, up to this point Shakespeare closely follows his source, Robert Greene's prose fiction, *Pandosto* (1595). Hermione's resurrection is not in the source and might be an "afterthought."[48] If so, then Hermione "is" dead until the idea of reanimating her changes the course of the story. In *Pandosto* the queen's death is decisive: "her vital spirits were so stopped that she fell down presently dead, and could be never revived."[49] The king has his wife embalmed, and entombs her and her son in a sepulcher that he then visits once a day. In Greene's tale, there is no redemption for the king, even though the child who was lost is found. In *The Winter's Tale* Leontes proposes that the queen and her son be buried in a single grave, asks to be brought to see their dead bodies, and plans to visit "the chapel where they lie" daily (3.2.238–9). This raises the question of whether Hermione is really dead and buried, and then resurrected. As Leontes asks at the end of the play, "how, is to be question'd; for I saw her, / As I thought, dead; and have in vain said many / A prayer upon her grave" (5.3.139–41).

The play's *mater ex machina* ending hints at the uncanny possibility that Hermione is the undead. Several critics have associated her statue with a funerary monument or tomb sculpture, suggesting that a commemorative icon comes to life.[50] Imagined in this way, her reanimation combines the miraculous with the horrifying. Whereas most critics dwell on the former, Kenneth Gross is willing to explore the darker possibilities. For Leontes "the 'dead likeness' of the queen is perhaps easier to dwell on than the thought of her literal return." Gross describes the statue and the play's ending as "haunted by . . . fantasies of return" allied with revenge and "intimations of a tragic economy that the play is eager to renounce." Gross argues that for both Camillo and Polixenes, "the statue-Hermione is not just a question mark but something taboo, and their words suggest a hovering suspicion that this moment of recovery cannot banish the thought of revenge," that, in other words, the animated statue is the vengeful ghost of the dangerous dead.[51] Critics who emphasize the play's Catholic resonances tend to play down such doubts and fears so as to celebrate grace and forgiveness. But the miraculous and vengeful need not be antithetical. Probing the Catholic associations in this final scene might lead us not only to forgiveness and redemption, but also to the anxieties about the uncanny that the play evokes in order to suppress and to the menace that is displaced from this female ghost.

In *The Comedy of Errors* the lost mother, presumed dead, becomes an abbess; in *Pericles* she puts on a "vestal livery" and is called a nun. Hermione, too, has complex Catholic associations after she is supposedly dead. Several critics have helped to position her statue within a Catholic culture of reverence for female figures.[52] The way is prepared when a servant praises Perdita as a creature who "would she begin a sect, might quench the zeal / Of all professors else; make proselytes / Of who she but bid follow" (5.1.107–9). Paulina responds, "How? Not women!" and the servant says, "Women will love her that she is a woman / More worth than any man; men, that she is / The rarest of all women" (5.1.110–12). But it will be Hermione, not Perdita, who has female acolytes and is adored as the rarest of all women. Perdita herself longs to kneel before her statue. Perdita's embarrassment about this desire accrues its need for apology—even in a play in which a Delphic Oracle figures importantly—from a post-Reformation iconophobia.

> And give me leave,
> And do not say 'tis superstition, that
> I kneel, and then implore her blessing. Lady,
> Dear queen, that ended when I but began,
> Give me that hand of yours to kiss.
>
> (5.3.42–6)

As both queen and mother, and object of devotion, Hermione certainly does resemble the Virgin Mary: "It is requir'd / You do awake your faith" (ll.94–5). Yet if we link Hermione to the Virgin, as many critics have done, we might also notice that the play leaves something out. The Virgin is a powerful figure as well as an accessible one; believers attributed to her the power to intercede on their behalf with her son and also to intervene directly, even violently, in the world. While Hermione does not seem to be vengeful, the Virgin Mary was often viewed as being so. One treatise defending Marian devotion warns that blasphemy towards Mary is "dangerously imprudent" since those who neglect or dishonor the Virgin fall into "poverty, misery, and disreputation, and confusion" and "come, after lives led in extreme obscurity of mind and misery, to end wretchedly in despayre."[53] Nor is Mary's vengeance always deferred and indirect. The Virgin also physically injures those who damage her image. Justus Lipsius' (1547–1606) much translated and discussed account of miracles attributed to the Virgin includes among its many miraculous rescues, resurrections, and rewards various instances in which the Virgin takes revenge against blasphemers and iconoclasts. A man who knocks off her statue's nose has his own nose shot off on the battlefield; Lipsius confides that "it was undoubtedly directed by the B. Virgin." Another who threatens to place the statue in a bonfire has his jaw shot off. "This was the Fortune of those that came to fight against the City of Halle, that is against the B. Virgin."[54] This Virgin is as vengeful as the Ghost of Hamlet's father, but she can exact revenge herself.

A lively debate in England over the miracles of Our Lady of Halle focuses on just this vengeful aspect of the Virgin's intercessions. In 1613, John Floyd, a prolific and passionate Catholic apologist, repeats Lipsius' stories of revenge against iconoclasts and argues that surely Lipsius could not have claimed that named persons in recent memory had lost noses if they manifestly had not.[55] Sir Edward Hoby, who frequently clashed with Floyd, scoffs that accounts such as Lipsius' depict the Virgin as a "hard-hearted Saint" and that if images are so vengeful (and powerful), how did it come to pass "when Popish Idols were suppressed in *England*, that no man lost his nose, nor received any harme, though many such woodden Ladies then lost their heades?"[56] For Hoby, Catholics present a Virgin who is too much like other women: splenetic, irrational, and bossy. Thus Hoby mobilizes misogyny as a resource for discounting the claims made for the Virgin's power. While anti-Catholic polemicists such as Hoby ridicule the idea of a vengeful virgin, Mary's staunchest admirers defend her rage as justified and recount her mutilation or murder of her opponents with reverence and gratitude.[57]

In contrast, the Hermione who is an animated statue, like the Hermione who appears to Antigonus in a dream, or even the "soul vext" stage walker who is fantasized by Leontes and Paulina, is not angry at her husband, not seeking revenge. Indeed, Leontes recognizes his wife in just these terms: "thou are she / In thy not chiding" (5.3.25–6). If the resurrection scene at the end of *The Winter's Tale* has Catholic as well as pagan resonances, then the evocation of Catholic belief is curiously partial and defanged. This Hermione may withhold her speech from her husband, but she does not shoot his nose off.

Hermione might be seen as a figure for the "Vanishing" Catholic, whose disappearance is a wish and whose return can be celebrated only if it serves to freeze the threat of an animate, powerful, and vengeful Catholicism into its most innocuous manifestation: the silent, loving, wrinkled mother. While the recent critical emphasis on Purgatory invites us to imagine a vanished Catholicism that longs to be remembered, I have hoped here to activate associations with women, revenge, and the undead in order to suggest how disturbing the specter of a clamorous and punitive Catholicism might be. This is a specter from which the stage turns away.

In this chapter, I have linked two questions: how is Catholicism—as cultural phenomenon more than as theology— itself a specter haunting post-Reformation England, feared and evaded rather than warmly remembered, precisely because it was not quite dead? And why are there so few female ghosts in Shakespeare's plays? The constellation of Catholic associations around the figure of Hermione illuminates the conjunction I have been suggesting. As I have argued, Catholicism was disturbingly vigorous rather than lamentably moribund. For centuries after the Reformation, it remained as vaguely defined and as undead as ever, going in and out of fashion, crucial to myths of nation-formation, animated by its association with ethnic difference, invaluable as a cache of images, objects, forms, and stories. Some attached themselves to their families through a cherished affiliation to their ancestors' faith; for others, Catholicism was a discovery, a choice, perhaps even a rebellion. Since Catholicism meant many different things, and because of that very indeterminacy proved mobile, adaptable, and resilient, it is premature to declare it dead and to be mourned in the late sixteenth and seventeenth centuries. Like the last Indians, Catholics did not vanish from the cultural landscape; instead, those who succeeded and dispossessed them later told stories that erased them. Catholics did not vanish from post-Reformation England, but rather from historiography of post-Reformation England. Consigned to the margins, they played the thankless roles of the losers and spoilers of history. When scholars began to look differently, to ask different questions, we saw them everywhere.

The rare appearances of women in ghost stories might mean either that dead women were rarely imagined to have legitimate claims on the living, or that the accusations and demands they might make were too horrifying to imagine. Perhaps this is why *The Winter's Tale* robs its female protagonist of rage and vengefulness even as it so provocatively links her to the spectral and the iconic. Focusing on what Hermione's apparitions do not do—accuse Leontes or vow revenge—might make it possible to imagine what early modern culture usually chose not to: the prospect of dead mothers or wives who return, of the repudiated mother church who wants to reclaim her properties and power.

The vanishing feminist?

When feminist work is clearly identified it is often so that it may be caricatured or dismissed in references to "the feminist reading of" a given work (as if there were only one and it is predictable) or "the feminist assumption that" all women are victims or all women are agents, that femininity is essential or femininity is constructed. Feminist work is also ghettoized through citation practices that suggest that scholarship on gender, women, and sexuality yields knowledge only on these topics and is only of interest to other specialists rather than to everyone working on politics or nationalism or print culture more generally. Yet gender is a question that might be asked even in studies that are not "about" it. When most ghost stories are about male revenants, then gender is a crucial category for understanding ghost stories and grief. When gender is a crucial resource in attacks on Catholicism, then it should be taken into consideration even by those who assume that they do not "do" gender. To sustain and extend the impacts of feminism, we need to resist removal to the "gender note." Such marginalization often precedes vanishing altogether.

The premise of this collection is that feminism is now so fully integrated into other knowledge making projects that it is no longer as sharply defined or isolatable. This would make feminism like the Indians and Catholics who appear to have vanished but have instead intermarried, metamorphosed, adapted, and survived. Survival is a good thing; invisibility and dispossession are not. Rather than mourn, we need to seek out, herald, and demand space for feminism's new manifestations.

Acknowledgements

I would like to thank Richard McCoy for the opportunity to present this essay for the first time as one of the CUNY Graduate Center Annual Shakespeare Lectures; Mario DiGangi for his illuminating response on that occasion; and CUNY faculty and students for the ensuing discussion. I am also grateful to Dympna Callaghan, and to audiences at the University of California, Davis, Loyola University of Chicago, and the NEH Summer Institute on "Inquisitions and Persecutions in Early Modern Europe and the Americas," at the University of Maryland, and especially Vincent Carey, Karen Nelson, and Adele Seeff for their helpful comments and questions.

Notes

1. Natalie Zemon Davis sees the rituals of All Souls' Day as striving, in part, "to keep the dead at bay." Natalie Zemon Davis, "Ghosts, Kin, and Progeny: Some Features of Family Life in Early Modern France," *Daedalus* 106 (1977): 87–114, esp. 93.
2. Peter Marshall, *Beliefs and the Dead in Reformation England* (Cambridge: Cambridge University Press, 2002), 15; Bruce Gordon and Peter Marshall, "Introduction," in *The Place of the Dead: Death and Remembrance in Late Medieval and Early Modern Europe*, ed. Gordon and Marshall (Cambridge: Cambridge University Press, 2000), 8.
3. Michael MacDonald and Terence R. Murphy, *Sleepless Souls: Suicide in Early Modern England* (Oxford: Clarendon Press, 1990), 44.
4. These terms for the dead come from the work of Nancy Caciola, "Spirits Seeking Bodies: Death, Possession, and Communal Memory in the Middle Ages," *The Place of the Dead*, 66–86, esp. 68; and "Wraiths, Revenants and Ritual in Medieval Culture," *Past and Present* 152 (August 1996): 3–45, esp. 37 and 30.
5. Caciola, "Wraiths, Revenants and Ritual," 33; Vanessa Harding, *The Dead and the Living in Paris and London, 1500–1670* (Cambridge: Cambridge University Press, 2002).
6. Marshall, *Beliefs and the Dead*, 89, 93–123.
7. Steven Mullaney, "Mourning and Misogyny: *Hamlet*, *The Revenger's Tragedy*, and the Final Progress of Elizabeth I, 1600–1607," *Shakespeare Quarterly* 45 (1994): 139–62, esp. 153–4.

8. Catherine Gallagher and Stephen Greenblatt, *Practicing New Historicism* (Chicago and London: University of Chicago Press, 2000), 141.

9. Pierre Viret, *The Christian Disputations*, trans. J. Brooke (London, 1579), fol. 104v; John Bale, *A Mysterye of Inyquyte* (Geneva, 1545), 54v, as quoted in Marshall, *Beliefs and the Dead*, 240; see also Peter Marshall, "Deceptive Appearances: Ghosts and Reformers in Elizabethan and Jacobean England," in *Religion and Superstition in Reformation Europe*, ed. Helen Parish and William G. Naphy (Manchester: Manchester University Press, 2002), 188–208, esp. 192.

10. Thomas Hobbes, *Leviathan* (1651), ed. C. B. Macpherson (Harmondsworth: Penguin, 1983), IV.47.712.

11. Arthur Marotti, "Shakespeare and Catholicism," in *Theatre and Religion: Lancastrian Shakespeare*, ed. Richard Dutton, Alison Gail Findlay, and Richard Wilson (Manchester: Manchester University Press, 2003), 218–41, esp. 219.

12. Ronald Hutton, "The English Reformation and the Evidence of Folklore," *Past & Present* (August 1995): 89–116; Elizabeth Mazzola, *The Pathology of the English Renaissance: Sacred Remains and Holy Ghosts* (Leiden: Brill, 1998), 101.

13. Anthony Milton, "A Qualified Intolerance: The Limits and Ambiguities of Early Stuart Anti-Catholicism," in *Catholicism and Anti-Catholicism in Early Modern English Texts*, ed. Arthur Marotti (New York: St. Martin's Press, 1999), 85–115, esp. 104.

14. Lisa McClain, *Lest We Be Damned: Practical Innovation and Lived Experience Among Catholics in Protestant England, 1559–1642* (New York and London: Routledge, 2004); Peter Lake and Michael Questier, *The Antichrist's Lewd Hat: Protestants, Papists and Players in Post-Reformation England* (New Haven, CT and London: Yale University Press, 2002), pp. 187–314; Alexandra Walsham, "'Yielding to the Extremity of the Time': Conformity, Orthodoxy and the Post-Reformation Catholic Community," and Michael Questier, "Conformity, Catholicism and the Law," in *Conformity and Orthodoxy in the English Church, c. 1560–1660*, ed. Peter Lake and Michael Questier (Woodbridge, Suffolk: Boydell, 2000), 211–61.

15. Eamon Duffy, *The Stripping of the Altars: Traditional Religion in England, c. 1400–1580* (New Haven, CT: Yale University Press, 1992) and "Bare Ruined Choirs: Remembering Catholicism in Shakespeare's England," *Theatre and Religion: Lancastrian Shakespeare*, ed. Richard Dutton, Alison Gail Findlay, and Richard Wilson (Manchester: Manchester University Press, 2003), 40–57; Scott Dudley, "Conferring with the Dead: Necrophilia and Nostalgia in the Seventeenth Century," *English Literary History* 66 (1999): 277–94; Ruth Vanita, "Mariological Memory in *The Winter's Tale* and *Henry VIII*," *SEL* 40.2 (Spring 2000): 311–37.

16. Keith Thomas, *Religion and the Decline of Magic* (New York: Charles Scribner's Sons, 1971), 493, 494.

17. Michael Neill, *Issues of Death: Mortality and Identity in English Renaissance Tragedy* (Oxford: Clarendon Press, 1997), 243–61; Stephen Greenblatt, *Hamlet in Purgatory* (Princeton, NJ: Princeton University Press, 2001), 17.

18. Jennifer Woodward, *The Theatre of Death: The Ritual Management of Royal Funerals in Renaissance England, 1570–1625* (Woodbridge, Suffolk: Boydell Press, 1997), 87–117; James I, *Trew Law of Free Monarchies*, cited by Woodward, checked against *The Political Works of James I*, Charles Howard McIlwain (Cambridge, MA: Harvard University Press, 1918), 69. See also Richard C. McCoy, "A Wedding and Four Funerals: Conjunction and Commemoration in *Hamlet*," *Shakespeare Survey* 54 (2001): 122–39, esp. 133; and Joseph Roach, "History, Memory, Necrophilia,"

The Ends of Performance, ed. Peggy Phelan and Jill Lane (New York: New York University Press, 1998), 23–30.

19. The magnificent tomb James I had built for Elizabeth in Westminster in 1606 placed her next to her Catholic half-sister, Mary, and in competition with an equally grand tomb for his mother, the Catholic Mary Stuart. Visiting Elizabeth's tomb, then, invited one also to pay homage to the two Catholic Marys. See Michael Dobson and Nicola J. Watson, *England's Elizabeth: An Afterlife in Fame and Fantasy* (Oxford: Oxford University Press, 2002), 46.

20. O. W. Furley, 'The Pope-Burning Processions of the Late Seventeenth Century," *History* 44 (1959): 16–23.

21. Huston Diehl, *Staging Reform, Reforming the Stage: Protestantism and Popular Theater in Early Modern England* (Ithaca, NY: Cornell University Press, 1997); Helen Hackett, *Virgin Mother, Maiden Queen: Elizabeth I and the Cult of the Virgin Mary* (London: Macmillan; New York: St. Martin's Press, 1995); Patricia Phillippy, *Women, Death, and Literature in Post-Reformation England* (Cambridge: Cambridge University Press, 2002); Alison Shell, *Catholicism, Controversy and the English Literary Imagination, 1558–1660* (Cambridge: Cambridge University Press, 1999), 23–55; Susan Zimmerman, "Animating Matter: The Corpse as Idol in *The Second Maiden's Tragedy*," *Renaissance Drama* n.s. 31 (2002): 215–43. In a series of connected essays, Zimmerman explores the rich significance of the gendered corpse in post-Reformation England, especially on the stage. See Zimmerman, "Duncan's Corpse," *A Feminist Companion to Shakespeare*, ed. Dympna C. Callaghan (Oxford: Blackwell, 2000), 320–38; and "Marginal Man: The Representation of Horror in Renaissance Tragedy," *Discontinuities: New Essays on Renaissance Literature and Criticism*, ed. Viviana Comensoli and Paul Stevens (Toronto: University of Toronto Press, 1998), 159–78.

22. See Abbe Blum, "'Strike all that look upon with mar[b]le': Monumentalizing Women in Shakespeare's Plays," in *The Renaissance Englishwoman in Print: Counterbalancing the Canon*, ed. Anne M. Haselkorn and Betty S. Travitsky (Amherst, MA: University of Massachusetts Press, 1990), 99–118; Laurie A. Finke, "Painting Women: Images of Femininity in Jacobean Tragedy," *Theatre Journal* 35.3 (1984): 357–70; Mary Beth Rose, *The Expense of Spirit: Love and Sexuality in English Renaissance Drama* (Ithaca, NY: Cornell University Press, 1988), 93–177; Valerie Traub, *Desire and Anxiety: Circulations of Sexuality in Shakespearean Drama* (London and New York: Routledge, 1992), 25–49.

23. All citations in this paragraph are to *The Norton Shakespeare*, ed. Stephen Greenblatt, Walter Cohen, Jean E. Howard, and Katharine Eisaman Maus (New York: W. W. Norton, 1997).

24. Catherine Belsey, *Shakespeare and the Loss of Eden: The Construction of Family Values in Early Modern Culture* (New Jersey: Rutgers University Press, 1999), 152, 173.

25. Katherine Eggert links posthumous affection for Queen Elizabeth I to what anthropologist Renato Rosaldo calls "'imperialist nostalgia,' that is, the longing of colonialism's agents for the very culture they have destroyed." See *Showing Like a Queen: Female Authority and Literary Experiment in Spenser, Shakespeare, and Milton* (Philadelphia: University of Pennsylvania Press, 2000), 133, 160, 161.

26. Jill Lepore, *The Name of War: King Philip's War and the Origins of American Identity* (New York: Knopf, 1998), 191–226, esp. 224.

27. Renée L. Bergland, *The National Uncanny: Indian Ghosts and American Subjects* (Hanover, NH and London: University Press of New England, 2000), 3.

28. Jean O'Brien, "'Vanishing' Indians in Nineteenth-Century New England: Local Historians' Erasure of Still-Present Indian People," in *New Perspectives on Native North America: Cultures, Histories, and Representations*, ed. Sergei Kan and Pauline Turner Strong (Lincoln, NB: University of Nebraska Press, 2006); *Dispossession by Degrees: Indian Land and Identity in Natick, Massachusetts, 1650–1790* (Cambridge: Cambridge University Press, 1997); and "'Divorced' from the Land: Resistance and Survival of Indian Women in Eighteenth-Century New England," in *After King Philip's War: Presence and Persistence in Indian New England*, ed. Colin G. Calloway (Hanover, NH: University Press of New England, 1997), 144–61. See also Brian Dippie, *The Vanishing American: White Attitudes and U. S. Indian Policy* (Middletown, CT: Wesleyan University Press, 1972); Karen Ordahl Kupperman, *Indians and English: Facing off in Early America* (Ithaca, NY and London: Cornell University Press, 2000), 239–40; and Susan Scheckel, *The Insistence of the Indian: Race and Nationalism in Nineteenth-Century American Culture* (Princeton, NJ: Princeton University Press, 1998).

29. John Gee, *New Shreds of the Old Snare* (London, 1624), sigs. H2–H2v.

30. Greenblatt, *Hamlet in Purgatory*, 108, 137. The first sentence of Greenblatt's *Shakespearean Negotiations* (Berkeley, CA: University of California Press, 1988) is "I began with the desire to speak with the dead"; he plays with this famous statement in his 2002 MLA Presidential Address, "'Stay, Illusion': On Receiving Messages from the Dead," *PMLA* 118.3 (2003): 417–26. Linda Woodbridge explores a "Protestant disinclination to speak with the dead" in "Afterword: Speaking with the Dead," *PMLA* 118.3 (2003): 597–603.

31. Gervase Babington, *The Workes of the Right Reverend Father in God, Gervase Babington* 2 vols. (London, 1622), 2: 189.

32. A. Anderson, *Shield of Our Safetie* (London, 1581), sigs. H3v–H4r. I found the Babington and Anderson passages through citations in Marshall, *Beliefs and the Dead*, 249.

33. Elizabeth Leigh at Arreton, Isle of Wight, 1619, as cited by Marshall, *Beliefs and the Dead*, 214, n. 149. Marshall also discusses epitaphs that envision post-mortem reunions between husband and wife (230–1), as does Jean Wilson, "I Dote on Death: The Fractured Marriage in English Renaissance Art and Literature," *Church Monuments* 11 (1996): 43–60.

34. Thomas, *Religion and the Decline of Magic*, 587–606, esp. 594, 597, 598. The case of the remorseful midwife, whose ghost reveals the bodies of two bastard children she killed, is recounted in *Great News from Middle-Row in Holbourn: Or a True Relation of a Dreadful Ghost Which Appeared in the Shape of one Mrs. Adkins* (London, 1679). For other discussions of this case, see Malcolm Gaskill, *Crime and Mentalities in Early Modern England* (Cambridge: Cambridge University Press, 2000), 218–19; and Laura Gowing, "The Haunting of Susan Lay: Servants and Mistresses in Seventeenth-Century England," *Gender and History* 14.2 (2002): 183–201, esp. 195–6. *A Full and True Relation of the Examination and Confession of W. Barwick and E. Mangall* (London, 1690) describes how, after Mangall drowns his pregnant wife, her silent apparition appears to her brother-in-law near the scene of the crime, leading him to suspect and then uncover the murder.

35. *The Works of Thomas Nashe*, 5 vols., ed. Ronald B. McKerrow and F. P. Wilson (Oxford: Blackwell, 1958), 1:383.

36. Marshall, *Beliefs and the Dead*, 253, 251–2, 259–61.

37. Gowing, "The Haunting of Susan Lay." The servant, Susan Lay, had borne children to the dead woman's husband and son. Gowing explores why the ghost appears to her servant, rather than her male relatives.
38. Marshall, *Beliefs and the Dead*, 133.
39. Jean-Claude Schmitt, *Ghosts In the Middle Ages: The Living and the Dead in Medieval Society*, trans. Teresa Lavender Fagan (Chicago: University of Chicago Press, 1998), 63, 130, 187–9, 221; Caciola, "Wraiths, Revenants, and Ritual," 38. For women ghosts in Greek and Roman texts, see Daniel Ogden, *Magic, Witchcraft, and Ghosts in the Greek and Roman Worlds: A Sourcebook* (Oxford: Oxford University Press, 2002), 146–66.
40. This stage direction reads: "The spirit of Susan his second wife comes to the bedside. He stares at it, and turning to the other side, it's there too." The appearance of his first, living wife and Frank's startled response cause the spirit to vanish. Most editors comment on the fact that, since Susan has already forgiven Frank, "it is unlikely that it is her ghost returning to torment him" (*The Witch of Edmonton*, ed. Peter Corbin and Douglas Sedge [Manchester: Manchester University Press, 1999], 4.2.69.2n); "Susan's ghost has not returned to accuse Frank, in all probability" (*The Witch of Edmonton*, ed. Arthur F. Kinney [New York: W. W. Norton, 1998], 4.2.69 sd); "there would be no real reason for her spirit to torment him here" (*The Witch of Edmonton*, ed. Etta Soiref Onat [New York: Garland, 1980], 356–7).
41. *The Second Maiden's Tragedy*, ed. Anne Lancashire (Manchester: Manchester University Press, 1978); See Zimmerman, "Animating Matter."
42. *The Woman's Prize, The Tragedy of Mariam,* and *The Duchess of Malfi* are all cited from *English Renaissance Drama: A Norton Anthology*, ed. David Bevington, Lars Engle, Katharine Eisaman Maus, and Eric Rasmussen (New York: W. W. Norton, 2002).
43. Ann Jones and Peter Stallybrass, *Renaissance Clothing and the Materials of Memory* (Cambridge: Cambridge University Press, 2000), 245–68, esp. 261. Marjorie Garber argues that while there are few female ghosts in Shakespeare many of the female characters are spectral. "Literal ghosts, portentous Senecan stalkers from the revenge tradition, tend in Shakespeare's plays to be male and paternal. But ... there is another whole group of ghost writers in his plays who are similarly under erasure, and these ghost writers are women—women marginalized by their gender, by their putative or real madness, or by their violation" (Marjorie Garber, *Shakespeare's Ghost Writers: Literature as Uncanny Causality* [New York and London: Methuen, 1987], 25).
44. Mary Beth Rose, "Where Are the Mothers in Shakespeare? Options for Gender Representation in the English Renaissance," *Shakespeare Quarterly* 42.3 (Fall 1991): 290–314, esp. 301.
45. In *The Knight of the Burning Pestle*, Jasper feigns his own death and thereby accomplishes a reconciliation with his beloved. Valerie Wayne argues that every wife praised as virtuous by Lady Julia in her defense of women in Tilney's *Flower of Friendship* "metaphorically jumps off a cliff. . . . the very best wife in this narrative is one who proves her love through her own annihilation" (Edmund Tilney, *The Flower of Friendship: A Renaissance Dialogue Contesting Marriage*, ed. Valerie Wayne [Ithaca, NY: Cornell University Press, 1992], 64).
46. William Shakespeare, *The Winter's Tale*, ed. J. H. P. Pafford (London and New York: Routledge, 1963), 3.3.16–17. Subsequent citations will be from this edition.

47. Greenblatt, *Hamlet in Purgatory*, 204; Garber also remarks upon "the similarity of this scenario to *Hamlet*" (*Shakespeare's Ghost Writers*, 15). Dorothy Osborne warns William Temple that she is going on a voyage by water and if she drowns "this will bee my Last Letter, and like a will. I bequeath al my kindenesse to you in it, with a charge never to bestow it all upon another Mistresse, least my Ghost rise againe and haunt you" (June 26, 1654, *The Letters of Dorothy Osborne to William Temple*, ed. G. C. Moore Smith [Oxford: Clarendon Press, 1947, letter 68, 170]).

48. Kristian Smidt, "Spirits, Ghosts, and Gods in Shakespeare," *English Studies* 77.5 (September 1996): 422–38, esp. 431; Lynn Enterline, "'You speak a language that I understand not': The Rhetoric of Animation in *The Winter's Tale*," *Shakespeare Quarterly* 48.1 (Spring 1997): 17–44, esp. 33, n. 31. See also Theodora Jankowski, " . . . in the Lesbian Void: Woman–Woman Eroticism in Shakespeare's Plays," in *A Feminist Companion to Shakespeare*, ed. Dympna C. Callaghan (Oxford: Blackwell, 2000), 299–319.

49. Robert Greene, *Pandosto* (1595), *The Winter's Tale*, ed. J. H. P. Pafford, Appendix IV, 198.

50. Bruce R. Smith, "Sermons in Stones: Shakespeare and Renaissance Sculpture," *Shakespeare Studies* 17 (1985): 1–23; Belsey, *Shakespeare and the Loss of Eden*, 111–12.

51. Kenneth Gross, *The Dream of the Moving Statue* (Ithaca, NY and London: Cornell University Press, 1992), 101, 103, 108. For another suggestive reading of the ending, see Laurie Shannon, *Sovereign Amity: Figures of Friendship in Shakespearean Contexts* (Chicago: University of Chicago Press, 2002), 185–222.

52. Ruth Vanita, "Mariological Memory"; Velma Bourgeois Richmond, *Shakespeare, Catholicism, and Romance* (New York: Continuum, 2000), 191–201. To argue that Catholic beliefs, practices, objects, and associations turn up in Shakespeare's plays—as elsewhere in post-Reformation culture—is not to say that he was or wasn't "Catholic." There is also an illustrious tradition of placing the statue in an Ovidian context: Leonard Barkan, *The Gods Made Flesh: Metamorphosis and the Pursuit of Paganism* (New Haven, CT and London: Yale University Press, 1986), 283–8; Lynn Enterline, *The Rhetoric of the Body from Ovid to Shakespeare* (Cambridge and New York : Cambridge University Press, 2000); Lori Humphrey Newcomb, "'If that which is lost be not found': Monumental Bodies, Spectacular Bodies in *The Winter's Tale*," in *Ovid and the Renaissance Body*, ed. Goran V. Stanivukovic (Toronto: University of Toronto Press, 2001), 239–59.

53. A. G., *The Widdowes Mite. Cast into the Treasure-house of the Prerogatives, and Prayses of our B. Lady*, including a prayer attributed to Sir Tobie Matthew (St. Omer, 1619), sigs. K4v, K5v, K5.

54. Justus Lipsius, *Miracles of the B. Virgin. or, an Historical Account of the Original, and Stupendious Performances of the Image, Entituled Our Blessed Lady of Halle* (London, 1688), sig. C. Although this translation was printed late in the century, Lipsius first published his text in Latin as *Diva virgo Hallensis* in 1604. Floyd and Hoby's responses to the text suggest that it was widely known by the second decade of the seventeenth century.

55. John Floyd, *Purgatories Triumph Over Hell, Maugre the Barking of Cerberus in Syr Edward Hobyes Counter-Snarle* (St. Omers, 1613), 128–35. William Fleetwood's *An Account of the Life and Death of the Blessed Virgin* (London, 1687) complains that "*Papism* has made Her a very pattern of Pride and Ambition, always aiming at Divine Honours; angry with all that pay them not, severely Punishing those that offend Her" (sig. D2v).

56. Sir Edward Hoby, *A Curry-Combe for a Coxe-Combe. or Purgatories Knell* (London, 1615), sigs. Ee2v, Gg3v.
57. McClain argues that the image of Mary as a warrior was specific to post-Reformation England; English authors "glorified Mary as a powerful warrior, capable of protecting the souls of those who venerated her through the rosary" (McClain, *Lest We Be Damned* 96, also 97–100).

12

No Man's Elizabeth: Frances A. Yates and the History of History[1]

Deanne Williams

"Shall we lay the blame on the war?"
Virginia Woolf, *A Room of One's Own*

Elizabeth I didn't like women much. She had her female cousin killed, banished married ladies-in-waiting (she had some of them killed, too), and dismissed the powers and potential of half the world's population when she famously addressed the troops at Tilbury, "I know I have the body but of a weak and feeble woman, but I have the heart and stomach of a king."[2] Of course, being a woman was a disappointment from the day she was born: it made her less valuable in her parents' and her nation's eyes, it diminished the status of her mother and contributed to her downfall, and it created endless complications for Elizabeth as queen, when she was long underestimated as the future spouse of any number of foreign princes or opportunistic aristocrats and courtiers. Elizabeth saw from a very early age the precarious path walked by her father's successive wives. Under such circumstances, who would want to be female?

Feminist scholars have an easier time with figures such as Marguerite de Navarre, who enjoyed a network of female friends and believed strongly in women's education; Christine de Pisan, who addressed literary misogyny head-on; or Margaret Cavendish, who embodies all our hopes for women and the sciences.[3] They allow us to imagine and establish a transhistorical feminist sisterhood. Elizabeth I, however, forces us to acknowledge the opacity of the past and the unbridgeable distance that divides us from our historical subjects. But this has not stopped us: the extent and range of feminist scholarship on Elizabeth illustrates how productive scholars have found placing her in a feminist context, and using feminist vocabulary to analyze her life.[4] As feminism has evolved, it has expanded to include the problematic cases such as Elizabeth.[5] And women's history does not confine itself to the silent, the submissive, the assimilable. Nevertheless, the

238

case of Elizabeth throws into relief the limitations of such a contemporary concept as feminism. Feminism is predicated on an assumption of rights and of equality—equality between men and women as well as equality among women. For Elizabeth, these assumptions would be utter nonsense.

One of the most influential studies of Elizabeth was produced by a woman who also had very little to say to feminism: Frances A. Yates. Published in the *Journal of the Warburg and Courtauld Institutes* in 1947, and reprinted in the 1970s and 1990s, Yates's article, "Queen Elizabeth as Astraea," describes

Figure 12.1 Photograph of Frances A. Yates. Reproduced by courtesy of the Warburg Institute.

the iconography of Elizabeth as Virgin Queen. It draws on the traditions of classical literature, European literature, drama, and the history of art and architecture, as well as religious history, to explain the literary and artistic processes by which, as she puts it, "the unmarried state of the Queen is exalted into a symbol of the imperial virgin Astraea which fills the universe."[6] Whereas previous studies of Elizabeth were confined to narrative history (from the prurient to the celebratory, and including, somewhere in the middle, the Victorian "girlhood" variety), Yates used "visual devices as historical documents in their own right."[7] Yates's methodology seems commonplace today: Renaissance scholars do not think twice about moving within and between disciplines; a knowledge of art, literature, music, and any number of other fields is not only *de rigueur* but necessary. In the 1940s, however, it was revolutionary. Yates's "Astraea" offered an early account of the intricacies of what the New Historicists called "representation," shaping not only Renaissance studies as a whole, but also the wave of feminist studies on Elizabeth that have emerged in the past two decades.

Yates would have shuddered to hear her work, much less herself, described as feminist. Although she was a member of the first generation of middle-class women to attend university, she did not see herself as participating in, or even representing, any kind of political struggle. She did not identify with women; she did not regard her work as a contribution to feminism; she did not go out of her way to mentor female students or cultivate friendships with other woman scholars. Instead, like so many female scholars of her time, such as the Shakespearean Muriel Bradbrook (1909–93) and the medieval historian Helen Maud Cam (1885–1968), she simply ignored feminism. Yates's intention was not to offer an account of what, today, we might call Elizabeth's gender trouble. For Yates, "Astraea" was an idea from the classical past that was pressed into the service of what she called "The Imperial Theme": an artistic and discursive system of monarchical representation that justifies the Reformation as well as England's nascent imperialism.[8] In "Astraea," virginity is an issue, as is Elizabeth's sex, but these issues are not regarded as part of a larger argument concerning ideologies or representations of gender. Feminism doesn't come into it at all.

Nevertheless, "Queen Elizabeth as Astraea" has had a profound influence on feminist scholarship on Elizabeth. Even as they proclaim their distance from Yates, scholars acknowledge the centrality of both her methodology and her claims.[9] For readers today, Yates explains how a public intensely conscious about having a queen processed and reformulated the problems posed by her gender—her femininity, her marriageability, and eventually her unmarried status—turning, after the feminist fashion, lemons into lemonade. For some, this may be a misreading of Yates's intentions. And it is possible that "Astraea" has since been read differently because apparent praise of empire is no longer acceptable. Nevertheless, just as literature is reconfigured as it is reinterpreted in different periods, so is criticism.

Yet we have lost sight of the original contexts in which the "Astraea" work was produced and read: the overwhelming losses of two world wars, the long interregnum between the first-wave feminism of the suffragettes and the bluestockings and the second-wave feminism of the 1970s, and the imposing legacy of Queen Victoria. Returning to the personal and historical events that shaped Yates's "Astraea" illuminates not only Yates's contribution to Renaissance studies but also our present interests and agendas. Like Elizabeth I herself, Frances Yates poses a challenge to the feminist scholar, requiring us to reexamine our current assumptions as well as our ideas about the past.

Et in Arcadia Ego

The Second World War had been over for about five months. Parts of London were rubble, and with rationing, power cuts, and other hardships, it still felt like war. Amidst the chaos of postwar London, the distinguished Renaissance scholar F. S. Boas invited Yates to give the Elizabeth Howland Lecture under the auspices of the Elizabethan Literary Society and the Streatham Antiquarian Society. Originally intended as an annual sermon, the Elizabeth Howland Lecture had been endowed by a great admirer of Elizabeth I's contributions to the Protestant cause.[10] The audience that gathered on November 17, 1945 for Miss Yates's lecture, an early version of the "Astraea" article, wanted to hear about the queen. Gathered in a hall that "was still suffering from the war and tattered blackout," they probably looked forward to reliving, via quotations of poetry, England's Golden Age. They wanted to hear about the Elizabeth of "merrie olde" England, identified with an optimism and certainty that, in the months immediately following the war, must have seemed a distant, though longed-for, ideal. They may even have wanted to indulge a collective fantasy about the current Princess Elizabeth, the heir apparent, who was expected to herald a return to national security and strength.

It was not well received. Recalling that evening, Yates put the problem down to interdisciplinarity: "it was an absolutely unheard-of thing in those days to use pictures in connection with a talk on poetry (poetic imagery having then absolutely no connection with pictures in the minds of the literary)."[11] Yet even if the audience did not mind her slides, Yates's learned formulations, linking Elizabeth to a wide-ranging collection of representations of chastity, would have sounded like an arcane, if not entirely foreign, language: "the just virgin is thus a complex character, fertile and barren at the same time; orderly and righteous, yet tinged with oriental moon-ecstasies" (33). Showing much-loved images of Elizabeth to be a mere assemblage of borrowed motifs and classical references, Yates was verging on sacrilege. Gesturing towards a bigger picture of elite, educated, and polyglot internationalism, Yates was also verging on the offensive. "Astraea" focused on

English culture, yet part of Yates's larger argument was that the French and the English constructed virtually interchangeable patterns of representation for their monarchs.[12] To an audience whose wartime suffering had been justified by a nationalist rhetoric, no one wanted to hear Yates deconstructing Queen Elizabeth *avant la lettre*, or implying that she had anything to do with the French. Even worse, Yates described Elizabethan paeans and praises as "propaganda": a word with associated with England's enemies across the Channel, and certainly not with its own monarchy.[13]

Yet Yates's intention was to be anything but divisive. Composed during the war, as she commuted from Surrey to the Warburg and British Libraries, "Astraea" is the product of research pursued in spite of air raids, ambulance volunteering, and other wartime dangers and stresses. As Yates recalls, in the unfinished autobiography she was working on when she died, "I was determined that Hitler should not prevent me from writing ... I went on working at it whenever possible."[14] Describing the process of constructing national identity and illustrating the importance of images in politics, "Astraea" is motivated by ideals of peace and unity. From its first paragraph, it accentuates the positive and eliminates the negative. Beginning with the catalogue of names for Elizabeth recited in Thomas Dekker's *Old Fortunatus*, Yates writes, "over Pandora as a name for Elizabeth we will not linger, but the Virgin Queen as Astraea is the subject of this essay" (29). Yet this optimism is superimposed on the inevitability of decline, as Yates recounts the appearance of Astraea in Ovid's account of the four ages: "War came, and brandished in its bloody hands the clashing arms. Piety lay vanquished, and the virgin Astraea, last of the immortals, abandoned the blood-soaked earth" (30). As Yates demonstrates the classical roots of the Astraea image, she also signals her own, more personal investment in Astraea as a figure for peace after war, and for unity after division. Yates expresses this longing to return to a Golden Age after a time of great destruction and hardship (or as she puts it, quite simply "the idea of sunshine after storms") in her little pamphlet, "Allegorical Portraits of Queen Elizabeth I at Hatfield House," which appeared in 1952.[15] Quoting Sir John Davies's *Hymns to Astraea*, she writes:

> Verses by the poets on Elizabeth as Astraea usually introduce the idea that she is restoring to England an eternal spring like that of the Golden Age ... Here the connection of the flowers of spring in the golden age with the spring, or golden age, of 'our state,' the state of England, is clearly made.

(218)

The idea of returning to a Golden Age is at once deeply nostalgic and intensely optimistic: the past becomes a pattern for reforming the present. Yates had personal reasons for idolizing the past. Her childhood seems, by all accounts, to have been quite close to perfection. Her family was remarkably unified and harmonious: her father was a successful naval architect; her mother presided over a well-organized household. Yates recalled that they lacked nothing. Although her father's salary was not large, her mother was frugal, and they had just enough for all the trappings of middle-class life: books and music, pets, parties, holidays. Most importantly, her family valued education: they sent Hannah to Girton College, Cambridge, Ruby to the Glasgow School of Art, and James to Hertford College, Oxford. As the youngest by eleven years, Frances was indulged by the entire family: her 1916 diary describes with great passion and detail the refurbishment of an old desk, which was installed in her very own "room of one's own" in the attic, which she dubbed "the studio," where she pursued her writing, painting, and photography.[16]

Yates's scholarly longing for unity constitutes a personal reaction to the First World War. As she recalls, "the 1914–1918 war broke our family; as a teenager I lived among the ruins."[17] As a 15-year-old, Yates confided to her diary:[18]

> My brother at this time was a school-master at St. Bees School in Cumberland. He was greatly beloved by the boys and when he left the school to join the army, the whole school house came to the station to see him off. He was a 2nd lieutenant in the 3rd Royal West Kent Regiment and was stationed at Chatham for training. My mother and I went down and stayed near him for more than a month. Soon after this he went out. He was killed on the 8th October 1915 whilst leading a bayonet attack. I shall not do more than state the bare facts of this event but of course it is a deep and lasting sorrow to all of us.

A much-loved schoolmaster and a published poet (a collection of his poetry was republished posthumously as *War Lyrics* in 1919), James Yates was filled with promise. With his sisters, he had enjoyed an excellent education, numerous professional opportunities, a loving and supportive family, and a complacent sense of certainty in his world and ambitions.

It has become something of a cliché to associate James's generation with the end of an era: a generation sacrificed along with an entire way of life. Many view the First World War as destroying a pan-European culture that, for all its faults and inequities, had been evolving since the Renaissance. The squalor of trench warfare overwhelmed the ideals of civilization and society with which soldiers on both sides had been raised. For Yates, the death of James was the death of childhood. Her diary laments, "It may seem to be a very selfish way of looking at it but why oh why, when I was just becoming more developed and when he would have been such a perfect companion & brother, when I was beginning to realize his real character, was he taken away?"[19] James's death also heralded the beginning of a kind of extended childhood. Frances and her sisters never married, never left their parents' household (although Ruby spent many years as a missionary in South Africa). The family remained frozen, as they were when James went off to war. As a result, Frances was able to pursue her scholarly life unhindered by marriage, childrearing, and housekeeping. She remained forever the baby of the family, with her sisters caring for her after their parents died. Frances's scholarly career, moreover, was a family enterprise: her parents went so far as to name their house in Surrey "New House" in honor of an admiring *TLS* review of Frances's first book on John Florio, which said that it cast "new and lively" light on the subject.[20] In this way, Frances replaced the promising, literary son that they had lost.

Yates was born in the penultimate month of the nineteenth century: a time when, as she described it, "The British Empire was at the height of its power and glory, the British Navy second to none in the world."[21] Taken outside for the first time on New Year's Eve, 1899, Yates felt as if she had experienced at firsthand a Golden Age of Innocence:[22]

> It seems to me now the Golden Age, in which the security and stability of the Victorian era were still intact and seemed the natural state of affairs which would continue for ever (though in a less severe and easier form). It was not, of course, a Golden Age for all, but for me it was a time of perfect safety and happiness when I first put down roots of experience and inquiry in a world which made sense.

Given her disciplined religious upbringing, the biblical structures of innocence and experience, and perfection and fall, come naturally, and are easily superimposed on Hesiod's notion of the Golden Age, which includes the inevitability of decline. Her account of hearing the news of the sinking of the *Titanic* crystallizes the sense of a threatened perfection that provides the motivation for her work:[23]

> We stood outside near the gate into the lambs' field whilst he told us about the *Titanic* disaster. In view of the kind of news which we were soon to hear and would continue to hear in unbroken crescendo throughout life, the loss of the *Titanic* might seem relatively unimportant, and yet it retains its impressiveness because it was the first piece of Frightful News, the first revelation that the whole rich world of 'modern civilization' was not so safe as it seemed, that things could go badly wrong.

The loss of the *Titanic*, the declaration of war (and the deeply symbolic crash of the gold sovereign), and, most tragically for her family, the death of James, cast a shadow over the Victorian solidity of Yates's domestic world. They prompted her scholarly efforts to recover and recuperate lost, and better, worlds: as she described it, "to return to idealism after it has been crushed; a desire for unity after dissension."[24]

"Astraea" emerged from the research that became *The French Academies in the Sixteenth Century* (also published in 1947). In what is considered to be one of her best books, Yates argues that the French academies that inspired Shakespeare's *Love's Labours Lost* contained a "whole encyclopedia," a vast pool of knowledge that was subsequently broken down into specialist subjects: "thus illustrating the breakup of the European mind into separate disciplines."[25] Her preface reads:[26]

> It is a book which ought to have been written in Paris, instead of from such sources as were available in war-time and post war-time London. Its excuse for appearing in the present form, without waiting for further findings from more detailed research in France, is that the conditions under which it was written, unsatisfactory from the scholarly point of view, were from the spiritual point of view perhaps not unrevealing. It might be difficult to recapture the atmosphere in which the French Academies of the sixteenth century first presented themselves as a steadying subject for contemplation in a disintegrating world.

Published in the same year as *The French Academies*, "Astraea" shows this ideal academy in action, revealing the mutually reinforcing disciplines and discourses of "music, art, rhetoric, or what you will." For Yates, the division of scholarly disciplines was symptomatic of a larger, almost metaphysical, division; in her work, she sought recovery and reunion. She wanted to return to the academy before disciplines, which she associated with an almost prelapsarian unity.

The Warburg Institute allowed her to replace her lost, happy childhood home with another. Established by Aby Warburg in the decades before the war, and moved from Hamburg to London in 1933, the Warburg offered a safe space for the pursuit of interdisciplinary scholarship before there was such a word. Ernst Gombrich's description of Warburg's "original vision of a unitary *Kulturwissenschaft*" illustrates how the Warburg answered Yates's psychological as much as scholarly needs.[27] Warburg's desire to assemble a library "uniting the various branches of the history of human civilization where [the student] could wander from shelf to shelf," and the library's flight from the Nazis in 1939, with the arrival, from Hamburg, of 60,000 volumes in a container ship on the Thames, resonated with Yates's longing to return to a scholarly utopia, and to reclaim a lost and threatened past.

As a result, Yates took deep, personal offense at any observation of disciplinary boundaries (a quality which disqualified her from the many academic posts for which she applied and, unfailingly, did not win). Sydney Anglo, who studied with her in the 1950s, recalls: "You did not dream of saying to her, 'Oh, but that's not History: it's French, or English Literature, or Italian, or Philosophy, or Science, or Medicine, or Magic,' or whatever. No boundaries, other than those of time and energy, were allowed to limit research."[28] Another distinguished former student, Sir Roy Strong, recalls her impatience with any expression of limitation: "When confronted with a thesis on Elizabethan Pageantry as Propaganda I said, 'I can't do that, it's English literature,' to which the reply came, 'A trained mind can do anything. You take the book from the shelf and read it.' "[29] Today it is fashionable, even ubiquitous, to call one's research "interdisciplinary," but at a time when disciplinary boundaries were honored, Yates would have nothing to do with them. She writes in the preface to the reprinting of *Astraea*:[30]

> My aims have hardly been conscious but I think that one of them has been crossing frontiers, crossing national frontiers in studies overlapping different national cultures, and crossing frontiers between disciplines, those artificial divisions between disciplines. I think that I have concentrated in history of ideas on ideas which cross frontiers and belong to mankind as a whole. One such idea which I have studied is that of 'universal harmony.'

Queen Bee

Like Elizabeth I, Yates's domestic life was surrounded by women, and her professional life spent talking with men. In her work on John Florio and Giordano Bruno, and her daily life at the Warburg, with friends such as Perkin Walker, Ernst Gombrich, J. B. Trapp, Fritz Saxl, and illustrious students such as Sydney Anglo and Roy Strong, Yates was in daily contact with important men, both dead and alive.[31] And she by no means deferred to them: as Strong recalls, "she ate bright young men, as you know."[32] And finally, like the apocryphal legend of Elizabeth dressing as a soldier to address the troops at Tilbury perhaps, there was a masculine aspect to Yates's appearance. Strong describes how "in attitude and appearance she... fits neatly into a gallery which includes Dorothy L. Sayers and Muriel St. Clare Byrne. To be intellectual was equated with the affectation of a certain mannishness."[33] Yates illustrates a phenomenon some feminists call "the Queen Bee": a woman who has enjoyed advantages enabled by her feminist predecessors, yet one who refuses to engage with or support feminism.

In Yates's papers I have found only one sidelong glance at the subject of feminism. Describing her father's relatively easy social mobility, Yates ventured: "though the injustice of discrimination between the sexes is (in my opinion) enormously over-emphasized to-day, there can be no manner of doubt that the Victorian Boy was in an unfairly strong position as compared to the Victorian Girl."[34] Yates's father's aspirations were possible because he was male, and exceptional; for him, as Yates put it, "a chink in the system appeared."[35] As a result, he could offer his daughters an education. Yates was a member of the first generation of middle-class women to attend university, and her experience as a correspondence student at University College,

London, does not seem to have produced the same sense of exclusion and rejection famously symbolized by boiled beef and stewed prunes in Virginia Woolf's *A Room of One's Own*.[36] Although her comment tacitly acknowledges it, Yates did not dwell on "the injustice of discrimination between the sexes." She had the education her mother longed for, and universities had been closed until quite recently to most boys as well as girls of her social class. Not wishing to appear ungrateful, and eager to get on with it, Yates does not dwell on the issue. Like Elizabeth, she simply wanted to be one of the boys.

Despite repeated accounts of past unity and high hopes for future harmony, Yates had little interest in overcoming specific social differences. Her work focuses on elite culture, the productions of an extreme minority of educated men and royalty. As she moved from "Astraea" and her studies of imperialism in the 1950s, to writing on the occult and Rosicrucianism in the 1960s and 1970s, her work became more and more concerned with rarified worlds. Her later books, such as *Giordano Bruno, The Rosicrucian Enlightenment*, and *The Occult Philosophy in the Elizabethan Age*, explore the magical systems that sought a return to the Golden Age. Whereas the imperial argument of "Astraea" was concerned with idealized representations of royalty in the interests of political unity, combining mysticism with a naïve, Kiplingesque sense of the benevolence of empire, her subsequent studies sought to recreate little islands of enlightenment in which more and more arcane forms of knowledge were pursued in the face of an increasingly worldly anti-intellectualism. [37] Towards the end of her career, she no longer even held herself accountable to reality. She writes in the Preface to *The Rosicrucian Enlightenment*:[38]

> The subject is fundamental because, basically, it is concerned with a striving for illumination, in the sense of vision, as well as for enlightenment in the sense of advancement in intellectual or scientific knowledge. Though I do not know exactly what a Rosicrucian was, nor whether there were any, the doubt and uncertainty which beset the seeker after the invisible Rose Cross Brothers are themselves the inevitable accompaniment of the search for the Invisible.

Yates's greatest hatred was for the barbarians at the gates. Her greatest attraction was to intellectual utopias that were threatened, unattainable, or virtual. Perhaps alluding to the lyrics of Ivor Novello's popular song "The Land Called Might Have Been," J. B. Trapp said, "Frances Yates was always at her best and most exciting when describing what might have been."[39]

This is not to say that Yates was entirely blind to social problems. In her account of her Victorian (and Edwardian) childhood, she grumpily anticipates a critical response by her imagined reader:[40]

> I hear in my mind's ear the mutterings of an angry reader. These oppressed grimy coalmen and patronized cooks and housemaids were the products

of a bad system. I was living, growls this reader, in a little island of bourgeois snobbery in one of the worst periods, and one of the worst areas, for the capitalist exploitation of the poor... I am not saying the system was not bad; it was bad: I am only trying to write an account, as honest as I can make it, of a family living in times which I can remember.

In her autobiographical fragments, Yates consistently and rhapsodically returns to this prewar period, which is inextricably tied to memories of her brother. This "little island of bourgeois snobbery" is, for Yates, a space of love and revelation and, as a result, she recalls it with intense nostalgia:[41]

I remember a primrose, newly opened, exquisitely pale and slender. My brother said, 'Look', so we looked at it... I have had the experience of looking at a primrose with a poet in an utterly unpolluted world. That primrose always comes to me with Vaughan's line, 'They are all gone into the world of light.'

Insulated from the Dickensian world of "grimy coalmen," Yates's childhood world was nevertheless defensible particularly because it was ideal and because it is lost forever. However legitimate a critique of Victorian class stratification and social injustice may be, this period, Yates implies, offered the vision of an "utterly polluted world." It was better than what followed. Moreover, as she conducted her research in the Warburg Institute, an organization that politics and prejudice had made unwelcome, Yates was reminded on a daily basis of the crisis in Enlightenment values that produced both world wars, and she believed that this kind of aggressive and appetitive barbarism destroyed (but also, as she later came to believe, crucially enabled) the Renaissance academies.

The women's movement also stalled between the wars. Alison Light's *Forever England* points out that an intense nationalism, which fueled an ensuing conservatism, derailed the process of advocacy for women's rights that was initiated in the latter half of the nineteenth century.[42] Yates's extreme idealism and reluctance to engage politically reflect this particular historical moment. Nevertheless, it seems counterintuitive that Yates's intellectual and professional craving for freedom should not dovetail with a commitment to feminism, with its overarching concern for self-determination. Yet with a temperamental hatred of restrictions, and a tendency towards mysticism, Yates would have been impatient with the primacy that first- and second-wave feminists placed on identity. As Diana Fuss explains, in *Identification Papers*, the process of identifying as one thing or another constitutes a form of longing for an absent and impossibly concrete and stable identity:[43]

Identification is a process that keeps identity at a distance, that prevents identity from ever approximating the status of an ontological given, even as it makes possible the formation of an illusion of identity as immediate, secure, and totalizable. It is one of the central claims of this book that it is precisely identity that becomes problematic in and through the work of identification.

Given Yates's historical experience, and her personal inclination to the ideal and the abstract, the idea of political action predicated on a particular form of identification would have seemed ill-advised, if not simply dangerous. Identities, from English or German to Jewish, feminist, lesbian, or Korean-American, can get people killed. Personal experiences with two world wars showed Yates that identities were less a source of power than a cause for division.

As a result, Yates's "Astraea" implicitly calls into question any kind of essential identity, as it traces how Elizabeth's identity as Virgin Queen was constructed by outsiders and consumed publicly. It shows how the shaping of identity is a process that has very little to do with individual agency: Elizabeth herself plays a role in her self-fashioning, but she is at best participating in a centuries-long conversation with learned men about queenship and power. Looking back, in the 1970s, on the contributions of "Astraea," Yates tiptoes around the idea of feminism, without committing herself to it:[44]

> The Tudor reform of the Church, carried out by the Monarch, allowed the propagandists of that reform to draw upon the traditions and symbolism of sacred empire for the glorification of the Queen. The image of her as Astraea, the Just Virgin of the Imperial Reform, was built up during her reign in the complex symbolism used of her, which incorporated the legend of the Trojan descent of the Tudors with the religious imperialism. This propaganda accustomed the public to think of a purified Church and Empire as a woman.

Elizabethans drew on an existing pattern for associating a spiritual empire with female power: like a cut-out dress for a paper doll, it was simply attached to the queen. Yet the cut-out does not come from a book about queens, or even women, but from a book about religious reform and imperialism. In a neat, almost sleight-of-hand way, Elizabeth's sex fades into the background, even as her gender (as the performance of queenship) is mobilized into a compelling political argument.

In Yates's day, however, sex and gender had yet to be split. While Judith Butler's lessons about gender performativity in the 1990s made the internal and external idea of "Woman" and the complexities of self-representation more of a conceptual issue, first-wave feminism hinged on identification. It concerned processes that required "identification" in the material, bureaucratic sense: the vote, labor, and property ownership. But Yates was more of a mystic than a utopian: she genuinely believed she was "living," through her scholarship, in the Renaissance. She was not concerned with how one might, in a political sense, achieve freedom or equality, or with imagining a social structure that would ensure that certain identities no longer produce deprivation or unjust privilege. She believed, instead, in the erasure of identity attendant on mystic union with the past. In her comments on her historical method, Yates describes the experience of absorption in archival work:[45]

> It has been life itself, the thing that makes life worth living because it increases life, enables one to live in many times and periods, instead of only one life in one period. The outlook of any one period is restricted, and can only be enlarged through absorption in outlooks of other times.

Even in her mysticism, Yates was first a scholar.

It might seem strange, then, to suggest that the example of Frances Yates has something to teach us about our students today. Feminist scholars proverbially lament the antifeminism (perhaps afeminism) of our students, who, for all of their desires and ambitions, refuse to attach themselves to feminism. They are, as Fuss would put it, resisting identification, refusing to align themselves with a feminist identity. But in post-millennial postmodernity, identities have come to be viewed as a virtual, superficial, occasionally cynical, and fundamentally protean act of manipulation. Like Yates, our students feel that any process that would identify them in a particular way, especially something they believe would undermine the endlessly inventive masquerade of femininity play that they enjoy, must be suspect. "Feminist" is particularly suspect as an identity as it is perceived (however incorrectly) as incommensurate with other, more porous opportunities for identity play, closing off such alternatives as diva, porn star, or soccer mom. Even worse, feminism has the temerity to critique these roles, spoiling the game entirely by apparently taking them all at face value, dismissing or disregarding the irony with which young people enjoy inhabiting (and discarding) roles. At a time when they are no longer children or even teenagers, they are motivated more by the opportunity to explore themselves as individuals. Given the restrictions of the Victorian society in which he was raised, James Yates did not send his daughters to university so that they could partake of a collective process; but so that they could develop as individuals.

No man's Elizabeth

Shekhar Kapur's film *Elizabeth* (1999) concludes with a striking scene in which Elizabeth, looking girlish and fragile, has her hair shorn by a weeping lady-in-waiting. Depicted, at the beginning of the film with flowing tresses and dewy blushes, Elizabeth now smears her face with stark white makeup, assuming the attitude of detached imperiousness which, Kapur implies, will define the next forty or so years of her reign. Kapur makes a very clear statement: that by remaining single, the queen preserved England's political autonomy. To this point, the film has traced the development of her touch-me-not empowerment through a string of rejected suitors. After breaking with the cross-dressing Duke of Anjou, Elizabeth returns to her banquet, Terminator-like, where she breaks with her English suitor, Robert Dudley, Earl of Leicester, because she is shocked to learn that he is married. At this point Elizabeth proclaims, to all present, that she will have one mistress and no master. And that she is, in a wonderful turn of phrase, "no man's Elizabeth!"

Kapur's treatment of history has been criticized for the rather Shakespearean liberties that it takes: Elizabeth's pronouncement comes too early in her reign, and it is presented as a revelation rather than an unfolding process of *faute de mieux*. Nevertheless, Kapur's film constitutes an imaginative account of the construction of a familiar public mask. It offers a narrative prehistory of our image of Elizabeth as Virgin Queen, an image foregrounded and anatomized by Frances Yates's "Astraea."

As I have shown, Yates's account of Elizabeth as "Astraea" is the product of a complex history that includes two world wars, the death of a brother, and the exodus of a priceless library. Her reconstruction of the iconographical machinery deployed by poets and artists to represent Elizabeth constitutes a process of recuperation that says as much about the history of the twentieth century as it does about the Renaissance. Yet the image of Elizabeth that comes out of Yates's work is very different from the image of Elizabeth that Yates herself grew up with. Yates's "Astraea" not only expresses nostalgia for the Victorian period, it reacts sharply against it. Perhaps Yates was more in tune with feminist optimism about the potential of modernity than many of her statements would lead us to expect.

Each age, it seems, has its own image of Elizabeth. It is possible that the image of "Astraea" that informed feminist studies of Elizabeth in the 1990s is now giving way to the waif-Elizabeth, celebrated in David Starkey's recent account of her life before she became queen.[46] When Frances Yates was a girl, the dominant image of Elizabeth was that of a solitary old woman, surrounded by courtiers, and horrified by her own mortality. The story that captured the Victorian imagination concerned Elizabeth's destruction of all of the mirrors in the palace (much as the story of Elizabeth's speech at Tilbury has captured ours: we love the idea of a cross-dressed, martial Amazon). As Nicola Watson explains, it was Augustus Leopold Egg's portrait, *Queen Elizabeth Discovers She is No Longer Young*, that started the trend. Highly praised from the moment it was first exhibited at the Royal Academy in 1848, its "realism" inspired a succession of unflattering Elizabeth portraits. For Watson, these images offer a potent antitype to the fecund domesticity (as mother of ten) that dominates representations of Victoria: it emphasizes the

temporal nature of Elizabeth—and hence the Elizabethan age—by contrast
to the ideals of a universal and eternal Victorian empire (on which the sun,
proverbially, never sets). Watson observes:[47]

> So obsessed did mid-Victorian culture become with the figure of the old
> queen, indeed, that Kingsley could observe ruefully in 1855 that 'it is
> much now-a-days to find anyone who believes that Queen Elizabeth was
> ever young, or who does not talk of her as if she was born about seventy
> years of age covered with rouge and wrinkles.' For the first time since
> her death, Queen Elizabeth was regularly pursued into the privacy of her
> bedchamber, to be triumphantly discovered in unflattering undress, all
> wrinkles and no rouge.

What was so threatening about Elizabeth? Whereas the Victorian period
invested its successes as an empire in the maternal productivity of its queen
(with the commonwealth figured as a "family"), the Elizabethan period had
tied its imperial might to virginity, with marriage to anyone but England
understood as a kind of national capitulation. The challenge Elizabeth
represented to Victoria meant repressing the heady combination of youth,
beauty, and virginity that produced "Astraea," and replacing it with the
Elizabethan body in all of its moral "truth" (as Falstaff puts it, in a play
that many like to believe was written for Queen Elizabeth, "old, cold, and
withered").[48]

Virginia Woolf's *Orlando* (1928) perfectly illustrates the barren grotesquerie
of the Victorian Elizabeth. Woolf describes Elizabeth as the resentful aged
admirer of the male Orlando, whom she spies kissing another woman in
the corridor. Orlando's experience of Elizabeth focuses on fetishized body
parts and accessories, expressing all of the horror evoked by the Victorian
portraits:[49]

> It was a memorable hand; a thin hand with long fingers always curling as
> if round orb or sceptre; a nervous, crabbed, sickly hand; a commanding
> hand too; a hand that had only to raise itself for a head to fall; a hand,
> he guessed, attached to an old body that smelt like a cupboard in which
> furs are kept in camphor; which body was yet caparisoned in all sorts of
> brocades and gems; and held itself very upright though perhaps in pain
> from sciatica; and never flinched though strung together by a thousand
> fears; and the Queen's eyes were light yellow...

Woolf figures the queen as animalistic, monstrous, half-bird (with skinny,
claw-like hands), half-cat (with yellow eyes and fur). Elizabeth's adorned,
caparisoned body, stiff with pain, represents the artificiality of the old world,
with all of its physical and psychological restraints. Woolf was particularly

drawn to the idea of the old furs, which she uses in her account of Orlando having sex with Elizabeth:[50]

> she pulled him down among the cushions where her women had laid her (she was so worn and so old) and made him bury his face in that astonishing composition—she had not changed her dress for a month— which smelt for all the world, he thought, recalling his boyish memory, like some old cabinet at home where his mother's furs were stored.

This masochistic experience, with Elizabeth as an aging Venus in furs, represents Orlando's immersion in and enslavement to an old world from which he must break free. The first in a series of sexual and romantic encounters that take place throughout history, Elizabeth represents the confinement in all senses (gendered, social, emotional) that Orlando flees. Woolf also associates Elizabeth with confinement in *A Room of One's Own*, in which she contrasts the power and optimism Elizabeth's reign offered Shakespeare and his contemporaries with the limitations it imposed on women. She imagines the life of "Shakespeare's sister," Judith. Equally talented (if not more so), Judith runs away from an unhappy and restrictive home to join the London theater scene; she ends up pregnant, alone, and suicidal: buried, eventually, in an unmarked grave in Elephant and Castle, a place "where the omnibuses stop."[51] The scenario that Woolf sketches, in her leisurely fashion, anticipates Yates's more terse comment on the respective lives of the Victorian Girl and the Victorian Boy.

Woolf uses Elizabeth as a marker for the Victorian period. Her descriptions of Elizabeth in *Orlando* draw on the conventional Victorian portraits—the *déshabillée*, the wrinkled skin, the cushions—which resisted and undermined the formality of sixteenth- and very early seventeenth-century portraits of Elizabeth, which depicted her, if anything, as more-than-dressed, in highly stylized and iconographically meaningful gowns. Using an ostensible realism to counter the idealized pretensions of their predecessors, the Victorian portraits accentuate the negative, just as Victorian biographies of Elizabeth draw out as much scurrilous speculation as possible, alleging sex, and lots of it, incest, and even an illegitimate child or two. As a result, the portraits tell us more about the prurience of the Victorian mindset than they do about Elizabeth. Woolf's Elizabeth thus associates the aging body of Elizabeth with a Victorian mentality obsessed with toppling Elizabeth from her pedestal, so menacing did it find an unmarried and childless queen. This is an age so threatened by female sexuality, that it had to fetishize it with furs.[52] *Orlando* rebels against the Victorian period by associating the body of Elizabeth not only with sexist social constraints, but also with its own sexual obsessions and repressions. The polymorphous Orlando pursues, instead, a pleasure-seeking and exploratory modernity. The rejection of Queen Elizabeth allegorizes Orlando's rejection of a past self; her aging body the antithesis of his androgynous future.

As near-contemporaries (Woolf was seventeen years older than Yates), Yates and Woolf would have shared experiences, such as working at the British Museum or attending an Oxbridge luncheon party, which Woolf describes in *A Room of One's Own*. They walked through the same Bloomsbury, and immersed themselves in the same London world.[53] Yet they saw Elizabeth very differently. Whereas Woolf uses the Victorian inheritance of the aging "private" Elizabeth in opposition to her modern feminist hero and heroine, Yates returns to the public image of Astraea to express her own desire for peace and harmony, wedded, of course, to great learning. As politics, ultimately, comes down to competing images, Yates's iconographic account renewed appreciation for the queen. It is curious, then, that the triumphant image of Elizabeth as "Astraea" should come from outside feminism, while Woolf's smelly old bird is bequeathed to us from one of feminism's patron saints. Yates, by bringing out what some might call the "goddess within," set the stage for feminist re-readings of Elizabeth as Amazon, as author, even as CEO. Yates's "Astraea" also reminds us where we came from, and how close we remain to the painful fragmentations of early twentieth-century history. Illustrating the power and vulnerability of optimism, as well as the peculiar beauty of nostalgia, Yates asks us to imagine the dissolution of all boundaries.

Notes

1. I would like to thank James Carley, Terry Goldie, Dorothea McEwan, Charles Hope, Ruth Morse, Stephen Orgel, Elizabeth Pentland, and J. B. Trapp for guidance and help. Clare Hall, Cambridge, and the Warburg Institute Library provided the ideal conditions for researching and writing this chapter.
2. *Queen Elizabeth's Speech to the Troops at Tilbury*, 1588 in *Elizabeth I: Collected Works* ed. Janel Mueller, Leah S. Marcus, and Mary Beth Rose (Chicago: University of Chicago Press, 200), 288.
3. For feminist discussions of Marguerite de Navarre, see Carla Freccero, "Patriarchy and the Maternal Text: The Case of Marguerite de Navarre," in *Renaissance Women Writers: French Texts/American Contexts* ed. Anne Larsen and Colette Winn (Detroit: Wayne State University Press), 130–40; "Voices of Subjection: Maternal Sovereignty and Filial Resistance in and Around Marguerite de Navarre's Heptaméron," *Yale Journal of Law and the Humanities* 5 (1993): 147–57; and "Marguerite de Navarre and the Politics of Maternal Sovereignty," *Cosmos* 7 (1992): 132–49. On Christine de Pisan, see *Christine de Pizan and the Categories of Difference* ed. Marilynn Desmond (Minneapolis: University of Minnesota Press, 1998); Susan Schibanoff, "'Taking the Gold out of Egypt': The Art of Reading as a Woman," *Feminist Readings in Middle English Literature: The Wife of Bath and All Her Sect*, ed. Ruth Evans and Lesley Johnson (London: Routledge, 1994), 221–45. On Margaret Cavendish, see Eve Keller, "Producing Petty Gods: Margaret Cavendish's Critique of Experimental Science," *ELH* 64 (1997): 447–71; Sujata Iyengar, "Royalist, Romancer, Racialist: Rank, Race and Gender in the Science and Fiction of Margaret Cavendish," *ELH* 69 (2002): 649–72; Rosemary Kegl, "'The World I have made': Margaret Cavendish, Feminism and *The Blazing World*," in *Feminist Readings of Early Modern Culture: Emerging Subjects*, ed. Valerie Traub,

M. Lindsay Kaplan and Dympna Callaghan (Cambridge: Cambridge University Press, 1996), 119–41; Bronwen Price, "Feminine Modes of Knowing and Scientific Enquiry: Margaret Cavendish's Poetry as Case Study," in *Women and Literature in Britain, 1500–1700*, ed. Helen Wilcox (Cambridge: Cambridge University Press, 1996), 117–39.

4. These include Helen Hackett, *Virgin Mother Maiden Queen. Elizabeth I and the Cult of the Virgin Mary* (London: Macmillan, 1994); Susan Frye, *Elizabeth I: The Competition for Representation* (Oxford: Oxford University Press, 1997); Katherine Eggert, *Showing Like a Queen: Female Authority and Literary Experiment in Spenser, Shakespeare, and Milton* (Philadelphia: University of Pennsylvania Press, 1999); *The Myth of Elizabeth*, ed. Susan Doran and Thomas S. Freeman (New York: Palgrave, 2003); Julia M. Walker, *Dissing Elizabeth: Negative Representations of Elizabeth I* (Durham, NC: Duke University Press, 1998) and *The Elizabethan Icon 1603–2003* (New York: Palgrave, 2003); Michael Dobson and Nicola J. Watson, *England's Elizabeth: An Afterlife in Fame and Fantasy* (Oxford: Oxford University Press, 2002).

5. Helen Hackett perfectly sums up the conundrum faced by Elizabethan scholars: "Feminist writers have generally had a somewhat more ambivalent attitude to Elizabeth, often finding themselves initially drawn to her as an attractive figure of female autonomy, only to become disappointed as they find out not only how little she did personally for other women, but also how little the very fact of having a woman on the throne changed the status of women in general." Hackett, *Virgin Mother Maiden Queen*, 240.

6. See Frances A. Yates, "Queen Elizabeth as Astraea," in *Astraea: The Imperial Theme in the Sixteenth Century* (London: Routledge, 1975 rpt. 1999), 29–87; 59. All references to this text are to this edition.

7. See the preface to *Astraea*, xii

8. Yates describes, "The Tudor reform of the Church, carried out by the Monarch, allowed the propagandists of that reform to draw upon the traditions and symbolism of sacred empire for the glorification of the Queen. The image of her as Astraea, the Just Virgin of the Imperial Reform, was built up during her reign in the complex symbolism used of her, which incorporated the legend of the Trojan descent of the Tudors with the religious imperialism. This propaganda accustomed the public to think of a purified Church and Empire as a woman." Frances A. Yates, *Shakespeare's Last Plays*, Selected Works, Vol. VI. (London and New York: Routledge, 1975 rpt. 1999), 4.

9. Hackett's *Virgin Mother Maiden Queen* distances itself from Yates (arguing that Yates's support came mostly from elegies rather than being produced in Elizabeth's time); nevertheless, her methodology and premise reflect her profound debt to Yates. Susan Frye criticizes Yates for a lacuna that is precisely the opposite of her claims. She writes, "Frances Yates saw the Queen's vitality, for example, as a 'powerful political weapon' without noticing that it was a weapon not always in Elizabeth's hands." See Frye, *Elizabeth I: The Competition for Representation*, 2. I have not found in Yates's work any suggestion of Elizabeth's agency: for Yates, Elizabethan representation is an impersonal process in dialogue with the past. Julia Walker's introduction to *Dissing Elizabeth* also observes the unwillingness of so many feminist scholars to acknowledge Yates's influence.

10. See Frances Yates, "The Genesis of 'Astraea', Autobiographical Fragments," in *Ideas and Ideals in the North European Renaissance* (London: Routledge & Kegan Paul, 1984), 321.

11. Yates, "Genesis of 'Astraea'," 321.

12. "The sacred One Ruler of these Catholic imperialist writers became in the hands of imperialist Protestant Elizabethan theologians the sacred One Virgin whose sword of Justice smote down the Whore of Babylon and ushered in a golden age of pure religion, peace, and plenty. The fact that Astraea for Dante is a symbol of imperial reform and is also the name of Elizabeth is more than a merely literary parallel." See *Astraea*, 47.
13. See *OED*. sv. "propaganda."
14. Frances A. Yates, "The French Academies," in *Ideas and Ideals*, 316.
15. "Allegorical Portraits of Queen Elizabeth I at Hatfield House," *Hatfield House Booklet* no. 1, 1952, London;. reprinted in *Astraea*, 215–19; 218.
16. Warburg Library Archive, "Frances A. Yates Papers". Family Papers. Frances Yates Diary. MS.
17. Warburg Library Archive, Frances A. Yates Papers. Collected Essays. Unused Essays Autobiography TS. See also Yates, "Early Life," *Ideas and Ideals*.
18. Warburg Library Archive, Frances Yates Papers. Family Papers. Diary entry, April 24, 1916. MS.
19. Warburg Library Archive, Frances Yates Papers. Family Papers. Frances Yates Diary.June 5, 1916. MS.
20. Frances A. Yates, "English Actors in Paris During the Lifetime of Shakespeare," *Review of English Studies* 1 (1925): 392–403.
21. Yates, "Early Life," *Ideas and Ideals*, 278.
22. Ibid., 291.
23. Ibid., 295.
24. In her acceptance of the Premio Galileo Galilei, awarded by the Rotary Italiani for a distinguished contribution to Italian studies, "though I have lived all these years in England, and in the same house, I am a citizen of the world through the Warburg Institute . . . To the best of my limited ability I have tried to work towards European understanding." See "The Acceptance of the Premio Galileo Galilei, Pisa, 8 October, 1978," in Frances A. Yates, *Renaissance and Reform: The Italian Contribution*. Collected Essays, vol. II (London: Routledge & Kegan Paul, 1983), 1–5; 5.
25. See Yates, "The French Academies," in *Ideas and Ideals*, 318. Yates's friend and colleague J. B. Trapp makes the following comment: "The tragedy—as Frances Yates felt keenly—was that once again Europe betrayed itself. Academic knowledge, thought and activity, bringing all the concerns of mankind into a harmonious whole, might have worked towards peace and toleration, but were thrust aside by the zealots and the politicians in the wars of religion. The academic ideal endured, however. It was active in the proliferation of academies in the seventeenth century, among the *philosophes* in the eighteenth, with their quest for the achievement of intellectual liberation and religious toleration through the dissemination of an encyclopedia, and finally in the nineteenth, when the creation of the Institut de France brought the academies, the arts and the sciences once again together." See J. B. Trapp, Foreword to Frances A. Yates, *The French Academies of the Sixteenth Century* (London and New York: Routledge, 1988), v.
26. Frances A. Yates, Preface to *The French Academies of the Sixteenth Century* (London and New York: Routledge, 1988), vii.
27. Gombrich continues, "Every section of the Library still reflects Warburg's original conviction that the responses of primitive man in language and imagery can lead to what he called 'orientation' in religion, science, or philosophy, or be degraded into magic practice or superstition; that the historian of literature and of art must

reflect on the nature of these responses in language and imagery; that no 'frontier police' should deter him from crossing these conventional borders of 'academic fields' " (323). See E. H. Gombrich, *Aby Warburg, An Intellectual Biography* (London: The Warburg Institute, 1970), 323.

Saxl describes Warburg's goal: "To give the student a library uniting the various branches of the history of human civilization where he could wander from shelf to shelf was his resolve." See Fritz Saxl, "The History of Warburg's Library," in Gombrich, *Aby Warburg*, 325–38; 326.

28. *Frances A. Yates, 1899–1981. A Memorial Volume*, ed. J. B. Trapp (London: Warbug Institute, 1982), 26.

29. Roy Strong, *The Roy Strong Diaries* (London: Weidenfeld and Nicolson, 1997), 306. Strong writes, "While one's contemporaries at the Institute of Historical Research seminars were slogging away at recusants in Cheshire, Mps in the parliament of 1581 or who did or did not pay Ship Money in Buckinghamshire in 1636, I was in full flight on triumphal arches, chariots, masques and ballets, and, even more, leaping through them into music, theatre, poetry, history of images and ideas, political and religious history, any tack to which the evidence led. The boundaries of knowledge widened dramatically. I was taught to think horizontally." Strong was Yates's student at the Warburg Institute in the fifties, and his books acknowledge his intellectual debt to her. See Roy Strong, *The Cult of Elizabeth* (London: Thames and Hudson, 1977) and *Gloriana: The Portraits of Queen Elizabeth* (London: Thames & Hudson, 1987).

30. Warburg Library Archive, Frances Yates Papers, "Notes on *Astraea*" (1975) TS.

31. The notable exception to the rule is Gertrud Bing, who was the director of the Insitute and married to Fritz Saxl. Yates dedicates *The Rosicrucian Enlightenment* to her.

32. See Strong, *The Roy Strong Diaries*, 287.

33. Ibid., 306.

34. Warburg Library Archive, Frances Yates Papers, "Memorial 1982" TS.

35. On the career of James Yates, see "From Wooden Walls to Dreadnoughts in a Lifetime," ed. Ruby W. Yates. *The Mariner's Mirror*. The Journal of the Society for Nautical Research 48 (1962): 291–303.

36. Virginia Woolf, *A Room of One's Own* and *Three Guineas*, ed. Hermione Lee (London: Chatto and Windus/The Hogarth Press, 1984).

37. "By claiming for the national church that it was a reform executed by the sacred imperial power as represented in the sacred English monarchy, the Elizabeth symbol drew to itself a tradition which also made a total, a universal claim – the tradition of sacred empire. The extravagant language used of Elizabeth need not necessarily imply that Elizabethan hopes went so far as to expect a world empire for the queen. The arguments for sacred empire—that the world is at its best and most peaceful under one ruler and that then justice is most powerful—are used to buttress her religious rights as an individual monarch. The monarch who is One and sovereign within his own domain has imperial religious rights, and he can achieve the imperial reform independently of the Pope. The lengths to which the cult of Elizabeth went are a measure of the sense of isolation which had at all costs to find a symbol strong enough to provide a feeling of spiritual security in the face of the break with the rest of Christendom" (*Astraea*, 58–9). Yates here is quite sensible on the distinction between a worldly and a spiritual empire; however, one cannot read this passage without thinking of England in the Second World War.

38. Preface, *The Rosicrucian Enlightenment* (London: Routledge & Kegan Paul, 1972 rpt. 1979), xiv.
39. See comments by J. B. Trapp in Biographical Memoirs of Fellows, vol. II. *Proceedings of the British Academy* 120 (2003), 538.
40. Yates, "Early Life" *Ideas and Ideals*, 287.
41. Ibid., 295.
42. See Alison Light, *Forever England: Femininity, Literature and Conservatism Between the Wars* (London: Routledge, 1991).
43. Diana Fuss, *Identification Papers* (London: Routledge, 1995), 2.
44. Frances Yates, *Shakespeare's Last Plays*, Selected Works, vol. VI (London and New York: Routledge, 1975 rpt. 1999), 4.
45. Frances Yates, "On Historical Method," Warburg Library Archive, Frances Yates Papers, TS.
46. See David Starkey, *Elizabeth: The Struggle for the Throne* (London: Chatto and Windus, 2000). Starkey's starting point also looks back to the Victorian tradition of "girlhood" literature.
47. See Nicola Watson, "Gloriana Victoriana. Victoria and the Cultural Memory of Elizabeth I," *Remaking Queen Victoria*, ed. Margaret Homans and Adrienne Munich (Cambridge: Cambridge University Press, 1997), 73–104; 85. See also *England's Elizabeth*, 147–78.
48. Shakespeare, *The Merry Wives of Windsor* V.v.154. *The Riverside Shakespeare*, ed. G. Blakemore Evans et al. (Boston: Houghton Mifflin, 1974).
49. Virginia Woolf, *Orlando* (Leipzig: Tauchnitz, 1929), 19. For further discussions of Virginia Woolf and the Renaissance, see Juliet Dusinberre, *Virginia Woolf's Renaissance: Woman Reader or Common Reader?* (London: Macmillan, 1997); and Sally Greene, *Virginia Woolf: Reading the Renaissance* (Athens: Ohio University Press, 1999).
50. Woolf, *Orlando*, 21.
51. Woolf, *A Room of One's Own*, 105.
52. Woolf clearly places the body of Elizabeth as a representation of History: "And as the first question had not been settled—What is Love?—back it would come at the least provocation or none, and hustle Books or Metaphors or What one lives for into the margin, there to wait till they saw their chance to rush into the field again. What made the process still longer was that it was profusely illustrated, not only with pictures, as that of old Queen Elizabeth, laid on her tapestry couch in rose-coloured brocade with an ivory snuff-box in her hand and a gold-hilted sword by her side, but with scents—she was strongly perfumed—and with sounds; the stags were barking in Richmond Park that winter's day" (*Orlando*, 85).
53. Cf. "London was like a workshop. London was like a machine. We were all being shot backwards and forwards on this plain foundation to make some pattern. The British Museum was another department of the factory" (*A Room of One's Own*, 25).

13
Women's Informal Commerce and the "All-Male" Stage

Natasha Korda

Recent feminist scholarship on early modern British theater history has begun to qualify the concept of an "all-male" Elizabethan stage by attending to the many instances of aristocratic female patrons, playwrights, and performers during the period, the impact of women spectators of varying classes in the commercial theaters, and the scattered examples of women performers in London and the provinces.[1] As I have suggested elsewhere, however, little critical attention has thus far been paid to the many ordinary women who worked within the networks of commerce surrounding early modern London's public theaters, in spite of the fact that a consideration of women's unexceptional status as workers both in and around the theaters may well allow for a more thoroughgoing critique of the all-male stage than has their exceptional status as players.[2] Such a critique would require that we extend the disciplinary boundaries of traditional theater history to include not only players, playwrights, and playhouses, but the heterogeneous forms of commerce that lent them support. For if we take into account the full range of social and economic interdependencies and collaborations that went into theatrical production, the all-male stage undergoes a metamorphosis and emerges as a network of commerce between active economic agents of both genders.

My focus in this chapter is women who worked in London's "shadow" or informal economy of crafts and trades, which flourished in the suburbs and liberties that gave rise to the commercial theaters. While important feminist work has been done on informal commerce in the early modern period, that work has focused primarily on the late seventeenth and eighteenth centuries.[3] Yet historians have acknowledged that the rapid expansion of the informal sector began in the late sixteenth century, when increasingly detailed statutes were passed in an attempt to regulate the growth of commerce outside of guild control. Such legislation, together with other forms of evidence, such as court records, account books, and popular pamphlets, ballads, and plays, provide important sources of information regarding

259

the parameters of informal commerce, and the extent to which women participated in this sector of the economy.

My aim is first to provide a theoretical framework that explores the usefulness of the concept of informality to an understanding of women's work, and then to consider the ways in which such work may have contributed to theatrical production. As such, this essay will build on recent feminist archival research into women's economic agency. Such research departs from earlier feminist work on the "traffic *in* women" (i.e. women as objects of exchange between men)[4] by focusing on the traffic *of* women (i.e. women as commercial actors or subjects/agents of exchange). This shift in the focus of feminist economic criticism has unquestionably necessitated what Dympna Callaghan terms a "return to the archives" to recover the many different forms of commerce in which early modern women were engaged. Yet it also requires the elaboration of new theoretical paradigms, such as the concept of "informality," through which such archival material may be reframed. This chapter will thus also consider the importance for feminist scholars in particular of maintaining a critical awareness of methodological problems raised by archival research, and of the interpretive paradigms we bring to bear on them.

That the material forms of women's work, and its intersection with theatrical commerce, have hitherto remained obscure may be attributed in part to an overly abstract and ungrounded notion of "The Market" that has characterized much of the new economic criticism of early modern drama.[5] Unanchored in the complex and heterogeneous forms of commerce that surrounded the theaters, and the diverse, material practices contributing to theatrical production, this monolithic view of "the placeless market"—first articulated in Jean-Christophe Agnew's groundbreaking and highly influential study, *Worlds Apart: The Market and the Theater in Anglo-American Thought, 1550–1750* (1986)—has obscured the socially differentiated and gendered subjects who worked within these networks of production and exchange. Thus, I would like to begin by revisiting the conceptual paradigm of Agnew's study, to understand better its occlusion of the material networks of commerce and credit upon which the theater depended and women's participation in them.

Agnew describes his book as an "intellectual history of two related *ideas*"— namely, the "idea of the market" and "the idea of the theater";[6] it sets out to analyze commerciality and theatricality as "abstracted properties" (xiii), rather than as material practices. Indeed, its fundamental aim is to unfold the history of this abstraction itself, insofar as its history of the idea of the market describes a "gradual displacement of concreteness" as this idea shifts from the situated phenomena of the market-*place*, with its "attributes of materiality, reality, [and] agency" (56) to an increasingly placeless and timeless market *process*, defined by "such detached and impersonal abstractions as exchange value," liquidity, and the money form (x–xi, 10). Agnew's history of the idea of the theater is likewise presented in terms of increasing abstraction. Here he draws on Anne Righter's account of meta-theatricality as the distinguishing feature of Elizabethan drama, defined as a theatrical form that was increasingly "confronting the conditions of its own performance," or what Righter terms the "idea of the play."[7] This idea is likewise abstracted from the material conditions of theatrical production: it is the idea of theatricality itself, as an abstracted property, which for Righter, as for Agnew, represents the object of Elizabethan drama's self-reflexive reflection. Agnew extends Righter's analysis in linking the idea of theatricality confronted by the theater to the emerging idea of commerciality—indeed, they appear to be two sides of the same coin. Thus, what Agnew terms "Protean Man" (the shape-shifting figure of the socially mobile actor [14]) becomes a theatricalized *alter-ego* of "fungible man" (122), and the "imaginative liquidity of the theatrical form" becomes a proxy or "formal analogue" of the "practical liquidity of the commodity form" (11–12).

The teleology of abstraction that governs Agnew's account, in defining the "situated phenomena" of the marketplace as residual, and the "placeless and timeless" market process as emergent (and ultimately dominant), privileges the latter over the former, which are dismissed as vestiges of a premodern past (x, 18, 28). Agnew himself admits, however, that the abstract concept of liquidity did not come to dominate the idea of the market until the end of the eighteenth century, and even then mainly among the elite (41–2). In positing liquidity as the defining trope of subjectivity in early modern English drama some two centuries earlier, Agnew effectively sets up a falsely universalized and anachronistic subject (i.e. "Protean *Man*") which effaces the heterogeneous, material conditions that defined market experience, and the ways in which that experience was shaped by a particular subject's positioning *vis-à-vis* the market—in accordance, for example, with his or her gender (54). The logic that governs Agnew's study, in privileging abstract properties such as liquidity and exchange-value over concrete forms of labor and modes of production, in turn privileges the "traffic *in* women" (i.e. marriage and prostitution) over the "traffic *of* women" (i.e. women's work and marketing activities): whereas the former is held to reflect an emergent market *process*, the latter is relegated to the situated phenomena of a residual market *place* (129).[8]

This erasure of female production and exchange is particularly evident in Agnew's historical account of the emergence of the "placeless market," which is attributed to the expansion and acceleration of what he terms "private marketing," or the informal and often unregulated transactions that took place outside the bounds of the marketplace, thereby resisting the restrictions and prerogatives of guild-regulated commerce, and thwarting the disciplinary intent of the Statute of Artificers (1563) (47–50). Agnew rather vaguely defines the agents of this "placeless market" as "middlemen" (48), their anonymity apparently a correlative of the "new and boundless silent trade" they purportedly practiced. Such trade, he maintains, was "[c]arried along on a tide of commercial paper that spoke 'voicelessly the utterances of the absent'" (50).

There is a single, brief moment in his study when Agnew does ground the abstract, *metaphorical* relation he posits between the idea of the market and the idea of the theater in a material contiguity, or what I would term a *metonymic* relation between the geographical location of such informal commerce and that of the commercial theaters: "It was no accident," he says, "that the common players of the English Renaissance sought the same immunities of London's liberties as the alien craftsmen who constructed their playhouses and fashioned their costumes" (54). Yet the relationship between the players and workers of the suburbs and liberties remains unexplored. It is this metonymic relation between the market and the theater to which I will now turn: the situated, material practices that defined theatrical commerce. In providing a more grounded, and therefore more bounded, view of the market, I hope in turn to produce a more porous view of the theater than that of traditional stage historians, who have typically portrayed the theater as an "enclosure" (125), or in Agnew's terms, a "world apart."

We have only begun to consider the ways in which the commercial theaters' imbrication in the informal market activities of the suburbs and liberties may have rendered them open to women's economic participation. Women whose economic activity was hampered by the licensed guilds often turned to London's informal economy of unregulated crafts and trades, becoming secondhand clothing dealers, pawnbrokers, peddlers, hawkers and regraters, forms of commerce on which, as we shall see, the public theaters depended heavily.[9] Women "found work where they could, flourishing in ad hoc businesses"; and while such informal commerce was disapproved of by the guilds, historical evaluation, as Beverly Lemire has argued, "should not end with the guildsman's assessment." For these "'disorderly' commercial practices were as common as they were reviled," she maintains, and formed a "vast network of commerce, which must be integrated into our concepts of the market" – and, I would add, of the theater.[10] To effect such integration, however, we must be willing to traverse disciplinary boundaries and take a fresh look at theater history in light of recent research by economic historians on the material practices of commerce and credit that made up the informal sector, and women's participation in them.

The high level of female participation in the informal sector is generally attributed to increasing restrictions placed on their labor in the licensed guilds. Thus, for example, in the case of the clothing guilds, according to Merry Wiesner, limitations imposed on female sempstresses, bleachers, and dyers applied only to their work on new cloth and clothing; articles of clothing that were already used and were being remade were not covered by these restrictions.[11] As the market in secondhand goods and clothing expanded over the course of the sixteenth and seventeenth centuries, however, attempts were made to restrict this sector of the market as well. In Leicester in 1573, a complaint was lodged by the city fathers against certain "Brogers or pledge women" who "vsed the trade of sellinge of apparel & howshold stuff" and who "have disorderlye used the same in hawkinge abrode from howse to howse."[12] The Leicester city authorities ultimately "determined that henceforth this trade should be conducted by its new male appointees 'and non other.'"

Of particular importance to an understanding of women's work in the informal sector surrounding the commercial theaters is recent work on early modern England's "culture of credit." With extremely limited amounts of gold and silver currency in circulation, England's economic expansion was fuelled by the increasing use of credit, much of which was informal.[13] Market exchanges were thus "far more eclectic than a simple trade of cash for goods."[14] Almost all commerce involved credit of one form or another and "it was credit, above all," Muldrew argues, "which dominated the way in which the market was structured and interpreted."[15] Most wealth circulated in the form of goods, rather than cash, such as clothing, plate, jewels, and other moveables. Yet there were, of course, circumstances in which money was needed (to reckon debts, pay rents, taxes, tithes, wages). Because cash was a scarce and valuable commodity in great demand, Muldrew observes, "interest was inevitably charged for its use" and "the price of interest was enormously high when it could be obtained."[16] This in turn led to new arguments justifying the charging of "interest" on economic grounds, and eventually, to the statute of 1571 tolerating interest rates of under 10 percent for the first time—a statute which, in William Ingram's view, played a crucial role in the rise of the commercial theaters. "The remarkable history of stage playing in the decade of the 1570s," he asserts, "can be better understood in tandem with the history of moneylending in the same decade,"[17] insofar as there is strong evidence that the first purpose-built theaters were financed with the aid of "many hundred pounds taken up at interest."[18] Yet, if credit was crucial to the initial outlay of large-scale funds for the building of the first commercial playhouses, it was likewise vital to the day-to-day operating expenses of theater people, who relied heavily on small-scale credit.

Recent scholarship by feminist economic historians has begun to detail the diverse and important roles women played in early modern England's informal economy through the provision and facilitation of small-scale credit. Women were active in informal networks of commerce and credit throughout England and the rest of Europe during the early modern period.[19] Wealthy widows and single women turned to pawnbroking as a "business, open to, and fit for, single women with cash in hand to use for stock in trade,"[20] as is evidenced by the lists of pawns found in their probate inventories.[21] The trade was carried out on a more ad hoc basis, however, and probably in far greater numbers, by women who worked as ale-wives, victuallers, inn- and tavern-keepers, and as petty retailers.[22] One finds numerous references to such women in plays, ballads, and popular pamphlet literature.[23]

Because the most commonly pawned item in the period was unquestionably apparel, the pawnbroking and secondhand clothing trades frequently overlapped. The shadowy world of used clothing also included "many of the same retail players as in the new," including shopkeepers, retailers, tailors, sempstresses, and menders of clothes. At the low end of these trades were the legions of itinerant traders who wandered about "calling their trade, haggling over goods, offering their wares for sale to passers-by, the very epitome of disorderly trade."[24]

Precisely how to define what constitutes informal commerce, however, remains a difficult question. The blurred contours of this sector have given rise to a host of descriptive terms—informal, irregular, black, hidden, shadow, parallel, secondary—that reinforce its penumbral or marginal status.[25] Recent theorists have seized on the purely relational aspect of "informality," arguing that it is "a specific form of relationship of production" whose contours or boundaries are in constant flux with respect to the "formal" economy,[26] varying in accordance with the vicissitudes of politico-economic regulations. "Hence, what is informal and perhaps persecuted in one setting may be perfectly legal in another," and the same economic activity will continually shift its relative location across the formal/informal divide according to a "variable geometry."[27] Far from marginal, informality is from this perspective "a fundamental politico-economic process at the core of many societies."[28] Participants in the informal sector likewise vary, incorporating a broad range of economic agents, from those who have been excluded from the formal economy, and who may have no other means of survival (e.g. the poor, women, immigrants), to informal entrepreneurs seeking ways to profit from the economic dynamism of unregulated commerce. Because the informal sector "cut[s] across the whole social structure," encompassing a broad range of heterogeneous economic activities and agents, it may incorporate relations of production that are progressive and exploitative.[29]

The informal networks of commerce and credit that surrounded the public theaters in early modern London have received comparatively little scholarly attention, perhaps because of the difficulty of recovering evidence about practices that by definition take place "off the books."[30] The important work that has been done on informal commerce in the early modern period, as mentioned above, focuses on the late seventeenth and eighteenth centuries. Yet historians have acknowledged, if only in passing, that the rapid expansion of the informal sector began in the late sixteenth century, when, "as prices and competition increased . . . more and more detailed regulatory statutes were passed in an attempt to slow the pace of change and to preserve the quality of merchandise as more and more poor households took up occupations outside of guild control."[31] By the seventeenth century, according to Muldrew, as much buying and selling was transacted privately—i.e. "abowte the streets of the cyttye," in households, shops, inns, alehouses, etc.— as publicly in marketplaces.[32] Attempts at regulation, however ineffective, provide an important source of information regarding the ever-shifting boundaries between formal and informal commerce. The repertories of the Court of Aldermen and the journals of the Court of Common Council for the City of London in the late sixteenth and early seventeenth centuries, for example, are filled with attempts to control such trade, attempts that were often directed specifically at women, such as the "womon brokers" who were ordered not to carry "abowte the streets of the cyttye any manner of apparel to be solde," and other itinerant hawkers of food and other commodities who sold their wares "in the streets" "not being licensed," and were accused of "disorder," and such market "abuses" as forestalling, engrossing, and regrating.[33] The complaints of "legitimate" crafts and tradesmen, voiced in pamphlets and petitions, likewise reflect the expansion of such informal commerce. In his 1598 treatise concerning abuses in the London markets, for example, Hugh Alley complains of the "Greedie kinde of people, inhabitinge in and about the city, & suburbs of the same, called *Haglers, Hawkers, Huxters,* and *wanderers,* uppe and downe the streets, in buyenge into their owne handes, to rayse the prices, for their owne luker, and private gayne."[34] Many of these itinerant hagglers, hawkers, and hucksters, as the illustrations that accompany Alley's treatise make clear, were women.[35]

The ubiquity of such informal commerce in the late sixteenth century did not suddenly render the market placeless, silent, and anonymous, but rather represented a growing diversification of the places, utterances, and actors that constituted it. The expansion of England's credit economy was not, as Agnew maintains, simply "[c]arried along on a tide of commercial paper that spoke 'voicelessly the utterances of the absent'" (50). Although various written instruments of credit, such as bonds, bills of exchange, and mortgages, were used by the late sixteenth century, Muldrew has demonstrated that "most credit extended for sales or services seems to have been remarkably informal," as one might expect "in a society with a high level of illiteracy."[36] Muldrew's research on early modern England's "culture of credit" has gone a long way to grounding our understanding of what constituted "the market" by detailing "how and where actual buying and selling were done, who was doing it, how often they were doing it, and what they thought of the activity of marketing."[37] He finds that most buying, selling, and credit arrangements were transacted through verbal acts of bargaining and reckoning conducted outside the bounds of the formal marketplace. Such bargains were far from "voiceless"; indeed, they "were extremely lengthy, often lasting late into the night, involving 'smooth words and fair speeches.'"[38] Thus, although many people used formal bonds at one time or another, commercial paper nevertheless represented "a minority of their total indebtedness." The culture of credit for ordinary men and women was "based on words."[39] In emphasizing the abstract and impersonal concept of liquidity as the defining paradigm of subjectivity in early modern drama, Agnew's influential paradigm has occluded the situated, material practices and heterogeneous modes of discourse that defined the culture of credit, and the diverse subject positions they encompassed.

It is, without doubt, extremely difficult to estimate the numbers of women working in London's informal economy as brokers, pledge-women, dealers in second-hand goods, and so forth. Even when documentary evidence attests to the existence of such women in large numbers, such evidence cannot always be taken at face value. Lemire, who has done the most extensive research on female brokers and secondhand clothing dealers in London, tends to view the scattered archival traces of this population as but the tip of the iceberg: "My work on the second-hand trade," she argues, "reveals that *untold* numbers of women functioned in informal commercial capacities, pawning and acting as brokers, accepting their neighbors' pledged clothing, sheets or cookware. Their often informal commerce was a vital facet of this economy" (my emphasis).[40] The temptation here is to assume that each example is exemplary, "typify[ing] the *countless* women... who cultivated commercial niches in the as yet unregulated credit environments of the West's growing cities" (my emphasis).[41] While it is true that certain types of evidence may indeed point to the existence of many more such women, we must also acknowledge that evidence of women working outside sanctioned forms of trade may at times augment their numbers to suit political purposes. Thus, for example, the author of a seventeenth-century polemical pamphlet arguing for stricter enforcement of market regulations, entitled *The Trade of England Revived,* complains of the proliferation of informal female hawkers and peddlers in London and elsewhere who "Profer Commodities... at Inns," blaming their increasing numbers for the decay of honest tradesmen and shopkeepers.[42] These informal female traders frequently served as convenient scapegoats for economic anxieties surrounding the "decay of trades."

An indirect indication of the increasing significance of London's informal economy in the late sixteenth and early seventeenth centuries may be found in the heightened interest of city and state authorities in regulating such unlicensed commerce. I will mention here only legislation directed at pawnbrokers and other traders in used goods and apparel; but it is important to remember that such legislation is but one facet of a much broader initiative to control informal market activities.[43] City authorities began to take a strong interest in controlling the commerce of informal "retailing brokers" in 1594–95. The Court of Common Council instituted two Acts during these years aimed at "diuers persons, called Retayling Broggers, Brokers or Hucksters, and others, such as use to buy olde Apparell, Householdstuffe, Bedding, Bookes, Endes, and Remnants of Silkes and Veluets, or of Linnen and Wollen cloth, or such like, to sell agayne."[44] The legislation institutes mechanisms of control through which such informal commerce may be regulated so as to generate revenue for the City's coffers: "hereafter there shalbe kept and written within this Cittie and Liberties thereof, true and perfect Register

ns.[57] The records of the haberdasher John Pope, mentioned
te the different ways in which women worked as interme-
ed pawnbrokers, moneylenders, and secondhand clothing
n, later in the seventeenth century.[58] In addition to his
op, Pope ran a moneylending and pawnbroking business on
omen served as facilitators of credit not only by organizing
nsactions, but by serving as intermediaries for unsecured
the latter context, they used their knowledge of women's
he community to vouch for their credit. Thus, for example,
relied on the judgment of a widow named Roberta Jones,
nore loans than any other man or woman in Pope's records,
to "[w]ool spinners, a silk weaver, a pin maker, mop makers,
s," after whose names appeared the phrase: "[Roberta Jones]
r word to se it payd."[59] Lemire found that "[w]omen relied
women than on men to assist in the getting of credit"—over
the women borrowers in Pope's accounts "relied on other
diate the credit process."[60] Fontaine speculates that female
ay have preferred to go to a female pawnbroker" or interme-
women specialized in handling female apparel and "to avoid
having compromised [their] sexual virtue."[61] The latter seems
he frequent references in popular literature to wives who pawn
d household stuff as sexually promiscuous, an accusation most
veled at women who "go to *Pawn alone* by themselves."[62] "[I]f
y time straightened for Money to spend abroad among her
ys one pamphlet, "then she carries Rings, or [her husband's]
he . . . *Pawn-Broker*, and makes the poor contented Cuckold work
Money to redeem them."[63] Male brokers such as Henslowe and
bly relied on female intermediaries because of their expertise in
he value of such goods, and because of their knowledge of the
y of female borrowers, knowledge that likewise enabled them to
rrower's credit.

's involvement in the credit activities of the theaters is further evid-
Henslowe's wife, Agnes, who was involved in his pawnbroking and
ding activities: she is listed several times in the accounts as lending
actors (as well as to friends, family, and other employees).[64] It is
alling in this context that Henslowe owed his initial investment
r his business and theatrical ventures largely to his providential
to Agnes, his former master's widow; so it is certainly not surprising
should have taken an active interest, and even played an active
his business affairs. Another example of a wife becoming intim-
volved in the financial side of her husband's theatrical affairs is
h Hutchinson, wife of Christopher Beeston, an actor and theater
eneur who owned the Cockpit theater. Beeston appointed his wife
d sole executrix" of his estate "by reason I doe owe many greate

bookes, by . . . honest and sufficient persons, being Free-men of this Cittie."
The register books function not only to prevent commerce in stolen goods
by listing the names and dwelling places of the brokers and their customers,
and a description of the articles sold or pawned, but also to enable the City
and its officials to profit from each and every transaction. For it stipulates
that the register books must list the amount of money at which each article
is valued so that the newly elected Registrars may collect a fee from the
brokers and from those wishing to peruse the record books in search of
stolen property. Additional revenue was generated by brokers who failed to
comply, to keep accurate records, or who were discovered to be receivers of
stolen goods.[45]

During the first year of James's reign, the expansion of the informal
sector was sufficiently apparent to become the focus of parliamentary legislation, and an Act was passed against retailing and pawnbrokers.[46] The Act
is unusual in that it provides a history of the broker's trade in London.
It claims that for hundreds of years, those bearing "the Name of Brokers,
and [who have] bene knowen called and taken for Brokers, and dealinge
in Brokerage and Brokerie," were "Freemen of the Citie" who were chosen
by a rigorous process of selection. In recent times, however, a new class of
persons has impertinently "assum[ed] unto themselves the name of Brokers
and Brokerage, as though the same were an honest and a lawfull Trade
Misterie or Occupation, tearminge and naminge themselves Brokers, wheras
in trueth they are not, abusing the true and honeste ancient name and trade
of Broker and Brokerage." This new class of "upstart Brokers," as they were
called, carried on a different sort of commerce: they "have and daylie doe set
up a Trade of buyinge and selling and taking to pawne of all kinde of worne
Apparell, whether it be olde or little the worse for wearinge, Houshold Stuffe
and Goods of what kind soever . . . findinge thereby that the same is a more
idle and easier kinde of Trade of livinge, and that there riseth and groweth
to them a more readie more greate more profitable and speedier Advantage
and Gaine then by theire former manuall Labours and Trades did or coulde
bring them." The Act further complains that these upstarts "are growen of
late to many Hundreds within the Citie of London, and other places next
adjoining to the Citie and Liberties of the same, and are like to increase to
farre greater multitudes, being Friperers, and no [true] Brokers, nor exerci-
seinge of any honest and lawfull Trade, and within the memorie of many
yet livinge such kinde of persons . . . were verie fewe and of small number."[47]
While the legislative history of attempts by city and state government to
regulate such commerce cannot tell us the precise extent of the informal
sector with respect to the formal economy, it gives us a sense of its perceived
and growing significance.

Further Acts of Common Council during James's reign reveal not only the
perceived exigency of the problem posed by the growing numbers of retailing
and pawnbrokers, but the inefficacy of attempts to control and regulate

them. According to an Act of 1622, the 1595 Act "establishing a Registry to bee kept . . . hath not taken such effect as was thereby purposed, and is to be wished it should haue done," and admits that none of the Council's prior legislative efforts had brought the brokers "to any conformitie."[48] A royal proclamation made eight years later by Charles I "for the suppressing of all secret and unlawfull practices of Retayling Brokers," however, reveals that the 1622 Act was no more effective than its predecessors, "but still the desire of unlawful gaine hath found meanes (in some ill disposed persons) to evade from the same."[49] Recognizing that the inefficacy of prior attempts to control such commerce lay not so much in the imprecision of the legislation, but rather in the difficulty of its enforcement, Charles's proclamation focuses its efforts, insisting "Wee straitly charge and command" that registry books be accurately kept and bonds of surety entered by all brokers.[50] Later in the seventeenth century, a proposal made to the House of Commons "For an Additional Tax to be Paid Upon Regulating and Licensing Pawn-Brokers" and other unlicensed traders estimates that by regulating, licensing, and taxing this sector, "these proposals by modest computation would raise £300,000 per Annum."[51] Whether or not this figure is exaggerated, the extraordinary sum it proposes gives some sense of the perceived proportions of the informal sector. A proposal for instituting charitable "banks of loan upon pawns" attempts to explain the failure of governmental regulation of pawnbrokers. The books of registry are avoided or evaded not only by thieves, who "giv[e] in false names," it maintains, but by "Merchants and Tradesmen . . . whose credit is of far greater consequence then their estate," and who in "pawn[ing] their Estates, and record[ing] their credit . . . so lose both."[52] That is, their names being publicly recorded and openly known not only to the Aldermen, Council members and Registrars, but to anyone who might pay the fee to peruse the registry, their credit is "exposed to jealousie and question, though they had enough to make good all." The proposal suggests that the informal credit provided by pawnbrokers had an important function in the larger economy, servicing not only the poor, but also those of middling status and the elite who depended on clandestine credit to maintain their reputations within the formal economy.

It is not surprising that the commercial theaters sought to profit from, and indeed were in certain respects themselves a manifestation of, the expansion of informal commerce. Because the professional playing companies and the entrepreneurs who backed them could ill afford the kind of lavish expenditure on new costumes and properties exhibited by entertainments at Court, they depended heavily on the pawnbroking and secondhand clothing trades. To what extent, then, did the theaters' proximity to and dependence on such trade render them open to the economic participation of female frippers, brokers, hawkers, and hucksters? Evidence of women's involvement in small-scale lending and borrowing, and in the secondhand clothing trade, in and around the commercial theaters may be found in Henslowe's "diary,"

some thirty pages of which a ness he managed between 159 listed in the accounts were wo identity is given, 78 percent wer pledging goods with Henslowe roles as managers of household of female to male borrowers in th London haberdasher named Pop women.[55]

Henslowe's accounts provide a economic activities of working wo and remind us that the webs of intertwined were hardly all-male pr in Henslowe's pawn accounts may market women to find ready cash, o hold economy, for some of these wo interest in the pawnbroking business as is listed 53 times in Henslowe's account sometimes up to five bundles in a sing September 1594 and January 1595, she i a half days, on average. Indeed, during th in which she figures, there are only eight goody Watson. It thus seems certain that hired by Henslowe as an agent, or was a entry in the accounts is in June 1594, wher "A manes gowne & A blacke Clocke tied until three months later, however, that she agent. On September 17, she pawns no fewe a diverse range of men's and women's appar 10s.[56] Several of these entries contain the cu goody watsones" or "goody watsones Intreste term "interest" here refers to interest that Hen term he ordinarily uses for this is "use," or a s in the margins of his accounts. Rather, it is mo to a more common definition of interest in the right or title to, a claim upon, or a share in . . . [a] uses or benefits pertaining to [that] property" (OE seem to suggest, then, that the bundles of goods t pawning with Henslowe on a regular basis in Sept in which she herself had a financial interest.

Such arrangements between large-scale pawnbrok intermediaries were quite common during the peri acted as "intermediar[ies] for a more important lender ation on potential lenders and borrowers" and se

for small-scale loa above, demonstra diaries to establis dealers in Londo haberdasher's sh the Bankside. W Pope's pawn tra loans as well. I reputations in Pope frequently who arranged including loans and laundresse douth pase he more on other 70 percent of women to m borrowers "m diary because suspicions of likely given their attire a frequently l she is at a Gossips," s Cloaths to hard to get Pope proba assessing communit assess a b Women enced by moneyle money t worth r capital f marriage that she role, in ately i Elizabe entrep "full a debtes, and am engaged for greate sommes of money, which noe one but my wife understandes, where or how to receaue pay or take in." Beeston's will suggests that his wife was involved not only in his credit activities, but also in the procurement of costumes; it directs "that my said executrix shall... prouide and finde for the said Companie [the King's and Queen's Young company], a sufficyent and good stock of apparell fitting for their vse."[65] It seems unlikely that Beeston would have entrusted his wife if she had had no prior experience in the procurement of costumes for the stage. Hutchinson would most probably have relied on the secondhand clothing trade to "provide and finde" such a "stock of apparell." Beeston himself is recorded in Henslowe's accounts as selling secondhand costumes to the Admiral's Men. There are many instances in his diary of Henslowe lending money to the Admiral's Men to purchase secondhand costumes, and of his selling them used costumes himself.[66] There is evidence as well that some of these costumes may have been unredeemed pledges from his pawnbroking business.

That Henslowe appropriated and resold unredeemed pledges at least on occasion is clear from an entry of March 1595, which reads: "dd vnto goody watsone... severalle garments of my owne to be sowld as followeth."[67] The entry then describes the articles and indicates the prices at which she will sell them. The six garments were in fact unredeemed pledges that Goody Watson had herself delivered to Henslowe some three to five months earlier.[68] Henslowe made a healthy profit on the transaction, charging between one-quarter and two-thirds more for the items then he had originally lent on them. We do not know how much of this went to Goody Watson as interme-diary; but she may well have profited from both ends of the transaction. The accounts further suggest that she was involved not only in pawnbroking, but had expertise as a secondhand clothes dealer as well. Henslowe may have relied on such female agents to help him estimate the value of second-hand clothing because most of the garments pawned with him were articles of female attire: in 1593, for example, of all the pledged items that are clearly identified, 82 items were women's and only 31 men's.[69]

If Henslowe indeed appropriated unredeemed pledges, or made more liberal use of the articles of apparel and other goods he kept in pawn, he would not have been out of the ordinary. There is a good deal of evidence that such activity was common practice among pawnbrokers of the period. The illegal use, renting out, and appropriation of pledges were among the most common offences for which early modern pawnbrokers were taken to task in court records, contemporary legislation, and popular literature. An Act of Common Council of 1595 stipulates that no pawnbroker "shall sell, lend, hyre out, or giue away, any pawne, pledge, or gage, before the same be forfeited for want or fault of redemption."[70] It is often assumed that early modern pawnbrokers could appropriate unredeemed pledges only after they had kept them for a year and a day; however, this rule became law only

272   *Natasha Korda*

in 1872, with the passage of the Pawnbroker's Act.[71] An Act of Common Council during James's reign stipulates a far shorter period, maintaining that pawnbrokers shall not "giue, sell, or do away" any pledged items "other then to the same person or persons that pawned or sold the same, till he haue kept such Plate & Jewels in his hands by the space of eight and twenty days."[72] In a contemporary case cited by Jeremy Boulton, Elizabeth Crowcher claimed that she had borrowed 24 shillings. from John Cleaborough, who, like Henslowe, was a Southwark pawnbroker, "upon a gown and taffety apron" and that "when she came to redeem her goods her apron was worn out for which she refused to receive her goods."[73] Similar cases appear in the Middlesex Sessions records, such as that of John Abbott, a victualler and alehouse-keeper, who was to appear in May 1610 "for selling before the time a poor man's clothes that were pawned to him"; or that of James Wilson, a broker who was to answer "Rebecca Evans, spinster, for detaining certain goods being pawned by her to him" in July 1612.[74]

Popular pamphlets likewise complain of pawns being "spoyled, imbezzled, altered, [or] changed" as a common experience.[75] A pamphlet of 1603 complains of the pawnbrokers in Houndsditch: "euery Moneth [a] pawne must be renew'd," and "if a day we swarue [i.e. are late in paying the interest], [a]ll will be lost, our garments are their owne."[76] A detailed account of such practices is given in a pamphlet entitled *The Devil and Broker*, which tells the story of a country bumpkin named John Plugg, who comes to London and is gulled into paying a £20 apprenticeship fee to a pawnbroker who promises to "make him free of the best trade in *London*."[77] Among the tricks of the trade that he learns, in addition to the art of usury, is the practice of appropriating the pledges of his customers: "And may I not wear the clothes when I have them in my keeping?" he asks. To which the broker replies, "Yes, and let them out too [i.e. rent them]." Yet another contemporary pamphlet implicates the wives of pawnbrokers in the practice of appropriating pledges, claiming, "If he has a good Pledge in his Hands" such as "a Ring of Value, or a Suit of laced Head-Cloths; it is forty to one but his Wife has the One on her Finger, and the other on her head, or in her Drawer," and when the "Person comes to pay the Principal, and Interest" he is told, "it has been sold."[78]

If Henslowe did sell, lend, or rent out apparel or other items left in his storage "Rome" to the Admiral's Men, this might account for the dearth of female costumes and small properties in their inventory of apparel "taken the 13th of Marche 1598." Of the 86 articles of clothing listed, only three are described as female apparel. It is indeed tempting to speculate that this absence was supplied by the many sumptuous female gowns listed in the pawn accounts. It is here that we confront the undeniably difficult, if not impossible, task of recovering evidence regarding informal commerce, which all too often and for obvious reasons takes place off the books. Yet this difficulty should not dissuade us from attempting to put the pieces of the puzzle together, even if some of the pieces are missing. For it was precisely the benefits of flexibility afforded by such informal commerce that may have made it ideally suited to the needs of women, who had fewer opportunities in the formal economy, as well as early modern theatrical entrepreneurs like Philip Henslowe. It is time to rethink our assumptions about the all-male stage, and our conceptualization of the relationship between the market and the theater, in ways that will allow us to account for the full range of women's economic participation in early modern theatrical production. In doing so, it is crucial that we attend to the theater's material ties to an entire matrix of informal commercial activity in which working women in early modern London played such a vital role.

Notes

1. See, for example, Susan Westfall, *Patrons and Performers: Early Tudor Household Revels* (Oxford: Oxford University Press, 1990); and David Bergeron, "Women as Patrons of English Renaissance Drama," in Guy Fitch Lytle and Stephen Orgel, eds., *Patronage in the Renaissance* (Princeton, NJ: Princeton University Press, 1981), and *Renaissance Drama by Women*. On female playgoers, see Michael Neill, "'Wit's Most Accomplished Senate': The Audience of the Caroline Private Theaters," *SEL* 18 (1978): 341–60; Richard Levin, "Women in the Renaissance Theater Audience," *SQ* 40 (1989): 165–74; Alan H. Nelson, "Women in the Audience of Cambridge Plays," *SQ* 41 (1990): 333-6; Jean E. Howard, "Scripts and/versus Playhouses," and "The Materiality of Ideology: Women as Spectators, Spectacles, and Paying Customers in the English Public Theater," in *The Stage and Social Struggle in Early Modern England* (London and New York: Routledge, 1994), 13. On women in court masques, see Suzanne Gossett, "Man-Maid, Begone! Women in Masques," *ELR* 18:1 (1988): 109. On non-aristocratic female performers, see Thornton Shirley Graves, "Women on the Pre-Restoration Stage," *Studies in Philology* 22:2 (1925): 184–97; and Ann Thompson, "Women/'Women' and the Stage," in Helen Wilcox, ed., *Women and Literature in Britain, 1500–1700* (Cambridge: Cambridge University Press, 1996); Stephen Orgel, *Impersonations: The Performance of Gender in Shakespeare's England* (Cambridge: Cambridge University Press, 1996), 4–9, and Pam Allen Brown and Peter Parolin (eds), *Beyond the All-Male Stage: Women Players in Early Modern England, 1500–1660*, ed. Peter A. Parolin and Pam Brown (Hants and Burlington, VT: Ashgate Press, 2005).

2. Portions of this essay represent a reworking of material in Natasha Korda, "Women's Theatrical Properties," in *Staged Properties in Early Modern English Drama*, ed. Jonathan Gil Harris and Natasha Korda (Cambridge: Cambridge University Press, 2002); and Natasha Korda, "Labours Lost: Women's Work and Early Modern Theatrical Commerce," in *From Script to Stage in Early Modern England*, ed. Peter Holland and Stephen Orgel (Basingstoke and New York: Palgrave Macmillan, 2004). I would like to thank Henry Turner for inviting me to present an earlier version of this paper at a conference on "Alternative Economies" held at the University of Wisconsin, Madison.

3. On the importance of the informal sector of the market in London in the late seventeenth and eighteenth centuries, see Colin Smith, "The Wholesale

and Retail Markets of London, 1660–1840," *Economic History Review* 55 (2002): 31–50; on women's role in the informal sector in England during this period, see Lemire, *Dress Culture and Commerce*; Pamela Sharpe, *Adapting to Capitalism: Working Women in the English Economy, 1700–1850* (New York: St. Martin's Press and London: Macmillan, 1996); *Women's Work: The English Experience, 1650–1914*, ed. Pamela Sharpe (New York: Oxford University Press and London: Arnold, 1998); for comparison with early modern France, see Olwen H. Hufton, *The Poor of Eighteenth-Century France, 1750–1789* (Oxford: Clarendon Press, 1974).

4. bell hooks traces the genealogy of this trope to first-wave feminism's problematic rhetorical appropriation of "the horror of the slave experience," and, in particular, the experience of being an object of property—"to enhance their own cause." bell hooks, "Racism and Feminism," in hooks, *Ain't I A Woman: Black Women and Feminism* (Boston, MA: South End Press, 1981). Within second-wave feminism, the trope gained renewed force through the influence of Claude Lévi-Strauss's structuralist analysis of the exchange of women according to the "principle of reciprocity" in *Elementary Structures of Kinship* (1949; Boston, MA: Beacon Press, 1969), 52–68. Among those who were influenced by Lévi-Strauss's paradigm, and who themselves strongly influenced subsequent feminist theory, are Gayle Rubin, Luce Irigaray, and Eve Kosofsky Sedgwick. See Rubin, "The Traffic in Women: Notes on the 'Political Economy' of Sex," in *Toward an Anthropology of Women*, ed. Rayna R. Reiter (New York: Monthly Review Press, 1975), 157–210; Irigaray, "Women on the Market" and "Commodities among Themselves," in Irigaray, *This Sex Which Is Not One* (1977; Ithaca, NY: Cornell University Press, 1985), 170–96; Sedgwick, *Between Men: English Literature and Male Homosocial Desire* (New York: Columbia University Press, 1985). For a more extended critique of the predominance of this trope within feminist scholarship on early modern drama, see Natasha Korda, *Shakespeare's Domestic Economies: Gender and Property in Early Modern England* (Philadelphia: University of Pennsylvania Press, 2002), 38–51.

5. See Jean Christophe Agnew, *Worlds Apart: The Market and the Theater in Anglo-American Thought, 1550–1750* (Cambridge: Cambridge University Press, 1986); and Douglas Bruster, *Drama and the Market in the Age of Shakespeare* (Cambridge: Cambridge University Press, 1992), 15. See also Michael Bristol's critique of the "placeless" market in *Big-Time Shakespeare* (New York and London: Routledge, 1996), 32–3.

6. Agnew, *Worlds Apart*, xii; my emphasis. Subsequent page references to this work will be indicated parenthetically.

7. Anne Righter [Barton], *Shakespeare and the Idea of the Play* (London: Chatto and Windus, 1962); see also Agnew, *Worlds Apart*, 11, 105, 144.

8. Thus, whereas "[w]omen had for centuries engaged in household [sic] marketing," he claims, "With the simultaneous growth in prostitution and in the marriage markets of the seventeenth century, Elizabethans began to look to the theater to represent a society thus opened to considerations of price." Agnew, *Worlds Apart*, 129.

9. Guilds restricted women's economic activity at the local level when there was a real or perceived labor surplus. David Herlihy thus cites a town ordinance in Bristol in 1461 forbidding weavers to employ their wives, daughters, or maids at the loom "lest the king's people [i.e. male subjects] . . . should lack employment." Cited in David Herlihy, *Opera Muliebria: Women and Work in Medieval Europe* (New York: McGraw-Hill, 1990), 178. On women's work in early modern England's informal economy, see Beverly Lemire, Ruth Pearson, and Gail Campbell eds.,

Women and Credit: Researching the Past, Refiguring the Future (Oxford and New York: Berg, 2001); Beverly Lemire, Dress, Culture and Commerce: The English Clothing Trade Before the Factory, 1600–1800 (New York: St. Martin's Press, 1997); and Lindsey Charles and Lorna Duffin, eds., Women and Work in Pre-Industrial England (London, Sydney and Dover, NH: Croom Helm, 1985).

10. Lemire, Dress, Culture and Commerce, 120.
11. Weisner, Working Women, 179–80.
12. Mary Bateson, ed., Records of the Borough of Leicester, 1509–1603, Vol. III (Cambridge, 1905), 147, cited in Sue Wright, "Churmaids, Huswyfes and Hucksters," 119n51, 147.
13. Craig Muldrew, The Economy of Obligation: The Culture of Credit and Social Relations in Early Modern England (New York: St. Martin's Press, 1998), 3.
14. Beverly Lemire, "Introduction. Women, Credit and the Creation of Opportunity: A Historical Overview," in Women and Credit: Researching the Past, Refiguring the Future (Oxford and New York: Berg, 2001), 5.
15. Muldrew, Economy of Obligation, 95. Because the supply of gold and silver was not great enough to meet the needs of the expanding economy, and because credit was so common, most economic transactions took the form of reciprocal debts, which were contracted between as many interested parties as possible, over a period of months or even years, which would then be "reckoned" or cancelled against each other at convenient intervals; money was then used only to pay the remaining balance. Ibid., 101, 107–8.
16. Ibid., 114.
17. William Ingram, "The Economics of Playing," in A Companion to Shakespeare, ed. David Scott Kastan (Malden, MA and Oxford: Blackwell, 1999), 316.
18. PRO, L. C. 5/133, pp. 50, 51. Cited in Ingram, "Economics of Playing," 316.
19. Laurence Fontaine, "Women's Economic Spheres and Credit in Pre-Industrial Europe," in Lemire, Pearson and Campbell, eds., Women and Credit, 24.
20. Holderness, "Widows in Pre-Industrial Society," 439.
21. Such as that of Edith Bide, who was owed £15 "upon pawnes" when she died in 1625. Sue Wright, "'Churmaids, Huswyfes and Hucksters': The Employment of Women in Tudor and Stuart Salisbury," in Women and Work in Pre-Industrial England, 111.
22. Garthine Walker, "Women, Theft and the World of Stolen Goods," Women, Crime, and the Courts in Early Modern England, ed. Jennifer Kermode and Garthine Walker (Chapel Hill, NC: University of North Carolina Press, 1994), see esp. 91–3. Kay Lacey has found evidence of women working as informal pawnbrokers and second-hand clothing dealers in London as early as the fourteenth century. Kay E. Lacey, "Women and Work in Fourteenth and Fifteenth Century London," in Women and Work in Pre-Industrial England, ed. Lindsey Charles and Lorna Duffin (London, Sidney, and Dover: Croom Helm, 1985, 24–78, esp. 52–3).
23. Recall, for example, Marion Hackett, the "fat ale wife of Wincot," to whom Christopher Sly is "fourteen pence on the score for sheer ale" (Ind., 2. 18–19) in The Taming of the Shrew, or Hostess Quickly, to whom Falstaff is indebted not only for his "diet, and by-drinkings," but for "money lent" him in the amount of "four and twenty pounds," in 1 Henry IV (3.3.71–2). By 2 Henry IV, his debt has risen to "a hundred mark" (2.1.30–1) and the Hostess brings suit against him, lest she herself be forced to "pawn both [her] plate and the tapestry of [her] dining-chambers" (2. 1. 239–40). In a seventeenth-century ballad entitled "Halfe a dozen of good Wives," a husband describes his third wife as "a drunken Sot,"

who would "pawne all things for Ale and Beere, / what ever she had got, / Shee scarce would leave a smocke, / or shooe unto her foot, / But at the Alehouse all these went, / and somewhat else to boot." Another ballad, entitled "Have Among You Good Women," tells of "drunken *Sue*," who "For drinke" will not only "sell all her smocks," but also "pawne [her husband's] shirt and his breeches," which she "spen[ds] at a sitting." Henry Chettle, in *Kind-Hartes Dreame*, speaks of landladies who, if their tenants "wanted money," would "on munday lend them . . . uppon a pawne eleven pence, and in meere pittie aske at the weekes end not a penny more than twelve pence." In George Bagshawe Harrison, ed., *Elizabethan and Jacobean Quartos* (New York: Barnes & Noble, 1966), 47.

24. Lemire, *Dress, Culture and Commerce*, 2, 116.
25. Thus, Castells and Portes argue, "The informal economy is a common-sense notion whose moving social boundaries cannot be captured by a strict definition without closing the debate prematurely." Manuel Castells and Alejandro Portes, "World Underneath: The Origins, Dynamics, and Effects of the Informal Economy," in *The Informal Economy: Studies in Advanced and Less Developed Countries*, ed. Alejandro Portes, Manuel Castells, and Lauren A. Benton (Baltimore and London: Johns Hopkins University Press, 1989), 11.
26. Ibid., 12.
27. Portes, Castells, and Benton, "Conclusion," in ibid., 298; Castells and Portes, "World Underneath," 26.
28. Castells and Portes, "World Underneath," 15.
29. Ibid., 11–12. See also Bryan Roberts, "The Informal Sector in Comparative Perspective," in *Perspectives on the Informal Economy* (New York and London: University Press of America, 1990), 23–42.
30. Philip Mattera, *Off the Books: The Rise of the Underground Economy* (New York: St. Martin's Press, 1985), 4.
31. Muldrew, *Economy of Obligation*, 48.
32. Ibid., 40–1.
33. For orders and other reports concerning women hawkers and "brokers" of apparel in the late sixteenth and early seventeenth centuries, see Corporation of London Record Office, Repertories of the Court of Aldermen (hereafter "Repertories"), 20:237, 21:274, 26/2:506, 29:163v, 30:68 and Journals of the Court of Common Council (hereafter "Journals"), 26:6-7v; concerning fishwives, see "Repertories," 21:115, 22:172, 24:48, 30:175, 30:310v and "Journals," 18:117v, 21:418, 22:378v-80v, 389, 406, 28:300-02; concerning herb-wives, see "Journals," 21:93v, 35:440; concerning hawkers of dairy products, see 19:325v; concerning forestallers, engrossers, and regrators, see "Journals," 25:150v–152.
34. Cited in Muldrew, *Economy of Obligation*, 41.
35. Hugh Alley, "A Caveatt for the Citty of London, OR a forewarninge of offences against penal Lawes," Folger MS V. a. 318, ff. 145.2. Reprinted in *Hugh Alley's Caveat: The Markets of London in 1598*, ed. Ian Archer, Caroline Barron, and Vanessa Harding (London: London Topographical Society, 1988).
36. Muldrew, *Economy of Obligation*, 3, 96.
37. Ibid., 37.
38. Ibid., 40, 42.
39. Ibid., 112, 156.
40. Lemire, "Introduction," *Women and Credit*, 8.
41. Ibid.
42. Cited in Lemire, *Dress, Culture and Commerce*, 99.

43. For an account of this broader initiative, see Archer, Barron, and Harding eds., *Hugh Alley's Caveat.*

44. Corporation of London, Court of Common Council, *Retailing Brokers* ([Acts & Orders, April 9, 1595] London: J. Windet for Iohn Wolfe, 1595), single sheet. STC 16715.

45. While the explicit aim of the legislation was to prevent the "Burgularies, Robberies, and Fellonies" encouraged by such brokers, the "reformation" it proposes is not outright prohibition, but rather a series of measures aimed at controlling, and even profiting from, what had clearly become a highly lucrative form of trade. The abuses cited by the legislation extend well beyond the "black market" in stolen goods to cover a gray area of informal, unregulated commerce. Such brokers, it maintains, "doe often, very secretely for unhonest lucre, and that most ordinarily, upon the Sabbaoth dayes, Festivall dayes, and other Holy dayes, whereon no markets ought to bee kept, nor bargaines, contractes, or sales to bee made . . . [trade] for very low prices, or small soms of money, divers [goods] . . . [a]nd the same doe presently sell againe, & transact sometimes to persons unknowne, sometimes to French and Dutch Brokers, who secretly conuay and make transportation thereof beyond the Seas." The legislation institutes mechanisms of control through which such informal commerce may be regulated so as to generate revenue for the City's coffers: "hereafter there shalbe kept and written within this Cittie and Liberties thereof, true and perfect Register bookes, by . . . honest and sufficient persons, being Free-men of this Cittie." The register books function not only to prevent commerce in stolen goods by listing the names and dwelling places of the brokers and their customers, and a description of the articles sold or pawned, but also to enable the City and its officials to profit from each and every transaction. For it stipulates that the register books must list the amount of money at which each article is valued so that the newly elected Registrars may collect a fee from the brokers (the amount of the fee depending on the value of the article sold or pawned) and from those wishing to peruse the record books in search of stolen property (the amount of the fee in this case depending on how far back in time the search extended). Additional revenue was generated by brokers who failed to comply, or to keep accurate records, or who were discovered to be receivers of stolen goods, who had to pay "the summe of five poundes of lawfull mony of England, The one halfe therof to be to the use and behoofe of the Mayor, Comminalty, and Citizens of London, the other halfe to the use of such Officers or persons as shalbe appointed . . . for the keeping of the said Register booke[s]." Ibid.

46. 1 James I, c. 21. Reprinted in *Statutes of the Realm*, vol. 4 (London, 1819), 1038–9.

47. The Parliamentary Act, unlike the earlier Act of Common Council, seems particularly concerned with "these kinde of upstarte Brokers, [who] under colour and p[re]tence they be Freemen of the saide Citie of London" presume it "to be lawfull for them" to give over their crafts and trades and profit from this more lucrative form of commerce.

48. The Act states that it had been "found by experience" that an Act of 1608, according to which brokers had to be "bound by Obligation (with good Sureties) in the summe of one hundred pounds" by the Registrar in order to practice their trade, was ineffective, insofar as "diuers persons, Brokers, Broggers, or Hucksters, and such other persons as use to buy or take to pawne old apparrell . . . or such like wares to sell againe, haue found diuers waies and meanes to auoid being bound." The Council nevertheless maintained it to be "verie necessarie and fit for

the good of the Commonwealth and publicke Weale of this Citie" to formulate "one cleare and plaine Law . . . free from ambiguity or contradiction, and easie to be understood and obserued" to regulate the "licentious trading of the saide Broakers, Broggers, & Hucksters." It goes on to reinstate the main provisions of the previous Acts, but goes into far greater detail as to how these are to be put into practice. It also makes clear that it is indeed the common*wealth* of the City with which it is concerned, for it institutes new and higher fees and penalties at each stage of the regulatory process. Ibid.

49. "A Proclamation for the better discovery and prevention of Burglaries, Robberies, and other Frauds and abuses, and for the suppressing of all secret and unlawfull practices of Retayling Brokers, and other which may occasion the same" (July 5, 1630). STC 8955. Reprinted in James F. Larkin, *Stuart Royal Proclamations*, vol. 2 (Oxford: Clarendon, 1983), 276.

50. This charge is commanded "upon paine of Our high displeasure and indignation, and upon such further Paines, Penalties and Forfeitures, as for such disobedience or contempt therein, shall or may bee imposed upon them and every of them. And for that end and purpose . . . Wee doe hereby . . . command Our Attorney Generall . . . to proceede in Our high Court of Starrechamber, or in any other course of Legall way against such offenders . . . And Wee doe further . . . command all Maiors, Sheriffs, Justices of the Peace, Constables, Magistrates and ministers of Justice whatsoever, to ayde and assist all and every the said Registers, and their Deputie or Deputies, in the due execution of the sayd dueties and Offices, for the better discovering, suppressing, and punishing of all such offences and Offenders." Ibid.

51. *A Proposal Humbly Offer'd to the Honourable House of Commons: For an Additional Tax to be Paid Upon Regulating and Licensing Pawn-Brokers; And All Manner of Persons Driving Trades or Occupations, That Have Not Served Apprenticeships, Or be Not Free of Some City or Town Corporate* (London, 1680), single sheet.

52. *Reasons for the Passing of the Bill Concerning the Settlement of Banks of Loan Upon Pawn to Prevent the Great Extortion of Brokers, And for the Easie Relief of Necessitated Persons* (London, 1662), single sheet.

53. The bulk of these records may be found in R. A. Foakes and R. T. Rickart (eds), *Henslowe's Diary* (Cambridge: Cambridge University Press, 1961), ff. 55r–61r, 73r–81r, and 133r–136r. However, there are other references to actors pawning their costumes with Henslowe scattered throughout the "diary," some dated well after 1596 (see 19v, 28v, 37r, 41v), and one as late as 1602. For a more extended discussion of Henslowe's pawnbroking records, see Natasha Korda, "Household Property/Stage Property: Henslowe as Pawnbroker," *Theatre Journal* 48:2 (1996): 185–95. See also Jones and Stallybrass, *Renaissance Clothing*, esp. chapters 1 and 7.

54. Of the total number of loans, 55 percent were to women, 15 percent to men, and 30 percent to anonymous debtors. Stallybrass and Jones calculate that there were some 59 named women (not including his female agents, discussed below) and 35 named men among Henslowe's pawnbroking debtors. Stallybrass and Jones, *Renaissance Clothing*, 31 and 285n91.

55. Lemire, "Introduction. Women, Credit and the Creation of Opportunity: A Historical Overview," in *Women and Credit: Researching the Past, Refiguring the Future* (Oxford and New York: Berg, 2001), 8.

56. Foakes and Rickert, eds., *Henslowe's Diary*, fols.78v, 79v.

57. Laurence Fontaine, "Women's Economic Spheres and Credit in Pre-Industrial Europe," in Lemire, Pearson and Campbell, eds., *Women and Credit*, 26.

58. Such women "channel[led] small bundles of garments into the stock of larger distributors," making a living buying goods on the London streets which were then resold to larger, more established traders. Lemire, *Dress, Culture and Commerce*, 114.

59. Ibid.

60. Ibid., 7.

61. Laurence Fontaine, "Women's Economic Spheres and Credit in Pre-Industrial Europe," in Lemire, Pearson and Campbell, eds., *Women and Credit*, 33.

62. *Four for a Penny: Or, Poor-Robin's Character of an Unconscionable Pawn-Broker* (London, 1678), sig. A2v.

63. *A Description of Devils* (London, n.d. [1687?]), sig. E3r. *Four for a Penny* likewise speaks of "Mrs. *Joan*, [who] when she is minded to see her Sweetheart . . . redeem[s] [her] . . . best Riggings out of Captivity" from the pawnbroker (sig. A2v). A contemporary ballad attributed to Martin Parker, *Have Among you Good Women* (London, 1634), portrays wives who pawn as drunkards, rather than sluts: "What thinke you of drunken *Sue*, / For drinke she will sell all her smocks, / . . . / Nay sometimes besides her own getting, / She'll pawne his shirt and his breeches, / Which all shall be spent at a sitting, / And thus she increaseth his riches: / What thinks her poore husaband of that."

64. Foakes and Rickert, eds., *Henslowe's Diary*, fol. 28v; see also fols. 28r, 38v, 42v and 124r.

65. Honigmann and Brock, eds., *Playhouse Wills*, 192–3.

66. Stallybrass and Jones, *Renaissance Clothing*, 184–6.

67. Foakes and Rickert, eds., *Henslowe's Diary*, fol. 19v.

68. Ibid., fols. 80r–80v.

69. Jones and Stallybrass, *Renaissance Clothing*, 31.

70. Corporation of London, *Retailing Brokers*, single sheet.

71. 35 & 36 Vict. c. 93. "Every pledge is redeemable within twelve months from the day of pawning, exclusive of that day . . . if not redeemed within the year and days of grace, [the pledge] becomes, at the end of the days of grace, the absolute property of the pawnbroker." *The Laws of England, Being a Complete Statement of the Whole Law of England* (London: Butterworth, 1912), 251.

72. STC 16728.5.

73. Jeremy Boulton, *Neighborhood and Society: A London Suburb in the Seventeenth Century* (Cambridge: Cambridge University Press, 1987), 88. Melanie Tebbutt has uncovered similar practices on the part of English laundresses, "who took the clothes of their clients to the pawnshops and, with the money they got for them, bought a number of goods to resell, so that, with the money they made on the sale, they could . . . reclaim the clothes and finally return them to their clients," thus completing the cycle. Cited in Laurence Fontaine, "Women's Economic Spheres and Credit in Pre-Industrial Europe," in Lemire, Pearson and Campbell, eds., *Women and Credit*, 29. Fontaine has studied similar complaints made against pawnbrokers in early modern Paris (many of whom were women), who were using, renting and reselling pawned items. She cites the case of a female broker, dame Bertrand, who was arrested in 1735, upon complaints that she kept, rented out, and resold items pawned with her. Ibid., 26.

74. Justices of the Peace, Quarter Sessions. *Middlesex County Records*. Calendar of Sessions Rolls 485-489 for the year 1610 (London: [British Library Typescript], 1925, 4:109, 10:136.

75. *Observations Manifesting the Conveniency and Commodity of Mount-Pietyes, or Publick Bancks for Relief of the Poor and other in Distresse upon Pawns, At a Certain Known Moderate Interest, and the Inconveniency and Great Discommodity of Continuing or Countenancing the Ordinary Pawn-brokers or Lenders upon Pawn* (London, 1661), sig. A2r. See also *Two Knaves for a Penny Or, A Dialogue Between Mr. Hord the Meal-man, and Mr Gripe the Broker. Wherein is Discovered the Unjust and Oppressive Practices of Those Caterpillers; To the Great Prejudice of the Kingdom, Especially the Two Cities of London, and Westminster. With Some Expedients Offered for the Future Prevention of the Same* (London, 1647), sig. A3v, and *Twelve Ingenious Characters: Or, Pleasant Descriptions, of the Properties of Sundry Persons & Things* (London, 1686), 16.

76. William Muggins, *Londons Mourning Garment* (London, 1603), sig. D1r.

77. *The Devil and Broker, Or a Character of a Pawn Broker in a Merry Dialogue. With their Manifold Frauds and Deceits Discovered* (London, 1677), sig. A1v.

78. *A Description of Devils* (London, n.d. [1687?]), sig. E1r.

14
Why did Widows Remarry? Remarriage, Male Authority, and Feminist Criticism

Jennifer Panek

> ... give me that lusty lad,
> That winnes his widdow with his well-drawn blade,
> And not with oaths and words: a widdows woing
> Not in bare words but should consist in doing.
>
> Widow Taffata, in *Ram Alley*[1]

Towards the end of Lording Barry's *Ram Alley* (1610), Widow Taffata illustrates the early modern theater's standard answer to the question 'why did widows remarry?' when she accepts young William Smalshankes for her husband based on his lascivious promise to "do her drudgery" and the phallic dagger he brandishes in earnest thereof. What might a feminist reader make of this scene? At first glance, it might look like "The Taming of the Widow": a male fantasy in which the poor but audacious William takes on the wealthy, independent widow and uses her lust to subsume her back into coverture and the patriarchal order, where she and her wealth will be under his control. (And if he threatens her with a dagger during courtship, we can imagine what kind of husband he'll make.) At a second glance, the scene reveals a textbook case of male anxiety: William, threatened by the potential that the richer, older, more experienced Taffata holds to become the kind of ungovernable wife that widows are reputed to make, compensates with violent sexual aggression that puts her, at least temporarily, in her place.[2] But what happens next? Taffata happily declares, 'I take thee to my husband' (2252), and the pair exit to ratify the contract in an offstage bed. They reappear shortly afterwards in a mood of mutual self-congratulation and proceed jointly to make fun of William's old father, who had wanted the widow for himself. *Finis. Enter the Epilogue.* We can, if we wish, take William's sexual mastery as shorthand for his promised success in other facets of husbandly rule, but that's not included in what we see. Insofar as we see William dominate Taffata, it is sexually and only sexually. Is it possible that William, in deciding to marry the Widow Taffata, is neither a successful patriarch-in-the-making nor a particularly anxious one? Might his ostentatious sexual mastery be not assurance of domestic mastery but in lieu thereof—an amusing theatrical gesture towards his prescribed role of dominance and government which he has no expectation of assuming? Reading the scene in this way requires us to discard an extraordinarily tenacious assumption: that early modern gender relations—and in particular those found in early modern marriage—are inherently oppositional. Husbands, with varying degrees of success and of anxiety, exercise the patriarchal privileges that serve their interests. Wives submit, resist, collude, transgress, or negotiate. The extent to which this assumption has informed feminist scholarship is indicative of its usefulness, even of its truth. But applied too sweepingly, it can obscure as well as illuminate.[3] In this chapter, I want to explore how widows' predilection for remarriage in early modern London[4] might best be viewed with a slight adjustment of the interpretive lens that is oppositional gender politics, and to focus on the possibility that remarriage was, at least for some men, a site in which the traditional gender hierarchy was simply neither expected nor desired to apply.

Investigating the finer cultural implications of second marriages would be a redundant exercise if early modern English widows were shown to be driven primarily by strong economic or social imperatives. The picture painted by economic and demographic studies of female remarriage, however, is one that is strikingly open to the intangibles of personal choice. There were certainly economic factors at work: Vivien Brodsky suggests that the active remarriage market for crafts- and tradesmen's widows in late sixteenth- and early seventeenth-century London was driven in part by widows' marginalization as participants in the thoroughly male-oriented London companies. Amy Erickson observes that widows of middling economic status were most likely to remarry, noting that gentry widows "could afford not to" and poor widows "could not afford to."[5] One is left, though, with the sense that although it was financially advantageous for some widows to marry, it was rarely a straightforward necessity. Continuing the craft or trade of her late husband was only one possibility for the widow who wished to remain single: moneylending could provide a "more than tolerable living standard" for women who inherited as little as 30 pounds, while civic officials routinely approved widows for retailing licenses which they refused to spinsters, and even assisted them with start-up loans.[6] Glimpses of individual lives suggest the variety of ways in which ordinary widows could support themselves. We find Alice Harvey, who obtained a lifetime license to work as a porter, hired a male laborer to do the work, and lived off her portion of the fees; Elizabeth Carlile, abandoned by her second husband, who reverted to the name of a widow and set up a shop of sewing supplies and tobacco, where she "thryved very well" (193r; 195r); and Anne Middleton, a bricklayer's widow and mother of the playwright Thomas Middleton, who supported herself and two children by managing her inheritance of about 300 pounds and the leases of several London properties. Both Carlile and Middleton, we might note, remarried men from whom they could expect little in the way of financial support, and who in fact turned out to be serious financial liabilities.[7] Moreover, if economic pressure towards remarriage is hard to pin down, moral or social pressure in either direction appears to have been negligible—all evidence suggests that early modern English culture regarded female remarriage and continued widowhood with similar equanimity.[8] The author of a 1574 treatise counseling a widow on her choice of husband perhaps best sums up the attitude: "not yt I mind to persuade or dissuade marriage with you, for therein you may best be your own judge, for you know best where your shooe wringeth you: neyther need you any counseller to bid you cut where it wringeth you."[9] Whatever the discomforts of the "shooe" of widowhood, a cut on the side of remarriage cannot be wholly explained by an ideological or economic pinch.

One does find, however, a certain ideological slant to the current debate among historians over the motives for female remarriage: namely, the belief that early modern marriage was inherently a patriarchal institution which served the interests of men, and which widows, fully aware of its limitations, re-entered with some reluctance. The most explicit statements of this belief appear in the context of a lively exchange between Jeremy Boulton and the feminist historian Barbara Todd over a later seventeenth-century decline in the practice of remarriage. While the percentage of brides described as widows in parish registers and records of marriage licenses reveals a great many remarrying widows in the late sixteenth and early seventeenth centuries, especially in London, their numbers gradually but significantly decrease through the Restoration period and into the early years of the eighteenth century. Boulton suggests that the decrease might be best explained by demographics, citing a change in the sex ratio of London's population towards a late seventeenth-century shortage of marriageable men.[10] Todd, objecting to Boulton's approach as a kind of 'demographic determinism' that denies female agency, challenges his data and considers reasons why women may have chosen not to remarry. Fundamental to her argument is a sense of the freedom of widowhood—a freedom constrained by a patriarchal society that sought to construct it as a widow's opportunity to devote herself to her late husband's memory, her children, or her God, but freedom nonetheless:

A married woman was legally and personally subject to her husband. A widow was free from such control. Even if she was poor, she was her own woman and could run her life as she saw fit. If she was lucky enough to have inherited or succeeded to property, she was able to control her independent means in her own interest and on behalf of her children and others for whom she chose to act.[11]

Thus, widows who contemplated taking a second husband would have been "aware of the consequences of their subordination should they marry again." As Elizabeth Foyster puts it, a widow's remarriage "represented the relinquishment of a position of relative freedom and even power over her own affairs, to one of subordination under a new husband."[12] The same idea implicitly informs other historians' interpretations of the lower remarriage rates found at higher social levels: "those least likely to remarry were the gentry widows, who could afford not to"; "[r]emarriage, when a possibility, was often an economic necessity; widows who were better off might choose independence"; "[m]ost gentry widows valued their economic independence too highly to risk remarriage."[13] Given that "[w]idows enjoyed the most extensive economic rights and privileges of any working women in the early modern period,"[14] the reflexive feminist position is to celebrate the widow who clung to those rights. Widows who remain so are choosing independence; those who remarry are choosing subordination. And since it is counterintuitive to think of a woman choosing subordination, it is tempting to focus on the economic factors influencing her decision, despite the fact that, for many widows, these fall considerably short of "necessity."

It is extremely difficult to know the extent to which early modern widows would have viewed widowhood and remarriage in these terms. What is easier to show, however, is how modern feminist readers have wanted to see that they did. For instance, if we trace the scholarly commonplace about gentry widows protecting their economic independence by refusing remarriage, we find its origin in a study which showed that 56 percent of the widows of sixteenth-century London aldermen did not remarry.[15] Leaving aside the rather substantial 44 percent who did remarry, and the fact that the study provides no information on the widows' ages, might not an equally plausible case be made that gentry widows were less prone to remarriage than women of middling status because they had *less* independence? After all, it is well known that the higher a woman's social standing, the more familial influence was wielded in the matter of her first marriage, and it is possible that similar pressure applied to her second. The active web of family interests and negotiations that spun the widowed Margaret Devereaux, *née* Dakins into a match with Sir Thomas Hoby may have in other cases constrained a woman from remarriage, even if only through limiting the pool of approved suitors.[16] The same tendency to celebrate widowed celibacy as motivated by a desire for independence appears in readings of Katherine Austen, one of the very few early modern widows who left a written record of her thoughts concerning remarriage. Austen's journal, kept between 1664 and 1666, reveals her apparently firm decision not to marry her suitor, a physician named Alexander Callendar. (I say apparently, because Callendar's courtship was cut short by his sudden death in 1665, not by any decisive action on Austen's part.) "[B]y far the most important factor," claims Todd, "was her awareness that marriage would rob her of her capacity to preserve and increase the fortunes of her daughter and two sons . . . It was this concern about losing her legal identity which eventually decided her against remarrying."[17] Austen's journal indeed mentions such a concern for her children's estates. However, this needs to be placed in the context of the worry to which she most frequently returns—not the legal disability of marriage *per se*, but the unsuitableness of this particular suitor. Callendar, in her view, is "a person of low fortune," and to marry him would be "to cast myself and a future issue into meanness when I may rise to [something] better." Moreover, she cannot shake off the suspicion that his interest in her is founded on her wealth, an issue she records them arguing about less than a fortnight before his death: "He then said to me and protested if I was a . . . beggar woman . . . I would have him, he would have me, and he would discourse with me all day. For he never talked with me but [he] learned something [from] me. I told him he was mistaken, and if I was [a beggar woman], he would not."[18] It is not at all clear that Austen would have similarly refused a man who offered the opportunity for her and her family to "rise to [something] better."

An example from the other side of the coin—the assumption that widows who did remarry were capitulating to patriarchy—appears in Loreen L. Giese's fascinating account of a 1611 matrimonial enforcement case brought by the actor John Newton against a widow named Joan Waters. Waters had been pregnant with her late husband's child during the courtship. She had also, according to the convincingly specific testimony of one witness, been extraordinarily assertive of her desires: "he verily beleeueth that the said Waters was then very much affected to him the said Newton in the way of marriage for that shee the said Waters did then with her lips sucke his the said Newtons necke in a manner of kindenes wherby shee made 3 red spottes arise whervpon the said Newton asking her what shee ment by it shee answering said that shee had marcked him for her owne." Waters' "marcking" of Newton, as Giese points out, constitutes a remarkable inversion of the patriarchal concept of the female body as male property. Yet a few lines later, she observes that by not remarrying, Waters would "disrupt patriarchal control since she would be creating a family without a male head," and adds that the widow's desire to marry before the birth of her child "can be seen to suggest her willingness to accept her place in the patriarchal order."[19] The phrasing is ambiguous as to exactly who would have seen the marriage in this light, but it seems rather unlikely, to say the least, that it would have been Joan Waters.

I do not mean to dispute that widowhood, for many early modern women, could be a time of considerable personal and economic independence, nor to discount the amount that they may have valued such independence. What I want to query is the reflexive equation of marriage—and particularly remarriage—with "the patriarchal order." When we celebrate widows' power and independence and ask what would lead them to relinquish it, we elide a question which has even more interesting implications for female agency: to what extent might the widow's position of power from which she enters a second (third or fourth) marriage remake the conditions of marriage itself? Brodsky hints at this possibility when she observes that "the union of older widows and younger men was a common pattern of city marriages" in Jacobean London, and adds, "[i]t cannot be doubted that such age inequalities must have given a bachelor-widow marriage a different character, providing greater opportunities for psychological and sexual dominance within marriage by the older woman."[20] Foyster anatomizes the ways in which such dominance—or at least attempts thereat—landed various couples in court, suing for marital separation. Disagreements over money are central to these disputes, as husbands contend that the widows they married refuse them access to the property they were promised, and remarried widows object to standards of living lower than those their previous husbands had provided.[21] The separation cases would not have surprised early modern moralists, who warn young men against marrying widows for precisely these reasons: "Let him marry a maide to the end hee may teach her good maners, and such other dueties, as are most beseeming and decent for a wife, for shee wil also be more tractable than a widdow, who will rather looke to be obeied, as wel for that shee hath been before acquainted with love matters, as also because for the most part they bring greater wealth unto their husbands, then the maides doe."[22] In my own work on remarrying widows on the comic stage, I have characterized such marriages as fertile ground for power struggles and male anxiety, and there is certainly evidence of both in any number of ballads, jests, and plays.[23] But what I find less than wholly satisfactory about these accounts, though, is their reliance on narrative genres that to a large extent revolve around contention and oppositional relations between men and women. Simply put, dramatic plots require conflict and contented couples don't go to court. And, as Foyster points out, a great many men clearly paid no attention to the moralists' advice about the dangers of marrying widows.[24] We might assume that they weighed the financial incentive against the hypothetical threat and decided to take their chances. No doubt some of them did. But the discrepancy between prescription and practice might also invite us to consider the couples who inhabit the gaps left by their culture's written traces, bachelors and widows as husbands and wives living peaceable, orderly lives in non-traditional re-arrangements of the domestic gender hierarchy.

If the inherently oppositional nature of most early modern narratives about marriage makes such arrangements difficult to trace, the language which I, as a feminist scholar, am accustomed to using—and indeed, the language that early modern texts tend to use about marriage—makes them even harder to talk about. To speak of the "dominance" or "power" of wives, and about husbands who are "submissive" or "subordinate" irresistibly evokes the inversion of patriarchal order, a state of things that all involved would have recognized as anomalous and disorderly. To speak of "egalitarianism" is slightly wide of the mark, because it erases the idea of a power differential; it is questionable, moreover, whether either sex in a culture so permeated with the necessity of hierarchy in every aspect of life would have viewed an egalitarian marital relationship as conducive to the orderly operations of a household. As Bernard Capp observes, "[e]quality for women may only be a realistic goal in societies where the general concept of equality is recognized and valued in the culture as a whole."[25] Perhaps the best way to put it is that the existence of a certain set of circumstances—the older, richer, maritally experienced wife with a younger, poorer, inexperienced husband—may have created a space where a wife's government of her husband could be orderly, accepted, and unremarkable.

Prescriptive literature, as one would expect, does not allow for much variation on the theme of domestic hierarchy. Expounding on a wife's duty to subject herself to her husband, William Gouge explicitly refuses to exempt couples who conform to the above-mentioned pattern:

> Obiect. What if a man of meane place be maried to a woman of eminent place, or a seruant be maried to his mistresse, or an aged woman to a youth, must such a wife acknowledge such a husband her superior?
> Answ. Yea verily: for in giuing herselfe to be his wife, and taking him to be her husband, she aduanceth him aboue herselfe, and subiecteth her selfe vnto him. It booteth nothing what either of them were before mariage: by vertue of the matrimoniall bond the husband is made the head of his wife, though the husband were before mariage a very begger, and of meane parentage, and the wife very wealthy and of a noble stock; or though he were her prentise, or bondslaue; which also holdeth in the case betwixt an aged woman and a youth, for the Scripture hath made no exception in any of those cases.

He goes on to condemn "the practise of such women, as purposely mary men of farre lower ranke then themselves, for this very end, that they may rule ouer their owne husbands: and others who being aged, for that end mary youths, if not very boyes."[26] One of the fascinating things about Gouge's vast treatise, though, is that his determination to shore up his position through sifting and countering every possible objection creates an unexpected window into other, arguably just as prevalent, currents of thought. The hierarchical nature of early modern society, as this passage makes clear, was not always to women's disadvantage: much as Gouge would like it to, gender does not necessarily trump the equally ingrained hierarchies of status, wealth, or age.[27]

The well-off widow of 30 who wed a 25-year-old "youth" straight out of his apprenticeship may well have assumed that she had the right to "rule" him to whatever degree and in whatever aspects of married life she deemed necessary.[28] But let us consider for the moment the idea that he, equally a product of his culture's hierarchies, might have assumed exactly the same thing. It is easy to believe when we read early modern marriage manuals that they are written to convince recalcitrant wives to obey and to instruct perplexed husbands on how best to enforce this obedience. For her, they are rigidly prescriptive; for him, helpfully informative, and to an extent, descriptive—of his ideals and aspirations, if not his actual situation. Based in the common-sense assumption that any position of power is inherently desirable, this view risks naturalizing the male drive to dominance in a way that we have long discarded when it comes to women and their supposedly "natural" place of subjection.[29] For instance, a recent study of the power of early modern women's informal networks states categorically that "[w]hile all men believed that male supremacy was necessary and right, many saw their superiority as constantly under threat, especially within the family."[30] Not all women, it goes without saying, were inherently inclined toward submission or fully culturally conditioned to accept their prescribed subordinate role. And along the same lines, I do not think we can unproblematically assume that men—all men—were inherently convinced of their supremacy and sought to rule. Much excellent recent work has focused on women's agency, and how they "found ways to limit, evade, or accommodate male domination";[31] at times, however, this formulation risks leaving such domination in place as a constant, as if "the rules" were automatically enforced in every household, to the same degree, with the variable consisting largely in the woman's submission, transgression, or negotiation. If the conduct books warned against male "tyranny"—men who tried to enforce obedience through harshness or violence—they also acknowledged male abdication: "if he be a milke-sop, and basely yield vnto his wife, and suffer her to rule, then, it may be, there shall be some outward quiet."[32] The pejorative labels should not distract us from the likelihood that, in certain circumstances, the "milke-sop" would not have considered himself a milksop any more than the domestic tyrant would have considered himself a tyrant. What kind of man would have gravitated toward the kind of wife endowed with qualities that entitled her to "looke to be obeyed"? The confident, no doubt, and the reckless, but also the man who set less store by mastery than by comfort and security, which offered their own kind of freedom.

Evidence for male acceptance of a kind of orderly inversion of the domestic hierarchy is fragmentary, but the fragments add up to enough to warrant consideration as something more than isolated exceptions that prove the supposed marital rule of either patriarchal domination or bitter power struggle. One glimpses such acceptance in the records of pre-marital settle-ments for separate estate, a means by which early modern widows kept legal control of some or all of their property during coverture in their subsequent marriages; Erickson estimates that widows were about twice as likely to make settlements as first-time brides.[33] What is equally significant, though, is that the visibility of these settlements in court records is rarely due to a dispute over the arrangements between the widow and her husband. Some can only be inferred from a discrepancy between the inventories of the husband's and wife's property upon their respective deaths, as in the case of Ann Smith, who died three weeks after her husband William with a will signed "Ann Tayler" (her name by her first husband) and an inventory worth £30 more than William's £36 estate, which had all accrued to her.[34] Others do appear in the context of a lawsuit, but the reason for these "was not ordinarily trouble with the husband who signed the agreement." Instead, the three cases Erickson describes all involve men who, after long and apparently untroubled marriages (two of them with widows), sue their wives' heirs, executors, or trustees for a greater share of her wealth. So it was with Charles Pressye in 1621, who, some twenty years earlier, had had no objection to the widow he married setting aside a substantial sum in trust with her son-in-law and marking the goods in her house (where he came to live with her) "soe shee might still keep hir owne stock and goodes whole, in apparancie to the world." "While it is possible to find evidence of disagreement," concludes Erickson, "it is unlikely that husbands invariably resented their wives' property claims. . . . The marriage settlements in early modern probate accounts seem to have been comparatively peaceably agreed to and carried out."[35]

Even records of more acrimonious relationships often testify, between the lines, to some unexpected norms. In 1610, Henry Bowles lost a matrimonial enforcement suit against the widow Susan Jason, but was depicted by his witnesses as having enjoyed a courtship that was very much on her terms: she invited him to dinner, talked to him of "the good that [he] shall receyve by [her]," informed him that she would not move from her own house after their marriage, and had him agree to a settlement in which he was bound not to "make away with" any of her property during her life and to leave her all but £100 of his if he predeceased her.[36] The question of this tale's veracity is less interesting than the fact that Bowles and his witnesses present it as completely unexceptionable behavior for both widow and suitor: neither Susan nor Henry, nor, presumably, the court officials, thought it at all unusual that she should court him, feed him, tell him where to live, and set her money off-limits while making demands on his. This all was to have resulted, had Henry had his way, in a happy marriage. Another matrimonial enforcement suit, this time brought by the widow herself, is strongly suggestive of the financial power a remarried widow could wield, even under coverture. As James Edwards, a London clothmaker and a widower, tried in 1626 to back out of his contract with the victualler Joan Nevill, he confided to his scrivener his fears that Nevill would get her hands on his money should she force him to marry her: he made his estate over to his children so that she should have "no benefite of or by [it]," and plied the scrivener with wine, "telling him that he would rather spend his money than let Joan have it."[37] Edwards' worries cast an ironic light on Gouge's confident pronouncement that "by our law [a wife] is so farre from gaining any property by her mariage in her husbands goods, as she loseth all the property she formerly had in her owne goods."[38] So too does the case of Ellen Charnock, whose neighbors "passed 'their verdict'" against her husband John in the couple's marital disputes, based on the fact that Ellen had been a wealthy widow and John had been "advanced in his Estate and Fortune" by marrying her.[39] Witnesses in marital separation cases where the complainant is a remarried widow regularly invoked the husband's misuse of "her" money: Henry Carlile was condemned as a man who "worketh little or not at all but liveth idly & hath spent and consumed his wife's substance w[hi]ch she brought him, she being before a widow." In a similar case, a witness approvingly informed the court that the abusive Edward Cleter "submitted him selfe to his . . . wife" after she took out a warrant against him.[40] There were circumstances in which the accepted order involved male submission.

One husband who, unlike Edward Cleter, seems to have lived peaceably in something resembling submission was the astrologer William Lilly. Lilly's marriage at the age of 26 to his master's much older widow is a memorable rags-to-riches story, especially since she left him her entire estate of almost £1,000 when he was 32 years old. One could presumably read Lilly as an exploitative fortune-hunter, but the details he discloses about their courtship and marriage tell a different story, one in which the great "Disproportion of Years and Fortune" between them mitigate any sense that his promotion to husband placed his former mistress in his power. The widow, we learn, was a shrewd and frugal financial manager, or, as he approvingly puts it, "a very Provident person, and of good Condition," who had no interest in "Gentlemen of decay'd Fortunes . . . for she was covetous and sparing." Only after much encouragement from her does he propose, to be promptly met by the reply that he was too young. His response is interesting: "I said nay; what I had not in Wealth, I would supply in Love; and saluted her frequently, which she accepted lovingly." Lilly's relative poverty,[41] which he conflates with the widow's reminder of his youth, requires a supplementary balance in his conduct. And it seems to have been no empty promise, as his description of their married life paints a picture of a man aiming to please a wife of "covetous and sparing" habits: "we lived very lovingly, I frequenting no Company at all; my Exercises were sometimes Angling, in which I ever delighted: My Companions two aged Men. I then frequented Lectures, two or three in a Week." Even more telling, however, is a detail that Lilly mentions almost in passing—for two years, he and the widow kept their marriage entirely secret, no doubt to forestall the "strong Suits of Law" subsequently brought against them by her first husband's kin. The secrecy, initially, was his idea (he feared that the widow's friends would advise her against marrying him), but the implications are startling: as there is no indication that Lilly went to work elsewhere, he and his wife evidently spent their first two years together living, in all outward appearances, as mistress and servant. How this influenced the power dynamic of their marriage can only be imagined. One gets no sense, though, that Lilly was unhappy.[42]

If Lilly offers evidence on an individual scale for non-traditional power structures within a contented marriage, William Rowley's city comedy, *A New Wonder, A Woman Never Vext* (*c.* 1614) elevates a similar arrangement to exemplary status. The play is notable for its old-fashioned didacticism, using a symmetrically structured cast of contrasting characters to teach a lesson in charity.[43] As George Cheatham points out, Rowley even presents his moral formula "within the context of the conventional medieval Christian world view, the so-called Great Chain of Being, which he explicitly evokes as a moral background for A Woman Never Vext."[44] The play matches the wise, patient, wealthy, and perpetually fortunate widow of the title with a bankrupt prodigal, safeguarding our estimation of her with the premise (treated exceedingly lightheartedly) that she seeks him out and invites him to waste her estate so that she might experience affliction for her spiritual good. In providential reward of the widow's charity, however, the planned affliction is transformed into an unexpected blessing: Stephen, the prodigal, suddenly reforms to become the perfect husband, and the two enjoy the ideal marriage. No critic, to my knowledge, has ever remarked on the extent to which this model marriage, in this play devoted to conventional morality, is punctuated by Stephen's deference to his wife, particularly in the financial matters that are so thematically central. The assumption, voiced by her clownish servant, that the widow is placing herself under a husband's control—he warns her to "take heede how you give away the head . . . [which] stands yet upon the shoulders of your widdowhood', and gloomily remarks after the wedding, 'hee masters you therefore I must be content"[45]—only points up the fact that Stephen does not master the widow or even try to, and that this is entirely unproblematic. In accordance with her plan for affliction, the widow explicitly hands over her money to her new husband (3.2.22–3); his response, in his newly reformed state, is to cast himself in the role of her steward: "my care are bent / To keepe your state, and give you all content. . . . I will o're-looke, and cast up all accounts, / That I may know the weight of all my cares, / And once a yeere give up my stewardship" (3.2.41–6).[46] And in this role he remains. When his wife instructs him to relieve Robert, his disinherited nephew, he acknowledges her authority in such matters: "I should have beg'd that bounty of your love / Though you had scanted me to have given't him" (3.2.68–9). She, on the other hand, needs ask no permission when she declares her intent to "send some Angels" to Jane Bruyne, should Robert win her hand in marriage (4.1.175). He asks her consent for the charitable expenditure of renovating Ludgate; when she decides to augment this project with the gift of a neighboring "faire tenement" inherited from her father, she says no more than "I'l give it freely" (4.3.131; 5.1.228). The closest the widow comes to asking for his consent is when she plans to forgive the £2,000 owed to her from two foolish gallants in exchange for a mere £200. Even here, though, her words are more of a polite suggestion than a request—"good Sweetheart, / Shall it [handling the debtors] be put to me?"—and Stephen's response is instant and unquestioning:

> Doe as you please;
> In all thy deeds th'rt govern'd with good starres,
> Therefore if thou cry'st peace, I'le not raise warres.
> E'ne order it how thou wilt.

(4.3.80–4)

The marriage upheld as an ideal is one which, in all practical matters, leaves "the head" firmly on the widow's shoulders. If *A New Wonder, A Woman Never Vext* evokes the Great Chain of Being, it is a chain that subordinates male privilege to the more complex and nuanced hierarchies of wealth, status, experience, and wisdom.

Not every stage prodigal who marries a widow reforms into a model of good stewardship like the exemplary Stephen. The happy endings of less didactic "prodigal son" plots, however, may invoke a less virtuous but equally unpatriarchal pleasure—the pleasure of freedom from responsibility. Alan Young has observed that prodigal son plays from around 1600 onwards are primarily concerned with the prodigal's relation to the single value of "thrift."[47] While the idea of thrift has the right economic emphasis, the sins of early seventeenth-century prodigal sons might be more accurately described in somewhat broader terms as a rebellion against government. That the prodigal has rejected being governed by his father or other authority figure goes without saying, but while filial disobedience *per se* may be the starting premise, it is rarely the continuing focus. Instead, the prodigal's central characteristic is that he willfully refuses to assume government of anything or anyone, including himself. Spendall, in *Greene's Tu Quoque* (1611), is handed the permanent management of a mercer's shop when his master is knighted: faced with this burden of privilege and responsibility, he changes from a model apprentice into an extravagantly generous *bon vivant* who splashes money and mercer's ware all over London until his master seizes back the shop and has him arrested for debt. Vallentine, in *Wit Without Money* (1614), begins the play ignoring the pleas of his late father's tenants who want him to redeem his mortgage and take over the management of his hereditary lands; according to the tenants, good government of the estate is an obligation which he owes them for their labor. Left in charge of his elder brother's house, Younger Loveless, in *The Scornful Lady* (1613), promptly uses his authority to command the elderly steward to bring him ale and wenches. In fact, each of the three vices which commonly define a Jacobean prodigal—drinking, dicing, and whoring—neatly represents a rejection of rule over each of the three things every man is required to govern: himself, for the drunkard allows drink control over his mind and body; money, for the dicer turns his control of his money over to chance; and women, for the cash-based relationship between whore and client is typically portrayed as her power to exploit him in an inversion of the conventional gender hierarchy. The prodigal's career, then, is specifically a rejection of the culture's prescriptive construction of manhood: the domestic patriarch who governs the resources and the subjects of his own little commonwealth.

When this career ends with the prodigal's marriage to a widow, the young man who has refused to govern finds himself comfortably installed in a household where he does not have to, because the widow, accustomed to managing her household and money independently, is fully equipped to assume this responsibility. All three widows are explicitly portrayed not only as wealthy, but as wise and eminently capable managers. Spendall is rescued from debtors' prison by 'the able and wel-minded' Widow Raysby, who displays a measured charity that contrasts sharply with his disorderly generosity;[48] in *Wit Without Money*, Widow Hartwell is shown directing the affairs of her younger sister, her maid, and three male servants; the unnamed widow in *The Scornful Lady* repeatedly warns Younger Loveless against the folly of selling his house to a usurer. In the latter play, too, we see a glimpse of how the kind of mutuality seasoned with male deference seen in *A Woman Never Vext* can operate even in a marriage where the husband is no paragon. When the widow instructs Younger Loveless to cast off his debauched companions who are mocking her plans to reform him and make him "civil," he persuades her to allow him to keep them, in a long and witty speech about how cheaply they can be kept on nothing but ale. The widow declares herself "half perswaded" and adds, "I'le take an order, meate shall not offend you, / You shall have Ale."[49] When the couple appear in the final scene, however, the companions are conspicuously absent for the first time since the play began, and no mention is made of them. The widow has had her way; the men are gone, probably starved out of her house. Younger Loveless's mock panegyric on ale-drinkers, moreover, allows him to save face in front of his companions while implicitly expressing his newfound distaste for their lifestyle. It may well be that with the "ale-only" diet, he himself is suggesting the means by which to be rid of them, gladly submitting to her wishes without letting the men realize it. Younger Loveless wants what the widow wants for him—comfort, security, civility, prestige—but he needs her to take him in hand and manage the change.

Wit Without Money and *Greene's Tu Quoque*, like *Ram Alley*, offer the more common resolution to the widow-marries-prodigal plot: a flourish of aggressive sexual bravado, much to the satisfaction of both parties involved. But when we take into account plays like *A Woman Never Vext* and *The Scornful Lady*, court records, and narratives like Lilly's that normalize the assertive, dominant remarried widow so feared by moralists, it becomes worth considering whether the sexual mastery of the widow opened a space in which an early modern audience might also enjoy it as a mere face-saving gesture, a light-hearted sop thrown to patriarchal prescriptive demands that the husband must exercise authority over his wife. Sexual mastery may be shorthand for all mastery, if one chooses to see it that way. Or it may be no more than sexual, for the extent of the suitor's dominance over the widow required for a happy ending may well have been more in the eye of the beholder than we have been willing to admit. The assumption of antagonism and oppositional relations between the sexes can obscure the fact that women's power did not always have to be in the teeth of men; to see it as inherently rebellious and disorderly is, in a way, to reproduce the very attitudes that we decry. Sometimes, the bedroom may be the only place where the man wants to be on top.

Notes

1. Lording Barry, *Ram Alley or Merrie-Trickes*, ed. Claude E. Jones (Louvain: Librairie Universitaire Uystpruyst, 1952), ll. 2248–51. All further references to this play are from this edition and appear parenthetically in the text.
2. On the lusty widow stereotype as constructed out of male fantasy and anxiety, see Linda Woodbridge, *Women and the English Renaissance* (Urbana, IL: University of Chicago Press, 1984), pp. 177–8; Katherine Jacobs, *Marriage Contracts from Chaucer to the Renaissance Stage* (Gainesville, FL, University Press of Florida, 2001), chapter 7; Ira Clark, *Comedy, Youth, Manhood in Early Modern England* (Newark: University of Delaware Press, 2003), chapter 4; Jennifer Panek, *Widows and Suitors in Early Modern English Comedy* (Cambridge: Cambridge University Press, 2004), chapters 2–3.
3. See Phyllis Rackin, "Misogyny is Everywhere," in *A Feminist Companion to Shakespeare*, ed. Dympna Callaghan (Oxford: Blackwell, 2000), 42–56; Lena Cowen Orlin, "A Case for Anecdotalism in Women's History: The Witness Who Spoke When the Cock Crowed," *ELR*, 31 (2001), 52–77, esp. pp. 73–7. Both Rackin and Orlin argue persuasively against the current scholarly tendency to assume "a history of men's anxiety in the face of female power, of women's disempowerment, and of outright misogyny" (Rackin, 42); both essays call for a more nuanced and complete picture of gender relations in early modern culture, but do so focusing mainly on women and touching only tangentially on the place of men in this revised paradigm. As Orlin asserts, there were early modern "women for whom the usual domestic prescriptions seem scarcely to be operative" (76). This essay invites us to consider the *men* who fit the same description.
4. On the high proportions of early seventeenth-century London brides who were widows, see Vivien Brodsky, "Widows in Late Elizabethan London: Remarriage, Economic Opportunity and Family Orientations," in *The World We Have Gained: Histories of Population and Social Structure*, eds. L. Bonfield, R. M. Smith, and K. Wrightson (Oxford: Oxford University Press, 1986), 122–54, esp. 126–34; Jeremy Boulton. "London Widowhood Revisited: The Decline of Female Remarriage in the Seventeenth and Early Eighteenth Centuries," *Continuity and Change*, 5 (1990), 323–55, esp. 326–9.
5. Brodsky, "Widows," 141–3; Amy Erickson, *Women and Property in Early Modern England* (London: Routledge, 1993), 196.
6. On widows who continued their husband's trade, see Amy M. Froide, "Marital Status as a Category of Difference: Singlewomen and Widows in Early Modern England," in *Singlewomen in the European Past 1250–1800*, ed. Judith

M. Bennett and Amy M. Froide (Philadelphia: University of Pennsylvania Press, 1999), 236–69; 244; Steve Rappaport, *Worlds Within Worlds: Structures of Life in Sixteenth Century London* (Cambridge: Cambridge University Press, 1989), 39–42. On moneylending, see Judith M. Spicksley, "To Be or Not to be Married: Single Women, Money-lending, and the Question of Choice in Late Tudor and Stuart England," in *The Single Woman in Medieval and Early Modern England: Her Life and Representation*, ed. Laurel Amtower and Dorothea Kehler (Tempe: Arizona Center for Medieval and Renaissance Studies, 2003), 65–96; 90. On widows obtaining licenses and loans, see Froide, "Marital Status," 245–6.

7. Froide, "Marital Status," 244; Panek, *Widows and Suitors*, 71, 65–6.
8. On societal approval of remarriage, see Panek, *Widows and Suitors*, chapter 1; Erickson, *Women and Property*, 198; Alan Macfarlane, *Marriage and Love in England: Modes of Reproduction 1300–1840* (Oxford: Blackwell, 1986), 234–6; Miriam Slater, *Family Life in the Seventeeth Century; The Verneys of Claydon House* (London: Routledge, 1984), 104–7. On similar approval of widow-headed households, see Froide, 'Marital Status'.
9. Andrew Kingsmill, *A Viewe of Man's Estate* (London, 1574), sig. I3v.
10. Boulton, 340–3.
11. Barbara J. Todd, "The Remarrying Widow: A Stereotype Reconsidered," in *Women in English Society 1500–1800*, ed. Mary Prior (London and New York: Methuen, 1985), 54–92, 55; see also Barbara J. Todd, "Demographic Determinism and Female Agency: The Remarrying Widow Reconsidered . . . Again," *Continuity and Change*, 9 (1994), 421–50, esp. p. 430.
12. Todd, "Remarrying Widow," p. 83; Elizabeth Foyster, "Marrying the Experienced Widow in Early Modern England: The Male Perspective," in *Widowhood in Medieval and Early Modern Europe*, ed. Sandra Cavallo and Lyndan Warner (Harlow: Pearson Education, 1999), 108–24, 113.
13. Erickson, *Women and Property*, p. 196; Laurel Amtower and Dorothea Kehler, "Introduction," in Amtower and Kehler, *The Single Woman*, ix–xx; xiii; Foyster, "Marrying," 112.
14. Froide, "Marital Status," 243.
15. For instance, Foyster, "Marrying," 112 n. 24 cites Todd, "Remarrying Widow," Erickson, *Women and Property*, and Brodsky, "Widows." Todd's data for remarriage in Abingdon show no significant difference between wealthier and poorer widows (68); Erickson cites Brodsky. Brodsky cites an unpublished PhD thesis by Steve Rappaport. There, presumably, Rappaport cites the same study he cites in *Worlds within Worlds*, 40 n. 46, which is N. Adamson, "Urban Families: The Social Context of the London Elite, 1500–1603' (University of Toronto, 1983), 188. Adamson provides the statistic that 56 percent of aldermen's widows remained single. But Boulton, "London Widowhood (326) points out that Adamson's figures are not broken down by age and might involve widows who are significantly older as well as wealthier.
16. On the Dakins–Hoby marriage, see Lu Emily Pearson, *Elizabethans at Home* (Stanford, CA: Stanford University Press, 1957), 492–3. Parental pressures were sometimes brought to weigh on the marital choices of middling-status widows: see Diana O'Hara, *Courtship and Constraint: Rethinking the Making of Marriage in Tudor England* (Manchester: Manchester University Press, 2003), 36–7. However, there are plenty of cases to support Margaret J. M. Ezell's assertion that 'in the matter of remarriage, widows often suited themselves' (*The Patriarch's Wife: Literary Evidence and the History of the Family* [Chapel Hill, NC: University of North Carolina

Press, 1987], 18); O'Hara, *Courtship* (76) records one such case from 1585, when Elizabeth Overie set her sights on the newcomer John Terrie and sent him two pieces of gold to "commend" herself to him and welcome him to the village of Littlebourne. In this case, it was the man's parents who involved themselves, encouraging the widow's suit to their son by sending her tokens and commendations.

17. Todd, "Remarrying Widow," 77. See also Sandra Cavallo and Lyndan Warner, "Introduction," in Cavallo and Warner, *Widowhood*, p. 12; Sara Mendelson and Patricia Crawford, *Women in Early Modern England, 1550–1720* (Oxford: Clarendon, 1998), 184.
18. Quotations from Austen's journal are from excerpts on Barbara Todd, "'I do no injury by not loving': Katherine Austen, a Young Widow of London," in *Women and History: Voices of Early Modern England*, ed. Valerie Frith (Toronto: Coach House, 1995), 207–37; 226–8.
19. Loreen L. Giese, "Theatrical Citings and Bitings; Some References to Playhouses and Players in London Consistory Court Depositions, 1586–1611," *Early Theatre*, 1 (1998), 113–28; 119, 121–2.
20. Brodsky, "Remarrying Widow," 127–8, emphasis in original.
21. Foyster, "Marrying," esp. 114–19.
22. Bartholomew Batty, *The Christian Man's Closet* (London, 1581), 97–8; see also William Gouge, *Of Domesticall Duties* (London, 1622), 190.
23. Panek, *Widows and Suitors*, chapter 2.
24. Foyster, "Marrying," 113.
25. Bernard Capp, *When Gossips Meet: Women, Family, and Neighbourhood in Early Modern England* (Oxford: Oxford University Press, 2003), 22.
26. Gouge, *Domesticall Duties*, pp. 272–4.
27. On the importance of age and wealth to a man's access to patriarchal privilege, see Alexandra Shepard, *Meanings of Manhood in Early Modern England* (Oxford: Oxford University Press, 2003), chapters 1 and 7.
28. Eighty percent of early seventeenth-century London widows who married bachelors were older than their husbands, with an average age difference of 4.5 years; see Brodsky, "Widows," 127. According to six early modern age schemes discussed in Shepard, *Meanings of Manhood*, 55, 25 is categorized variously as "youth," "staied youth," "young man," and "adolescence".
29. That men are naturally designed for dominance is a routine assertion in early modern prescriptive texts: see William Whately, *A Bride-bush, or a Wedding Sermon* (London, 1617), 18; Thomas Smith, *De Republica Anglorum*, 1583 (Menston, Yorks: Scholar, 1970), 12–13.
30. Capp, *When Gossips Meet*, 20.
31. The quotation is from Capp, *When Gossips Meet*, 2. Use of an oppositional model of gender relations in feminist work is often a factor of the genre or subject being studied: for instance, the anti-masculine jests in Pamela Allen Brown, *Better a Shrew than a Sheep: Women, Drama, and the Cuture of Jest in Early Modern England* (Ithaca, NY: Cornell University Press, 2003), which function as "one of the 'oppositional practices of everyday life,' a means for ordinary people to contest social practices that ordain them as subordinates" (8); or female resistance to marriage in Theodora Jankowski, *Pure Resistance: Queer Virginity in Early Modern English Drama* (Philadelphia: University of Pennsylvania Press, 2000); or the segregated female spaces in Corrine S. Abate, ed., *Privacy, Domesticity, and Women in Early Modern England* (Aldershot: Ashgate, 2003), which "are not always subversive or

spiteful, dangerous or disorderly, [but] ... are no less threatening for that" (2). Arguments against the assumption that female agency is inevitably expressed in opposition to patriarchy tend to be found in recent work on women's writing: see Danielle Clarke, *The Politics of Early Modern Women's Writing* (Harlow: Pearson Education, 2001), pp. 2–3; Suzanne Trill, "Spectres and Sisters: Mary Sidney and the 'Perennial Puzzle' of Renaissance Women's Writing," in *Renaissance Configurations: Voices/Bodies/Spaces, 1580–1690*, ed. Gordon McMullan (Basingstoke: Palgrave Macmillan, 1998), 191–211, esp. 197–9.

32. On how prescriptive authors imagined male abuses of power, see Shepard, *Meanings of Manhood*, 78–82, 86; the "milke-sop" quote is Gouge, *Of Domesticall Duties*, 286; see also Whatley, *A Bride-bush*, 18–19.

33. Erickson, *Women and Property*, 149; also 123. Moralists, one should note, seem to have had no objections to this practice: see Gouge, *Of Domesticall Duties*, 291.

34. Erickson, *Women and Property*, 144.

35. Erickson, *Women and Property*, 123, 148. The disputes about money described by Foyster, "Marrying," 114–17, are additional evidence in separation suits where the primary cause is cruelty or adultery.

36. Laura Gowing, *Domestic Dangers: Women, Words, and Sex in Early Modern London*, (Oxford: Clarendon Press, 1996), 158.

37. Ibid., 170.

38. Gouge, *Of Domesticall Duties*, 300. Recent work suggests that many ordinary married women felt a strong sense of property ownership, despite the legal fiction of coverture: see Natasha Korda, *Shakespeare's Domestic Economies: Gender and Property in Early Modern England* (Philadelphia: University of Pennsylvania Press, 2002), chapter 1, esp. 38–47; Orlin, "A Case for Anecdotalism," 76; Capp, *When Gossips Meet*, 30

39. Foyster, "Marrying," 117.

40. London Metropolitan Archives, DL/C/219/194r; DL/C/218/325; for further instances, see Panek, *Widows and Suitors*, 71–2.

41. By ordinary standards, Lilly was hardly poor: his master had bequeathed him a lifetime annuity of £20. See Lilly, *Last of the Astrologers*, p. 18.

42. William Lilly, *The Last of the Astrologers: Mr. William Lilly's History of His Life and Times From the Year 1602 to 1681*, ed. Katharine M. Briggs (London: Folklore Society, 1974), 9–20. Lilly's marriage is also discussed in Brodsky, "Widows," 126–7.

43. See Alexander Leggatt, *Citizen Comedy in the Age of Shakespeare* (Toronto: University of Toronto Press, 1973), 16–17; George Cheatham, "Introduction," in William Rowley, *A New Wonder, A Woman Never Vexed* (New York: Lang, 1993), 1–40, 23–33.

44. Cheatham, "Introduction," 24.

45. William Rowley, *A New Wonder, A Woman Never Vext*, ed. Trudi Laura Darby (New York: Garland, 1988), 1.2.11–12; 3.2.9–10. All subsequent quotations from the play are from this edition and appear parenthetically in the text.

46. See also 3.2.87–90, where Stephen calls his use of his wife's money "borrowed bounty" and asks her consent; and 3.2.101–13, where he promises to take all cares off her hands and invites her to take her ease, doing "ought that may seeme good / To [her] owne will."

47. Alan Young, *The English Prodigal Son Plays: A Theatrical Fashion of the Sixteenth and Seventeenth Centuries* (Salzburg: Institut für Englische Sprache und Literatur, Universität Salzburg, 1979), 243–7.

48. J. Cooke, *Greene's Tu Quoque or, The Cittie Gallant*, ed. Alan J. Berman (New York: Garland, 1984), 15.2168.
49. Francis Beaumont and John Fletcher, *The Scornful Lady*, ed. Cyrus Hoy, in *The Dramatic Works in the Beaumont and Fletcher Canon*, vol. 2, gen. ed. Fredson Bowers (Cambridge: Cambridge University Press, 1966–96), 449–565, 4.2.103–4. All subsequent quotations from the play are from this edition and appear parenthetically in the text.

15

"I desire to be helde in your memory": Reading Penelope Rich through Her Letters

Grace Ioppolo

Lady Penelope Devereux Rich (1563–1607) seems to have had the particular ability to distress men, including her brother, Robert Devereux, second Earl of Essex and her 'star-lover', Sir Philip Sidney, on their deathbeds. As Essex's inevitable execution for his rebellion in February 1601 approached, he blamed his treachery against Elizabeth I on "my sister, who did continually urge me on with telling me how all my friends and followers thought me a coward, & that I had lost all my valour."[1] Perhaps Essex had taken his cue from his old friend and step-cousin Sidney, who confessed as he lay dying in October 1586, "There came to my remembrance a vanity wherein I had taken delight, whereof I had not rid myself. It was my Lady Rich. But I rid myself of it, and presently my joy and comfort returned."[2] Both accounts, each a secondhand report by a male observer, almost certainly exaggerated Rich's siren-like command of the moral downfall, and subsequent loss of comfort and joy, of these two self-assertive and self-absorbed men.

But the men closest to her were not the only ones to contain and represent her in these damaging ways, for even after her death she was the subject of continual gossip in letters or accounts by aristocrats, courtiers, minor poets, and common balladeers. The contemporary author who wrote "imaginary" epistles between Rich and Sidney described her as "doomed (as in deede shee was) . . . amongst many *that* admired her perfections," precisely because she possessed "sweetnes and beauty; witt and demeanour, incomparable."[3] In fact, most of what we know about Penelope Rich, poetic muse to Sidney, sister to Essex, wife to Robert, Lord Rich, and mistress to Charles Blount, Lord Mountjoy (later Earl of Devonshire), comes through these men or later male historians and literary scholars, who construct her through these men.[4] Sidney canonized her as an erotic demon, her brother denounced her as an emasculating shrew, her husband proclaimed her an adulteress, and her last lover died exhausted from a long and futile battle to nullify her reputation as "an Harlot, Adulteress, Concubine and Whore."[5] In each case she has been seen as betrayed by the men whom she herself was supposed to have betrayed. In effect she was an emotional or physical cuckoldress of all the men who loved her.

But if the men around her castigated Penelope Rich as "a fair woman with a black soul," as King James called her,[6] women often pitied and ultimately disempowered her by viewing her as the victim of patriarchy. Queen Elizabeth may have shared her eventual successor's view of a morally and spiritually blackened Rich, who was one of her maids of honor, her cousin through the Boleyns, and her goddaughter.[7] But, remarkably, Elizabeth had excused Rich for a number of potentially or genuinely treacherous acts, including writing and circulating an audacious letter to her, conspiring with James against her, and living in open adultery with Mountjoy,[8] not to mention assisting Essex in his planned *coup d'état*. Elizabeth's repeated forgiveness of acts for which other maids of honor, aristocrats, and her cousins, Mary, Queen of Scots, were banished from court, tortured, or executed may have stemmed from a mix of affection and frustration with the beautiful and charming Rich. But perhaps Elizabeth recognized that the strong-willed and unusually assertive Rich had, like her queen, been unable to conform to a culture that entrapped and eviscerated women who had too much to do or say. During her reign, Elizabeth never fully reconstituted this culture from patriarchal to matriarchal, but it seems that she did not fully wish to prevent those like Rich from trying.

In the succeeding centuries, women seemed equally loath to analyze Rich's character and power, and it was left to male scholars to re-create her image as a sexually indiscriminate betrayer of brothers, lovers, husbands, and monarchs. William W. Ringler epitomized this view in acknowledging that Rich "possessed all the courtly graces and accomplishments," was interested in literature, and took "a far more active part than other women of her time in the delicate and dangerous game of courtly intrigue and political manoeuvring." He added that "she was courageous, loyal to her brother, and without scruple when what she thought his or her own advantage was at stake." Yet he felt compelled to "judge" her, concluding, "We are left partly admiring her courage, partly deprecating her departure from the moral standards of the day."[9] It is important to remember here that Ringler's praise and censure came from studying her in the reflection of Sidney, not on her own terms. In 1983, Sylvia Freedman seemed determined to rescue Rich from such an anti-feminist judgment in an admirably researched and informative biography. But in choosing James Joyce's epithet of "Poor Penelope" for the title of her book, Freedman betrayed her subject by further canonizing her as both pitiful and pitiable. In fact, Freedman's hagiography repeatedly institutionalizes the simultaneous view of the "irrepressible woman of immense vitality, able to live her life in defiance of convention" and the poor victim who should not be held responsible for her many actions, including personal and political treacheries and betrayals.[10]

Jeanne Robertson, Katherine Duncan-Jones, and Mary Ellen Lamb have been some of far too few literary scholars who have insisted on reintegrating these contrary views of Rich to argue that she was not solely patronized or exploited by men, but existed outside and beyond their reflection. Duncan-Jones has especially emphasized that Rich was the intellectual, and not sexual, center of a powerful literary circle and that her "patronage of poets, translators and musicians shows her taste to have been exceptionally sophisticated."[11] However, some male scholars continue to frame Penelope Rich solely through the reactions of men who used or exploited her.[12] All in all, since her death in 1607, we have been encouraged time and again to accept her brother's chilling warning that "she must be looked to, for she had a proud spirit."[13]

But in looking to her, we look away, for her "proud spirit" and deficiencies, such as her declining "moral standards," to use Ringler's terms, have almost always been represented through others' words, and not her own. Surely the truth of Rich's life, character, and influence must lie somewhere between the two extreme views epitomized by James and Elizabeth. In this chapter I will attempt to allow Lady Penelope Rich to evaluate and present herself by letting her speak in her own words through the many letters in her own hand. Freedman and a handful of others have quoted from her letters in part, but there is no study or literary analysis of the letters in print, although transcriptions of many of these letters appear in various manuscript catalogues.[14] None of the letters appears in the standard edition of Devereux family letters in which her father, Walter Devereux, first Earl of Essex, and her brother Robert figure prominently.[15] This is particularly remarkable given the importance of her 1600 letter to the queen in defense of her sick brother, imprisoned for his unauthorized return from the Irish wars. It is time to let Penelope Rich speak for herself. We do not need to read or listen to the Earl of Essex, Sidney, Lord Rich, Lord Mountjoy, or even King James to understand her. Instead we can read and listen to Penelope herself. Once we hear her voice in these autograph letters, we can recognize how that voice is used in her powerful letter to the queen.

'She is very pleasant in hir Letters'

Although she was a very prolific correspondent, only a fraction of Rich's autograph letters are extant, and only one particular letter, that written in 1600 to the queen on behalf of her brother, survives in multiple scribal copies. The majority of her autograph letters are among the Cecil family papers at Hatfield House. The unusually high survival rate is due to the conscientious preservation of the archive by Sir Robert Cecil, Elizabeth's principal Secretary of State, and later Lord Treasurer, and one of Rich's most frequent correspondents and patrons. But I also suspect that some of these letters, which are not directly addressed to Cecil, are extant at Hatfield because Cecil seized or collected them, as he did in the case of her brother, after her arrest in February 1601 for her part in the rebellion. In fact, some of her letters (*c*.1599) to Henry Wriothesley, Earl of Southampton, another conspirator in the Essex rebellion, or letters about Rich from his wife are also at Hatfield and were probably seized by Cecil along with Southampton's other papers after his arrest for his part in the conspiracy.

Other letters in Rich's hand are in the Anthony Bacon papers at Lambeth Palace, in various collections at the British Library, and among State Papers at the National Archives (formerly the Public Record Office), Kew, and at least one is in a continental library. For the most part, then, these letters are among the papers of the original recipients. Others that were dispersed and sold are now at the Bodleian Library, Oxford, and possibly elsewhere. Although I want to focus on the letters Rich wrote, it is useful to look at what others wrote about her letter-writing in their own letters. This is especially important because Rich was preoccupied with corresponding with such powerful figures as James VI of Scotland (prior to his accession to the English throne in 1603), Cecil, and Southampton on behalf of the suits of various friends and servants whom she patronized. Thus, their responses, and the gossip about such responses in others' letters, establish the context for Rich's writing and her own voice.

Ringler and Duncan-Jones have each made a strong case for Rich's extensive education, intellectual ability, and sophisticated taste in literature. James made the same judgment about her abilities as author, for he reportedly "commended muche the fynnes of hir wit the Invencyon and wele wrytyngs." The occasion of this praise was a congenial attempt on her part in 1589 to ingratiate herself and her brother with the Scottish king in anticipation of his becoming Elizabeth's successor. However, Elizabeth's advisors evidently saw the situation differently, as a potentially dangerous interference in matters of succession,[16] and as possibly even a wishful conspiracy to depose an enfeebled queen and replace her with the much younger James. Thus Elizabeth's spies intercepted letters, paid informers, and planted spies in the Scottish court to monitor the relationship of Rich and Essex, among others, with James.

According to the letter reporting James's flattering assessment of Rich's "writings," she had devised an elaborate cipher with code-names for all the participants in her plot so that they could exchange letters without arousing suspicion. Thomas Fowler anxiously informed William Cecil, Lord Burghley, Robert Cecil's father and predecessor in office as principal secretary, that Rich called herself "Rialta" or "Ryalta," her husband was "Ricardo," and James was (hopefully perhaps) named "Victor." Fowler reports that he had read her private letters to her friend Richard Douglas,

> where by she Remembers him of his charge for his frendes and a nykname for every one that as partake in the matter wherefo thie sayd master Richard hathe a long Scrole an as an alphabet of Sipher to vndersand

them by. She is very pleasant in hir Letters and wryghtes the most part thereof in hir brothers behalfe so as they shall be shewed to the King w*hi*ch they were.

It is only when the "darke partes," or more coded passages, are "expounded" to him that James commends Rich's fineness of wit and her inventive and "well" writings.[17]

This "matter," as Fowler terms it, can be viewed as Rich's harmless exercise to ingratiate her family with the man whom they anticipated would be the next English monarch, or as Rich's conspiracy against a woman whom she considered to be too old and feeble to remain on the throne much longer. In fact, Elizabeth did not officially name James as her successor until shortly before her death fourteen years later. In either view, Rich's behavior was impolitic and presumptuous in 1589, although she reaped the rewards when James ascended English throne in 1603, as he immediately named her an attendant to his pregnant wife, Anne.[18] Rich later received a number of other honors from James and Anne, with whom she performed in Jonson's *Masque of Blacknesss* in 1605. We can therefore assume that her correspondence with James did not cease in 1589. However, it is striking that Rich is "commended" here in Fowler's letter for her extraordinary abilities to deceive, manipulate, and, more precisely, to obscure the truth in such an equivocal way. Even more remarkable is her confidence that she would not be seriously challenged or punished by the queen or her officials. In this, Rich was prescient, fortunate, or sensible. This was not the last time she and her friends enjoyed the use of ciphers. Several letters between Sir Robert Sidney, brother of Philip, and his servant Rowland Whyte employ similar codes, particularly in discussing court intrigues in which Rich is attempting to manipulate the queen into bestowing favors on friends.[19]

"I remaine your frende very affectionate": Rich's autograph letters

No poems or other literary works attributed to Rich are extant, although it is possible that she was involved as author or co-author of works written by the Sidney Circle.[20] So we must look to her autograph letters to give her a voice and thus reassess her not simply as a beautiful and charming seductress, but as a shrewd analyst and accomplished practitioner of written discourse on her own terms. In 1986, Clark Hulse cited a modern printed text of one of her letters to argue that "the letters that survive from her own hand, mostly written around the fateful years of 1600 and 1601, show her to have had a rather invertebrate but effective prose style."[21] However, her surviving letters span the period 1588–1605, with the majority falling in the mid-to late 1590s, not 1600 and 1601. Nor should the citation of one letter be used to judge her style as "invertebrate": anyone reading her autograph letters in manuscript would recognize her as far from spineless. In 2001, George Klawitter also misrepresented Rich by repeating dubious claims drawn from an unreliable and partly fictionalized 1911 biography. These included the statement that a "mutual attraction" between Sidney and Rich began in 1576, and "as a girl she promised herself to Philip Sidney," and that "three events" in Sidney's life "steered Rich away from Sidney" as a potential husband.[22] All that we know for certain about the early relationship of Rich and Sidney is that they knew each other through their families; her late father had expressed his wish that the two should marry, but her guardian matched her instead to Lord Rich.[23] In fact, when Mountjoy tried to convince James in 1606 that Rich should be allowed to divorce, he stated that she had "married ag*ainst* her will unto one ag*ainst* whom she did protest at the very solemnity."[24] In no part of this document or in any of her own papers is there a mention of her romantic interest in or rejection of any other man at the time, including Sidney. Nor is there any reliable information that proves that Rich and Sidney were lovers before or after her marriage to Lord Rich.

Many of her letters have survived simply because they record attempts to gain favors for a variety of friends and servants. Although she profits in some way from these favors, she seems to want to bestow the types of privilege that she herself enjoyed as the daughter of an earl, the stepdaughter of an earl, the wife of a baron, later an earl, and the mistress of a baron, later an earl. This is most apparent in her correspondence with the Cecil family: first, Lord Burghley, Elizabeth's close advisor and Lord Treasurer, and then his son, Robert. Both men were powerful political figures who had direct access to the queen. They were also linked with the Devereux family in a variety of ways, from the friendship between Burghley and Rich's father, to Burghley's guardianship of her brother Robert, to Robert Cecil and Robert Devereux's constantly shifting alliances and quarrels over many years.

The earliest extant letter from Rich to Lord Burghley appears to be a request of 1588, urging him to fulfill a promise he had made to her late stepfather, Robert Dudley, Earl of Leicester, in granting a wardship to the son of friend. This letter is far more direct and aggressive than the later ones, because she seems fatigued, possibly due to pregnancy or childbirth. She writes:

> I beseche your L*ordship* to make me so much bound vnto you as to set it so forwarde as that I may shortly hope to see an end of it, and I will acknowledge it euer as proceeding from your L*ordship's* greate fauour and will imploye my selfe bothe to desarue it and to shewe all thainkfullnes for so great a benifit.[25]

Rich's exasperation is directed either at herself or Burghley, whose delay has prompted her to bring up an old subject. However, her letter is far more congenial and gracious than two patronizing and indiscreet letters written to Burghley by Rich's sister Dorothy in 1583, demanding that she receive her dowry, withheld because when a maid of honor to the queen she had married Sir Thomas Perrott without permission.[26] Rich had acted as a go-between between her sister and Perrott before their marriage, according to an extant letter in the State Papers.[27]

Although Rich's relationship with Robert Cecil became strained in 1600 over the queen's response to her letter, he was her frequent correspondent and benefactor, as his father had been, and their letters seem genuinely cordial and affectionate, as in this request for his help as in 1595:

> Worthy Sir Ro: Cissill, I knowe your minde to be honorably constante towards your frends, amonge which number I desire to hould place, as on that doth make greate estimation of your affection, I must intreat you now to fauour this berar so much as to procure him ether your fathers letter, or my Lord Admiralls, to my Lord of Harforde in a very resonable cause, wher in I praye you to forther him all you may since it consernes him as much as he is worth, the matter I refar to him selfe to let you vnderstand, and so wishing you all contentment I remaine your frende very affectionate
>
> Penelope Riche

In a postscript she adds, "I desire to be comended to my La*dy* and to contenu in her faire frendshipe."[28] As is common with women of this period, Rich writes in an italic hand, not the secretary hand more commonly used by men. However, her italic resembles in some letters the predominantly italic hand used by her brother, and it is possible that they had the same writing tutor as children, at least before their father's death, when Essex was sent to live with his guardian, Burghley. However, her handwriting is much neater and more legible, in fact semi-calligraphic, than that of her brother, who only partially forms or entirely omits some letters when writing cursively. Although her letters look neat enough to be fair copies of original drafts, they do contain sufficient corrections and revisions to suggest she did not necessarily copy her letters, but sent the originals. The semi-calligraphic style implies that she wrote slowly and carefully, to present her language in the most effective way. In fact, Rich's letters rarely run longer than one side of a bifolium, and when she does run on, she turns the paper sideways and continues writing lengthways in the left margin rather than on the verso. She adds the address of her recipient herself in an elaborate and flourished style, writing it on the fourth page of the bifolium and, as is customary, seals the letter with ribbon or wax seals.

That Rich usually confines herself to short, one-page, neatly written letters suggests that she was very concerned with the visual impact of her writing, seeing it as fixed and set into one single, unified space. Even so, she is not economical in her language, and often embellishes her praise or compliments, even with such frequent correspondents as Cecil. But her letters do lack the extended metaphors and excessive numbers of dependent clauses that are notable in her brother's letters, and in her letter to the queen. In fact, Rich is usually succinct, possibly because she constantly asks her correspondents to "entertaine me in your memory" and to "hould me in your worthy minde," or more simply, "I desire to be helde in your memory."[29] In none of these can she be accused of being tedious, repetitious, or boring. Her bonds to Robert Cecil stem not just from the friendship of their families but his ability to relay private information about the success or failure of her brother's various military exploits, particularly in the 1590s, as well as gossip about his standing at court. In short, she and Cecil had a mutually beneficial bond: each provided the other with important gossip or sensitive information about Essex, the figure whose ascendancy and fall dominated court politics from the early 1590s to 1601 and some years afterwards.

At times in her letters, Rich's self-absorption cannot be disguised. In 1599, she writes a striking letter to Cecil, most likely dating from mid-December when her brother was still under house arrest at the home of Sir Thomas Egerton, the Lord Keeper, after his unauthorized return from Ireland in September 1599. Rich begins by reminding Cecil that he has already done a "favor" for Essex's wife, Frances, most likely allowing her access to Essex on December 13. Rich insists that it is her turn for a favor and she asks Cecil to speak "earnestly" on her behalf to the queen for leave to visit her brother at least once. Rich had evidently already asked the queen but had been refused on the grounds that "if she granted me leue, my sister would louke for as much." By "sister" Rich is probably referring to Dorothy, now married to the Earl of Northumberland, as she refers in the letter to Frances as "my sister of Essex." Rich then ingenuously argues that even if her sister also demands access to Essex, it "need be need be no argument against me, since her Ma*jes*ty being content to permit that fauour but to some fewe, I may if [it] please her obtaine it before others, because I haue humbly and ernestly made the first sute, for which I haue laide my hopes vppon your selfe." Rich then politely concludes by reminding Cecil that she will "euer remaine your most affectionate frende."[30]

It is difficult not to fault Rich here for a minor act of treachery against her sister. According to Rich's logic, because she made the first suit to the queen to see Essex, she should be obliged, whereas her sister, making the second suit, should be denied. That the two women were frequently living together at Essex House during this period does not appear to Rich to suggest that she owes Dorothy any loyalty or generosity. In any case, Essex was not allowed to meet either of his sisters or any family members other than his wife during his confinement at the Lord Keeper's. However, he had convinced Egerton to let him exercise in the walled garden, at which time he could be seen by his mother and other worried relatives and friends when they peered at him from the windows of a house overlooking the garden.

The logic of Rich's argument here must have failed to persuade Cecil, for some time later Rich again writes to Cecil:

> I haue bine a very importunate sender vnto her Majesty for leue to see my vnfortunate sicke brother and haue reseued so much comfort of her, though she hath not granted it, as I may hope to obtaine it, if you will vowchsafe me so much fauour as to mediat my humble sute, which I praye you very ernestly to do for her that will neuer be vngratfull in acknowledging your Kindneses, don in so distressed a tyme.

Rich adds in a postscript, "If you had bine hear I wuld haue intreated your fauour with my owne presence, which I am forced to do by thes hasty lines."[31] Perhaps Cecil was well aware that Rich's powers of persuasion were even more forceful and intimidating in person than in writing and was glad not to have been entreated with her "owne presence."

Throughout her life, Rich's relationship with her brother was mutually dependent and mutually destructive. She seemed unable to resist even his most selfish entreaties. At one point, probably in 1599, she is woken by a messenger carrying a letter sent by Essex, who is obviously ill or in crisis, perhaps immediately after his unauthorized return from Ireland when he was still at court and not yet confined to Egerton's house. She then writes to his servant Thomas Downhall to report:

> my brother wold haue me come to the courte in the morning erly, I am here scarse well and in my night clothes, hauing nothing else hear, but yet I will come and desire not to be seene by any one, him selfe, wherfore I praye you come, for me as erly as you thinke good, and deuise how I may come in very priuately.[32]

Despite her lack of clothing and her illness, she pledges to hurry to Essex at his insistence, more concerned with safeguarding his rest than her own, as she notes in a postscript:

> if it had not bine for importuning my brothers rest I would haue come in the night to haue kept my selfe from any others eyes, good Master dounall let me not faile to see you erly, I would not write to my brother because I thought he would be asleepe before the messenger came.[33]

Although she had being woken by a messenger in the middle of the night, she refuses to allow her brother to suffer the same disturbance. More interesting here is her ironic statement that she is so concerned at being supplied only with nightclothes that she would have preferred to have sneaked in the dark into her brother's rooms at one of Elizabeth's palaces. But it is her modesty and not her vanity she is protecting. Ultimately, she protects her brother and travels by day when she will be on public display, dressed in the only clothes available to her.

In less troubled periods, long before or after her brother's difficulties with the queen, Rich did not use her letters only to seek help from possible benefactors but to convey her sincere affection and regard for friends and relatives. In an autograph letter (*c.*1589) written in French to Leicester's former secretary, Jean Hotman, she is gracious, flirtatious, and utterly charming:

> Je luy souhaitte les bonne graces de sa maitresse et à monsieur Palevesin bon vant, et à monsieur de Sydnye, qui ne croye pas tout ce que l'on luy dict, et à monsieur Constable, qu'il ne soit plus amoreux, et a vous mesme d'aymer bien vostre femme et a tous d'estre constants jusque à vendredy.[34]

Perhaps her claim that Robert Sidney, her step-cousin through the marriage of Sidney's uncle, Leicester, to her mother, does not believe everything one tells him ("qui ne croye pas tout ce que l'on luy dict") is meant to forestall any gossip he might hear about her. In any case, this is as affectionate as a 1599 letter to Southampton, whose wife, Elizabeth Vernon, is staying with Rich, who is also her cousin. Rich assures him, "nothinge shall make me neglecte to yealde you all the ernest assurances I can of my affection and desires to be helde deare in your fauour whose worthy Kindnes I will striue to merit by the faithfullest endeuours my loue can performe towards you." In a postscript, Rich sweetly adds, "your *Lordship's* Daughter is exseading faire and well and I hope on your fair sonn to winn my wager." From this letter Southampton and any other readers can easily picture Rich pinching the cheek of Southampton's little daughter and betting his wife that she will soon deliver a boy. This and other letters from this period have been misdated 1603 in a contemporary hand, perhaps by one of Cecil's secretaries to disguise the fact that they had been seized after Southampton's arrest in 1601.

Throughout her letters, Rich manages to display compassion and concern for her friends; though whether this is genuine or politic is not always easy to determine. Having promised that she would stand as godmother to Robert Sidney's child, she was not dissuaded by a risk to her health. Rowland Whyte reported to Sidney in 1595:

> When I told her that my Lady and the child had measles, she replied that after 8 days there was no danger and it should be no occasion to keep her from doing Sir Robert Sydney and his lady a greater kindness. I besought her to take a longer time to think on the danger, which she did till the afternoon; and then coming to her to Essex House, she told me she was resolved.[35]

Such concern appears to demonstrate her deep commitment to her friends, but in fact, it was not her fear of catching measles that delayed the ceremony. In another pointed letter from Whyte to Sidney, he claims that "Lady Rich is come to town, but the christening is put off till New Year's eve. She says it was at Lord Compton's desire. But I doe rather thincke yt to be a tetter [i.e. blemish] that sodainly broke out in her fayre whyte face . . . that keapes your son from being christened."[36] Perhaps it is not ironic that Rich was more frightened of the risk of a displaying a blemish than of catching measles. She had a more serious risk to her beauty and health in 1597 when she became seriously ill with smallpox. Although it was first reported that "the small pox has much disfigured Lady Rich," it was later noted that she recovered "without any blemish to her beautifull face."[37] Evidently, the news was unanimously greeted with joy.

Rich also learned to forgive and forget, whether for political or personal reasons. Two years after Cecil helped to prosecute and execute her brother for treason, Rich pledges to Cecil that "your noble fauours towardes your absente frende and my selfe hath longe since oblidged my affection in the hyest degree, which I profess vnto you increaseth dayly so as you may dispose of me as assuredly as of any frende you haue liuinge." She also reminds him that "the passages of our fortunes, and tyme shall witnes the sinserety of my mind." If one of these passages of fortune is Essex's death, Rich does not give in to bitterness but proceeds to ask Cecil to offer a commission to her friend, Sir John Townsend.[38] Yet Rich's resilience had a more immediate cause: her lover, Lord Mountjoy, now elevated to Earl of Devonshire, had succeeded Essex as leader of the English forces against the Irish and is the "absente frende" to whom Rich refers.

Together, Mountjoy and Rich played important roles, he as a trusted courtier and military leader, she as a royal confidante and servant at the court of James, the man whom "Ryalta" had teased and impressed in her "well writings" so long ago. In fact, Mountjoy's accomplishments and prowess mirrored those of his friend, her brother, with whom he had frequently competed at court for Elizabeth's favors: in loving Mountjoy, Rich loved a mirror image of Essex. Rich and Mountjoy sought the legalization of their union and their children, and to this end succeeded in convincing James to allow Lord Rich to divorce his wife on the grounds of adultery. Although James's assent did not include remarriage for either, Lord and Lady Rich each immediately took another spouse. As punishment, James declared the marriages illegal, and Lady Rich was especially castigated for betraying the reputation and honor of Mountjoy. In 1606 Mountjoy wrote his own letter, or more precisely a steely discourse, "in defense of his Marriage with the Lady Rich," which was also printed.[39] It seemed to have been as ineffective as the letter Lady Rich had written to her monarch in 1600, although it provoked the same type of censure. Mountjoy died before the year was out.

Yet, Rich remained sincere in her concern for her old friend and benefactor, Cecil, writing to him in 1606 that she has hurried to her home in London due to "the rumors of your siknes." She has since received news of his "safe recouery," beseeching him, "beleue that no frende you haue liuing doth papticipate more your grife, or ioye, then my selfe whose affection you haue so infinitly obleged, with your constante fauours." She closes her letter with news of her family's visit to his son and other family members, touchingly noting, "my mother I thinke will growe younge with ther companye."[40] Rich died in the following year, predeceasing both Cecil and her mother, Lettice Knollys, who had been first married to Walter Devereux, then to Leicester, and finally to Christopher Blount, who lost his head with her son after the 1601 rebellion.

'My Lady Ritches Letter to the Queene'

Rich is most famous, and indeed infamous, not for the many extant letters in her own hand but for one that exists only in the hands of others. It is time for her authorship of this letter to the queen in 1600 in defense of her brother and the circumstances surrounding it to be reassessed in the context of her autograph letters. If the original was indeed sent to the queen, it would have been kept in the State Papers, but there is no trace of it there. Scribal copies, at least twelve in number and each slightly variant, can be found at the British Library and at the Bodleian, Inner Temple, and Folger Libraries and elsewhere; most of the copies date from the 1620s and 1630s. Any or all of these later transcripts appear to have been made from other manuscript copies, rather than the 1600 unauthorized printed text, which was immediately suppressed. Thus these scribal copies are at some distance from Rich's autograph letter.

It has been assumed that Rich wrote the letter during late 1599/early 1600, when her brother was ill and confined to York House, home of the Lord Keeper. Essex had been placed there immediately after his arrest in late September 1599 for his unauthorized return from Ireland, where he had commanded the army unsuccessfully trying to suppress the Earl of Tyrone, as well as for other misdeeds against the queen. By December, Essex was seriously ill, but by January 1600 had begun to recover, at which time the queen reconsidered his case. She finally allowed him to move back into his own London home, Essex House, in March, where he remained under house arrest; after being formally interrogated some months later, he was finally given his full liberty in August.[41] Rich's letter to the queen indeed asks for the release of her "unfortunate brother," either to return to Elizabeth's service or to live a private life, free from the infamy and blemish to his reputation being spread by his enemies.

However, Rich's letter may have been composed anytime between late September 1599 and February 2, 1599/1600, when Rowland Whyte reported to Robert Sidney that "my Lady Rich was called before my Lord Treasurer or Mr. Secretary, for a letter she had wrytten to her Majestie."[42] Although one scribal copy of the letter (British Library Stowe MS 50) dates it "January 1,

1599" (i.e. 1600), Rich provided no information about the actual date of composition. The queen was exceptionally angry when the letter was written and again when it was published. The blame fell squarely on Rich and not her brother, according to Whyte, who complained in May 1600, "Yt is sayd that my Lady Riches letter to her Majesty is alsoe printed, which is an exceeding wrong donne to the Earle of Essex."[43] Elizabeth finally demanded that Cecil and Thomas Sackville, Lord Buckhurst, who was then Lord Treasurer, formally investigate the publication. Evidently Rich had already provided written excuse for her actions, but the document did not satisfy Elizabeth. Buckhurst was then ordered to interrogate Rich in person, forcing her to answer a number of charges. This second set of answers was sent to the queen, along with another letter from Rich which she requested remain private and confidential, a request that Elizabeth, surprisingly, granted.

Cecil's outline of the result appears in an extant autograph letter (now at Hatfield House) to Buckhurst. This letter is so heavily revised as to be illegible at places, and it does not appear to carry an address; it is therefore probably Cecil's first draft before it was fair-copied by one of his secretaries and sent to Buckhurst. However, the many layers of revisions suggest that Cecil used exceptional care and effort, particularly in his choice of words. Among other points, Cecil tells Buckhurst that he has shown this new "declaration" of Rich's answers to Elizabeth, "which it pleasde her to reade deliberately her selfe./divers thinges passed which I forbeare vntill I meet you because they are not necessarie for the present, most of them tending to her mislike." Yet Cecil begins discussing some of these "divers thinges" which he had planned to withhold from Buckhurst, namely Buckhurst's long deferment, that is, delay, in dealing with the matter, evidently because he was

> still so apt to excuse my ladyes course in her former answeares by imputing *tha*t to feare only in her of giuing further offence, *w*hich rather shewed a proud disposition & not much better then a plaine contempt of her Ma*jes*ty and yourselfe.

Perhaps Buckhurst's indulgence was partly due to the fact that, like Elizabeth, he was a cousin of Rich's through the Boleyns.

Cecil finally summarizes the matter as it now stands: the queen has read Rich's declaration and noted Rich's many regrets, including her "sorrow" at her monarch's "displeasure," her "feare to offend further," her "humble and obedient spirit to satisfy all doubts," as well as her "great desyr" to recover her majesty's favor. Cecil tells Buckhurst to inform Rich that

> it is true her Ma*jes*ttie was displeasde as she had Cause, to see that she [i.e. Rich] being a Lady to whom it did not apperteyne so to meddle in such matters, would be so bold to write in such a style to her, especially when the best interpretacions *w*hich she doth make can not free her from

stomach & presumption when she writ and when her former careless and dry answers shewed how little she valued her majestys comandments.

Cecil then relays a moral lecture from the queen to Rich, who has been "far from desire to Improve her faults hauing given her all advauntages to make the best excuses which tyme or new counsayle could aford." Although irritated with this earlier behavior, the queen was now confident of Rich's "resolution to cary her self as becomes her to all persons hereafter, to give her leaue to dispose of her selfe as may best agree with her owne health or other respect." In this last statement appears a veiled threat that further behavior of this kind will provoke a punishment that might indeed injure Rich's health.

The queen then graciously suggests that she is willing to "free" Rich from the "directe desire or purpose" of having had the letter printed, if she

is well able to proue whene she hath given copyes by which meanes it hath been printed, and If it is no worse then that she was only so negligent that others might come by it her error was not so excusable but that shrewd circumstances might be inferred, vppon such a voluntary negligence (wherevppon hath fallen so strange a consequence).

In other words, it seems that Rich's "sinceritie of obedience," by which she has now "soght to make amends," has given the queen some leeway and leniency about her punishment. In fact, here Elizabeth deftly outmaneuvers Rich, so well known to James and the Sidneys for the cleverness of her secret ciphers and covert literary strategies. Elizabeth generously suggests that the printing must have occurred for one of two reasons: either Rich distributed copies of the letter to others who had it printed, or she was so "negligent" with the original that others were able to "come by it" and take it to a printer. Elizabeth claims the second reason to be the lesser "error," but that neither reason leaves Rich blameless, and both implicate her in a shrewd, voluntary, and deliberate plot against the queen.

Elizabeth mentions one more matter: she assures Rich that her private letter enclosed with the declaration "hath passed the eyes of noe other creature." The queen's expertise in manipulation here lies in the fact that this news is delivered to Buckhurst and thence to Rich by Cecil himself, the one man, as Elizabeth's most trusted aide, who should have seen this confidential letter. Cecil confirms this fact: "soe it is true I protest to God, for her Majestie caused it to be burnt without giving me any manner of light whoe it may be." Cecil then peevishly adds, "whereof I was not inquisative for although my name hath been bulked for fashyon in respect of my place, yet I doubt not but I was and am in her ladyships contemplacion the person on whom all the figures of that lettre dyd principally play."[44] In other words, Cecil believes that Rich's attacks in her original letter to the queen about unnamed enemies of her brother alluded to him "principally," and he is not happy about such an accusation, even though he was directly responsible for dealing with Essex's case. Whether Cecil's reaction stems from personal hurt or political anxiety is not made clear. In any event, he implies that the charges by Rich, a woman with whom he had an affectionate personal relationship and correspondence, constitute a personal betrayal, as do her successful attempts to ensure that he had no access to the second letter.

The surviving scribal copies of Rich's first letter to the queen in defense of her brother suggest that the original was elegant and eloquent, occasionally punctuated with the common poetic tropes and images of the period. It is also a masterpiece of rhetoric in managing simultaneously to praise the queen's generosity, divinity, and "sacred clemency," and to slander her brother's "combined enemies" who labor to build his "ruin," while reasserting her brother's devotion of his "love, his life, and his service" to Elizabeth.[45] To Rich's apparent courage in sending the letter we must add her skill as author here, particularly in the opening of the letter which employs the exceptionally ingratiating and fulsome language of so many other supplicants to Elizabeth in this period. Yet, I want to argue that this letter may not originally have been written by Rich but, rather, by her brother, Essex. While she certainly copied it in her hand, with which Elizabeth would have been familiar, before it was sent to the queen, I suspect that Rich did not compose the letter.

I draw this conclusion about the authorship from two sets of evidence. First, the language and style do not resemble those she used in her surviving autograph letters, but do closely resemble those in her brother's many autograph letters to the queen. Essex could have written this letter any time between late September, when he was imprisoned, and early December, when he became seriously ill. Second, in Cecil's letter to Buckhurst, and in other accounts of the matter, both the queen and Cecil suggest that Rich has *not* told the truth about the provenance of her letter and that some "shrewd circumstances" and "so strange a consequence" are involved in its composition and circulation. Rich's attempt to evade interrogation by fleeing to the country, noted by John Chamberlain among others, in February,[46] her "dry answers" to Buckhurst's first inquiry, and her later reluctance to explain her actions also imply that she was afraid to detail the circumstances in which the letter was written. Despite Cecil's preoccupation with "her ladyships contemplacion" in the letter, he and the queen seem to have been hoping that Rich would confess that she did not, in fact, write the letter. The queen's magnanimity in excusing Rich for her behavior, especially in reiterating possible reasons for it, may have derived from Elizabeth's conviction that Rich was shielding her brother. Thus, Rich received more indulgence than Elizabeth commonly gave such transgressors, as in the case of John Stubbes's 1579 letter attacking the queen's proposed marriage to the Duc d'Alençon, which resulted in him and his printer losing their right hands on the scaffold.[47]

I am not suggesting here that Rich was incapable of such poetic and rhetorical scope shown in the letter. Her autograph letters, along with her patronage of poets, display that she did indeed possess the wit, invention, and finesse as a writer and author with which James credited her. My argument stems instead from my transcription and study of over 50 autograph letters of her brother to the queen, most of which are found in a volume from the Hulton family (British Library Additional MS 74286).[48] Numerous other autograph and scribal letters by Essex to other correspondents are also extant, but my concern here is only with his original letters (and copies made by his secretaries) to Elizabeth. The imagery, vocabulary, style, and tone bear striking resemblance to those used in Rich's letter to the queen. These similarities are most evident in Essex's letters written between 1599 and 1600 begging for the return of Elizabeth's favor after he had willfully lost it, the same circumstances in which Rich's letter is sent. Of course, some similarities can be explained as shared or common conventions of the time, as when Essex repeatedly ends his letters with the wish that his words may "Kisse your Majesties fayre hands" (Hulton letters, ff. 6, 84, 99). Rich concludes her letter with the humble request, "I presume to kisse your faire handes." Such an expression may have been routine in addressing Elizabeth; however, the more distinctive cadence, rhythm, and style of Essex's letters recur in the letter purportedly written by Rich.

Rich's 1600 letter also draws on or repeats a number of ideas and images that Essex used in previous letters as well as in those written during his imprisonment, just before his illness. For example, in an undated Hulton letter, Essex tells Elizabeth,

> My lyfe was neuer deere vnto me for I preferred the least occasion of doing your Majestie seruice before that my seruice cold neuer challenge any meritt butt wher your fauour was a partiall iudg. (f. 29)

In Rich's letter, she tells the queen that her brother's

> loue, his life, and his seruice to your beauty and the state, had deserued noe absolution after soe hard punishment, or soe much as to answer in your faire presence, who would vouchsafe more iustice and fauour then he can expecte of partiall iudges.[49]

In a letter of 1591, Essex painfully reminds Elizabeth that his brother Walter has died in battle with him against the French Catholics:

> I find thatt your Majesties indignation threatens the ruine and disgrace of him, thatt hath lost his deerest and only brother spent a greatt part of his substance ventured his owne lyfe and many of his frends in seeking to do your Majestie seruice. (f. 21)

Rich's letter makes the same points but adds the earlier death of her father in Ireland to that of her brother in France:

> his posteritie maie not repent their fathers were borne to soe harde a destine; Two of them pirishinge by beinge imployed in owne contry where they would haue done yow sirvis to the shedinge of theire last bloode.

Certainly Rich would have been as concerned as her brother with the deaths of their father and Walter, but she repeatedly makes her points in the letter by focusing on the same issues of "infamy," "ruin," and "reputation" as found in Essex's own letters. Other similarities are more trivial, but nevertheless striking. He blesses Elizabeth's "princely & angellik nature" and her "gracious, princely, and diuine nature" (National Archives SP 12/174/39, 274/95), as does Rich, who commends Elizabeth's "owne princely Nature." In the Hulton letters, Essex calls Elizabeth his "goddesse" and speaks of her "bewty," her "excellent perfections," and her "fayre eyes" (ff. 96, 105, 110, 119, 99, 75). Rich calls Elizabeth her brother's "sacred goddesse" and compliments her on her "excelent beauties and perfections" and her "fayre Eyes." Essex and Rich share the same view of his salvation; Essex claims in 1599 while miserable in Ireland, "Thatt any man shold leaue purgatory to go to paradize yt is nott strange" (Hulton letter, f. 111), and Rich claims that Essex's enemies will force him to "goe through purgatory to heauen."

Rich's letter appears in fact to be constructed on the same rhetorical strategies that Essex employs in various letters written to the queen before 1600. Essex tells Elizabeth in an undated letter, "I see your style all redy changed, & nothing but gathering of clowdes & fowle weather after me" (Folger MS V.b/214, f. 202), while Rich draws the same image more subtly and cautiously:

> Early did I hope this morninge to haue had my eyes blessed with your ma*jes*ties: beauties, but seeinge the same depart into cloude, and meetinge with spirits who presaged by the wheeles of their chariots, some thunder in the aire.

Nonetheless, in a Hulton letter, Essex still acknowledges of Elizabeth's commands, "I do reuerence the oracle" (f. 29), while Rich calls her a "diuine oracle." Essex, who appeared to suffer from depression, and perhaps mania, complains frequently that the queen's various withdrawals of her favor have plunged him into "despaire" and "misery" (Hulton letters, ff. 9, 12, 5–16, 105, 110; Folger V.b.214, f. 202; National Archives SP 12/274/138). Rich focuses less specifically on the "afflicted," by which she means her brother, "that must despaire in time" who "feele the miseries of Hell."

In fact, a despairing Essex once told Elizabeth, "when I looke into myself and examin whatt thatt capitall fault shold be thatt I had com*m*itted, I find nothing except *that* to a fault to striue to do her Majestie more seruice then she cares for" (Hatfield House CP 40/67). In her letter, Penelope more ambiguously laments her "vnfortunate Brother whome all men haue libertie to defame as if his offence were capitall." The ever self-absorbed Essex informs Elizabeth in 1599, probably during the early months of his imprisonment, "I was neuer prowde, till your Majestie sought to make me too base. And now since my destiny is no better: my despaire shall be as my loue was with out repentaunce" (f. 110). He blames his enemies for the fact that he was a "once happye but now most sorrowfull creature," with a "sentence giuen to ruyn & disable him who dispyseth lyfe when he shall be made vnfitt for your service" (National Archives SP 12/174/39). Rich laments that her brother's sullied reputation must "disable him for euer seruinge againe his sacred goddesse." Rich calls her brother "soe base detected a creature," and claims that all this is due to "those combyned enimies that labor upon false grounds to buylde his ruyne." Such a view of victimization is common in Essex's letters, as in his claim to Elizabeth, "yf your Majesties fauor be no more assured to me then thatt slander and suspicion, which are the basest enemies a man can haue, dare threaten to take yt from me I haue liued too long" (Hulton, f. 29).

Essex's reputation is paramount, even early in his career when he worries that coming home from the French wars "without doing any thing wold vutterly ouerthrow my poore reputation" (Hulton f. 21). In another letter from May 1600, some months after Rich sent her letter to the Queen, he repeats this rhetoric, claiming, "Nowe I do not only feel the waight of your Majesties indignacion, and am subiect to their malicious informacions that first envyed me for my happiness in your favor" (National Archives SP 274/138). Essex writes repeatedly in this vein, especially in 1599, claiming, for example, "to be subiect euery ower [hour] to base and vile imputations is as impossible for me as yt is vntollerable" (Hulton letter f. 117). Essex was particularly fond of seeing his loss of the Queen's favor, or any other decline in fortune, as an "overthrow," a term he uses in the letter cited above and in several others (Hulton, ff. 12, 21, 90; Hatfield House CP 65/29). Rich complains of the "particular malice and counsels" of Essex's enemies, who "haue practised only to glutt themselues in there priuate reuenge," so that the can "rise by this overthrow." Rich begs that "though hee may not returne to the happines of his former sirvis to liue att the feet of his Admired Mistris yett hee may sitt downe to a priuate life with out this imputation of infamye." At Elizabeth's feet was where Essex once belonged; during the French wars he writes that he wishes "as a reward of my seruice to be soone att home att your Majesties feete. whence nothing butt death or (your vnconstancy which is nott in rerum natura.) can driue me." In his letters during and after this imprisonment he also requested that he be allowed to return to die at her feet, but to no avail.[50] Finally, it was not Elizabeth's inconstancy but his that drove him into a "private" life, shunned by Elizabeth and the court, which he continually bemoaned from September 1599, when he had his last meeting in person with Elizabeth, and February 1601, when he was executed for treason.

Perhaps Rich came to all these conclusions in her letter to Elizabeth because she had recently received a bitter and angry letter from her brother. Although the letter (British Library Additional MS 64081) is undated, it was clearly written while he was ill and despondent, almost certainly in late 1599 or early 1600. In it Essex offers a number of platitudes, defining envy as "the humor of him that will be glad of the reversion of an other mans fortune and reuenge the remedy of such fools as in iniuries know not how to keepe themselves afore hand." Her receipt of this letter may have prompted her letter to the queen. In fact, his deep-seated resentment and paranoia seemed to have infected or poisoned her own life and language for some years, as in a 1596 letter she sent to Cecil asking for news about Essex's welfare during his expedition against the Spanish at Cadiz:

> I would faine here [hear] for ther ar some allredy out of ther owne base enuye seekes to detract what they can from his honor, though ther words retorne to ther owne disgrace, rather then his disprais, when I see you I will let you vnderstand what I knowe of this matter.[51]

Even though such language resembles that in her letter to the queen, Rich cannot sustain in this letter the rhetorical tropes, imagery, and power of the other letter, especially as these charges come within a paragraph of mundane gossip. In fact, the sentence cited above seems oddly inserted into the letter as the type of platitude so favored by her brother in his own written and spoken language.

The most striking feature that Essex's and Rich's letters share is a complete inability to claim, or accept, responsibility or blame for Essex's disobedience to the queen and his other offenses. Both try to argue that Essex was conspired against and forced into treacherous behavior by others, and the inclusion of Cecil in these conspirators is more than implied. But given the way she succeeded in charming Elizabeth with contrition and repentance after the letter was printed, Rich would surely have been wise to write her original letter to the queen as a simple and submissive apology for her brother. Instead, she brashly ranted at length, in fact much more than she needed to, about her brother's "enimies." According to Cecil, she employed subtle and shrewd diplomacy when appealing to the queen after the letter was printed; this type of subtlety and shrewdness appear only in the brief but exceedingly flattering opening and closing of this two-page letter. That she repeated her brother's common and usual complaints against the queen's courtiers throughout the body of the letter, without showing any contrition or repentance on his part, would suggest that Essex was primarily responsible for the letter. If she did write all or most of the letter, the usually subtle, shrewd, and self-composed Rich badly misjudged her audience.

The relationship between the siblings was unusually close; not only did Essex allow his sister to live in open adultery with Mountjoy in Essex House, but he entrusted her with many more secrets and confidences than he offered his wife, Frances, or his other sister, Dorothy. The two extant letters from Essex to Rich suggest an exceptionally close and dependent relationship.[52] But Essex also exploited Rich's sexual charm to procure and seduce allies and supporters, no matter the consequences for her, as on the eve of his 1601 rebellion when he sent her to the home of Edward, Earl of Bedford, so that she could beg him to meet with Essex. She even insisted that she escort Bedford back to Essex House in her coach, clearly not giving him any opportunity to decline, or so he reported when charged in the conspiracy.[53] Whether Rich went to Bedford's house on her own initiative or her brother's is not made clear, although gossip at the time suggested that she had encouraged the participation of other potential conspirators.

Rich, along with Frances, was in the house when her brother rode through the streets of London on February 8 calling for support in his rebellion against the queen's supposed enemies. Rich was still in the house when Essex returned in defeat. When officials came to arrest him, he managed the safe removal of Rich, his wife, and the other women in the house before surrendering. But, due precisely to his accusation that Rich had "urged" him into the rebellion by calling him a "coward," she was also arrested as a "conspirator" and placed under the charge of Henry Sackford, Keeper of the Privy Purse. She was eventually released without charge,[54] perhaps in deference to her relationship with Mountjoy. In a letter to Charles Howard, Lord Nottingham, the Lord Admiral, she apologized for aiding her brother, claiming, "I haue bine more like a slaue then a sister, which proseeded out of my exseeding loue, rather then his authority."[55] This letter displays the graciousness and humility lacking in her 1600 letter to the queen. Essex's confession that he had proceeded with this plot only because Rich called him a "coward" may not have been the first time that he used his sister as equivocation for his act of disloyalty. Rich's 1600 letter to the queen surely derived from the same type of circumstances. If Rich wrote all or part of the 1600 letter, she usurped her brother's masculinist rhetorical style and strategy in order to do so. Perhaps she did not live *for* her brother but *through* him, the only way possible for an exceptionally smart woman to live in a patriarchal society.

Conclusion

We can fully understand Rich through her only surviving letter that appears to have an extant response. Her correspondent was Anthony Bacon, who frequently lived at Essex House, Rich's principal residence in London, even after her marriage to Lord Rich. It is important to read both letters in whole in order to judge the power and effect of Rich's writing without interrupting her. On May 3, 1596, when Essex was about to embark on the Cadiz expedition, Rich sent a letter, addressed in her hand to 'my Esspetiall frende Mr Bacon at Essex house'. The letter reads:

Worthy Mr Bacon, ther ar many resspects which leads me to an extreordenary estimation of your vertus, and besides your curtesis towardes my self, incresethe the desire I haue to requite your frendshipe, and to do you all honor, praying you, to beleue my wordes, since your merits doth chaleng, more then I can acknowledg, allthough I do with much affection, estime your worth, and while I am in this solitary place, wher no sound of any news can come, I must intreat you to let me here something of the worlde from you, espetially of my Brother, and then what you knowe of the frenche affaires, or whether ther go any troupes from hence to ther ayde, and so wishing you all contentment I remaine Your frende very affectionate

Penelope Riche

I would faine here what becomes of your wandering nayghbure.

Bacon's reply, dated May, 5, was addressed "To the right honorable my especiall good Ladye the Ladye Rich," and reads:

Most honerable worthie Lady, My right humble & dutifull thanks are the least & yet the most I can render your good Ladishipp for the honor of your good opinion & kind conceipte of me which I humbly beseech your Ladishipp to beleiue. I shall allwayes be no Lesse redy the gladd to acknowledege my all obedience & acceptable seruice to me possible, for the first fruitts whereof may it please your honor to be aduertised that I exspect howerlie to hear from the noblest Earle your deare Brother & will not faile to acquaint your Ladyshipp with any good news that I shall euer heare from his Lordshipp or of him by others:——For the french affayres her Majestie at the last is entered into treatie & is brought allmost to condiscend to the sending of thre thowsand men into France to be payde by her for fiue monethes, & that their shall be certaine french noble men sent to remaine heare as hostages for her Majestys your reimborcement further as yett I heare not to be proceded your Ladyshipp may well call my neighbour wandring if you knew as I doe against my will what strange bypathes his thoughts walke in which fester eury day more & more in his mind by my lordes silence & the continuall alarums that sounds in his eares of the Queenes displesure. The Duke of Bouillon presseth him to be in redines to returne with him but he refuses to goe with out my Lords priuitie & consent. This is all Madame at this instant that I know worthy the addvisment which I most humbly besech your honor to accept & to dispose freelie of my poore seruice for so many respects intirelie vowed vnto you. And so I most humblie take my leaue. your honors in all humble & faythfull affection to obey yow.[56]

The "wandering neighbour" to whom they refer is Antonio Perez, a notorious informer on his previous employer, Philip II of Spain.[57] What I find remarkable is the way in which Rich writes a seemingly simple letter asking to hear "something of the worlde," lightly punctuates it with some apparently sincere flattery, and succeeds in receiving much more information than she seemed to request. For example, she makes a brief and seemingly innocent query about Perez and acquires a significant amount of politically useful and indiscreet news in response. Certainly Bacon is dependent on her good favor, and through her, the good favor of her brother, hence he obliges her in every possible way.

But I suspect that the reason that all of the extant letters that Rich wrote, including this one, run to one page or less is because she was an expert manipulator of other people's language without using very much of her own. That is, she had perfected the skill of drawing confidential and private confessions from her correspondents while she remained reticent and self-contained, and I assume that the letters she received tended to be as detailed, informative, useful, and long as Bacon's. Although her letters are intimate in tone she does not proffer intimate revelations or confessions about herself. This is usually the case with correspondents below her rank, such as Bacon, and those above it, such as Burghley or Cecil, and most probably with Elizabeth, as in the second letter in 1600, which the queen destroyed at Rich's specific request. The other letter written to Elizabeth in 1600 to which Rich put her name in defense of her brother does not display any of these skills of manipulating the use of language. I do not believe that Rich's extant autograph letters reveal her as being shy or self-restrained in person, for much of her life was marked by the same excessive passion, enthusiasm, and vivacity as her brother's. But as a woman constantly admired and praised for her physical beauty, she expertly managed to maintain and project the idea that she was merely an image, effigy, or icon, even in her own writing. Thus, she learned to offer as little as necessary in order to receive as much as possible, whether in letters or poems or any other form of discourse written by or to her. Perhaps, then, we should recognize that in choosing Lady Penelope Rich for the Stella so beloved by Astrophil, Sidney did not simply represent a cold, aloof and unattainable mistress of love, but an expertly self-crafted master of rhetoric whose real skill was in provoking language rather than providing it.

Notes

1. Godfrey Goodman, *The Court of King James I*, ed. Brewer, 2 vols (London: Richard Bentley, 1839), 2:17.
2. George Gifford, "The Manner of Sidney's Death," in *Miscellaneous Prose of Sir Philip Sidney*, ed. Katherine Duncan-Jones and Jan Van Dorsten (Oxford: Clarendon Press, 1973), 169.

3. See Josephine Roberts, "The Imaginary Epistles of Sir Philip Sidney and Lady Penelope Rich," *ELR*, 15 (1985), 59–77.

4. For various other poets who celebrated or derided Rich's charm, see Tom W. N. Parker, *Proportional Form in the Sonnets of the Sidney Circle: Loving in Truth* (Oxford: Clarendon Press, 1998), esp. 205-6, n. 33.

5. Sylvia Freedman, *Poor Penelope: Lady Penelope Rich, an Elizabethan Woman* (Abbotsbrook: The Kensal Press, 1983), 179.

6. Ibid., 168.

7. M. Margretts, "A Christening Date for Lady Penelope Rich," *Notes and Queries*, 239 (1993), 153–4.

8. Mary Ellen Lamb argues that "perhaps the engagement of the Queen's own sexuality, on some level, in the flirtatious relationship between Elizabeth and the earl [of Essex] worked to create Rich's relative impunity from gender ideology" so that she could conduct her affair with Mountjoy "without incurring any obvious censure from the Queen or her court," *Gender and Authorship in the Sidney Circle* (Madison, WI: University of Wisconsin Press, 1990), 15. However, what is more striking is Rich being absolved from her obvious complicity in Essex's rebellion.

9. Commentary: *Astrophil and Stella, The Poems of Sir Philip Sidney* (Oxford: Clarendon Press, 1962), 443, 446. For a more recent study of Rich's possible involvement in the publication of Sidney's poems, see H. R. Woudhuysen, *Sir Philip Sidney and the Circulation of Manuscripts, 1558–1640* (Oxford: Clarendon Press, 1996).

10. Freedman, *Poor Penelope*, vi.

11. Duncan-Jones, *Sir Philip Sidney, Courtier Poet* (New Haven, CT: Yale University Press, 1991), p. 246. Duncan-Jones offers a number of important readings of Rich's abilities in several articles and in introductions to various editions of Sidney's work, as does Woudhuysen in *Sir Philip Sidney and the Circulation of Manuscripts*.

12. See, for example, Parker, *Proportional Form in the Sonnets of the Sidney Circle*, esp. 205–6, n. 33.

13. Goodman, *The Court of King James I*, ed. Brewer, 2:17.

14. I have been unable to consult Michele Margrett's unpublished PhD thesis, entitled "Stella Britanna: The Early Life of Penelope Rich," which I assume takes up her early letters.

15. W. B. Devereux, *Lives and Letters of the Devereux, Earls of Essex, in the Reign of Elizabeth, James I, and Charles I*, 2 vols (London, 1853). The editor, Walter Devereux, includes letters from the queen and other important women of the period, but limits mention of Rich to biographical information involving her brother and other male relatives.

16. See Paul E. J. Hammer's discussion of this episode in *The Polarisation of Elizabethan Politics: The Political Career of Robert Devereux, 2nd Earl of Essex* (Cambridge: Cambridge University Press, 1999), 91.

17. Hatfield House CP 18/50; for a transcription, see *Historical Manuscripts Commission: Report on the Manuscripts of the Earl of Salisbury*, 24 vols (London: Her Majesty's Stationery Office, 1883–1976), 3:438. Hereafter cited as *HMC: Salisbury*.

18. Hatfield House CP 99/133; *HMC: Salisbury*, 15:56.

19. See, for example, *Report on the Manuscripts of Lord De L'Isle & Dudley preserved at Penshurst Place*, 6 vols (London, 1925–66), 2:253, 273, MSS 3/19/97, 4/30/97, cited as *HMC: De L'Isle*.

20. On this point see Lamb, *Gender and Authorship in the Sidney Circle*, 15.

21. Hulse, "Stella's Wit: Penelope Rich as Reader of Sidney's Sonnets," in *Rewriting the Renaissance: The Discourses of Sexual Difference in Early Modern Europe*, ed. Margaret

W. Ferguson, Maureen Quilligan, and Nancy J. Vickers (Chicago: University of Chicago Press, 1986), pp. 274–5.

22. Klawitter, "Barnfield's Penelope Devereux, Exalted and Reviled," in *The Affectionate Shepherd: Celebrating Richard Barnfield*, ed. Kenneth Borris and George Klawitter (London: Associated University Presses, 2001), 62, 65.

23. On Penelope's match with Rich, see the letter of her guardian, Henry Huntingdon, to Burghley, British Library MS Lansdowne 31, f. 105.

24. "Discourse written by the Earl of Devonshire in defense of his Marriage with the Lady Rich," British Library MS Lansdowne 885, f. 86.

25. British Library MS Lansdowne 57, f. 118.

26. See British Library Lansdowne MS 39, f. 172, 181. In the first letter, for example, she pleads unsuccessfully, "I know your Lordship is so entertained with great publike causes as myne though in respecte of ther vnhappynes as great as priuate causes may be, yet in so much as it is very harde for any other to haue the feling of our owne esstate as wee haue our selues." It would not be difficult for Burghley to respond that her private crisis was not as pressing as the "great publike causes" of the day.

27. See National Archives SP 12/161/22.

28. Hatfield House CP 30/ 96; *HMC: Salisbury*, 6:75.

29. Hatfield House CP 32/ 95, 87; *HMC: Salisbury*, 5:239, 236.

30. Hatfield House CP 68/10; *HMC: Salisbury*, 10:21.

31. Hatfield House CP 75/83; *HMC: Salisbury*, 9:428.

32. Hatfield House CP 206/95; *HMC: Salisbury*, 14:101.

33. Hatfield House CP 206/95; *HMC: Salisbury*, 14:101.

34. The letter, now in a continental collection, is cited in full by Joan Grundy in her edition of *The Poems of Henry Constable*, ed. Joan Grundy (Liverpool: Liverpool University Press, 1960), 28. The letter reads: "Je baisse en toute humilité les mains de ma cherre clarté et à monsieur de Buzenval. Je luy souhaitte les bonne graces de sa maitresse et à monsieur Palevesin bon vant, et à monsieur de Sydnye, qui ne croye pas tout ce que l'on luy dict, et à monsieur Constable, qu'il ne soit plus amoreux, et a vous mesme d'aymer bien vostre femme et a tous d'estre constants jusque à vendredy. La plus constante de ceux, qui sont nommez en ce papier, hors mis une Penelope Riche."

35. *HMC: De L'Isle & Dudley*, 2:194, MS 12/5/95.

36. *HMC: De L'Isle & Dudley*, 2:204, MS 12/26/95.

37. *HMC: De L'Isle & Dudley*, 2:265, 268, MSS 4/13/97, 4/18/97.

38. Hatfield House CP 103/50; *HMC: Salisbury*, 15:87.

39. See British Library Additional MS 73087, ff. 82–105.

40. Hatfield House CP 193/15; *HMC: Salisbury*, 18:394.

41. There are a variety of biographical accounts of Essex's life. For the period up to 1597, see Hammer's excellent book; for the period after, see Robert Lacey, *Robert, Earl of Essex* (London: Phoenix Press, 1971). Also see Hammer's entry on Essex in the new *Dictionary of National Biography*.

42. *HMC: De L'Isle & Dudley*, 2:435, MS 2/2/99.

43. *HMC: De L'Isle & Dudley*, 2:461, MS 5/13/00.

44. Hatfield House CP 181/62; *HMC: Salisbury* 10:167–8.

45. A transcription of one of the copies of the letter to the queen (British Library Additional MS 40838 ff. 9v–10r) reads: 'The Coppie of a letter written to the Queene from the Lady Riche. Early did I hope this morninge to haue had my eyes blessed with your majesties beauties, but seeinge the same depart into cloude,

and meetinge with spirits who presaged by the wheeles of their chariots, some thunder in the aire. I must complaine and expresse my feares to that high ma*j*estie and diuine Oracle from whence I receiued a doubtfull answere vnto whose power I must sacrifice againe the teares and prayers of the afflicted that must despaire in time; If it be too soone to importunate heauen when wee feele the miseries of hell, Or that words directed to y*o*ur sacred wisdom should out of season deliuered for my vnfortunate brother, whom all men haue libertie to defame, as if his offence were capitall, and he soe base a deiected a creature, that his loue, his life, and his seruice to your beautiy and the state, had deserued noe absolution after soe hard punishment, or soe much as to answer in your faire presence, who would vouchsafe more iustice and fauour then he can expecte of partiall iudges, or those combined enemies who labour upon false grounds to builde his ruine; vrginge his faults as criminall to your deuine honour; thinking it a heauen to blaspheme heauen; whereas theire owne particular malice and counsailes, haue practised only to glutt themselues in there priuate reuenge, not regardinge your seruice or losse, soe much, as their ambitious mindes to rise by this overthrow. And I haue reason to apprehend, that if y*o*ur faire handes doe not checke the course of their vnbridled heate, the last course wilbe his last breath, since the euill instruments that by their office and cunninge prouide for the feast, haue sufficient poyson in their heartes to infecte the seruice, which shalbe easy to taste till it bee digested, and then will it proue a strong preparatiue of great mischiefe concyt=ed among such craftie workemen, who will not only pull downe all the obstacles of their greatnes but when they are in full strength, like the Giants, make warr against heauen it self. But your ma*j*esties most gracious conclusion in giuing hope of ye voydience, is all the comfort I haue, which if you hasten not before he take a full surfitt of disgrace, they will say the spotts they haue cast on him are too fowle to be washed away, and soe his blemished reputation must disable him for euer seruing againe his sacred Goddesse whose excellent beauty and perfection will neuer suffer those faire eyes to turne soe farr from comparison, but that at the least if he may not returne to the happines of his former seruice to liue at the feete of his admired M*i*stris: yet he may betake himsele to a priuate life, without this imputation of infamie: That his posterity may not repent their ffarthers were borne of soe harde a destiny; Two of them perished by their imployment in one country when they would haue done you seruice to the shedding of their last bloudes, if they had not beene wonded to the death by them (with faction) that care not on whose neckes they vnuistly build the walls of their owne fortunes, which I feare will growe more dangerously high then is yet discouered, If God doe not hinder th*e* worke as the tower of Babell, and confounde theire tounges that vnderstande one an other too well. And lastly seeing out of your Ma*j*esties owne Princely Nature and vnstained vertue, there must needs appeare, that mercy is not farre from such beautie; I most humbly beseeche you to make it your owne worke, and not to suffer those to take aduantange that lye in ambushe; thinking soe soone as they discouer a relenting compassion in your worthy minde to take the honour vpon them as a meanes of our saluation; not of any charitie, but of pride, that all must be attributed to them, and your sacred clemency abuse, by forcinge vs to goe through purgatory to heauen. But lett your Ma.ties: deuine power be noe more ecclipsed then your beautie, which hath shined through th*e* world, & imitating the highest in not destroying those which trust only in your mercy, with which humble request I presume to kisse your sacred handes vowinge all obedience and endles loue of your most Loyall and obedient subiecte P. R."

46. John Chamberlain reported to Dudley Carlton on February 22 that "the Lady Rich hath ben called coram [before the court] again about her letter, but she excused herself by sicknes and (as the Scottish man sayes) did not compeer." Shortly afterward, Carlton replied, "the Lady Rich who hath been once more summoned to appeare about her letter, excused herself by sicknes and is now stollen into the cuntrie to be further owt of harmes way." National Archives SP 12/274/48, 86.

47. On this case, see Peter Beal, "Philip Sidney's *Letter to Queen Elizabeth* and that 'False Knave' Alexander Dicsone," *English Manuscript Studies 1100–1700, Volume 11, Manuscripts and their Makers in the English Renaissance*, ed. Peter Beal and Grace Ioppolo (London: British Library, 2002), 1–51.

48. I discuss these letters in "'Your Majesties most humble faythfullest and most affectionate seruant': The Earl of Essex Constructs Himself and his Queen, Elizabeth I, in the Hulton Letters," in *Queen Elizabeth I and the Culture of Writing*, ed. Peter Beal and Grace Ioppolo (London: British Library, 2006).

49. For all citations from Rich's letter I use British Library Additional MS 40838 ff. 9v–10r, the text of which I provide in n. 24.

50. In a 1600 letter that was widely copied and circulated (printed in 1651), he concludes of his long request to return to her favor, "To your Graces acceptance I commmend yt, and with all humble, and reverent thoughts that may be, rest ever to be commanunded to dye att your feete." For copies of the letters, see, for example, Folger Library MSS X.c.11, V.b.214 (f. 106), also V.a.239 (f. 50), V.b.234 (38–41).

51. Hatfield House CP 48/49; *HMC:Salisbury*, 6:562.

52. Both letters are described by Arthur Freeman in "Essex to Stella: Two Letters from the Earl of Essex to Penelope Rich" (Boston: Godine, 1971). One is now in the British Library (Additional MS 64081), and the other at the Bodleian Library. The undated BL letter reads: "Deere Sister I wold haue made more hast vnto you but that yesternight I was surprised with a feuer and this morning I haue such an humor falne downe into one side of my heade as I dare not looke out of my chamber. This Lady hath intreated me to write a fantasticall letter but I am so dull with my sicknes and some other more feuer causes as I will rather choose to disp/rayse those affections with which none but women, apes, and horses are delighted. Hope for that which I haue not, is a naiue expectation, so delight in that which I haue, is a deceauing pleasure, to wish the returne of that which is gone from me is womanish vnconstancy. Those thinges that fly me, I will not loose labor to follow. Those that meete me I esteeme as they are worth, and leaue when they are noughte worth. I will neither bragg of my good happ nor complaine of my ill for secrecy makes ioyes more sweet, and I am thee most vnhappy when an other knowes that I am vnhappy. I do not cruy, because I will do no man that honor to thinke he hath that which I want, nor yet am I not converted because I know some things that I haue not Loue I confesse to be a blind god more for the pour sakes that were hir god fathers then for any pouer I see that he hath Ambition fitt for hartes what allready confess themselues to be safe, Enuy it is the humor of him that will be glad of the reversion of an other mans fortune and reuenge the remedy of such fools as in iniuries know not how to keepe themselues afore hand. Iealous I am not for I willbe glad to loose that which I am not sure to keepe. Yf to be of this mind be to be fantasticall than ioine me which three that I find reckned but *tha*t they be yong and hansome which the first find so I take my leaue being not glad to write more for payne. Your brother what loues you deerly R. Essex'. The Bodleian letter reads: 'To my

deere Sister the Lady. Penelope Rich. Deere sister Because I will not be in your debt for sending of a footman I haue directed this berer to Leas to bring me word how yow do. I am malencholy, mery, some tymes happy and often vnfortunate the Court of as many humors as the rayne bow hath collors. the tyme wherin wee liue, more vnconstant then womens thoughtes, more miserable then old age itself and breedeth both people and occasions like to itself that is violent, desperate and fantasticall. Myself for wondring at other mens strange aduentures, haue not leysure to follow the wayes of mine owne hart but by still resoluing not to be prowde of any good that can come because it is but the fauour of chaunce nor to throw downe my mind a whit for any ill that shall happen because I see that all fortunes are good or euill as they are esteamed. the preacher is ready to begin and therefore I he shall end this discourse though vpon an other text. Your brother that deerly loues yow R. Essex."

53. See Hatfield House CP 76/67 (*HMC: Salisbury* 11:51), in which Edward, Earl of Bedford confesses to the Privy Council on 8 February 1601: "Sonday in the morning, preparing myself according to my vsuall manner, with my famylie & in my howse to performe the duety of that day by serving god, After x of the clocke, prayer being ended & a sermon begonne The Lady Riche came into my house, desyring to speke with me spedelie, which I did in the next roome to the place where the sermon was, her Lady then telling me the Earl of Essex would speke with me. / wherevpon I went presently with her in her coche, none of my famylie following me owt of the sermon Roome, and so departed with her vnknowne to my said famylie. About xi of the clocke I came to Essex howse where shortly after the Earle of Essex with otheres of his company drewe themselues into [erasure] secrett conference," etc.

54. See, for example, Hatfield House CP 76/56 (*HMC: Salisbury* 11:44), in which Captain Thomas Lee includes "La. Rich" in a list of February 12, 1601 of conspirators. Her arrest is also documented in various 1601 State Papers at the National Archives.

55. Bodleian Library Tanner MS 114, f. 139. Freedman reproduces the letter in *Poor Penelope*, 150.

56. Lambeth Palace Bacon MSS 657, ff. 61, 133r-v.

57. I am grateful to Paul E. J. Hammer for explaining the significance of this reference; also see *The Polarisation of Elizabethan Politics*, 180–1. I am also grateful to Peter Beal for supplementary information on Essex's career and letters.

16
Hormonal Conclusions

Gail Kern Paster

In response to a volume of feminist essay whose central concern is whether or not feminism has become absorbed beyond recognition into other critical practices, I propose the "after" word *hormones*. My interest is specifically in female hormones, even early modern female hormones (as I will try to make clear) and all that early modern hormones may be said to stand for. What exactly they could signify—and why feminism should care—is precisely the question I wish to make visible. As far as I am able to determine, hormones have not yet been explicitly mentioned in this volume, unless one counts R. S. White's speculative description of Shakespeare's Gertrude as possibly post-menopausal (p. 109). The reason for the omission of female hormones needs to be considered because hormones are, after all, the bodily basis for the emotions and, historically, female emotions have been an important topic in traditional critical discourse and hence a target for feminist deconstruction.

What would it be to think seriously about early modern women's hormones, and why is it that we generally resist doing so? Admittedly, I am using the term "hormones" somewhat provocatively here to metonymize the realm of the biological *tout court*.[1] And I am responding affirmatively to philosopher Paul Griffiths's aggressive proposition that if emotions cannot be studied empirically, then "there is an important sense in which the emotions do not really exist."[2] I believe that critical resistance to naming hormones, let alone to thinking seriously about them, is directly related to the central theoretical occlusions of postmodern feminism and its well-founded suspicions of notions such as the universal and the natural. It was certainly the case that reference to the self-evidently universal and natural in traditional humanist criticism was rhetorically a move to closure and theoretically a move beyond the explicable to the self-evident. But, as I will explain, there seems to me no necessary or even logical connection between citation of these categories and the endpoint of feminist analysis. Our desire as feminists to insist on the manifold effects of gender and other forms of difference has led to a theoretical disregard for the possibility of forms of universality that may nevertheless permit secondary or perhaps supplemental forms of difference. The problem is that feminism as practiced, for example, by brilliant philosophers such as Judith Butler or anthropologists such as Catherine Lutz has so thoroughly theorized the biological, so thoroughly subsumed the biological into the ravening maw of the cultural domain—the cultural domain now substituting in post-modernism for the place once held by the universal—that it has become increasingly difficult to consider behaviors and emotions as biologically determined at all, let alone give them meaning and importance on that basis in the experience of women.[3] But, with respect to the emotions, there is good reason to suppose that some of them—hope, fear, anger, sadness, desire—are universal and widely recognizable across cultures, while others are culturally and historically quite specific.[4]

The distinction between the two categories of universal and historically specific is important for literary historians generally, and perhaps for early modern feminists especially, because of the broad assumptions about women's emotions that—paradoxically perhaps—have always characterized attacks on and defenses of women. The emotional lability often associated with women takes the blame for what is assumed to be women's impulsivity, changeability, and readiness to weep; but it also produces general assumptions about female compassion, tender-heartedness, and natural capacity to love. The cruel mother is a monster of nature, a figure of myth. Clearly the linkage between women and emotions is rightly felt to be insulting to women, a denigration of their powers in maturity to manage often large households, run businesses, work in sometimes abusive conditions of service and even—in the case of Elizabeth I—reign charismatically for most of 45 years. Women's emotional lability becomes the ground for paternalistic protectionism, for second-class citizenship, for denials to women either by statute or by custom of full participation and self-representation in law, property, and business.

Thus, hesitantly because heretically, I introduce the thought of early modern female hormones in order to suggest the possibility of a new utility for the twinned ideas of the universal and the natural in a reconstructed feminist practice. I want to consider the possible role of biological determinants in the behavior, thought, and emotions of early modern women—even if we have to look for evidence of those biological determinants in literature of undoubtedly misogynistic purport. Whatever else we know (or do not know) about early modern women such as Penelope Rich or the possibly pregnant Persian lady whose enigmatic portrait Pamela Brown wishes to decode, we have to believe that their behavior in life (like ours) had a strong hormonal and biological component, just as it had a rich cultural component derived from such factors as religious belief, life experience, family position, erotic predilections, and romantic destinies. It follows, I think, that the behavior of female characters in literary fictions—even in fictions to be enacted on-stage by young male actors—allows us (admittedly contingent) glimpses of a biological substratum for emotions and for actions and for specific, highly variant cultural responses to them. Though this biological substratum—as Butler rightly insists—cannot be known apart from signification or articulated as if it were prior to discourse, the biological helps to determine the emotional and behavioral texture of women's lives in ways that cannot simply be subsumed into a discourse of gendered performativity,[5] because the latter in its own way has become a move toward closure too. Thus I welcome R. S. White's speculations about whether we should consider *Hamlet's* Gertrude as post-menopausal or not—a speculation that I have not encountered in such clinical terms before, even though the question matters greatly to a play as preoccupied as *Hamlet* is with dynastic transition and with the biorhythms of women's sexual appetites. Gertrude's question to Hamlet in the closet scene—"What have I done, that thou dar'st wag thy tongue/In noise so rude against me?" (3.4.38–9)— in this context is a sturdy defense of the naturalness of her sexual appetite, just like the Duchess of Malfi's plainspoken defense of her marriage: "Why might I not marry?/I have not gone about, in this, to create/Any new world, or custom"(3.2.109–11).[6] Such defenses should come as no surprise in what Valerie Traub has called the "sex-positive" culture of early modern Europe, but I think it is important to underscore the two women characters' invocation of natural appetite and the realm of biological sexuality.[7] When Gertrude's mood changes to one of guilt-ridden remorse for her sexual activity and she begs Hamlet to "speak no more" (88) of her remarriage, her guilt arguably derives more from his nasty representation of all sexual activity and of the affective contagion of disgust than from any admission of the unnaturalness of sexual activity by "matrons."[8]

The idea of hormones thus seems to me a useful way to think about the biological because we can take it for granted that highly variant and class-specific cultural practices in birthing, wet-nursing, and contraception strongly affected the production and expression of female hormones—thus creating a hermeneutic space for seeing interactions between the cultural and the biological. And enough is known generally about the production and expression of hormones to extrapolate from historical and perhaps even from literary evidence. The whole arena of reproduction is a rich area for such an exploration, because we know that practices such as wet-nursing allowed wet nurses themselves, suckling their nurse children on demand, to lengthen the intervals between their own pregnancies even as it condemned upper-class mothers who sent babies out to frequent pregnancies that must have exhausted and debilitated them. We have found it relatively easy, from this historical distance, to see the role of a misogynistic ideology in shaping ostensibly neutral medical writing about obstetrics and female physiology and to see the role of status and position in determining women's choices. But we have been reluctant—for fear of committing the intellectual errors of presentism and a retrospective form of cultural imperialism—to think about the emotional entailments of grim biological realities.

In writing about the wet-nursing culture in early modern England, I and other feminist critics have typically emphasized the overarching irony of a cultural practice that empowered lower-class women at the expense of the health and well-being of upper-class women.[9] We based feminist arguments on lactation as a historically well-known contraceptive as well as on the painstaking reconstruction by Dorothy McLaren, Valerie Fildes, and others of baptismal and other historical data.[10] We wanted above all to construct a culturally and historically specific picture of the experiences of early modern mothers—emphasizing the role of cultural expectations in shaping and determining their experiences and insisting on the role of patriarchy in constraining their reproductive choices. In such discussions culture's shaping of natural processes rightly loomed large. But if we allow ourselves to focus instead on the hormones of continually pregnant elite women, we ought to be willing to infer from the gynecological facts a surge in hormonal activity and emotional lability that accompanies pregnancy and the post-partum period. Such biological reasoning might allow us in turn to become more sensitive to the likely emotional tumultuousness of early modern women's reproductive years—*as a general rule*—even apart from whatever we know through diaries and other documentary records of specific women's hopes and fears. The result might be a more resonant and historically specific context for evaluating the otherwise exhausted commonplace association of women and emotionalism. In reading John Donne's valedictory poems addressed to his wife, for example—especially "A Valediction Forbidding Mourning"—we could remember Ann Donne's twelve pregnancies in sixteen years of marriage. Here are biographical facts that suggest both biological and emotional possibilities. Considering the poet's several protracted stays abroad and a period of London lodging—times of enforced sexual separation—it seems fair to infer from all these pregnancies that Ann Donne found it easy to conceive.[11] While Donne's biographer John Carey suggests that Ann remains largely unknowable as a personality, it is hard for me to imagine that a married life of almost continual pregnancy amid circumstances of penury and disfavor would not have produced in her a high degree of emotional lability, whether or not she ever expressed it or found herself able to overcome it. Ann Donne's passions in such circumstances— could we but know them—would add significant resonance to the picture of mutual passion of grief and reunion that declares itself so powerfully in the poems. When Donne's speaker in the *Valediction Forbidding Mourning* suggests that they "melt and make no noise, / No teare-floods, nor sigh-tempests move," I think we are allowed to contemplate Ann's emotional lability.[12] We may not know what it is *natural* for Ann Donne to feel in her circumstances, but we need to admit that those feelings would have a basis in nature—a nature that includes the hormones accompanying the twelve pregnancies that must have resulted from cultural practices discouraging contraception among elite—even if impecunious—women.

We can speculate, for example, that Ann Donne would have suffered from post-partum syndrome. The domestic conduct books emphasize the privileges—emotional privileges among them—allowed to mothers' lying-in.[13] Jacques Guillemeau urges the new mother to protect herself from emotional distress: "Let her shun anger, melancholy, griefe, and other such passions of the minde: Let her keep herself quiet, not much stirring or troubling her body."[14] The result of such protectiveness was, of course, a carnivalesque form of invalidism, again for more affluent or middling-rank women with extensive support networks, during a protracted lying-in that we now know cannot have contributed beneficially to their physical recovery. But we might also venture a guess about what such enforced inactivity may have contributed to their rate of emotional recovery from post-partum depression. Guillemeau's warning about the danger of negative emotions on the new mother—a warning perhaps directed more or less sternly at the new mother herself to eschew negative emotions—allows us to infer that post-partum letdown was as much a concern in early modern English culture as it is today. The female gossips' celebrations of a new mother's successful birth may have been designed to ward off negative emotions following childbirth. And while the churching ceremony that welcomed the new mother back into the congregation may, as have I argued earlier, been a pollution ceremony marking the end of her lochial flow, it too may have had the positive goal of countering the negative effects of post-partum blues.[15]

As a student of early modern Galenic humoralism, I have come to the conclusion that humoralism permitted, reflected, or produced a greater expectation of emotional lability than seems to me characteristic of post-Enlightenment psychology and western culture generally.[16] The high value placed on emotional constancy widely evident in both literature and philosophy during the period may well be traceable to this preoccupation with the passions. Susan James has argued that "the interest in the emotions that so pervades seventeenth-century philosophy is itself part of a broader preoccupation in early modern European culture with the relations between knowledge and control, whether of the self or others."[17] Certainly, early modern culture associated certain stages of life with greater emotional volatility than others, just as they associated certain kinds of people with greater emotional volatility than others. It is not at all surprising to feminist critics that women and children are singled out, usually pejoratively, for their emotional lack of control or that adolescence—in both sexes—is associated with emotionalism. As Rosalind playing Ganymede tells Orlando in *As You Like It*, she has cured love-stricken youth by aping women's overemotional behaviors:

> would I, being but a moonish youth, grieve, be effeminate, changeable, longing and liking, proud, fantastical, apish, shallow, inconstant, full of

tears, full of smiles; for every passion something, and for no passion truly anything, as boys and women are, for the most part, cattle of this colour . . .

(3.2.409–15)

Of course, the idea of one's emotions being affected by the phases of the moon—a belief reflected in Ganymede's self-description as a "moonish youth"—is one most of us no longer accept. But recent work on the developmental specificity of adolescent emotions and—as we have been told lately—even of the adolescent brain suggests accepting some sort of biological basis for adolescence as a life-stage rather than merely labeling it an invention of permissive modern western culture. So too, I am arguing here, we should be willing to allow for the fluid interaction of biology and cultural practice in identifying emotional specificities for early modern women based on what we know of their lives—their relative degrees of empowerment, their marital expectations, their obstetrical and gynecological probabilities, and so forth. It is just this combination of physiological and cultural factors that so recommends Robert Burton's analysis of virgins' melancholy in *The Anatomy of Melancholy* when he paints a deeply sympathetic portrait of sad young gentlewomen who "out of a strong temperament, innate constitution, are violently carried away with this torrent of inward humours, & though very modest of themselves, sober, religious, virtuous, and well given (as many so distressed maides are) yet cannot make resistance."[18] And he inveighs against those who turn a deaf ear to "the teares, sighes, groanes and grievous miseries of such poore Soules committed to their charge" (1: 417).

I am not suggesting that Burton's picture of wailing virgins has any simple or direct basis in social or biological fact. He himself denies the evidentiary basis of his analysis immediately after presenting it, and his tendency to proliferate endless forms of melancholy as a way of denying his consummate self-absorption also undercuts the persuasiveness of any single form of it in his book. But there is a strikingly high number of sad young women throughout the literature of the period, and Michael Macdonald does report a statistically significant number of young women who sought out physician Richard Napier because they were forbidden by parents or employers to marry the men they loved.[19] It seems to me entirely too easy to discount literary sadness as the product of heteronormativity and generic necessity—of the requirement that young female protagonists must start out sad in order to become happy by finding the right hero to wed. I am suggesting instead that sadness is generically part of an emotion script specific (though not exclusive) to young women in the period, and that we would do well to look in those texts for language that directs us—as Burton does—to the recognition of a biological component complicating social despair. That biological component may be thoroughly saturated with socially inflected nuance and may be based on an altogether erroneous basis in medical or biological fact. But it is the description of an interaction between the physical and the cultural, the biological and the social—an interaction much like what Burton describes—that gives our own feminist speculations an appropriate theoretical heft and gravity.

In this respect, my aims in this afterword parallel Gil Harris's because, like Harris, I believe that historicism—including feminist historicism—has "become wedded to . . . the assumption of an absolute temporal difference between past and present" (p. 35 above). The refusal to admit the "natural" and the "universal" as potentially useful intellectual notions is integral to such an assumption. My overarching interest is in allowing the natural and the universal as categories to return to feminist analysis without sacrificing our well-honed interest in historical and cultural specificities. By doing so, we would not only give ourselves a better theorized ability to identify with the women—fictional and real—whose experiences so command our attention as feminist historians, but we would also be able to see much more common ground and draw firmer analogies between the experiences of seventeenth-century women, ourselves as western-trained feminists, and our female contemporaries elsewhere in the world today.

Notes

1. In this respect, my interest aligns with Mary Thomas Crane's salutary reminder in cognitive criticism that brains are our bodies' text-producing organ. See *Shakespeare's Brain* (Princeton, NJ: Princeton University Press, 2001), 3–35.
2. Paul Griffiths, *What Emotions Really Are: The Problem of Psychological Categories* (Chicago and London: University of Chicago Press, 1997), 1.
3. See, for example, Judith Butler, *Bodies that Matter: On the Discursive Limits of Sex* (New York: Routledge, 1993); and Catherine Lutz, *Unnatural Emotions: Everyday Sentiments on a Micronesian Atoll and Their Challenge to Western Theory* (Chicago: University of Chicago Press, 1988), 3–13.
4. For a fuller explanation of this point, see *Reading the Early Modern Passions: Essays in the Cultural History of Emotion*, ed. Gail Kern Paster, Mary Floyd-Wilson, and Katherine Rowe (Philadelphia: University of Pennsylvania Press, 2004), 9–13.
5. As Ian Hacking has asked provocatively, "*What* is said to be constructed, if someone speaks of the social construction of gender?" See *The Social Construction of What?* (Cambridge, MA: Harvard University Press, 1999), 9.
6. Quotations from Shakespeare follow *The Riverside Shakespeare*, ed. G. Blakemore Evans (Boston, MA: Houghton Mifflin, 1997). In quoting from John Webster, I follow *The Duchess of Malfi*, ed. John Russell Brown (Manchester: Manchester University Press, 1997).
7. Valerie Traub, *The Renaissance of Lesbianism in Early Modern England* (Cambridge: Cambridge University Press, 2002), 95.
8. The term *matron* is Hamlet's when he apostrophizes "shame" mutinying in "a matron's bones" (3.4.83). On the contagiousness of disgust, see William I. Miller, *The Anatomy of Disgust* (Cambridge, MA: Harvard University Press, 1997). On disgust as a primary emotion, see Silvan S. Tomkins, *Affect, Imagery, Consciousness. Vol. III: The Negative Affects* (New York: Springer, 1991), 19, 21–5.

9. See Gail Kern Paster, *The Body Embarrassed: Drama and the Disciplines of Shame in Early Modern England* (Ithaca, NY: Cornell University Press, 1993), 198–208.

10. See, for example, Dorothy McLaren, "Fertility, Infant Mortality, and Breast Feeding in the Seventeenth Century," *Medical History 22* (1978), 378–96; Valerie Fildes, *Breasts, Bottles, and Babies: A History of Infant Feeding* (Edinburgh: Edinburgh University Press, 1986), 175—8. Both cited in *The Body Embarrassed*, 199, nn. 82 and 83.

11. See John Carey, *John Donne: Life, Mind and Art* (New York: Oxford University Press, 1981), 74–5.

12. Quotations from Donne follow *The Complete Poetry of John Donne*, ed. John T. Shawcross (New York: Doubleday, 1967).

13. See William Gouge, *Of Domesticall Duties* (London: 1622), 401–2.

14. Jacques Guillemeau, *Child-birth, or The Happie Deliverie of Women* (London, 1612). 224.

15. For my earlier discussion of churching, see Paster, *The Body Embarrassed*, 193–6. See also David Cressy, *Birth, Marriage, and Death: Ritual, Religion and the Life-Cycle in Tudor and Stuart England* (Oxford: Oxford University Press, 1997).

16. I make this case especially in *Humoring the Body: Emotions on the Shakespearean Stage* (Chicago: University of Chicago Press, 2004), 19–20.

17. Susan James, *Passions and Action: The Emotions in Seventeenth-Century Philosophy* (Cambridge: Cambridge University Press, 1997), 2.

18. Robert Burton, *The Anatomy of Melancholy*, ed. Thomas C. Faulkner, Nicolas K. Kiessling, and Rhonda L. Blair, 6 vols. (Oxford: Clarendon Press, 1989–2000), 1: 416–17.

19. Michael Macdonald, *Mystical Bedlam: Madness, Anxiety, and Healing in Seventeenth-Century England* (Cambridge: Cambridge University Press, 1981), 94.

Index

city comedy 18–19
  location in 118–19, 120–5, 130–2
  London comedies 117–18
  mistaken identity in 136n
  see also brothel comedy
Civil War, English 11, 138
Cixous, Hélène
  affinity with Margaret Cavendish 34–6, 40–2
  and Cleopatra 33–4
  and corporeal matter 44
  écriture feminine 33, 35, 36–7, 38–9
  "Sorties" 33, 36, 38
  "The Laugh of the Medusa" 36
  "The Sex That Is Not One" 39
  Vivre l'orange 36
Clarke, Mary Cowden 97
class hierarchy 6, 7
  contested 197–8
  Victorian 248
  see also social rank
Cleaborough, John 272
Cleopatra
  identifications with 33–4, 47
  portrait of Lady Ralegh as 184, 185
Cleter, Edward 290
Clifford, Lady Anne, Countess of Cumberland 139, 152
Clifford, Margaret, Countess of Cumberland 152, 153, 158, 161
Cockpit theater 270
Colet, John, *Grammar* (with Lilly) 201
Collace, Katherine 144
Comedy of Errors, The 228
commemoration 213
commerce
  and blurring of gender norms 131, 132–3
  London as centre of 117, 123–4, 129–31, 133
  retail licenses 282
  retail shops 124, 129
  women in 24–5, 123, 124, 282
  see also informal economy
confession
  auricular 55–6, 57
  private 56–7
consent, in marriage ceremony 3, 4, 7
consumption 124
contiguity 39

conversion, trope of 119
  in brothel comedy 125–32
  in Turk plays 125–6, 133
Cooke, Joshua, *How to Chuse a Good Wife from a Bad* 222
Copley family, Gatton, Surrey 11
Corneille, Pierre, *Pompey*, translation 76–7, 78
cosmology
  Aristotelian 43
  "worlds-within-worlds" 41
Cotterell, Sir Charles 76
Country Wench, in brothel comedy 126–8
coverture, law of 5, 288–9, 297n
Cranmer, Thomas, Archbishop of Canterbury 56
credit
  culture of 263, 265–6
  loans to women 269, 275–6n
  small-scale 263–4
  women as lenders 269, 275–6n, 283
  see also pawnbrokers
Crowcher, Elizabeth 272
Culpeper, Nicholas 107
cultural participation, feminist revisionist view of 5
cultural performance 1, 12–13
  marriage ceremony as 2–3
Cumberland, Countess *see* Clifford, Anne; Clifford, Margaret
Cust, Lionel 173–4

Dakin, Margaret, widow 284
Dalby, Mrs Dorothey 53
d'Aragona, Tullia 177, 188
Davies, Sir John, *Hymns to Astraea* 242
dead
  Catholic view of 214–15
  changing beliefs about 221
  fear of 213
  see also ghosts
decorum 74
Dekker, Thomas 122
  The Honest Whore 128–9
  Old Fortunatus 242
  The Roaring Girl (with Thomas Middleton) 125
Dellasega, Cheryl, *Surviving Ophelia* 102
Devereux, Dorothy 305, 306, 318

340   *Index*

rhetorical figures – *continued*
  gendered   85–6
  ironia (irony)   82–3
  meiosis   82
  micterismus   82
  orismus   83
  paragon   83
  ploche   81, 82
  sarcasmus   82
Rich, Lord   304, 309–10
Rich, Penelope, Lady   26–7, 299–320
  affection for friends   308–10
  arrest (1601)   302
  correspondence with Anthony Bacon
      318–20
  correspondence of   301–3
  divorce from Lord Rich   309–10
  education and intellect   302
  friendship with Cecil   306, 309–10,
      317
  handwriting   305
  letter to Elizabeth in defense of
      brother   310–18, 322–3n
  letters from Essex   317, 324–5n
  marriage to Mountjoy   309
  moral character   299–301
  prose style   303–4, 305–6, 314, 317,
      320
  relations with brother (Essex)   307–8,
      317, 318
  request for favors in letters   306–7
  use of ciphers   303, 312
Richardson, William, *On Shakespeare's
    Imitation of Female Characters* (1788)
    95
Richmond, election (1678)   29n
Righter, Anne   261
Ringler, William W., on Rich   300, 302
ritual, loss of Catholic   215–16
Roman Catholic church *see* Catholicism
rope dancers   12, 13
Rowlandson, Mary   144, 145
Rowley, William
  A New Wonder, A Woman Never Vext
      291–2, 293
  Birth of Merlin   190n
Russian Formalism   68, 86–7, 88

Sackford, Henry   318
Sand, Georges   97

Saxl, Fritz   246
Sayers, Dorothy L.   246
Second Maiden's Tragedy, The   222
Selby, Sir George   79
self, Reformation and   214, 215
servants, household   124, 140
sewing and mending, in Hamlet   108
sex, and gender   249
sexual desire   25, 124
sexual transgression   25
  bisexuality   38–9, 49n
  fluid standards (London)   129
sexuality
  Cixous and   38, 48n
  and female biology   328
  and gender   17
  and remarriage   25–6, 281–2, 294
Shakespeare, William
  Cixous's reading of   38
  and Globe Theatre   123
  women in   94–5, 216–17, 224
  see also individual plays
Shandler, Sara, *Ophelia Speaks*   102
Shirley, Sir Anthony   189n
Shklovsky, Victor   86, 88
  "Art as Technique"   67, 68
Showalter, Elaine   98
Sidney, Mary   86
Sidney, Sir Philip   26, 27, 75
  and Penelope Rich   299, 304
Sidney, Sir Robert   303, 308–9, 310
sins
  remission of   56
  of women   58
Smith, Ann and William   289
Smithson, Harriet   99
social rank   4, 20, 150, 162, 165
  and childbirth   328–9
  and education   195–8
  and remarriage   282, 284
souls
  "Conversation" of   39
  movement of   34, 40
Southampton, Elizabeth Vernon,
      Countess of   179, 191n, 308
Southampton, Henry Wriothesley, Earl
      of   179
  letters from Penelope Rich   302
Spanish Tragedy, The   59–61
spinsters   3, 6

whores
common and private (distinction)
119
conversion to respectability   128–9,
131
distinguishing clothing   122
transformation of wives into   128–9
see also brothel comedy; prostitution
Whyte, Rowland   303, 308–9, 310
widows
ambivalent status of   222
economic independence of   282
freedom of   283–4
sexuality and remarriage   25–6
and younger husbands   281–2, 296n
see also remarriage
wilderness, notion of   144, 146
Wilkins, John, parish clerk of
Whitstable   9
Williams, Raymond   86
Wilson, Thomas   84
Winter's Tale, The   23, 224–30
Catholic resonances   228–9
resurrection scene   229
Wise, Sir Thomas   221
Wit Without Money   292, 293
Witch of Edmonton, The   222, 235n
witchcraft   215, 221
women   18–22
adolescent   101–4
association with Catholicism   216
in commerce   24–5, 123, 124, 282
dead   216–17
as dedicatees of writings   53, 71–2,
74, 162
education of   195–6
freedom in London   124–5
as ghosts   219–24
as head of household   124
lack of legal identity   4, 7
nature of relationships   141–2
as patrons   152, 158, 165
penitents   59

as readership   73–4
revisionist view of status of   6
as scholars   24
social inferiority   4
unmarried majority   3, 6
and unregulated desire   124
as victims   99–100
see also mothers; pregnancy
women writers   20–1, 26–7, 85–6, 188
and location   139, 147
and patronage   152
playwrights   259
travellers   143–6
Woodman, Marion, *The Owl was a
Baker's Daughter*   100–1
Woolf, Virginia   24, 42, 50n
A Room of One's Own   238, 247, 253,
254
Orlando   252–3
Wroth, Lady Mary   74–5, 188
Urania   178

Yates, Frances A.   14, 21, 23–4, 239
*The Occult Philosophy in the Elizabethan
Age*   247
education and career   242–6
*The French Academies in the Sixteenth
Century*   245
Giordano Bruno   247
and interdisciplinarity   241–2, 245–6
on *Portrait of an Unknown Lady*   174,
186
"Queen Elizabeth as Astraea" (1947)
239–40, 241–2, 245, 249, 251, 254
rejection of feminism   246–7, 248,
250
The Rosicrucian Enlightenment   247
Yates, James   243
youth revolution, Hamlet as
embodiment   104

Zucchero, Federigo   173
Zwingli, Huldreich   56